The Soul of Success

Published by CelebrityPress®, Orlando, FL

CelebrityPress® is a registered trademark.

Printed in the United States of America.

ISBN: 978-0-9961978-3-0
LCCN: 2015941221

This publication is designed to provide accurate and authoritative information with regard to the subject matter covered. It is sold with the understanding that the publisher is not engaged in rendering legal, accounting, or other professional advice. If legal advice or other expert assistance is required, the services of a competent professional should be sought. The opinions expressed by the authors in this book are not endorsed by CelebrityPress® and are the sole responsibility of the author rendering the opinion.

Most CelebrityPress® titles are available at special quantity discounts for bulk purchases for sales promotions, premiums, fundraising, and educational use. Special versions or book excerpts can also be created to fit specific needs.

For more information, please write:
CelebrityPress®
520 N. Orlando Ave, #2
Winter Park, FL 32789
or call 1.877.261.4930

Visit us online at: www.CelebrityPressPublishing.com

Dina!   11.9.15

The
Soul of
Success

I'm SO grateful for our
connection and I look
forward to working with you
on something amazing really
soon. If I can ever support
you in any way, just say the
word! Love you!

CELEBRITYPRESS®
Winter Park, Florida

Dina!

11.9.15

I'm SO grateful for our connection and I look forward to working with you on something amazing really soon. If I can ever support you in any way, just say the word! Love you!

Mandy

CONTENTS

CHAPTER 1

THE SOUL OF SUCCESS

BY JACK CANFIELD

We are all capable and worthy of achieving extraordinary levels of success in our lifetime. I know this because I have literally helped millions of people from all walks of life and from all over the world achieve their dreams. After I achieved incredible results in my own life with the *Chicken Soup for the Soul*® series having sold hundreds of millions of copies in 47 languages, I decided to share the secrets of my success with the rest of the world.

It had all started forty-five years ago when self-made multi-millionaire W. Clement Stone took me under his wing and taught me what he called "The Success System That Never Fails." As soon as I started applying his teachings, I started to have amazing success in my life. I wrote a book on self-esteem for teachers that sold 400,000 copies. I took my income from $8000 a year to $100,000 a year in just a few short years. I founded a successful personal development retreat center in Amherst, Massachusetts, from which I launched a successful educational consulting practice. I later moved to California, where I eventually started Self-Esteem Seminars, which evolved into today's Canfield Training Group. And then came *Chicken Soup for the Soul*® and my role in the movie "The Secret." Everything I ever wanted to manifest came into fruition.

Along the way I became fascinated with the topic of success, and I spent forty years researching, studying and interviewing successful men and women, looking for the thinking patterns, beliefs, habits and principles that allowed them to produce such extraordinary results. What I discovered was a set of timeless principles that always worked when people identified, assimilated and applied them with persistence and consistency.

As I taught these principles to others and saw the phenomenal breakthroughs they created, I vowed to devote my life to teaching people how to be more successful in all areas of their lives—from their careers to their relationships. This led to my life purpose, which is *to inspire and empower people to live their highest vision in a context of love and joy in harmony with the highest good of all concerned.* I inspire people through stories like those found in the *Chicken Soup for the Soul®* books, and I empower them through my Breakthrough to Success trainings, our Canfield Coaching program, our Train the Trainer programs, and books like *The Success Principles™: How to Get from Where You Are to Where You Want to Be.*

When I first started teaching about success, my definition of success was "being able to create whatever results you wanted in life—both internal states (like self-confidence and happiness) and external results (like being the top salesperson in your company or becoming a millionaire)." Later, as my understanding of true success evolved, my definition of success became "fulfilling your soul's purpose."

I believe everyone is born with a unique self that is yearning to fully express itself, to fulfill its unique purpose. We all have a unique set of talents that we have been given in order to fulfill that purpose. Lately, in all of my seminars, workshops and trainings, I have been asking people to look deeply inside and ask the question, "What is wanting to emerge through me at this time? What is it that is seeking a more full expression in my life?" Take a moment to ask yourself that question right now. Perhaps there is a part of you that is seeking expression that you have been ignoring. Maybe you're even afraid of it.

I remember when I began to realize that compiling and editing the *Chicken Soup for the Soul* books was no longer fulfilling me. The excitement and passion for the work had begun to die. I felt like I was becoming jaded. I wasn't sure what I wanted to do next, but I knew this wasn't it anymore. It was scary. We had sold hundreds of millions of books and I was making a multi-million dollar a year income from the book royalties. If I stopped, I had no idea how I could affect as many people or make as much money doing something else.

If you want to reach out for something new,
you must first let go of what's in your hand.

~ Sonia Choquette

I remember once talking to a trapeze artist who told me that the hardest thing for someone learning trapeze was letting go of the bar they are holding onto and trusting that the other bar will be there for them to catch. Well I did let go, and after a few months of being open to what wanted to come into expression, I rediscovered my passion for training and writing about success. I remember sitting in bed one morning with my laptop and spending three hours making a list of all the principles I believed had led to my success, and then deciding to write a book about it. I then spent several months interviewing 75 of America's most successful people to make sure that these principles were universal and weren't just unique to me. As it turned out they were universal.

As a result of writing *The Success Principles*, which was eventually translated into 27 languages, I began to be invited to speak all over the world—from Germany, Russia, Greece and Slovakia to India, Thailand, Singapore and Japan—to teach these principles. And now we've developed a Train the Trainer program and trained more than 500 people from 40 countries to teach these principles to others. Let's just say it has all worked out very well.

Don't ask what the world needs. Ask yourself what makes you come
alive and then go do that. Because what the world needs is people who
have come alive.

~ Howard Thurman

My purpose in sharing all of this with you is to assure you that you can trust the universe to support you if you take the risk to follow your true passions as they evolve. And how will you know your true passion, your true purpose, what you are being called to do? You will know from your experience of joy as you do the thing you are meant to do. Joy is your built-in GPS system. When you are experiencing true joy, aliveness and a sense of expansion, you are on course to fulfilling your purpose; when you are not, you are off course.

GET CLEAR ABOUT WHAT MAKES YOU COME ALIVE

One of the best ways to get clear about what makes you come alive is to conduct what I call a Joy Review. Make a list of the times in your life when you have felt the most joy, the most excited, the most happy, the most passionate, the most alive. For me, it is when I am learning new things and when I am teaching others about what I have learned. For Patty Aubery, the president of my company, it is when she is helping people take what they love to do and helping them figure out how to monetize it.

I recently had dinner with a man from England who was attending one of my workshops. He told me he was a very successful businessman making a seven-figure income running a company he had started. He said he wasn't as happy as he wanted to be, and that he felt he hadn't found his purpose. I asked him when he had felt the most joy in his career. He said it was when one of his employees had come to him with a very difficult and challenging personal problem she was facing and he had spent an hour successfully coaching her using some techniques he had learned at an NLP workshop.

I suggested that maybe what was crying for expression in him was coaching others through the difficult times in their lives. He answered, "I think you're right, but I don't see how I could make a seven- or high six-figure income doing that." I suggested he could let his current business partner take over running the business or he could hire a qualified business manager to come in and run it, take a percentage of the profits as the founder and co-owner of the business, pursue a career in coaching and training, and still end up making the same amount of total income. His face lit up and he became a lot more animated as we strategized the various ways he could go about this. His new sense of freedom and aliveness was the feedback that this course of action was aligned with his true purpose.

Once you become more aware of what your purpose is, there are some other success principles that will help you manifest it more easily and more quickly.

I. TAKE 100% RESPONSIBILITY FOR YOUR SUCCESS

Your decisions cause your rewards and consequences. You are responsible for your life, and your ultimate success depends on the choices you make.

~ Denis Waitley

Here's the deal—there's only one person ultimately responsible for making sure you live the life you were meant to live. That person is YOU.

If you want a meaningful, purposeful life filled with financial freedom, loving relationships, rewarding work, exciting leisure time, a successful business, and everything else that makes up an ideal life, you have to take 100% responsibility for creating that life.

From the state of your health to the state of your finances…from the quality of your relationships to the people you associate with…from your emotional health to the opinion you have of yourself—you are ultimately responsible for all of it! Embracing this level of responsibility is not easy, but once you do, your life and your results will skyrocket.

Taking 100% responsibility means you must give up all blaming, complaining and making excuses when things don't immediately go the way you want. Instead, you need to ask yourself the question, "How did I create that or allow it to happen?" Because if you can see how you created or allowed it, you can un-create it and recreate it the way you want in the future. It's amazing how most people don't get this. They blame others for everything that doesn't work in their life.

Jan Quintrall of the Spokane Better Business Bureau recently wrote about a complaint they received. It read "I want to file a complaint against (blank) Bar. Here is what they did to me. I was there last weekend and they served me too much to drink, and made me write them a check to pay for my drinks. I did not have enough money in my account, so the check bounced. Then the bank charged me fees that plunged my account deeper into the hole and more checks bounced. I don't know why the bank charged me, it was not my fault, and it was the bar's fault, they made me drink too much! But my real problem is now I don't have enough money to pay my rent, but part of the problem there is my boss does not pay me enough so it is always hard to pay my rent. But those people at the bar made it impossible, them and the bank. I want the bar to pay my rent this month and send a letter to the bank admitting they made this happen so the bank gives me back all those charges they took from my money."

Can you believe it? And here's a story that's even more amazing:

In 1992, Ricky Bodine, a 19-year-old high school graduate, along with three other friends (one of whom had a criminal record), decided to steal a floodlight from the roof of a high school gymnasium. Ricky climbed the roof, removed the floodlight, lowered it to the ground to his friends, and, as he was walking across the roof, fell through a skylight. As a result of the injuries he received, Bodine sued the school for his injuries! In other words, a burglar fell through a skylight and blamed the skylight's owners for his injuries. What's more amazing is that he ended up getting a settlement of $260,000 plus $1200 a month for life!

While these are extreme and seemingly absurd cases of placing responsibility for our circumstances outside of yourself, how many times a day, perhaps in smaller ways, do you the place blame on others outside of yourself for the situations you find yourself in? Have you ever blamed the traffic, your parents, your spouse, your kids, your neighbors, the government, or the economy for why something in your life isn't working? Did your blaming get you more of what you wanted? Probably not. Here's a useful formula that will explain why.

$$E + R = O$$
Event + Response = Outcome

Every Outcome (O) you get in life is a direct result of your earlier Response (R) to an Event or Events (E) that occurred.

Blaming is a Response (R) to an Event (E) that doesn't change the Outcome (O). The only thing that will change the Outcome is to think new, more positive and responsible thoughts, visualize more positive images, and engage in different, more effective behaviors.

Remember, you always have two choices. You can either blame the event or you can change your thinking and your behavior. Continuing your old patterns of thinking and behavior will keep producing the same results in your life. 2+2 will keep producing 4. If you want something different, you will have to do something different. If you want 5 (a better outcome), you will have to do 3 instead of 2. Here's another thought to ponder. If what you were currently doing in life would give you more of what you want, that more would have already showed up.

If you want something better, you have to change your responses. Change your self-defeating thoughts (I don't know how, I'm not worthy, I'm not smart enough, I don't have enough time, I don't have enough money, I'm a victim) to self-empowering thoughts (I can find out how, I deserve, I am smart enough, I have everything I need to create anything I want). Change the way you "see" yourself in your mind's eye from negative images of rejection and failure to positive pictures of acceptance and success. Replace your non-productive activities with productive work habits as well as focused and consistent effort.

II. CREATE A VISION OF YOUR IDEAL LIFE

Once you have a sense of what you are excited about doing and have assumed 100% responsibility for making it happen, take time to sit down and write a detailed vision of everything you would be experiencing in all areas of your life if you were living that dream. Be as detailed and specific as possible. And at this stage, don't worry about whether or not it is possible or how you're going to make it happen. Just let your deepest and true self describe exactly what you want.

III. TURN YOUR VISION INTO SPECIFIC, MEASURABLE GOALS

Goals are dreams with deadlines.

~ Diana Scharf Hunt,
Author of *The Tao of Time*

Next, turn your vision into a set of measurable goals. By measurable, I mean "how much, by when." How can you measure it (it needs to be a specific number such as units sold, dollars earned, people impacted), and by when will you accomplish it (a specific date like June 30, 2017)? Write your goals down. Map out all the steps you would need to take to achieve those goals as best you can. (If you don't know what steps to take, ask someone who has already done it—in person or by reading their book or taking their seminar.) Choose someone to share your goals with, and commit to a consistent time when you will give them a regular progress report on how you are doing. There is now a great deal of academic research that shows that writing your goals down, sharing them with others, and having someone hold you accountable with a regular reporting process greatly increases your achievement of your goals.

IV. VISUALIZE YOUR GOAL(S) AS ALREADY COMPLETE

Set aside five minutes every morning and again in the evening to close your eyes and visualize your goals as already complete. Imagine what you would see if you were looking out through your eyes at something that would let you know you were fulfilling you purpose, living your vision and had already achieved your goals.

After we sold Chicken Soup for the Soul Enterprises and I had created my vision of writing and teaching about the success principles, I spent a few minutes *every day* visualizing bookstore windows full of *The Success Principles* books, seeing the book listed on all the major bestseller lists, seeing myself being interviewed on morning television shows like *Today* and *Fox & Friends*, speaking at large corporate conventions, training rooms full of excited and committed students, and conducting trainings in Europe, Asia and the Middle East—all of which have since come true.

I encourage you to take the time to do the same, and when you do, make sure to add in the feelings you think you would feel if you had already accomplished your vision. Make the feelings as real and as intense as you can. Think of the picture you create like the destination programmed into the GPS system in your car, and the emotions like the fuel that actually drives the engine. The harder you push on the gas pedal, the faster the car goes—the stronger the feeling, the quicker the result.

V. THE MAIN SECRET TO SUCCESS IS TAKING ACTION!

Look at a stonecutter hammering away at his rock, perhaps
a hundred times without as much as a crack showing in it.
Yet at the hundred-and-first blow it will split in two, and I know
it's not the last blow that did it, but all that had gone before.

~ Jacob A. Riis

The main thing that separates the "winners" from the "losers" in life is that the winners constantly take action. In today's world, ideas are not enough. Timely execution is what matters. Yet, it's surprising how often I see people get trapped in planning, deciding, investigating and other preliminary activities—when what they should really be doing is taking action on their goals. When you take action, the Universe responds and rewards that action with feedback about what worked and didn't work, and by constantly course correcting, you can quickly move toward the completion of your vision.

VI. THE WORLD DOESN'T PAY YOU FOR WHAT YOU KNOW. IT PAYS YOU FOR WHAT YOU DO!

Have you ever had a great idea—only to see it turned into a successful business or a new invention or a popular product *by someone else* because they took action on it and you didn't? Dreaming is important, but it is not enough. You must take action.

And please remember, all actions don't pay off *immediately*. In most all things there is a learning curve. It takes time to *master* anything. There's a lot of research that says it takes 10,000 hours (between five and seven years) to master anything. Brian Tracy says that we are try-fail-learn, try-fail-learn, try-fail-learn, try-fail-learn, try-fail-learn, try-fail-learn, try-fail-learn, try-fail-learn, try-succeed machines. I agree. I find it encouraging to remember that "every master was once a disaster."

Give yourself permission to take the time to learn how to do—and eventually master—whatever new thing you decide to do. In my own career I have literally read thousands of books and taken a lot of seminars on speaking, writing, training, coaching, motivation, management, leadership, humor, money management, meditation, communication skills, sales, enrollment, marketing, online marketing, advertising, branding, team building, networking, social media, public relations and customer service.

VII. PRACTICE THE RULE OF 5

When *Chicken Soup for the Soul* was first published, everyone on our team wanted it to become a *New York Times* #1 Bestseller. With that goal in mind, we interviewed dozens of book-marketing experts and sought the advice of numerous bestselling authors. We even read a book called *1001 Ways to Market Your Book*. And with literally thousands of strategies we could pursue, to be honest, our goal began to feel a little overwhelming.

Then one day, I was talking to a friend who reminded me that even the largest tree could be felled simply by swinging an ax at its trunk just five times a day. "Eventually," he said, "the even the largest tree would have to come down."

Out of that advice, we developed The Rule of 5: do five things every day that will move you closer to completing your goal. In the case of *Chicken Soup for the Soul,* it meant doing five radio interviews a day . . . Or sending out five review copies to newspapers. Or asking five ministers to use a story from the book in their sermons . . . Or calling five network-marketing companies to sell them a copy for every one of their sales associates . . . Or sending out five press releases a day. And on and on . . . everyday . . . for more than 2 years. Not only was it worth it, but the book went on to reach #1 on the *New York Times* and *USA Today* bestseller lists, sold more than 210 million copies in 47 languages, and spawned a series that has sold more than 500 million copies around the world.

And now we're using that same Rule of 5 to reach our current goal of selling a million copies of *The Success Principles* by 2016 and to train one million Certified Success Principles trainers by 2030. And once again, we are on track to fulfill both those goals.

If you want to achieve the fulfillment of your life purpose, realize your highest vision and achieve all your goals, I encourage you to read the 10th Anniversary Revised Edition of *The Success Principles* and check out the Success Principles Train the Trainer program at www.JackCanfield.com.

About Jack

Known as America's #1 Success Coach, Jack Canfield is the CEO of the Canfield Training Group in Santa Barbara, CA, which trains and coaches entrepreneurs, corporate leaders, managers, sales professionals and the general public in how to accelerate the achievement of their personal, professional and financial goals.

He is best known as the coauthor of the #1 New York Times bestselling *Chicken Soup for the Soul®* book series, which has sold more than 500 million books in 47 languages, including 11 New York Times #1 bestsellers. As the CEO of Chicken Soup for the Soul Enterprises he helped grow the Chicken Soup for the Soul® brand into a virtual empire of books, children's books, audios, videos, CDs, classroom materials, a syndicated column and a television show, as well as a vigorous program of licensed products that includes everything from clothing and board games to neutriceuticals and a successful line of Chicken Soup for the Pet Lover's Soul® cat and dog foods.

His other books include *The Success Principles™: How to Get from Where You Are to Where You Want to Be* (recently revised as the 10th Anniversary Edition,) *The Success Principles for Teens, The Aladdin Factor, Dare to Win, Heart at Work, The Power of Focus: How to Hit Your Personal, Financial and Business Goals with Absolute Certainty, You've Got to Read This Book, Tapping into Ultimate Success, Jack Canfield's Key to Living the Law Attraction,* and his recent novel—*The Golden Motorcycle Gang: A Story of Transformation.*

Jack is a dynamic speaker and was recently inducted into the National Speakers Association's Speakers Hall of Fame. He has appeared on more than 1000 radio and television shows including Oprah, Montel, Larry King Live, the Today Show, Fox and Friends, and 2 hour-long PBS Specials devoted exclusively to his work. Jack is also a featured teacher in 12 movies including *The Secret, The Meta-Secret, The Truth, The Keeper of the Keys, Tapping into the Source,* and *The Tapping Solution.*

Jack has personally helped hundreds of thousands of people on six different continents become multi-millionaires, business leaders, best-selling authors, leading sales professionals, successful entrepreneurs, and world-class athletes while at the same time creating balanced, fulfilling and healthy lives.

His corporate clients have included Virgin Records, SONY Pictures, Daimler-Chrysler, Federal Express, GE, Johnson & Johnson, Merrill Lynch, Campbell's Soup, Re/Max, The Million Dollar Forum, The Million Dollar Roundtable, The Entrepreneur Organization,

The Young Presidents Organization, the Executive Committee, and the World Business Council.

He is the founder of the Transformational Leadership Council and a member of Evolutionary Leaders, two groups devoted to helping create a world that works for everyone.

Jack is a graduate of Harvard, earned his M.Ed. from the University of Massachusetts and has received three honorary doctorates in psychology and public service. He is married, has three children, two step-children and a grandson.

For more information visit: www.JackCanfield.com

CHAPTER 2

SUCCESS IS A SEVEN-LETTER WORD

BY ROBERT H. SHOLLY

Success is many things to many people. The foundations of my successes were paved with my insatiable curiosity as a child and the influence of several significant family members. I had a magical life with doting parents and grandparents who modeled and coached me in the fundamentals needed for success in life while making sure I understood that no one can become a success all on their own.

When I was a child I was a typical boy and didn't like chores. I would fail to pick all the weeds in the garden and my grandparents made me go back and do it over again until I got it right. At age twelve, I still resisted giving it my all at times. Once my dad and I were building a garden and had to haul the excess dirt away. My dad showed me where he wanted me to dump the dirt, but I thought it would be good enough to dump it about three fourths of the way in what I thought was a better spot. However, I was firmly told that I needed to dump it where he had identified and that if I had done the job right the first time, I would not have had to double haul the dirt and would have been finished much earlier. That may have been when I finally got the message, do it right the first time.

When I enlisted in the Army as a private, my supreme goal was only to make sergeant. When I made sergeant, I was encouraged to become an officer, which I was able to accomplish by attending Officer Candidate School. The tremendous mental and physical effort required to graduate successfully from that institution stretched me as a human being and jump-started my desire to make the Army a career and gave me another set of life standards. As I reached each rank, I focused on the basics of doing whatever job I had to the best of my ability. I observed officers senior to me so I could have a better understanding of their responsibilities in the event I was promoted to that grade some day. In the military, I recognized that you are promoted not only on how well you do your job at your current rank, but also on how your superiors see your potential for greater responsibility. The same is true in civilian life.

I studied the biographies of the great leaders, read all the pertinent books and other materials that were available, and volunteered for service schools that would enhance my skills and my value to the Army. This preparation paid off when I was privileged to lead men in combat in Vietnam. After that, my career was a series of assignments that prepared me to command higher-level units. Considering my early beginnings as a private, retiring as a colonel was a great personal success. No matter how forceful, intelligent, clever or innovative I may have thought I was, I knew that my every success was the result of having been lifted on other's shoulders to reach the next rung of the ladder, and I was grateful for all the help along the way.

After my military career, I entered the corporate world. At times even colonels have to start over again. I did. I began by writing project proposals from a small cubicle and providing my expertise on various foreign countries. Through perseverance, I eventually became a project manager on projects in remote parts of the world and under hostile conditions. As my value to the Fortune 500 Corporation increased, I was provided the opportunity to become the General Manager of a newly-created subsidiary company. I considered myself extremely successful while at the helm of this great little company, but success was not accomplished without teamwork, dedication and outstanding efforts of all the staff and employees. The many team-building activities we enjoyed together helped to strengthen our working together. Our team went to the gun range together, canoed in the bayou, had family picnics, and much more as we grew into the proverbial "well-oiled machine."

Success is borne of a multi-faceted approach. For the purpose of clarity, I offer the acronym SUCCESS, to be used as a guide.

- Strategize

- Understand
- Commit
- Compete
- Enhance
- Study
- Support/Share

1. <u>Strategize</u> – You must have a plan. In the military, a goal is established and then things like terrain, enemy, and friendly forces are considered. Once all the pros and cons of these aspects are reviewed, the commander selects the best course of action to take the objective. Parallels can be drawn in civilian life. Before the final objective goal is reached, however, there will be numerous smaller objectives that need to be addressed. Some can be accomplished simultaneously, while others will need to be done sequentially. You must define your goal, learn everything you can about the task at hand, practice, gain expertise and prepare. However you do it, remember that the way to eat an elephant is one bite at a time.

2. <u>Understand the journey</u> - Too many people over-think what it will take to be successful. They get overwhelmed by all the minutiae they imagine, and never get started. It is good to play the "What if…" game, but only in the context of identifying the challenges so you can overcome them. Approach tasks with a positive attitude and BELIEVE deep inside that you will be able to accomplish them. Be realistic about what the personal costs may be in terms of finances, time, emotions and mental and physical effort. You must recognize there can be setbacks, but "You aren't a failure unless you never try or until you quit before reaching your goal." If you fall, get back up on your feet – you are still standing and that in itself is an accomplishment."

3. <u>Commit to the task at hand</u> - Keep the goal in mind, focus and concentrate. Don't get sidetracked, don't scatter your energies or resources and don't go down rabbit holes that have nothing to do with your long-term goals. Sometimes you have to sacrifice the "now" for something larger in the future. That doesn't mean become a workaholic. You must recognize the need for balance in your life between work and personal recharging. It is wonderful when you can blend your work with personal enjoyment, but many of us will not

find that perfect condition. You may not be the quickest, strongest, smartest, most agile person in the world, but Aesop had it right when he created the tortoise and the hare story. The tortoise kept his eye on the goal, while the hare lost focus and played along the way.

4. Compete – Everything is a competition, whether it is against your peers and colleagues, or just against your own standards. Successful athletes and businesspersons pit themselves against personal standards to build strength and abilities. To do something well, you have to believe you can do it. That takes confidence. Confidence is a mighty tool and each achievement will strengthen and increase your abilities and mark you a winner. Do whatever is necessary to build your confidence. Dress like those who have achieved similar objectives. People like people who look, talk and seem to think like themselves, not above them. Do not become a clone, but if you can blend in with people, you can learn from them.

   a. Network with those who can support and assist you. Jack Canfield says, "Meet influential people and learn from them." One aspect of competing in order to develop confidence, is to always act as though you have already achieved your objective. It is important that you are never a user and never act in an arrogant or superior manner. As you develop confidence, you will start to take on the attributes of someone who is smart, strong and successful. If you believe it, you can attain it. The power of visualization can give you confidence and an advantage over your competitors.

   b. Another useful tip is, "Don't burn bridges." Sometimes you need to draw upon other's expertise to augment your own. I doubt there is a successful person who has never needed something from someone or some organization with whom they have worked in the past. A momentary gratification of anger may cut off something that may be useful in the future.

5. Enhance skills: – My father told me to learn everything I possibly could from everybody and everything everywhere. He encouraged me to learn to type. I have used that skill all my life and it has made a difference time and again. If you have computer or mobile device skills, learn more. If you have social media skills, develop them to a greater degree. Learn public speaking, not only in front of an audience

but also impromptu speaking, which is a most valuable skill. Absorb speaking techniques such as motivational, persuasive, humorous and storytelling. Learn the basics of videography and sound. If you understand the principles of sitting or talking before a camera, you will do well when the time comes. Develop writing skills that present you well. Whether they are electronic or on paper, your words tell a great deal about yourself.

People skills may be even more important than technical skills. As I have already mentioned, you can learn much by associating with already successful people. Their experiences and other associates can provide you with valuable insights and possible mentoring.

6. Study - Study successful people who have gone before you. Learn constantly and develop your technical background. Read everything you can that pertains to your selected industry, including the biographies of the giants in your field. As you have time, read the giants in other fields as well to gain exposure to new ideas and ways of thinking. Their stories will not be yours, but they will have something you can use. There are basic commonalities used for success in various endeavors. By reading stories, you will begin to recognize how these basics apply to you. In gaining expertise, you not only have to read, you need to learn something from everyone you meet. It is amazing how many little things you can pick up from casual acquaintances that will come in handy later on.

7. Support and share - This is something all successful people do. They recognize their duty to give back. Whether their sharing is in the form of mentoring, donating money, time or effort, all successful people do it. If you help your colleagues and community, it will come back to you in a positive form.

There are many perspectives and numerous guidelines for success, whole books have been written about them. Read all those you can and take away what feels right for your situation.

I heard a very successful author say, "I became an overnight success, but it took me ten years to do it!" That is what many people forget. Overnight successes are rare.

Most of us pay dues to make it to the top in our chosen field. Those dues generally consist of learning and practicing the basics. To quote the old Chinese philosopher, Confucius, "Success depends upon previous preparation, and without such preparation there is sure to be failure." Studying and learning the basics holds true in all areas of life. You can understand something intellectually, but unless you internalize it, it will fail you when you most need it.

Good or bad luck is just a manifestation of probabilities. It has nothing to do with omens, lucky charms, fortune cookies or magic. It has to do with sustained hard work and your belief that you can achieve a certain goal. Put a working plan together to provide the necessary tools and resources. Prepare yourself properly and the probability of achieving success is increased many fold. Recognize opportunities when they come, and if you have prepared and stayed the course, your dreams of success can come true.

That being said, as the great motivational speaker, Zig Ziglar said: *"I'll See You at the Top!"*

About Robert

Robert H. Sholly is a Nobel Peace Prize Winner (shared with other UN Peacekeepers). Colonel, USA (Ret.) and a Hall of Fame Inductee, U.S. Army Officer Candidate School. He is also a Sports parachutist D-268. Middle East, Africa, South Asia specialist. Speaks five (5) languages. Corporate executive. General Manager of a wholly-owned subsidiary of a Fortune 500 corporation. National Racquetball champion. President, 8th Infantry Regiment Society. ActiVets Board Member. Best Selling Author. Winner of 21 Literary Awards. VP of Membership, Mid-Pearland Toastmasters. Professional Speaker.

This highly-decorated, distinguished soldier-citizen was born in Santa Fe, New Mexico in 1938. As the first-born of a park ranger and his school teacher wife, Sholly was raised in national parks, lived in tar paper shacks, and was home-schooled. He was then educated in a one-room school house with 12 other students of various ages and grades. During this grade-school education, the only pastimes available were reading the dictionary, the encyclopedia, or playing geographical games on the world map.

Sholly's high school education required he live with his grandparents in California, a transition from 12 classmates to 3,000. This endeavor prepared him to deal successfully with the many moves his future held.

After high school, Sholly attended Texas A&M University as a member of the ROTC. That part of his education was short lived, and as his old New Mexico rancher stepfather used to say, "He discontinued his matriculation."

As many young men did, he joined the Army. Advancing through the enlisted ranks to Sergeant, he applied for Officer Candidate School and graduated a Second Lieutenant of Infantry. He later left active duty to return to college. In order to maintain his military affiliation, he joined a local National Guard unit.

During the break in active duty, he got married and enthusiastically took on additional responsibilities. About this time, the Vietnam War became more active. Because of his training and patriotism, he felt compelled to return to active duty with assignment to Vietnam. After his first tour, he obtained Masters degrees in History and English from the University of Texas at El Paso.

At the completion of 35 years of service, he retired a highly-decorated Colonel with a Silver Star and the Defense Superior Service Medal and a graduate of the US Army's War College.

Using his transferable skills, Sholly entered the corporate world as a consultant, became a project manager, and eventually a general manager. He spent 15 years in corporate life, retiring again in 2006. Unable to "do nothing" Sholly proceeded to fulfill his lifetime passion to write a book: *Young Soldiers Amazing Warriors*. He is now a best-selling author, an entrepreneur and a professional speaker. The best-selling memoir of his first tour of duty in Vietnam has won 21 awards.

Robert Sholly also enjoys hiking, racquetball, traveling, and mentoring. He shares the knowledge he gained throughout his careers through workshops and public speaking.

Sholly's full bio is available at: www.youngsoldiersamazingwarriors.com

Contact Robert H. Sholly at: robert@robertsholly.com

YouTube Book trailer: http://tinyurl.com/oo8upgv

Social Media - Follow Sholly on Facebook, Twitter @vietnamwarriors, Linked-In and Instagram

CHAPTER 3

NAVIGATING RETIREMENT'S TURBULENCE

BY ROBERT NORTON

Imagine you are going to fly from New York to San Diego but there is only enough fuel on the plane to get to Denver. When would you think it would be best to address this issue? Over Denver, when you are now out of fuel? Or, on the ground in New York?

You would obviously want to deal with this issue before you left the ground. A successful retirement works the same way. You do not want to be five - ten - fifteen years into retirement only to realize you are now out of money.

According to a study by Wells Fargo, of 1,000 middle class Americans, 70% of those with a written retirement plan are confident they have enough money for retirement. Of those without one, only 44% are confident. An even more pronounced finding was that those with a written plan had three times as much saved as those who did not. This does not have to be an eighty-page document. A concise overview will work in all but the most complex cases.

A "successful" retirement has a different meaning for different people. Does it mean more time to devote to grandkids, or more time for leisure and travel? Getting your golf handicap down to single digits? Or it could mean being able to devote your time to charitable enterprises or starting a new business. Whatever it means to you, the first step is to identify your income needs and developing a plan to meet those needs.

The previous generation's retirement was a simpler process. Many retirees worked for one company for the majority of their careers. At age 65, they would get a retirement party along with a gold watch and a pension. The pension plus their Social Security was their income. And often the pension would have a cost of living increase much like Social Security, so that income would continue to increase over time. Today, few companies provide their employees a traditional pension. It is up to the employee to make sure they have saved enough for their retirement. More importantly, it is their responsibility to make sure they don't outlive their retirement savings!

Combined with the fact that we are living longer, the challenge of providing a secure retirement becomes ever more daunting. We are now faced with having to provide an income stream that may have to last 20 to 30 years or longer. Remember that inflation will continue to drive the cost of living increasingly higher.

So where to start? The first step in solving any problem is to assess where you are at the current time. Are you already in retirement or are you looking to retire in the next 1, 5, 10 or 15 years? How much have you put away towards your retirement? This should include all retirement, investment, bank and annuity accounts. You may even have whole life insurance policies that could provide income in retirement. Do you have investment properties or business interests that will continue to provide income during your retirement?

TAKING BENEFITS

One very important thing to consider is your Social Security benefits and how and when you will begin taking them. There are 567 ways a married couple can take their benefit payments. Making a mistake in how you claim these benefits can be extremely costly. Anyone who starts their benefits or spousal benefits prior to their full retirement age will receive a reduced benefit for life. Full Retirement Age (FRA) is based upon your year of birth. For those born in 1937 or earlier, FRA is 65 years old. FRA increases by two months for every year from 1939 - 1942. (i.e. 1938 FRA = 65 years 2 months, 1939 FRA = 65 years 4 months ...) If you were born in 1943 - 1954 your FRA is 66 years old.

Birth years of 1955 - 1959 again increase by two months for each year. Anyone born in 1960 or later has a FRA of 67 years old.

The natural inclination for most people is to start taking benefits as soon as they are eligible. I recommend that you do an analysis of your benefits to determine when and who takes their Social Security benefits. The wrong choice can cost you tens of thousands of dollars or more over the course of your retirement. When I do a Social Security analysis for clients, they are often amazed at how large a difference the different claiming-strategies make in their long term income. Depending on when you were born, retiring at age 62 could cost you up to 30% of your benefit. It is definitely worth the time to make sure you are using the proper strategy for your particular situation. As a side note, widows and divorcees should always determine if the spousal benefits would be a more advantageous means of collecting.

The Social Security Handbook has over 2,728 separate rules governing your benefits. They will provide you no guideline as to which claiming strategy would be most beneficial for your circumstances. You alone must determine your claiming strategy and it will be the one with which you must live. This is a complex area that has far-reaching implications for a solid retirement income. It is worth the time to do an analysis to determine the most beneficial way to collect these lifetime benefits for you and your spouse. You have spent your entire working life paying into Social Security, it only makes sense to try and get the most benefit that you can.

Now you need to determine how much you will need to cover your living expenses. This could be a percentage of your pre-retirement income or an aspirational number. I recommend that the first number to come up with is a basic needs number. By this, I mean how much is required to pay all necessary expenses. Think of this as all the monthly expenses that won't change whether you are still working or not, including your mortgage, if you still have one, taxes, insurance, car and utilities. You will probably still want to eat, so food should be in there too. Now, without any additional luxuries, you will have a baseline number to solve for. Using this number you can determine how far ahead of the game you are, or if some modifications may need to be made.

This is where you gauge how much fuel you have in your plane (i.e. retirement plan) and where you plan to fly. You can make adjustments.

How far can you fly, how fast? Can you bring friends along and make multiple stops along the way? Knowledge is power. This is the information you need to know before you go on your long and hopefully very enjoyable journey through retirement. Knowing where you are and where you are going can provide a great deal of peace of mind. I think this is the key to a "successful" retirement. You don't want to be constantly fretting over your retirement. You want to have a solid grasp on your situation and the long-term prospects for your future. You want to have a map to follow on your journey.

LOOKING FORWARD

Okay, so now you know where you are and where you want to go. What's the best way to invest your assets to accomplish your goal? What is the best plan? Much like a diet, it is a plan you are comfortable with and one you will stick to. There are multiple strategies people use to accomplish these goals. There is a bucket strategy and a 4% withdrawal strategy. Many people will dedicate a portion of their assets to create a personal pension. They can create their personal pension to provide an income stream to cover their base expenses. This income will last for their lifetime and can increase over time. The key again, is to find a plan you are comfortable with and can stick to.

Work with an advisor. Find someone whose approach and plan makes sense to you. Think of him or her as your co-pilot on your journey to help you set your course. Advisors help to make sure the equipment is running correctly, the wheels are properly inflated, the wing tabs and rudders are functioning. We watch the radar for turbulence or storms and help navigate through these difficult times. Good advisors are constantly scouring to find opportunities and potential pitfalls that may affect clients. This information is used to make sure retirement plans remain on course.

The advisor-client relationship is important. You will be disclosing much personal information. For an advisor to do as good a job as possible, we need to have a very good picture of your needs and goals. So find someone who you would be comfortable enough with to sit down and share a meal together. Ideally you will be working together for many years. I still work with my very first client from 1992 when I started at Merrill Lynch.

I am always surprised when I meet someone who has not, and who is unwilling to spend a couple of hours to plan for a retirement that can last decades, though they will spend hours planning for their vacation. Putting our heads in the sand like an ostrich and hoping for the best is not a plan or strategy. Do the work and get your plan on track. Once you are up and running with a solid long-term plan you will have done the bulk of the work. Now you, along with your advisor, will monitor your plan and any changes in your life, and adjust accordingly. When you have a plane up in the air and cruising along on a proper flight path, the hardest part is done. Now you need to monitor the equipment and watch the weather so you can make any needed adjustments.

PREPARE FOR THE FINISH LINE

One other area that is vitally important and often overlooked in a solid plan regards your estate and end of life. Ben Franklin said, "In this world nothing can be said to be certain, except death and taxes." We will all succumb to the ravages of time eventually. Our loved ones will be left behind to grieve and miss us. They will also be required to wrap up our financial affairs. Having a few key documents in place prior to becoming ill or incapacitated, can alleviate a lot of pain and heartache for our loved ones.

A Will, financial and medical Powers of Attorney, and a Living Will should all be part of your planning. Your Will directs the disposition of your assets: who you want to get what and how much. The powers of attorney will allow someone to make financial and medical decisions for you should you be unable to do so for yourself. Whether you become incapacitated for a brief or very long time, decisions will need to be made regarding your financial and medical affairs. Without your powers of attorney, your family will have to go through the legal process of guardianship to get someone appointed for you. It would be much better for you to have these in place to eliminate wasted time and additional expense for your family.

A Living Will or advanced healthcare directive allows you to plan for the extent of the life-saving measures you do or do not want taken. Three years ago, I lost my mother and ten months later, my father. My dad's situation was such that we had to make a decision no one ever wants to make. My dad had a Living Will. My brothers, sister and I knew what he wanted done. It was there for us to read in black and white. In one of the saddest and difficult days in our family's life, our dad had lifted some of the burden from us. We knew what he wanted and we did as we were told.

Death and illness is always a sad and difficult time for a family. Planning for life's inevitable decline and end can alleviate many of the burdens of this time. Make your wishes known and get the proper documents in place so your family can focus on what is important.

Do these things now, get your plans in place and you can fly off into your retirement with confidence.

Sources:

Wells Fargo Study, *Middle Class Americans Face a Retirement Shutdown.* 10/23/2013

www.social security.gov

About Robert

A financial professional since 1992, Robert Norton started his own financial firm in 2000, intent upon providing the unbiased investment-management and retirement-planning services retirees and pre-retirees need to pursue their financial goals.

"My mission," Robert says, "is to work with people in an environment of mutual respect and enjoyment of each other's company. I want to be a useful partner, in helping my clients gain financial confidence, so they can focus on what is most important in their lives."

In addition to over 20 years of experience, Robert brings to clients a Bachelor of Science Degree from Clemson University's School of Commerce and Industry as well as his Series 7 and 24 Securities registrations, held through LPL Financial. His experience and training have made him a versatile professional capable of helping clients with a variety of financial needs.

As an independent advisor, Robert works exclusively for his clients – not for financial companies or brokerages. He is free to make sure his clients' needs are always the top priority.

Robert's honors include appearing as a guest on 1210 WPHT's "The Big Talker" and the former WWAC TV. He's also a multi-year winner of the Five Star Wealth Manager Award*. The greatest tribute to him, though, is a loyal and growing clientele.

Away from work, Robert enjoys spending time with his six wonderful nieces and nephews, and with his near-constant companion and best friend, Bohdi, the dog.

CONTACT INFORMATION
Robert Norton
LPL Registered Principal
Norton Wealth Management
18 South Second St., Hammonton, NJ 08037
21 Broad St., Charleston, SC 29401

Phone: 609-704-0444
Or: 843-277-8767

Fax: 888-710-2470

E-mail: robert.norton@lpl.com
Website: www.nortonwealth.com

WWW.RETIREREADYSC.COM
WWW.RETIREREADYNJ.COM

DISCLOSURES

Securities Offered Through LPL Financial, A Registered Investment Adviser. Member FINRA/SIPC.

*Five Star Wealth Manager Award Winner 2012, 2013, 2015
Award based on 10 objective criteria associated with providing quality services to clients such as credentials, experience, and assets under management. Prior to 2012, award was based on client satisfaction. Respondents evaluated criteria such as customer service, expertise, value for fee charged and overall satisfaction. The overall score is based on an average of all respondents and may not be representative of any one client's experience.

CHAPTER 4

HOW TO THRIVE IN MEDICAL SCHOOL AND ACADEMIA

BY THOMAS J. CUMMINGS, M.D.

When I was in high school I knew my number one goal in life was to go to medical school. No one in my immediate or extended family was a physician or was connected in any way to the medical profession. My parents divorced when I was in second grade, and neither attended college. None of my childhood friends came from a family of doctors or had any aspiration to become a doctor. How then could I have possibly become so focused to do something that seemed like it should've been nothing more than a dream, a longshot fantasy? I believe three events from my youth played a major role:

(1). My seventh-grade English teacher wrote to my mother and told her I had a gift for writing. She also pulled me aside after class one day and told me the same. I still have that simple, handwritten note, and four decades later that compliment remains vivid. The confidence and encouragement I received from this unassuming gesture continue to influence me.

(2). At the age of thirteen, I went to my pediatrician for my annual check-up. In the waiting room, he noticed I was reading The Journal of the American Medical Association rather than the other common doctor office magazines. I told him, "I want to be a doctor." He replied, "You must read every day for the rest of your life." "I'll do

SOUL OF SUCCESS VOL. 1

it, I promise," I answered. He smiled and said, "Stay focused. Don't let anyone distract or discourage you."

(3). During sophomore year of high school, my mom was working for a costume jewelry company in an attempt to make ends meet. One frigid January evening the company hosted a seminar featuring Mr. Jim Rohn. We rode the subway and took a bus to get there. The title of the seminar was, "Developing a Winning Attitude." I know that was the title because I still have the cassette tape I purchased, and it was the best five dollars I've ever spent. That night changed my life. In Mr. Rohn's dynamic lecture I learned to write down my goals, focus on them, and take action to achieve them. In his distinct style I remember him saying, "Don't wish it were easier, wish you were better."

Although Mr. Rohn is no longer with us, I still consider him (and Mr. Jack Canfield, of course) to be my success coach, and his teachings remain with me today. Mr. Rohn also taught me to keep a journal and to write things down: ideas, thoughts, quotes, and anything else worth keeping. That sparked my habit of always having a pen and notepad in my pocket, and I do mean always. It was also in that conference room that I knew I wanted to go to medical school more than anything in the world. Did it matter that I had zero knowledge about what it meant to be a doctor or what it took to become a doctor? Did it matter that I had no medical pedigree?

Maybe you are able to recall similar situations in your life that made a positive influence. They must be guarded and treasured, for they open the door of opportunity for us. Perhaps we can teach our children to be aware of this and to recognize the potential difference-making moments in their own lives. The following account of my journey through medical school, residency and fellowship, and the climb from assistant professor to tenured full professor at a major medical university, is interchangeable with any profession. I made it, and so can you, even if the odds for success do not seem to be in your favor.

Herein, I will tell you the <u>five</u> concepts that are the core and the soul of my success. These are the methods I used to accomplish my goals. These methods are not novel. They are the foundation, and they have stood the test of time. Everything here has already been lectured or written by the great personal development teachers over the years. The key concept is that sometimes the important first step of success is to commit to the basics and the fundamentals, even if they appear vague and oversimplified. Here they are. Why not give them a shot?

1. *Find out what format works for you. Trust it, believe it, and stick with it. Distance yourself from the negativity of others. Know when to accept advice, and when to ignore it. Evaluate and modify your plan if things aren't working.*

My situation is my situation. Your situation is your situation. Our individual journeys are unique. I believe that I am exactly where I am supposed to be at every given moment, and that everything that has happened to me is as it was meant to be. My method of learning may differ from your method of learning. I chose to attend almost every class in college and medical school; I never wanted to miss a day. Along the way, many laughed and proclaimed that going to class was a waste of time. Maybe they were right, maybe they weren't. There isn't necessarily a right or a wrong answer. I respect their opinion, and it is their choice how they will spend their time. The point is, I knew what was right for me. I learn best when I'm in a lecture taking notes from a professor who knows a lot more than I do. They'd also laugh about how taking notes was a waste of time since everything was already written down in the book. I ignored them, and I went to class and took notes, every day. I knew what format worked for me. I trusted it, believed it, and stuck with it. Of course, if things aren't working, you must know when to evaluate, modify, and change your plan if necessary.

2. *Focus, pay attention, listen, work hard, and don't quit. Persevere.*

Clues and opportunities to your dreams and future could possibly be as close as a friend or family member or as random as a chance lecture that influences you in a positive direction. Focus. Pay attention. Listen. In the martial arts there is a saying: All black belts were once white belts; the difference is the black belt did not quit. Similarly, all professors were once students. If you are a student and you struggle with a subject, consider getting a tutor. Sometimes we need a coach, a tutor, or a teacher. I still seek out my mentors and senior professors on a daily basis to learn from them; they too are both masters and master students. Our coaches and teachers are invaluable, and we must choose them wisely. And, of course, I continue to read every day, and I do mean every day, to be the best I can be for my patients, and to honor the promise I made to my pediatrician.

Albert Einstein attributed his success to the fact that he would stick with a problem for years and return to it again and again when all others had given up. If your goal is to go to medical school, and your application is rejected, what will you do? There are two options: you either keep trying, or you quit and choose another career. You can keep trying by attending a medical school in a different country, or, by improving your grades, admission test score, and curriculum vitae, and then apply again. It really is that basic, the difference between reaching your goal and not reaching your goal. I realize there are other factors that come into play, but if you want to achieve your goal, you must find a way to go forward and keep your dream alive.

> 3. *Find out what your weaknesses are, and improve them. Conquer your fears.*

I used to have a great fear of speaking in public. Throughout grade school and high school I did whatever it took to avoid having to make a presentation in front of others. I deliberately chose to attend a large undergraduate university, knowing I could fill my schedule with classes in big lecture halls that would provide me anonymity and a safe haven from public speaking. But I knew I couldn't run forever, and that I had to address and fix the problem. I also knew I couldn't survive medical school and residency like this, where almost every day you have to make a presentation in class, on rounds, or at a conference. I did some research, and I determined the best option for me to overcome my fear was to attend a Dale Carnegie public speaking workshop. There, I learned how to speak with confidence, how to conquer my fear, and how to thrive in speaking situations. Similar to the night I met Mr. Rohn, the night I graduated from the Dale Carnegie workshop was one that significantly transformed my life. I now knew my goal was within reach and nothing could stop me. I learned that if you want to achieve something great, there are no shortcuts. Today, I consider public speaking to be one of my strong skills, and I never shy away from an opportunity to embrace it.

> 4. *Dare to achieve your goals. Make your own breaks. Be patient. Ask. Be reliable. Be confident. Be great.*

Once I made it to medical school, I knew I wanted an academic career, a career filled with teaching, writing, traveling, and service, and a career where I would be involved with something bigger than myself. In medicine you have two basic choices: private practice or academia.

There are pros and cons to both. I wanted an academic career, where one of the highest recognitions comes in the form of promotion to the rank of Professor with Tenure, and a career focused more on the outcome than on the income.

During my residency, fellowship, and early years as an attending physician, I actively sought out all opportunities to teach. I wanted to learn as much as I could in my specialty and to become known as an international expert. It is said the definition of an expert is one who has hung around long enough to have made every mistake. One way to work towards this is to teach the practice of medicine, especially your specialty, to others. With thanks and gratitude to my newfound confidence in public speaking, I soon won a few teaching awards voted by my peers and my students. Next, in academia you have to make your own breaks. You cannot sit by the phone and wait for it to ring. You must pick up the phone and make the calls. I would contact session coordinators at national and international academy meetings and ask if they had room for one more speaker. I promised them I would give an all-star game worthy lecture, and I would be the most reliable speaker they ever had. Soon, I was an invited lecturer to meetings around the world on six continents, and Antarctica is not yet out of the question.

When doing this, be confident, not smug or conceited—and know the difference, for it is a big difference. Stay unassuming and humble. Study as much as you can. Prepare your lecture to be great, whether it's for five medical students or for five hundred international experts. I recall an interview with The Harlem Globetrotters basketball team declaring the commitment to excellence is the same for a crowd of a few people as it is for a crowd of thousands of people. That's respect. That's being great.

5. Use your talent to serve the greater good.

A favorite biblical quote of mine is that we are to use our gifts to serve others. If you are reading this book, you are likely to be a person dedicated to success. And one noble form of success is to use your talent to serve the greater good. In my career I'm able to teach and mentor, volunteer for medical mission work, and serve my patients. However, if I believe my seventh-grade English teacher and the biblical quote, it becomes clear that I should use my gift of writing to serve the greater good. I strive to do this in my novel *The Shoulder-Ride Gift*. To learn more, please visit my bibliography page.

About Dr. Cummings

Dr. Thomas J. Cummings, M.D. was born and raised in Brooklyn, New York. His attraction for writing began in the seventh grade when his English teacher told him he had a gift for telling stories with written words. Decades later, he hasn't forgotten that simple, encouraging, life-changing compliment. Throughout high school, college, and medical school, Thomas worked to improve his writing skills, with the goal of fulfilling his belief that we are to use our gifts to serve others. He is grateful to his family, friends, teachers, and coaches who helped him along the way and who are far too many to mention here.

Thomas J. Cummings received his M.D. degree from Rutgers Robert Wood Johnson Medical School in Camden, New Jersey, and then completed a residency in Anatomic Pathology and a fellowship in Neuropathology at Duke University Medical Center in Durham, North Carolina. Dr. Cummings is currently on faculty at Duke University Medical Center where he is tenured Professor of Pathology and Professor in Ophthalmology. He lectures extensively on Ophthalmic and Neurological Pathology around the world on six continents (and Antarctica is not out of the question). He's written and co-authored more than one hundred medical manuscripts and book chapters, won multiple teaching awards, and is sole author of the textbook, *Ophthalmic Pathology: A Concise Guide,* published by Springer Medical Publishing Company.

The Shoulder-Ride Gift is Thomas J. Cummings' first work of fiction. Its premise is that shoulder-rides are uplifting — literally — for children and adults. The goal of the story is to inspire others to get involved and connect with a child through the gift of a shoulder-ride — either their own child, or, by volunteering at orphanages, hospitals, or any other place where there is a child in need. Shoulder-rides are free, and no special equipment or set-up is necessary, somewhat analogous to why football (soccer) is the sport of the world. Even if only for a few minutes, a simple shoulder-ride could be the highlight of a child's day, especially a child who is disadvantaged, ill, bullied, or lonely. A shoulder-ride can also be the highlight of the day for the adult offering it; indeed, they are some of Thomas' most treasured memories of being a parent. The motto of the story is: The Shoulder-Ride Gift: Give One, Receive One.

The Shoulder-Ride Gift is coming soon to wherever books are sold, with the goal of transforming this basic, simple concept into a thriving global reality. *The Shoulder-Ride Gift: Give Leprosy a Lift;* and, a children's book version of *The Shoulder-Ride Gift,* are Dr. Cummings' current works in progress. Proceeds from these books will be dedicated to helping others locally and globally with physical disabilities, mental disabilities, cancer, leprosy, tropical diseases, other illnesses, and social disadvantages.

If you want to learn more, please visit: www.theshoulderridegift.com. Thomas J. Cummings is managed by Peter Miller, the "Literary Lion", at Global Lion Intellectual Property Management, Inc. (www.globallionmanagement.com).

[Disclaimer: I, Thomas J. Cummings, M.D., confirm that I have no financial obligations or conflicts of interest to declare with respect to any of the individuals or enterprises mentioned herein. T.J.C.]

CHAPTER 5

DAILY COMPASS

BY BENTLEY MURDOCK

Do what you love and give passion the stage
As you calmly embrace the real you.
Your life will be happy and loving you back,
But only if you love what you do.

CORE VALUES

Success, to me, is enthusiastic progress toward the realization of balanced, worthwhile endeavors. In other words, success can be achieved at every step of the way while accomplishing your goals.

An intangible key element of any successful reality is obtained by *embracing* one's own unique set of personal core values. These become the roots, which feed our passions from within. As such, they deserve our most focused and disciplined attention.

Also known as standards or virtues, core values are just as unique as the individuals to whom they belong. These profound and deeply personal truths are treasures we gather along the way in life, working feverishly to make known their existence and purpose. When nourished, these values become our most reliable muscles, both emotionally and psychologically.

Those who enjoy more frequent success in their lives allow themselves to be guided from within. They passionately govern their own lives, functioning in harmony with their core values. Every human in all of creation is gifted with free agency, infinite potential and the ability to be led by an intrinsic mechanism of her or his own design - a literal Daily Compass. Many are convinced they can somehow ignore their deepest values, neglecting their conscience. (The universe, however, has a unique way of reminding us, every thought, action, and word gets evaluated.)

Our personal values are anxious to arrive on the scene whenever we stray from what we intrinsically know is good and right. Most people only allow their values to emerge after their emotional walls have come down, often only in the company of those to whom they trust revealing their most vulnerable selves. Courageous and wise are those who hear that tender plea from within, beckoning toward those higher roads of choices and decisions. Each of us is able at any time to tune in and hear that inner voice whispering. Many do hear it clearly and listen carefully. Others choose to become acquainted with bitter tinges of guilt and regret, pretending they don't know any better.

Fully embracing your core values will ignite your own sparks of passion and dedication, introducing you to your best self. They will guide you through setting and achieving goals, yielding for you the greatest abundance of success and happiness your life has ever known.

MY STORY

I grew up in a large, Christ-Centered Family, with seven awesome brothers, one remarkable sister, and two lovingly dedicated parents. We were (and still are) a unique group of very eclectic individuals! Over time, I truly began to grasp how fortunate I was (and am) within such a family. All were quickly taught important values: sacrifice, patience, and teamwork. But above all, there was ONE leading the others. My family planted within me the seed of my first core value: INTEGRITY.

I knew I wanted to do incredible things, making a difference in the world. I knew it was critical that I integrate myself with my Creator, my Savior, my Family and others to whom I turn with admiration and respect. I wanted to function and contribute as part of something greater than myself, to keep my imperfections and inadequacies from limiting my accomplishments. The roots of integrity fostered within me other equally valuable morals and virtues.

I was raised with the knowledge and understanding that we are all truly unique and infinitely valuable children of God. I was taught, and more importantly I know, each of us has within us seeds of infinite greatness capable of miraculous accomplishments. I became determined to help others nourish their own seeds of potential by sharing with them my second core value: FAITH.

Life is for learning and I've navigated through plenty of my own struggles. But I've always held a passionate certainty regarding who I am (and whose I am), where I came from, why I'm here, and where I'm going. The trunk of my faith is the permanent reality that I am a creation of Infinite Intelligence and can do anything with my mind and energy. My life's goal is to help others discover the purpose of their own existence and potentially bright future.

As a child, I developed a rare bone disease called "Legg Perthes", which inhibited healthy growth. The medical solution was to wear corrective leg and hip braces until growth resumed. They were awkward, painful, embarrassing, and unnaturally bowed my legs, causing me to waddle like some weird alien-duck zombie. I became the target of ignorant discrimination. Thankfully, we lived in Hawaii, surrounded by sympathetic locals, who lovingly treated me like family. My parents, siblings, friends, and teachers gently introduced me to my third core value: COMPASSION.

As I nourished that seedling of the purest kind of giving, other similar branches began to grow: understanding, charity and kindness. I am eternally thankful for those leg braces, my family, and people like my best friend, Arnold Ngatuvai. They warmly embraced me for who I was and gently introduced me to the person I eventually became. Every relationship in my life is beautiful and priceless because I've been taught by example to treat others with compassion.

When down in a gully and can't see the stars,
When fear is all that's in fashion;
Chart new directions that nourish new virtues.
Your compass is found in compassion.

When a husband and wife are one with their Creator, they resonate a three-fold harmony capable of healing the past, embracing the present, and changing the future. As my wife and I begin raising our own children in truth and light, we more fully understand the purpose of putting first things first. I lovingly thank my wife, Michelle, for re-introducing me to my fourth core value: UNITY.

When I've chosen to ignore my core values, I've suffered. I've heard those inner pleadings begging me to make things right yet chose at times to be selectively ignorant. I've often called on the assistance of other values: passion, confidence, forgiveness, and humility. Only then has lasting momentum been able to regenerate. The combinations of uniquely personal values are specific to each individual. The atmosphere of teamwork among my own core values is largely responsible for granting me the success I currently enjoy.

Consider the most successful, balanced and wholesomely influential people in the world; you'll find one predominant core value governing their daily thoughts, words, and actions. Derived from the Greek phrase 'En Theos' meaning "With God" (What better partnership?!); my fifth core value: ENTHUSIASM.

Similar to plants responding to sunlight, water, and rich soil, all aspects of our lives become invigorated through vibrant enthusiasm. When I choose to embrace my core values, the branches of my life produce abundant and delicious fruit, energized by this Mother of All Virtues. As I've introduced my own core values, hopefully some of yours have begun to surface.

UNIVERSAL LAWS

Functioning perpetually, regardless of our acknowledgement of their existence, these universal laws govern all energy, determining the irrefutable outcome of all actions. Understanding their purpose can be immediately applied to accomplishing goals.

The first universal law determining your success is *The Law of Attraction*. It states: All thoughts held in the mind will eventually materialize into reality. Charging thoughts with focused energy speeds up this process (hint: enthusiasm). Achieving results not yet experienced requires willingness to do things you've never done. Most people have only a foggy idea of what might be a nice reality to enjoy someday. Few access within themselves the disciplined art of focusing only upon that which they desire. The task is to determine what your ideal reality would look and feel like and to relinquish all thoughts not in harmony with those outcomes. The result of a regimented diet of the mind is more rewarding than most could ever conceive.

The second universal law applying to personal development is *The Law of Compensation*. It states: What you give will inevitably return to you greatly multiplied. Our thoughts, words, and actions become boomerangs of amplified energy returning back to us more of whatever we've been contributing. Each boomerang magnetizes to it additional thoughts, similar experiences, material things, and even people – all in harmony with its initial energy. While applying patience for your desires to materialize, keep in mind that limitations of time are determined by our own perception.

Our experiences find us by virtue of what we observe in ourselves and extend unto others. These become our contributions. Earl Nightingale guided me to my own conclusion: The compensation we receive in life will always be in direct proportion to the quality and quantity of our genuine contribution. Those who fully understand this truth quickly become known for habitually going the extra mile.

Utilizing *The Law of Attraction* and *The Law of Compensation* are essential to your success. The universe demands perfect balance. Our awareness of irrevocable law launches our journey of prioritized sacrifice toward that which we desire. What we GIVE in facilitation of our goals is just as crucial as what we GIVE UP. What are YOU willing to give and/or give up in exchange for that which you desire? . . . (Speed-Readers, STOP! Go back and re-read the previous sentence, writing down the exact details that leap forward in your mind. From those words will stem your first bold action steps!)

Grant yourself permission to prune all negative thoughts, bad habits, incorrect beliefs, limiting behaviors, and detrimental associations from your tree of life. Liberate yourself in every way from the heavy guilt of their collective influence. Positive and constructive thinking habits create a bed of rich soil, where universal laws and core values coexist and flourish harmoniously.

DETERMINING YOUR CORE VALUES

Understanding your own personal core values is essential to the swift arrival of your ideal reality. Which standards, virtues and values of yours have come to mind as you've been reading? What personal experiences could assist you in determining your own core values? What qualities do you admire most in a spouse or business partner? Questions like these are intended to reveal which strengths are most valuable to you. The traits you seek, most often in others, are those you must begin to master first. (More information about determining your own core values is included in Bentley Murdock's Bio, found at the end of this chapter.)

Take a moment to recall any interests in your life, originally responsible for stirring passion within you. Recover the innocence you enjoyed as a child, permitting you to confidently draw, sing, and dance, as if destined only to do so. Allow yourself the privilege of accessing boundless, imaginative thought. This process is paramount for the re-introduction of your innermost values.

APPLYING CORE VALUES

Embracing core values is an awkward dance, at first, stepping on our own toes and trying to blame it on others. Feeling foolish with our initial inability to remain in harmony with our core values is natural. Go easy on yourself, leave room for stumbling, be quick to forgive, and remember, it's a process of building emotional muscles, which takes time.

One misconception about core values tells us to have a different set we take to work, while the seemingly incompatible ones hang out at home with the kids. Your values are, and should remain, the very core of your soul. Nothing about your existence should be permitted to function independently from your core values. Double lives lead only to double trouble. When applied consistently, core values serve as a built-in set of converters, harmoniously streamlining your home-life, personal relationships, and professional endeavors.

The transformation and re-sculpting of one's character will often be met with resistance. Selectively ignorant family and friends are often willing to fabricate excuses and justifications for mediocrity, while the majority of limitations we encounter originate from ourselves. Comfort zones of all kinds become enemies to any healthy progress and should be quickly exposed and quarantined. When confidently driven on a mission toward the achievement of your goals, your core values act as your undeviating compass.

Feed your heart and mind only constructive input, which motivates and inspires. Write and record, in your own voice, uplifting affirmations, filling your mental dialogue with personal, present-tense, positivity. Imagine and create a physical vision board, displaying images of your ideal reality. Create a personal, professional or family mission statement, outlining core values, focus points, ideals and long-term goals. These action steps are all ingredients to your success, calculated to synchronize you with your goals and values.

MENTORSHIP

When we call ourselves to action, and hold ourselves accountable, we begin embracing tangible change as reachable. Even though you're capable of phenomenal accomplishments, this is where I invite you to seek counsel from those who are already living lives similar to your ideal reality. Ask for the cooperation and assistance of those who already enjoy that which you desire. Research, seek out, and select your own personal and professional Mentors.

The Greek words, "Men" and "Tor", combine to create the meaning "Mind Tower", which paints an image of elevated respect toward those of influence. A Mentor is a guide, leading by example and teaching from personal experience, those who seek her or his specified learning. Mentors coach others to do closely as they have done in order to achieve similar results. Who is currently living the lifestyle you seek for your ideal future? Who do you greatly respect, emulate, and admire and why? Who would you consider approaching to be your personal and/or professional Mentors? I invite you to reach out to them with an open mind, a teachable heart, and a willingness to embrace the concept of duplication. Lend yourself to their counsel only when found entirely consistent with your core values and you'll begin taking steps toward the reality of your ideal future.

FAITH IN YOURSELF

Become willing to submit yourself to specific action steps. Inspiration will continue to find you as your subconscious realigns itself with new images of your ideal reality. Doubts can return, fears might linger, and worries may creep in, but stay focused and they will continue to atrophy. Busy your mind with only the thoughts of what you desire, what you're willing to give toward the achievement of your goals, and exactly how it feels to be enjoying your future accomplishments.

As you become your best and most balanced self, old comfort zones will loosen their grasp, allowing intrinsic motivation to take root. Continue embracing a perpetually more youthful and confident reality, driven by priceless core values. By doing so, you'll always be guided on each step of your joyful and successful journey.

I have faith in your abilities and I wish you only the best in all you endeavor to accomplish. Enjoy the adventure and give it all you've got . . . You deserve a life you love.

Mahalo

About Bentley

Bentley Murdock is a Certified Transformational Trainer of Jack Canfield's *Success Principles*. He is also an inspirational speaker, author, musician, mentor, and life coach. He dedicates his time and energy to helping others confidently and youthfully pursue and achieve that which they greatly desire. His philosophy is rooted in the understanding and proper application of universal law, in harmony with one's personal core values.

Growing up in a large family and recognizing his desire to be perpetually youthful, Bentley gravitated toward working with youth. The intrinsic confidence and creativity of the young-at-heart deeply fascinated him. He became driven to unlock the mystery as to why the process of becoming an adult so often suppresses those remarkable attributes.

Utilizing live, musical performance as an avenue of connecting with youth, Bentley has successfully educated and awakened in the lives of thousands, a genuine interest in reviving that bold and confident, youthful state. His original "feel good" music is wholesome, family-friendly and created to lift and inspire all who hear it. For more information about Bentley's original music, live performances and speaking engagements, please visit www.BentleyMurdock.com.

While pursuing an education in child-to-adolescent development and behavior, Bentley has traveled, speaking and performing in both English and Spanish, for audiences of any size and of all ages in The United States, Mexico, and Canada. He regularly addresses topics ranging from goal setting, confidence building and core values, to managing addictive and compulsive behavior, drug and alcohol abuse prevention, peer pressure, and bullying. Bentley is also a Certified Confidence & High Ropes Course Facilitator & Mentor, and is currently pursuing his Doctorate of Philosophy Degree in Advanced Human Behavior and Psychology.

Bentley put his creative, social-media marketing skills to use while working for Publicis Groupe, one of the largest multinational, public relations and media-marketing firms in the world. He served as Social Media Ambassador for California's Central Coast and learned much of the hands-on, inner-workings and politics of the demanding Corporate World.

Bentley now trains corporation leaders and professional management teams of all kinds, to harmoniously streamline employee culture with customer expectation. He helps his clients set specific goals and action steps, establish individual and company core values, create mission statements, and become willing to allow each individual within their teams to do the same. (An extensive list of potential core values is available at: www.DailyCompass.com.)

As a life coach, personal mentor, and professional musician, Bentley meets with individual clients of all ages and demographics, to work on uniquely customized personal development coaching. Whether in person or over the phone, the process he facilitates caters to the distinct needs of each individual. For more detailed information about Daily Compass Life Coaching, Personal Development Workshops, Transformational Core Values Training, Personal and Professional Mentorship, and speaking engagements please visit: www.DailyCompass.com or feel free to contact them directly.

Bentley Murdock
Owner & Founder

DAILY COMPASS INTERNATIONAL
Perpetual Success - Coaching & Mentorship

866-396-8742

PO Box 1388 Midway, UT 84049

info@BentleyMurdock.com

info@DailyCompass.com

www.DailyCompass.com

www.BentleyMurdock.com

www.facebook.com/bentleymurdock

www.facebook.com/bentleymurdockmusic

www.facebook.com/dailycompassinternational

www.twitter.com/bentleymurdock

www.linkedin.com/bentleymurdock

www.instagram.com/bentleymurdock

www.youtube.com/user/bentleymurdock

CHAPTER 6

SMALL WORLD, BIG CONNECTIONS

BY BRENDA R. McGUIRE

A journey is measured in friends, rather than miles.
~ Tim Cahill

Blazing like a giant red Christmas ornament, the sun seemed to float on the glowing horizon as the Peace Boat sailed toward the African country of Eritrea where we were to make harbor. It was early Christmas morning, and I had gone up on deck to sort through my mixed feelings. It was hard being away from home at Christmas, and yet the anticipation of experiencing a holiday in an exotic culture left me with a feeling of excitement. Traveling was not new to me, and I usually felt 'at home' wherever I was in the world, but on such a special day, I was feeling homesick. Still, my travels had taught me how welcoming and hospitable people could be in this small world.

When the ship docked, the joyful refrain of "Jingle Bells" accompanied by banging drums being played by a large group of women dressed in white Tigray dress warmed my heart. Christmas in Eritrea was so special as local villagers opened their hearts and homes. Although they had very little to call their own, they generously shared what they had and helped remind me of the true meaning of Christmas. At a local orphanage, fellow shipmates handed out presents that I'd helped gather and wrap on Christmas Eve. The children's eyes glistened with hope, and laughter filled the room when Santa handed out the gifts. They were simply amazed by the "man in the red suit," having never met Santa before! Later, when I was seated on a tour bus and we were getting ready to leave, a woman took off what was obviously a much-worn and beloved, beaded leather necklace and handed it to me through the window. Without words, her sacrifice and gift from the heart brought tears to my eyes—her gesture was so generous and loving that even though it was my only Christmas present that year, Christmas felt complete.

Later that day, as we pulled out of Eritrea at sunset, I leaned over the wooden railing of the ship and waved goodbye to my new friends, reflecting on how my life had brought me to Africa. So far from home, my thoughts drifted back to my childhood growing up in rural Iowa. Back then, I used to stare out over the fields of green corn that moved so much like the waves of an ocean, and dream of exploring the world and meeting people in faraway lands. While in high school, I became best friends with an exchange student from Norway and was fascinated by the stories of her culture. That relationship further sparked a curiosity to see the world and connect with different cultures—an interest that continued to grow in college.

Without a passport, having limited funds, and knowing almost no one who'd traveled overseas, I had no idea how to make my travel dreams a reality. Then one day, in 1992, I saw a poster on my college campus about *Semester at Sea*, an academic world voyage, which ultimately would change my world forever. Little did I know when I signed up that this opportunity would set me on a path to every corner of the globe and allow me to connect with people from diverse cultures. At the time, I never dreamed that the connections I was about to make over the next decade would allow me to live, work and travel the world, and eventually, lead me back home.

After working hard to overcome the obstacles and financial challenges of going on my first global adventure, Semester at Sea, I set sail on the U.S.S. Universe. My destination—THE WORLD! During our 102-day academic voyage of discovery and exploration, we visited 12 countries on four continents. I came home forever changed, as I had quickly learned that we live in a small, kind-hearted and globally connected world. With this experience and just a little money, a backpack and a dream, I had the courage to move by myself to Australia, England and Ireland. While living and working in these countries, I took every opportunity to immerse myself in each culture. Eventually, my heart called me back to Japan—something I'd wanted to do since visiting there during Semester at Sea's first port of call. I headed for Osaka, to face the challenge of making a life in a non-English speaking country with a culture very different from my own. The first connection I made in Japan ultimately would lead to a myriad of life-changing connections that continue to impact my life and shape who I am today.

Shortly after my arrival at Osaka's Kansai airport, I went to the information counter to find a place to stay. A young Japanese woman, sporting a familiar yellow and purple Lion's Club jacket, caught my eye. Interested in what her story might be, I struck up a conversation with her. Her name was Akiko, and she was delighted to share her experience—she'd just returned from a wonderful stay with a host family in Indiana and wanted to somehow reciprocate the hospitality. Before I knew it, she invited me to her home for the night. Amazingly, she and her family's invitation turned into a home-stay of nearly two years. My priceless friendship with Akiko, a true 'soul sister,' led to a job, a home, a church, and valuable links into the Japanese community.

One day, while walking down a busy street in Osaka, I saw another poster that would further change my life. It was advertising 'Peace Boat'—a non-governmental organization that took Japanese passengers around the world to promote peace and cultural understanding. Eventually, I accepted a teaching job on Peace Boat—sailing around the globe, meeting people on six continents, and marveling at the kindness of strangers. While the places I saw were amazing, it was the people I met—like the woman in Eritrea on Christmas—that made the experience richer. In particular, one woman, who I became friends with on Peace Boat, Yayoi, would eventually impact my future, although I didn't realize it at the time.

After Peace Boat, I felt drawn back to Australia—the first foreign country that I'd lived and worked in after college—to pursue a master's degree in International Communication. Once again, I learned not to underestimate the power of connections and what I like to call the 'small world effect'—the amazing way life seems to have for bringing people together again in the most unexpected ways and places—even when doing so seems to defy the odds.

I relocated back to Sydney, Australia, just in time for the 2000 Olympics and Yayoi came for the world event. While out socializing one night, she introduced me to someone from Malaysia who introduced me to his boss from Iowa. Through this introduction, I eventually met my future husband who, coincidentally, also was from small-town Iowa. Ironically, he was working for the same company as my mom back in Iowa! We'd both moved to Australia at nearly the same time and met during the Closing Ceremony of the Olympics while watching a magical fireworks show from a balcony overlooking the twinkling Sydney Harbor. Four years later, on the eve of the Athens Olympics, that Iowa guy got down on one knee and proposed to me on the romantic Greek island of Santorini at sunset on a cliff overlooking the Aegean Sea. Amazingly, in yet another 'small world' moment, the first people to congratulate us were some of my Japanese friends from Peace Boat, who we ran into in Athens at the Olympics the next day.

We got married in Maui and my friend Yayoi, a native of Hawaii, helped us plan and celebrate our beach wedding, which was attended by friends from all over the world. During our reception, as I went around the room recounting how each guest had impacted my life, I couldn't help but marvel at the ripple effect of the connections I'd made that led me halfway around the world to meet and eventually marry a fellow Iowan.

After a decade spent living, working and traveling overseas, life soon brought me full circle back home to Iowa. When I started my global journey as a naïve, rural Midwestern girl, I never dreamed that through my connections I would sail around the world three times, live in six countries, travel to over 70 countries, oversee a multimillion-dollar business division for a Fortune 500 company, and lead one of the world's largest cross-cultural training organizations.

Filled with the knowledge of the value of connections, my personal experiences and education, I soon founded and became the CEO of two international companies, WorldWide Connect® and Global Gals®. Both companies help people connect with cultures and countries around the world—whether personally or professionally. WorldWide Connect, a cross-cultural training firm with a team of over 100 trainers on six continents, has helped thousands of business professionals, travelers, and expatriates handle the challenges of navigating a culturally diverse world. Global Gals empowers and educates women who want to live, work and travel around the world. While we emphasize how women can be smart, safe and savvy travelers through our workshops, retreats and events, our most important gift is to help them meet and travel with other women around the world.

Looking back, the series of connections I've made—most poignantly the friendships I formed with Akiko and Yayoi—make it clear to me that the most precious part of my world travels is the people I've met and the friends I've found. They led me to my husband, led me home, and led me to follow my dreams of helping others bridge cultural gaps and get the most out of their international experiences.

While memories of breathtaking vistas may fade, it is the people you meet and the kindness of strangers that will stay with you forever. Travel is an investment you can make, which no one can ever take away from you. The relationships you build with people open doors, broaden minds, and lead to opportunities you never thought were possible.

Below are some tips that I've found to be most effective in cultivating professional and personal connections, and discovering friends—both locally and globally.

THE 4 C'S FOR CREATING CONNECTIONS IN A CROSS-CULTURAL WORLD

1) Connecting

My experiences have taught me that the people you meet will be, by far, the most priceless gift of your international experiences, so don't miss out on the magic! As one of my trusted mentors says, "I've learned that friendships don't have to cost, they can actually pay, by making life richer and more exciting." Your experiences will be enriched when you open your heart, your mind and your soul to meeting people from different cultures, backgrounds, viewpoints, and ways of life.

In the business world, it's important to recognize the importance of taking the time to develop relationships with your clients, colleagues and customers, and understand that in some cultures, building trust and respect must happen first before 'getting down to business.' A U.S. business executive once admitted to me that he lost out on a multimillion-dollar deal because he overlooked the importance of building a long-term relationship with his Asian client.

2) Caring

So often when people think of traveling overseas they think of what they see on international news networks and view the world as a 'big and scary' place with potential threats lurking around every corner. Through my travels, I've learned that the world is overwhelmingly kind-hearted. Repeatedly, during my most distressing times of need, total strangers offered me help, kindness and support. Once while stranded in a small village in Japan, someone generously gave me several hundred dollars to get a train ticket back to Osaka!

In 2013, my father was diagnosed with cancer just 13 days before he passed away. As messages of caring and concern poured in from around the globe, the most important lesson was clear—the friendships you make and keep are one of the most important things in life. Over the years, I introduced my Dad to my international friends, and he made his own friends around the world, but in the end he was moved by all the lives he realized he'd touched. As a legacy to my father, I established Global Gals to help other women connect with cultures, countries, and new friends around the world.

3) Cultures

Whether you're moving to a new country, traveling for leisure or conducting business globally, it's important to understand the culture you're operating in. Each country has its own customs, social etiquette and cultural do's and don'ts. For example, when you arrive at your destination, do you know the appropriate attire? Do you know how to negotiate effectively or whether or not it's polite to make direct eye contact? When meeting someone for the first time, do you know whether you should kiss, bow or shake hands?

Through my international business experiences, I've learned the importance of understanding the culture you're working with in order to avoid making embarrassing and costly cultural mistakes, which can lead to lost business opportunities, damaged relationships, and lost revenue. A company's 'bottom line' can be negatively impacted if its employees aren't equipped with the appropriate cross-cultural skills needed to build and develop effective business relationships around the world.

4) **Coincidences**

Time and again in my travels, I've experienced the uncanny serendipity that often seems to dictate the paths of many a traveler. On multiple occasions while visiting one country, by coincidence, I've run into an old friend or acquaintance from another country across the globe. For example, early in my career, I moved to London without a job. As I was walking down the street, I ran into my old boss from Australia, whom I hadn't seen in two years. She had an opening at her new office across the street, and within an hour, I was gainfully employed!

I've met so many people who have experienced similar stories that it inspired me to launch www.smallworldstories.com where people can share the 'small world' coincidences and kind-hearted gestures they've experienced first-hand.

* * *

I often wonder how different my life would be if I hadn't had the courage to strike up a conversation with a complete stranger at the Kansai Airport. That single interaction with Akiko caused a ripple effect that would change my life forever and impact both of our destinies. If I hadn't met Akiko, I know that my life wouldn't be nearly so exciting or so rich. Without a doubt, my understanding of the importance of making and maintaining relationships, wherever I go, has helped me get to where I am today. More importantly, it has given me the opportunity to help others connect around the world.

My journey has taught me just how true the anonymous quote is: *There are no strangers in the world, just people I haven't met yet.*

About Brenda

Brenda McGuire is an avid globetrotter, entrepreneur, and global business and travel expert whose global journey has taken her to over 70 countries on six continents. Wherever she is in the world, whether it's backpacking in Europe, exploring the Amazon rainforest, interacting with the locals of Morocco or traversing the Australian outback, she feels right at home.

As a young girl, Brenda had limited opportunities to see a world beyond her small, rural Iowa town, but that all changed after she participated in the Semester at Sea program, visiting 12 countries in 102 days. She returned home a "citizen of the world," and spent the next 20 years turning her global dreams into reality.

During her global career, Brenda has lived and worked in Japan, Australia, the United Kingdom, Ireland, the United States and Switzerland, with positions in the corporate, academic, non-profit and government sectors. In New York, she led a multimillion-dollar division of a Fortune 500 company, overseeing one of the world's largest intercultural and global workforce development organizations. A recognized cross-cultural expert in her field, she has taught thousands of individuals and companies in more than 50 countries how to effectively live, work and travel—across diverse cultures, time zones, and language barriers.

Brenda is the Founder and CEO of WorldWide Connect®. With an extensive global network of over 100 consultants on six continents, they deliver cross-cultural training, global business and leadership effectiveness programs, and expatriate support to international companies. Brenda also founded and is the Chief Global Gal of Global Gals®, which empowers and educates women to reach their travel dreams through workshops, retreats, cultural training and networking events.

Brenda is a frequent international speaker at conferences, corporate meetings, and industry events and has served as a guest lecturer aboard several cruise ships. An internationally recognized speaker, she won the acclaimed Speakers EXPY® Award. Sharing her experience and knowledge, she gives audiences the tools to succeed in business, travel, and cross-cultural understanding. Along her journey, she has connected with fascinating people whose own stories broadened the depths of her cultural awareness. She created www.smallworldstories.com for people to share the kind-hearted and coincidental 'small world' stories they've experienced.

Due to her international travel and business expertise, Brenda has won many awards and was selected as one of America's PremierExperts®. Brenda is a No. 1 best-selling author and recently co-authored, *Answering The Call: Entrepreneurs and Professionals Reveal How They Said Yes to Success and You Can Too*, which immediately hit three No.1 best-seller lists. Brenda was featured in over 350 media outlets, including CNBC and *The New York Times*, as well as on ABC, CBS and NBC affiliates for receiving the Best-Selling Author *Quilly*® Award. In addition, she was invited to share her expertise on a US Airways in-flight video, which aired on 1,700 flights.

She has an MA in International Communication from Macquarie University in Australia and a BS in Psychology and International Relations with Distinction from Iowa State University.

Connect with Brenda:
brenda@worldwideconnect.com
www.globalgals.com
www.worldwideconnect.com
www.facebook/globalgals
www.twitter.com/theglobalgals

CHAPTER 7

FIVE SIMPLE RULES TO SHARPEN YOUR THINKING

BY CHRISTIAN G. KOCH, CFP®, CPWA®, CDFA™

"The right thinking pays dividends when all other assets have faltered. Clarity in life comes from engagement." This was one of the comments I provided to the Wall Street Journal for an article published in December 2014 entitled: "What Makes You Successful in Today's Economy." And for those unfamiliar with the article, the terms "right thinking" refers to a deep unconventional understanding of complex situations, while engagement refers to being present in the moment with laser-like focus. Sit tight, more on that topic comes later. For now, write down these five simple rules:

1. *Gather ALL the facts: Ask yourself the question: What are the facts?*

2. *Determine what is true and what is false or just opinion.*

3. *Take a moment and pause. Be confident once you have determined a course of action.*

4. *Don't be afraid to make a mid-course correction if the facts or circumstances change.*

5. *Make ALL decisions based on principle.*

My story begins in 1984. I was 14 years old and had just completed the 8th grade. At that time, I was unhappy with my academic and social situation in Atlanta. My parents suggested I look into attending high school in St. Louis at The Principia. It had a good reputation as a rigorous Christian boarding school and my father had attended when he was my age.

One balmy day in early August, my father and I hopped in the car to embark on the nine-hour journey to a city and school foreign to me. As we drove through the front gates of the campus, I began to question whether I had made the right choice abandoning all that was familiar. A few hours later, my dad said goodbye as I settled into the boy's dorm—my new home.

As I moved into the dorm that August day, I could never have imagined the wisdom and perspective that would be injected into my life. What I took from the experience was a clarity and sense of intuition that I, to this day, find irreplaceable.

The Principia is a co-ed boarding school with primary mission to teach, develop and educate young individuals in foundational principles. One of the core concepts is developing the "whole man." This framework is not only focused on a rigorous academic environment, but is also based on spiritual, mental, physical and social development. The understanding of these principles is that true education is to train a child to think intelligently using more than just numbers and literature known in much of the academic systems across the country.

After high school graduation, there were four elements of my education that I was able to apply:

- How you think and what you think determines your experience
- Above all else in your thinking process, be curious
- Don't be afraid to be different, as conformity is a social disease that brings mediocrity
- Being unique and result-oriented makes a person very valuable.

The experience had been successful in training my young mind to think, perceive and act based on principle. The qualities and attributes of principle are: alert, accurate, anchored, clear, consistent, discerning and genuine.

Sixteen years later, I found myself in Cambridge, Massachusetts attending the Advanced Management Program at the prestigious Harvard Business School. Like Principia, HBS was a life-altering and career-changing experience that accelerated both my personal and professional growth with the mission of developing business leaders that make a difference in the world. I learned leadership is about thinking clearly, acting with confidence and recognizing patterns that others can't see. Harvard Business School is well-known for the case study method of teaching, which is learning based on real-world companies and situations. Learning from this standpoint further developed my practical judgment.

At HBS, our daily goal was to read several cases which already had an established storyline. Our job was to determine the facts, understand the main themes and business dynamics and reach a conclusion. Each professor would always make us give our recommendation before we learned the outcome of the case. Working three case studies per day, I achieved a solid understanding and exposure to a variety of business models and situations of managements' success and failures.

From my perspective, what we need most in our lives is the correct framework to tackle any problem. You need to breakdown the issue to its smaller parts and assess the facts one at a time to see if they make sense, just as we approached the case studies at Harvard with logical and sequential steps. Listening and adhering to the party line can be a backwards step. For those unfamiliar with the idiom, *toeing the party line*, it refers to a person who thinks and conforms to a specific agenda. Make assessments as to which facts are true and which should be discarded.

The first time I flew to San Francisco was a clear day, with the city, Golden Gate Bridge and Alcatraz as miniature figures from my window seat on the plane. Two days later, when I flew back, the flight was stormy with bad visibility. I could see nothing out of my window seat. However, I still knew that the objects and buildings I saw two days prior were all there. The absence of a clear view did not change my perspective of reality. This example illustrates the importance of understanding that we may not always have clear visibility for decision making. However, having the confidence that the facts have not changed despite the current picture may help get us to the next stepping stone.

HAVING THE RIGHT MENTAL ATTITUDE

Southwest Airlines has a unique boarding procedure of first-come-first-served seating. As you can imagine, this was not the ideal policy for our family of seven flying to Atlanta from Denver over Christmas vacation. To make sure our family was able to sit together on the plane, I purchased one advance seat. This put me in the group of the first 30 individuals to board the plane. My mission was to save seven seats together (may the force be with me that day and for all others in this situation). The rest of my flock would board in the last section. The gate agent, of course, gave me the "party line" and said that we could not board the plane early together. If I had not purchased one early boarding ticket, I am sure we would have been split up on the airplane with lots of tears on our return flight.

The Southwest Airlines experience of planning ahead and anticipating problems is an example of how right thinking and right acting can make a difference and improve our daily experience. Now don't forget those five simple rules I had you write down.

PRACTICAL APPLICATION FOR A FINANCIAL EXPERT

To this day, I use a similar decision framework in my business by providing wise counsel on retirement and investment issues based on a set of client facts. These are my modern-day case studies. The way one interprets, understands and sees those individual facts and their interrelationship determines what financial strategies to execute for success. I have developed a solution that is far better than any large financial company could think of doing with individuals. Creating a success strategy is about building personal relationships with clients and in-depth conversations about life issues.

I have developed a unique process that each client works within to achieve their desired goals and objectives. It is designed to be a comfortable framework for each step of the process. Experience has taught me that individuals seeking financial advice are at different points of their life cycle. Those points are constantly changing and evolving. My unique retirement planning process has four steps:

1. Develop A Retirement Vision

2. Build the Optimal Retirement Portfolio

3. Focus on Retirement Distribution Strategies

4. Estate and Wealth Transfer Planning

Step 1: Starts with having an honest one-on-one discussion about what

78

the individual's goals and objectives are in retirement. For me, this is the most important part of my process. It gives me a chance to listen, and then listen again, to see if this person is a good fit. The stock market can be extremely volatile and I want to make sure that this person has the right temperament to weather the storm. Similar to not being able to see out my airplane window, long-term value investing requires very much the same skill of confidence in your initial facts and findings. For example, the intrinsic value of a company may rise 5% per year backed by fundamental data on sales, earnings and book value growth, but the price action of the stock may move 20% up or down depending on perception, expectations and other events.

Step 2: Begins with building a customized retirement portfolio with individual securities (stocks and bonds). Depending on the individual's age and income need, the portfolio is built brick-by-brick or stock-by-stock with the focus on Total Return (dividend income plus price appreciation). I don't believe in diversification, so portfolios tend to be concentrated with a range of 25 to 30 companies. I have diversified away all the unsystematic risk after incorporating 15 to 17 companies in the portfolio. This runs contrary to the beliefs of the modern portfolio manager and is an unorthodox view, but one that I believe to be sound, based on my 20 years of investment research.

Step 3: The focus is now on withdrawing your wealth and tax-efficient withdrawal strategies. One case study at Harvard Business School had a dramatic impact on me as a financial expert. David A. Garvin, who teaches courses on leadership, general management and operations, taught a case study on Mount Everest and how several experienced climbers died because they did not prepare for the descent correctly. This analogy supports the risks in the withdrawal phase of retirement. In the case study, the Mount Everest team spent all of their time planning the climb up and no time planning their return down. Based on the case study, accidents happen on the descent after the summit has been achieved. I believe converting your investment portfolio into retirement income, or the descent of your investments, is critical. This requires a different financial strategy just as the climbers needed to adapt to return home.

Step 4: Begins with a discussion on wealth transfer issues and setting up the best structure for passing on multi-generational wealth. I do this in conjunction with an estate planner who is an expert on family limited partnerships, trusts, and estate tax issues. Updated IRA beneficiary forms are also a critical element in this discussion. One of the ratios I use in my practice is the TPA/TGE ratio. The numerator is "TPA"- total pre-tax assets like IRAs, 401(k)s and 403(b)s. The denominator is "TGE" - total gross estate. This is a good indicator of the percentage of your total estate that is infested with taxes. Most people don't realize they will have to pay a toll in the form of income taxes to receive their own money.

In sum, several decades ago,Thomas A. Edison established this challenge: *The most necessary task of civilization is to teach men how to think.* From my experience, decision-making is both an art and science. It involves conscious analytic and unconscious intuitive elements. Good decision-making can be easily improved with my five simple rules. When it comes to making wise investment choices, most individuals are self-taught as decision-makers. My unique four-step retirement planning process creates a comfortable framework for individuals to optimize critical financial decisions during their golden years.

About Christian

Best-Selling Author, Christian Koch, CFP®, CPWA®, CDFA™, is recognized as one of the top thought-leaders and private wealth experts in the money management industry. He has co-authored the book, *Get in the Game*, which describes his unique four step investment process and five principles that can help individuals in the journey to be successful long-term investors.

When it comes to the investment consulting process and creating portfolios for retirement, you need an experienced wealth management professional. Christian Koch's expert knowledge and approach to traditional investments, individual security selection, retirement income distribution planning and more, can help you face the future and the intricacies of your investment portfolio with a fresh new outlook.

Christian has a unique investment process and a retirement planning system that has served clients for years: develop the vision, build the optimal portfolio, focus on distribution strategies and then evaluate wealth and estate transfer planning. He says asset location is extremely critical to maximizing efficiencies, especially during a slow-growth economy, and minimizing taxes are a significant component of success.

Christian is a Harvard Business School AMP graduate and former investment research analyst. He also holds the prestigious Certified Financial Planner™ professional, Certified Divorce Financial Analyst™ and Certified Private Wealth Advisor® certifications, placing him in a select group of financial professionals.

In 2013, 2014 and 2015, Christian's credentials and work was rigorously examined after which he was honored with a coveted Five Star Wealth Manager Award.

Christian is on the Board of Directors of Rotary Club of Buckhead, and is involved in the Harvard Business School Club of Atlanta.

You can connect with Christian at:
Christian@kamsouth.com
www.kamsouth.com

CHAPTER 8

DESERVE TO SERVE™

BY DR. ANTONIO CIGNO

IT'S ALL IN THE PERSPECTIVE

I see that my professional role is to touch peoples' lives and help them change. I want to guide them to improve the way they express themselves to the world in the most comfortable, confident, positive and loving manner. What may surprise you is that this is not the pat idealism of a psychologist or an educator - not even of a pageant finalist! This is how I approach the otherwise tense and occasionally even emotionally isolated world of general dentistry.

This attitude formulated the basis of not only my professional but also my personal world. I credit all my success to this mindset of approaching life with the question, "How can I support others in their journey toward self-expression?" The truly powerful aspect of this concept is that it is so simple in nature: it begins with a capacity and willingness to listen.

WHERE THE STORY BEGAN

My motivation to empower others didn't hit me like a bolt of lightning in the middle of the night; it was an evolutionary process that took ten years to become truly clear. The son of a dentist, I left my father's practice in St. Louis to optimistically build my own in Milwaukee. While the acquisition of the Milwaukee practice made sense on paper, it was devoid of humanistic appeal. The doctor I bought the practice from did his part to contribute to every negative emotion associated with the profession of dentistry: his practice was almost the embodiment of butchery and greed. That culture of dread and isolation is what has led dental professionals to rank consistently highest on the list of suicides for a profession.

Perhaps it was ordained that I was confronted with this challenge; it may have been the impetus for a change in attitude and awareness. Whatever its origin, the result is not to be denied.

It wasn't long before I adopted the philosophy "you must serve in order to deserve." I knew that as a *physician*, I had to earn the right to care for my patients; to minimize their sense of violation and replace it with trust derived from a genuine sense of interest in them as human beings. While my effectiveness lay in my patients' perception of my professional capabilities, it did not mean that I couldn't simultaneously achieve my goal to make a person-to-person connection with them.

PAPER OR PLASTIC?

I first put this seemingly simple philosophy into play one day at the grocery store. Standing in the checkout lane, I noticed that both the cashier and patrons were robotic, avoiding anything that might resemble eye contact or true connection.

When it was my turn to check out, I decided to try something different. In an energized and loving tone, I exclaimed to the cashier, "Hi, Maria! How are you today?"

She looked up stunned and answered the question. Throughout our interaction, I continued to gaze at her and give her my undivided attention, absorbing her surprised reaction. When she was finished and it was time for me to leave, she said, "Thank you so much. I was having such a bad day and this interaction changed everything right there." It is amazing how just one genuine connection a day can make all the blank, empty or bad ones go away.

And all I did was say "hello" and take the time to care.

BUILDING MOMENTUM

That experience prompted me to ask myself, "How do I create something bigger, that enlivens even more people? How do I create a lifestyle of touching and inspiring others?"

I was suddenly confronted with something that has become all but forgotten in our society: the realization that I had a choice. I could choose how to live, how to behave and how to treat others. We're often asked as children what we want to be when we grow up, but perhaps this question is better put to us as adults. Despite the challenges everyone encounters, we all have the opportunity to step into the power of being the person we *choose* to be rather than the person we are programmed to be.

For instance, I wanted to be confident and this required some definition. *What does a confident person look like? How does he dress, stand and walk? How does he communicate with others?* The question, "What do you want to be when you grow up?" doesn't ask what you want to *do*, it asks what you want to *be*. That question is still relevant to adults and it was especially relevant to me at the time. It had nothing to do with labels. I was a husband, a father, a doctor and a man; these were only a few of the labels I lived up to, but there was so much more.

CONSTANT REINVENTION

As I grow older, I continually re-invent myself to fulfill each of my roles. I know that if I'm not growing forward, I'm moving backward... which looks a lot like dying. With that in mind, I applied my "BE" philosophy to everything and everyone around me.

I had to develop a clear vision and honest relationship with myself; if I didn't, I knew that nothing would change. I had to grow personally before I could help others, whether they were members of my family or my dental practice. I know that if I help the people around me grow, their growth will ultimately contribute to even more people and the community at large. That is how we affect change.

I began within my own sphere, in my office. I listened to my patients, asking them what was important to them. I learned about them not just as patients, but also as people. What brought them to my office? What was his or her past experience with the dentist? What was most important to them in life and why do they want to find a dental home?

As I listened and discovered the goals and desires of my patients, I learned to connect their medical health with their dreams and desires. From there, I was able to show my patients how the two are directly related.

I believe I have no business touching somebody's mouth until I've touched his or her heart. I have to **_earn the right_** to help them and to be so intimate with their medical health. This is what Deserve To Serve™ is all about. While there are lots of great dentists out there, our patients come to us specifically because we take care of them as people. Teeth are easy! My practice is about so much more than teeth.

My team follows this philosophy as well. We have worked with a great coach, Wes Jankowski, for over a decade to focus on becoming better versions of ourselves so we can better serve others. We read personal development books constantly throughout the year. We focus on communication within ourselves, with one another and with the patients.

At the end of the day, I want to matter. That "mattering" begins quite often with my team, each member of which is as dear to me as family. I've developed a hierarchy for my relationships; with God, myself, my wife and daughter, my teammates and then the people out in the community, the patients and their entire community.

I think we all have an obligation to live a life of example, whatever that means to each individual. One of the most important requirements of success is that you release judgment of self. If you fall into a judgment trap, you are very likely to fall short of all your goals. If you must compare, compare yourself to your God-given potential: do your actions stack up to the greatness you have within you?

If you cultivate a practice of questioning yourself in this way and stay focused and patient, your potential is unlimited. Some people achieve great things against all odds and despite facing seemingly insurmountable challenges. There must be some integrity behind that, obviously. (Note: If you separate the word be-lieve and drop an "e" you are left with Be–Live. It is not faking it until you make it, but instead it is about having a vision in your mind and 'Being the vision'.)

Three years ago marked the completion of a new dental office eight years in the making. It was a stressful process that involved an entirely new set of rules with which I wasn't familiar at all. Essentially, I felt as though I was starting over from the very beginning and rebuilding my business from scratch.

Not only was the environment physically different but the practice went from a team of three to a team of eight individuals. This took some adapting. I had to figure out what the person who led that team would "**BE**" like. I had to learn how to communicate my vision of how a dental office can change people's lives, how to sift through and choose the right team mates that could work together as one living, breathing entity. I had to learn how to listen to them and trust them as a representation of who I am and who we are at Cigno Family Dental. This couldn't be done by just choosing random bodies who knew how to scrape teeth. I had to hand-pick people that saw possibility in the world and understood the beauty and fulfillment that they could bring to their own lives by mattering to those they served.

That's what really made a difference in my business. Cigno Family Dental builds relationships and takes care of people; that is very important to us and it is the responsibility of everyone on the team. We breathe as one, we move as one and we serve as one. We are one.

None of us, not even me in the role of doctor is as great as all of us working together. Together as a unit we are a force to be reckoned with and we change the world. The spotlight often shines on one individual, but the truth is that nothing great has ever occurred without the strength of a cohesive team behind it.

The concept of "Be-ing" is hard for some to grasp. It can be discovered, uncovered and inspired, but it has to come from desire within to make a difference. Consequently, I developed a team of leaders who can take care of things in a manner that speaks for my philosophy. This is what sets our business apart from the other dental options in Milwaukee, and it's why my patients choose to be members of the Cigno Family Dental community.

THE END RESULT

It's crucial that you continue to grow so that you can honestly answer the question, "What difference am I making in my life and in the lives of others?" For many years I have used slide presentations to illustrate this. It begins with a picture of a gun and the sound of a shot fired. The caption reads, "Bang you're dead."

How's that for an eye opener? It leads to big questions: What difference did you make? Did you matter? Whose life did you touch? Whose life is better off because you were here? Did you create magical moments or were you too stressed and just trying to get through the day? Did you have the courage to take risks and grow, or did you just live in fear? It was your life, now it's over. Does anyone care?

Those are the questions we must ask one another and ourselves on a regular basis. At some point it becomes about legacy: how will we leave the world a better place?

I take very seriously the statement, "Built in the image of God." I let this phrase guide me in thought, word and action: it's about being "Godlike" in ever-expanding growth as a person who is earning the right to be here every day. It's about taking risks. It's about supporting people, and helping people see themselves as bigger in the world, helping them understand that they are only limited in their realm of possibility by what they "Be-live" about who they are, who they are meant to be and why they are here.

Reaching your goals, dreams and desires is never going to happen if you are afraid to show the world who you are. We are here changing lives. Teeth and smiles are the avenue through which we get to do so.

None of this can ever happen unless I take time to ask questions and listen to what the person's ultimate dreams and desires are. It is only when I take the time to ask the probing, hard, and sometimes awkward questions that I can really take care of them as their doctor instead of just another tooth mechanic.

Sometimes patients come into my office and I can tell by the look on their face that it's not the day to perform dental work. I have my time scheduled for them, so I may as well try and be useful. They talk and I listen. Now this doesn't happen on a daily basis, but with a little sensory acuity you can tell how to match each patient at his or her level.

It doesn't matter if we're just cleaning teeth or rebuilding the entire mouth. I want my patients to feel better about who they are as people in the world. When they walk out of my office, they're better for having stopped in.

We all want things from life, whether it is the respect of others, peace of mind, loving relationships, 15% body fat, a Ferrari, or a multimillion dollar bank account. We can have it all no matter what our background is, but first we have to decide what a person that has all of these things looks like. What type of action do they take? Who do they 'be'?

People often ask me, "How much is enough?" People assume it is the material things that motivate my business. Material things take care of themselves when you are being enough. The being is the access to the having.

My dream is to make a big footprint in this world before I go. I believe that my life bank account will be the most abundant in every way by serving others. I express this through the work that is done at my dental office, through my writing and speaking engagements and as a part of my everyday life. It is my obligation to earn the privilege to be on this Earth through serving others.

That is **Deserve to Serve**™

That…is success.

About Dr. Tony

Dr. Antonio (Tony) Cigno has been practicing dentistry for 25 years. Since the age of five, he knew he wanted to be a dentist when he saw how happy his father, also a dentist, was able to make his patients. To this day, Dr. Cigno prides himself on his philosophy of patient-centered care.

Dr. Cigno received a DMD from the Washington University School of Dental Medicine in St. Louis, Missouri. Dr. Cigno is also finishing a Fellowship and Mastership at the Academy of General Dentistry and has written several published articles. He is a member of the Academy of General Dentistry, American Association of Functional Orthodontics, and the International Association of Orthodontics.

Dr. Cigno works at one of the most technologically-advanced dental facilities in the state, offering not only intraoral but digital and 3-D imaging, providing you with the safest most accurate diagnostic tools available today.

Dr. Cigno was Wisconsin's very first and Premiere Provider of Fastbraces.

Committed to continuing education, Dr. Cigno has completed over 600 hours of additional courses in implant dentistry, orthodontics, endodontics, periodontics, fixed prosthodontics, myofascial pain/occlusion and operative dentistry. He also has another 400 hours in interpersonal communication training.

In his free time, Dr. Cigno enjoys designing and building guitars, writing and performing music, spending time with his wife and daughter, and participating in outdoor activities such as snow skiing, triathlons and cycling.

CHAPTER 9

THE C.A.R.E. PRINCIPLES OF SUCCESS:
HOW CONNECTING, ASPIRING, AND REWIRING CAN EMPOWER YOU TO ACHIEVE THE SOUL OF SUCCESS

BY DENNY FLODEN

When I opened the door, my Alaskan Malamute, as always, greeted me with his tail wagging and with what looked like a smile on his face. He followed me to the sofa and curled up at my feet as I read the Flint Journal. I don't think he understood, but he certainly noticed when I exclaimed loudly, "That's what we do!" I was reacting to an article about a young veteran who was blinded in Vietnam and wanted to find a job where he could "help other people and contribute something positive." That's how I learned about Howard Myers, but this isn't where the journey began.

I didn't know much about my father; I recall seeing him around four or five times during my childhood before I was placed in the foster care system at the age of thirteen. Like most foster children, I bounced around from house to house finding the whole episode difficult and lonely.

Growing up without a stable environment and without the guidance and direction of a father or mother, I didn't feel that anyone truly believed in me, that there was no one who could guide me toward success.

That all changed with my high school coach Dick Fetters, who was the closest thing I had to a father. Coach Fetters was special. He started the Riley High School swimming team even though we didn't have a pool in the school. We practiced at the YMCA in downtown South Bend, Indiana very early each morning before school. Under Coach Fetters' tutelage, we won the Indiana State High School Swimming Championships as a team and I won five individual state championships.

More importantly, he cared about us and guided us towards becoming responsible and productive men. He taught me more than how to compete; he taught me discipline and structure, and how to survive. He challenged me to become a better person and not to let my childhood circumstances stop me from succeeding in any endeavor. Because Coach Fetters believed in me, I began to believe in myself.

After my junior year, Coach Fetters left Riley High School for a job in Florida. Although his departure left a big void, he didn't forget me. He was still thinking of me as he wrote letters to universities recommending me for an athletic scholarship. Those letters were critical. In my last two years of high school, I was in a group living arrangement at the Children's Aid Society of Indiana. I was on my own and simply had no financial ability to attend college without an athletic scholarship.

After accepting a full ride to the University of Michigan, I visited Coach Fetters to thank him for all he had done for me. In my naive exuberance, I told him, "Coach, someday I'm going to be a millionaire and repay you for all you've done for me." He looked at me with his sly understanding smile and said, "If you really want to repay me, just do for someone else what I have tried to do for you. That's the best way to repay anyone."

I followed in Coach Fetters' path and became a swimming coach for a short time. Later, I started selling life insurance for Mass Mutual where I met my mentors, Frank Comins and Joe Shomsky. They picked up where Coach Fetters left off, giving me advice and guidance. They taught me that selling was, or at least should be, telling the truth in the most attractive manner. The motto for Mass Mutual back then was: "We Serve." Joe and Frank lived by that motto.

Later, my responsibilities were expanded to recruiting and training life insurance sales agents. That's when I read about Howard. I called him, identified myself as a recruiter for Mass Mutual and that I wanted to discuss the possibility of his becoming one of our insurance agents. His first response was, "I've never heard of your company."

"That's okay," I responded, "They haven't heard of you either."

We made a connection and agreed to meet the next day.

I asked Howard if he was comfortable sharing how he lost his eyesight. He told me that he was a machine gunner on an Armored Personnel Carrier and April 26, 1967 was a "stinking hot day." They were driving out of the jungle near Cu Chi and Howard remembers that he was munching on a pineapple. As they approached a shaded clearing, Howard yelled to the driver, "Hey Lonnie, don't pull over there. That's where the enemy hides land…"

KaBOOM!!!

"I lost my baby blue eyes in the explosion," he continued, "and I lost my pineapple, too."

I was sincere in offering a job opportunity to Howard; but I soon realized that I had reacted based on my emotions. As we explored the possibilities of working with Mass Mutual and becoming a successful Life Insurance agent, it dawned on me that there were monumental hurdles in Howard's path. For example, the rate book that we used to calculate premiums was more than three inches thick. Even with good eyesight, everyone had trouble reading the extremely small print. This was before laptop computers were invented and we did not have any of the productive and assistive tools that are available today. I felt that Howard should have a full-time assistant, but we were not in a position to provide one.

Howard said that everyone who had interviewed him suggested, "Don't call us, we'll call you." But his phone never rang. I was growing more doubtful every second so I told him, "You won't have that problem with me. You'll have to call us because I don't think we'll be calling you." And, as graciously as possible, I concluded the interview.

When I returned to the office, I told Joe about meeting Howard and that

SOUL OF SUCCESS VOL. 1

I felt bad because I had probably given him false hopes.

"What should I do now?" I asked.

"Well," he said, "you better hope he doesn't call."

But he did call. During our interview, Howard said that he wanted to be treated "like everyone else, not like a disabled blind guy." So I proceeded with the usual hiring process and gave Howard the six pre-contract training books, complete with tests, every potential recruit had to complete before they were hired. This weeded out a lot of people and I guess that, subconsciously, I thought it would weed out Howard as well.

Weeks, then months, went by with no word from Howard. I had dodged a bullet – "problem solved," I thought.

But he did call and said, "I read the books, what's next?"

Stunned, I suggested he drop by the office and prove that he knew the answers to the test questions. Not only did Howard know the answers, but he would also call out answers even before I finished asking the questions.

I ran down to Joe's office and asked what I should do next. "What would you normally do at this point?" he asked. The look on Joe's face told me this was my problem and I had to find the solution.

I called to schedule an exam with the State of Michigan so Howard could obtain a license to sell life, health and accident insurance. "And one more thing" I told the lady, "we need someone to read the questions to Howard."

"Why?" asked the lady.

"Because he's blind," I said.

"Oh no," answered the lady, "we don't allow anyone in the testing room except the Proctors and the person taking the test."

This was 1969, a long time before the American Disability Act was passed in 1990.

I didn't know how Howard could master everything necessary to be successful in the life insurance business and the State of Michigan

Insurance Exam could give me the excuse to let Howard down gently. But I didn't do it. When the lady said that Howard couldn't have someone read and record the answers to questions, I had an unexpected immediate response.

I told the lady that I appreciated how helpful she had been and that I wanted to protect her from losing her job.

"What are you saying?" she asked.

I told her that she should explain to her boss that based on existing policy, she had just denied a Vietnam veteran, who lost his eyesight fighting for his country, the right to take a state-licensing exam. I suggested that if her boss was comfortable answering questions from every newspaper, radio and TV station in Detroit, Flint and Lansing, MI, she probably would not hear from me again.

She called back in less than two hours and we were able to schedule Howard's exam. He passed with a score of 92!

Coach Fetters had planted a seed to help someone else as he had helped me, and finally, after nearly ten years, it started to sprout. I had the opportunity to show how much I believed in Howard the same way that Coach Fetters believed in me.

On the job, Howard insisted he wanted be treated just like everybody else; so I did just that -- NO EXCUSES! He participated in every training that was offered, and, just like everybody else, Howard was held accountable each week for the number of sales calls, interviews and closings he made. I went on some joint client calls with Howard for training purposes. It was clear, however, that I was neither his taxi driver nor his secretary, and that if he was to succeed, it would be based on his efforts, not mine.

We talked about goals and what it would take to be considered successful in his first year. I informed him that the ultimate honor was to be among the "Freshman Five," the top five new Mass Mutual agents in the United States in their first year.

"Were you in Freshman Five?" he asked.

I told him I might have been one of the Freshman Ten, but I did not qualify to be one of the Freshman Five.

"Good. I'm going to be Freshman Five then," resolved Howard.

He not only accomplished this goal, I seem to recall he was number two in the nation.

Howard and I lost touch over the years, until his son, Chad, called me to say that he was starting a personal and professional development company in honor of his father. He was excited and wanted me to know that I was a large part of his father's success.

That phone call would soon lead to a re-connection with Howard and we began sharing our story to a variety of audiences, bringing hope, inspiration and motivation to thousands. Eventually, we founded the Mindworks Performance Group as a vehicle for Howard to share how, through focused attention, he had literally re-wired his brain for a positive "Blind Vision" of success.

As he grew up, Chad had wondered why his father was so successful even though he was blind. Chad eventually became a teacher, earned a Master's degree in Education and became a Certified Personal Coach. Together with his friend Chris Veihl, who holds a Master of Arts in Counseling and is a Licensed Professional Counselor in Michigan, they began researching how and why Howard was able to go from the depths of depression to a heightened sense of confidence and self-awareness.

Howard has always generously credited me with being his mentor. Candidly, I was barely one step ahead of him and probably learned as much from him as he learned from me. In essence, we mentored each other. Chad and Chris studied what "the two old guys did" and then researched the latest scientific information to provide a sound basis for the C.A.R.E. Principles for Success that we teach.

C: CONNECTION

Whether it is with your customer, your spouse or your children, a solid connection is key to attaining desired results. Coach Fetters and I formed a deep connection through his ability to empathize when I felt defeated and isolated. I was empowered to mirror his vulnerability and courage as he led me through life without making any judgments. He believed that I did not have to be a victim of my past. He believed in my ability to rise above challenges. He believed in my whole being. This belief helped me to break free from my circumstances.

Connecting through empathy requires vulnerability and courage to honor one's journey without judgment. It takes belief in another's worth to begin the process of change and growth. Coach Fetters believed in me and I believed in Howard. Win-win for everyone involved.

A: ASPIRATION

To aspire is to breathe, to eagerly desire, to rise up and soar. To become a leader, parent, coach, manager, or mentor requires imagination and creativity; but these two qualities are inhibited by a victim mindset.

Howard burst into my office one day. . . steaming mad, red-faced and speaking angrily about the Social Security Administration. I calmed him down as best as I could and asked what the problem was. "Those !@#$% just cut off my Social Security Benefits." he responded.

"Why?" I asked.

"They say I'm making too much money to be disabled!"

I asked Howard if, in view of his success, he still felt that he was truly disabled. He stared at me, turned, slammed the door shut behind him and the subject never came up again.

Howard had finally gotten rid of "dis", and from then on, stayed focused on "ability." He was no longer a victim. My belief in him was the foundation for Howard believing in himself, just as Coach Fetters' belief in me was the basis of my self-confidence.

Part of focusing on ability is visualizing what you want to happen. Howard lives in his mind without the need for any visual input. As he frequently says, "You don't have to have eyes to have a vision."

R: REWIRING

Chad and Chris researched the neuro-science behind what happened with Howard and me. Simply put, Howard was forced to re-wire his brain from that of a sighted to a sightless person thereby creating new neural pathways.

Today we are aware of Neuro-Plasticity – our mind's ability to change our brain. For Howard, it was a matter of survival. If a blind guy can re-wire his brain for survival in a sighted world, is there any reason we can't re-wire our brains for success in the same world? Of course we can and what a joy it is to teach someone how to do that.

E: EMPOWERING

When we truly connect with people, aspire for something better and re-wire our brains for success, we are able to focus on our abilities instead of our limitations. We gain power from having a positive vision, and we begin to live a life of gratitude where we give hope and help for others. When we are empowered, we can empower others to succeed. It is then that we have truly developed the Soul of Success.

Written with gratitude to Coach Fetters, Joe Shomsky and Frank Comins: You planted the seeds and showed us the way. Hopefully we are honoring you with our efforts to share with others what you gave to us.

About Denny

From rather humble beginnings, Denny Floden launched a success-oriented path by studying what made people successful and applying these concepts and principles to his own life. He has a history of achievement since childhood. He won five Indiana State High School Championships in swimming, and was inducted into the South Bend Riley High School Hall of Fame and the Indiana State High School Swimming Hall of Fame.

In college, he was a member of three NCAA National Championship Swimming Teams and earned three Collegiate All-America selections at the University of Michigan, while studying to become a teacher. He finished with a BA and an MA in education.

Leaving teaching for the financial services industry, Denny started as an insurance agent for Mass Mutual. He quickly rose through the ranks becoming Staff Supervisor and, finally, Assistant General Agent. Later he moved to E. F. Hutton & Company to become a Senior Financial Consultant. He is a Chartered Life Underwriter and a Life Member of the Million Dollar Round Table.

Venturing into Hot Air Ballooning, Denny is Owner, CEO and Chief Pilot for Capt. Phogg Enterprises, LTD. He became the first World Hot Air Balloon Champion and won the United States National Hot Air Balloon Championship. He also won the Heineken International Balloon Championship as well as the Seven-Up International Balloon Championship. He served 22 years as Chief Pilot for Kellogg's Tony the Tiger worldwide balloon program and was the subject of a popular children's book, *Capt. Phogg® and The GR-R-REAT Tony Balloon* by Suzanne Tate. In 2014, Denny was inducted into the United States Ballooning Hall of Fame.

His "retirement" is a combination of a very successful real estate business based in Bradenton Beach on Anna Maria Island, Florida and the development of the Mindworks Performance Group (MPG). Denny is a Founding Member of the MPG for Personal Development, Corporate Seminars, Workshops and Keynote Addresses designed to teach and share the fundamentals of re-wiring the brain for continued success. He has shared the stage with fellow MPG members for many keynote presentations such as "Enlightened Journey towards Self Leadership" for the Georgia Nursing Association Professional Development Seminar, "Illuminating Peak Performance Seminar" for the Cornerstone Title Realtor Seminar in Sarasota, Florida, and the State of Michigan Community Health Spring Conference Keynote and Workshop. The Mindset Makeover

Workshops for Farm Bureau, Farmers Insurance Group and Mass Mutual round out his most recent speaking engagements.

You can connect with Denny at:
Mpgdenny@gmail.com
www.mindworksperformancegroup.com
www.twitter.com/mpgdenny
www.facebook.com/DennyFloden

CHAPTER 10

THE PERFECT FINANCIAL PLAN

BY FRITZ ENGELS

What is the perfect financial plan?
And . . . two different stories that say it all.

Hello, I am Fritz Engels. I have been doing financial planning and estate planning for over 30 years. The question, "What is the perfect financial plan?" is the million-dollar question! Not understanding how that question has many answers can cost millions of dollars!

The answers to each client's needs are different. Let's just take a look at two different clients that I have worked with over the years. These may have been prospective clients that hired me or they did not "heed" my advice and went with another planner, but either way, I can never forget them. I will use different names, of course, to protect their privacy.

THIS IS THE STORY OF MR. AND MRS. JONES

The Jones family comes to me with $3,000,000 in investable assets and both are healthy and happily married at the age of 65. Both their parents and grandparents lived well into their 80's and 90's. They are expecting to both live very long lives. They are not averse to losing some money, but decided that they will never want to have less than $2,000,000 and we even went more conservative than that after spending 2 months in planning. We chose an 80/20 plan. This means that no matter what happens, they want 80% of the $3,000,000 at $2,400,000 to never have any risks to a loss. They then could relax and know that even if they lost 100% of the remaining $600,000 that is the 20% in a variable program, they could stay retired and still make ends meet.

As the years went by, the $2,400,000 that was 100% safe grew to about $7,000,000 when they turned 90. Of course they lived off of these funds, they paid taxes, they paid for long-term care and all of the ordinary expenses of life that naturally occur over 25 years. The $600,000 in the variable program sometimes outperformed the fixed and safe side, and of course, in 2001 and 2008 they lost 50% of the $600,000 "bucket" of money. But, they stayed the course! They always had more than they needed; they kept their eyes on the plan!

As they passed away in their mid 90's, they left millions of dollars to their Trust which then took care of the death taxes, and final expenses and then this set up income programs for their children and grandchildren. This was a very happy story.

NOW, HERE IS THE STORY OF THE DAVIS FAMILY:

Mr. and Mrs. Davis were also 65 years old and also had $3,000,000. They also expected to live very long lives and I gave them all the same advice that I gave the Jones family. But, the Davis family wanted to get rich fast! "Fritz, we want to turn our $3,000,000 into $6,000,000 in 10 years and $12,000,000 in 20 years." "We have many friends that made their fortunes in the stock market in the 1990's." I taught them about the "cycles" of the stock market. I taught them about safe money versus "less safe money" planning. I taught them that it may be a lesson to be "heeded" that 100% of all of their investable assets at age 65 being at risk would be unwise. I even suggested maybe a 50/50 plan as a compromise, even though I strongly believed in the 80/20 plan that the Jones family adhered to.

But, the Davis family was unhappy with my advice and went to another planner. That planner did not discuss the risks and for a little while, "he was the Good Guy." I was the "Bad Guy." Thus, I stood for what I believed and even advised the 50/50 plan. Well, I guess you know what happened. These clients frequented my office over 25 years just to say hello, but their advisor had the relationship and kept telling them to "stay the course" at age 70, 75, 80 & 85. Sadly, between some health problems with no long-term care planning, a lawsuit without strong legal planning and huge losses due to the Stock Market in 2001 and 2008, a lot of bad things occurred. They lost all of their retirement. They lost their home and were on Medicaid at age 80. They only had Social Security. At the end of their lives, there was no Trust, there was no legacy or inheritance for the children and grandchildren. Actually, Mr. & Mrs. Davis lived with all of their children and grandchildren for the last 10 years of their lives. Sadly, they were a burden to their family, and died with no assets and debts that approached $1,000,000.

These are two very real stories. Estate Planning is critical. I advise all of my clients to sit down with a reputable and qualified planner with two+ decades of experience or more. Never put all of your assets after age 60 in the stock market. There are many steps to a great financial plan and finding a great planner.

- First, the planner must have experience.
- Second, the planner must have great references and a solid planning history with his clients.
- Third, the planner should be a fiduciary and a wealth adviser.
- Fourth, the planner should understand the clients' long-term goals and risk tolerance.
- Fifth, the planner needs to have a written plan based on the available funds, pensions, and Social Security based on a realistic budget of now and into the future.
- Sixth, that planner needs to express very seriously what it means to go slowly and surely versus fast and risky. No plan should be so fast and unsafe so that a Jones family can become a "Davis Family."
- Seventh, the planner needs to do legal, tax & financial estate planning.
- Eighth, the planner needs to address the cost of living in the future, with the increased cost of taxes and inflation.
- Ninth, the planner needs to address how long the client may live to be, future stock market crashes and the world economy.
- Tenth, the planner needs to have 5, 10, 15, 20, 25 year cash-buckets to address all of the above-mentioned needs and then needs to address the cost of long term care. Most clients do not

know that up to 90% of what has been saved, can be wiped out in the last two years of life due to long term care costs. Thus, and in conclusion, a planner needs to "see the big picture." The planner needs to put together a plan that covers all the unexpected costs and increasing costs of living as we age.

Thus, "What is the perfect financial plan?" It is a plan that fits your situation. It is a customized plan that addresses real life costs and connects that plan to your age, your health and longevity, your risk tolerance, and what is your accumulation value. But, the perfect plan comes from sitting down with a planner of great experience, education, and knowledge. Don't be like the Davis family. Be like the Jones family. Get a great financial planner and take his advice.

Thank You!

Fritz Engels

The Engels Financial Group

About Fritz

Fritz Engels is well known in the Northwest Georgia area where he has taught safe retirement principles and full financial planning for over 30 years. He uses his expertise to educate his clients through detailed financial analysis and investment and tax planning strategies to preserve and grow estates and wealth-planning programs. Fritz Engels is not only a financial planner, he is an asset conservationist and estate planner that understands IRA's, taxes, tax laws, and the government systems that can affect us as we age. He founded Engels Financial Group to provide retirement and estate planning to retirees and those nearing retirement.

As an independent licensed financial planner and wealth adviser, Fritz is able to do what is in the best interest of his clients and not a specific company. He provides a high level of business integrity that his clients can trust. His goal is to provide his clients with the potential for positive returns in all types of market conditions, with no risk of loss of principal and guaranteed lifetime income for those with specific economic and conservative needs as well as full financial planning for those well beyond the conservative phases of wealth building.

Fritz assists families in Atlanta and NW Georgia and the surrounding area to preserve their capital, increase their income and organize their portfolios for more profitability. People who consult with Fritz find that they lower their tax bills as much as 50%, eliminate taxes on their Social Security income, increase their fixed monthly income, avoid government and court interferences, avoid all losses and obtain better protection for their financial future. Fritz offers FULL financial planning, including taxes, legal, investments, TRUSTS, fixed income, pension planning and tax-free income programs providing CPA and Lawyers from his staff.

Fritz is also involved in the local community, serving as a member of Heritage Presbyterian Church. Fritz is a highly sought-after motivational speaker and a teacher at a local university. Fritz and his wife and family live in Acworth, GA; Fritz has two college degrees; one from LSU and the other from KSU.

Fritz is considered a veteran financial planner and his present client base has been very happy with his work for over 30 years. THE ENGELS FINANCIAL GROUP has an A+ BBB rating. Fritz is a caring individual who is committed to building strong and lasting relationships with his clients and has earned the respect and friendship of many individuals in his community. Just as these clients have come to know and believe in The Engels Financial Group, you are sure to be pleased with Fritz's services as well.

CHAPTER 11

THE MEME FACTOR

BY HAGOP EMRAZIAN

When I was about to finish high school, I kind of expected and hoped that something or someone was going to help me pursue my dreams and put together that master plan for my education, personal growth and development. I expected a lot from others while being under the impression that I deserved all good things to come my way, and why not? Right? How naïve of me!

I got hit with a big wall called reality, where my only option at that time was to work in a workshop, welding and fabricating metals day-in and day-out. Despite my resentment of the idea at that time, I now truly appreciate the time spent there as it really helped me learn about different types of people and working under pressured circumstances. It helped me a year later in my first corporate job in a bank as a teller, with one difference – I was wearing a suit in an air-conditioned office.

May I ask you to take your eyes off the book and look around you. Who are these people? What did they do today and what will they do tomorrow? Who do you think is more successful than the others? Why do you think so? Is it the way they look, dress or behave? Is this the way they might be looking at you?

But who really decides on what success is?

To the majority of the people, it might be accomplishing a better financial and social status, for some it could be fame, and to others it could be getting through the month with a ceiling over their head and the bills paid.

After 20 years in corporate, meeting different people from different backgrounds and in different contexts, it became clearer that no one success story is the same and not all can be replicated in the same way. They are different, so are you.

A few years back, I was so trapped in the maze of doing it all to get it all, and spending longer hours at work, which was my daily routine for feeling accomplished as the Regional Director of Learning and Development for a major logistics company. One day flying back from a short business trip, I decided to drive home from the airport although I was jetlagged and tired, but the voice in my head almost mumbled, "... you can do it, go ahead you busy bee."

Apparently I slept, because when I opened my eyes my car was already skidding on a concrete barrier of a highway bridge like a speeding train, but with the wheels spinning in the air, hitting the brakes hard didn't do any good. I closed my eyes and didn't know what to expect or to be ready for, the no-thought process was going a-mile-a-minute and all I remember was me asking God to take care of my daughter and my wife. The car didn't flip over the bridge because it hit a traffic sign pole, which stopped it.

This was my wake up call. This was my stop-and-start call.

We sometimes get caught in too many details and focus on the wants, and neglect the most important things. For me, it was family and friends. My priorities changed and my comprehension of being successful got a different twist with more focus on human relationships, inspiration and perseverance

I summarize it as the **MEME** factor.

- Meaningful
- Entertaining
- Memorable
- Educational

Meaningful

Anything that you get involved in, practice or preach has to be meaningful, otherwise why are you putting your energy and time in doing it? It is important to be candid about our own strengths, there is a big chance that our skills, knowledge and attitude need an update, as when we get into the trap of routine, our years of experience could be merely the duplication of what we did in our first year, with a slight change of scenery!

During my training workshops and speeches, people often vent that they feel stuck and there is no way around for progression; I remember this particular learner who complained of not getting what she deserved and how everyone else was getting the credit for her work and all the five managers she worked with over the years did not give her the chance she deserved. Sounds familiar?

In such cases I believe we have three options and we need to make a decision. A friend of mine, Robbie, shared this with me a few years back when I was stuck:

1. Getting proactive and discussing with the stakeholders what needs to be done to help our and our group's performance and productivity, it has to be a win-win. Explore what it is that's important, relevant and urgent to you and the people you are dealing with.

2. One of our least favorite options would be accepting the *status quo*, especially when we have obligations and can't afford to move around or out, while keeping an eagle eye on the opportunities around us, yet it is important not to lose focus on the job in hand. I had my share of people who day dreamed about their next job and forgot that they have an actual one that needs their attention!

3. Leaving to get another challenge. This could be in the same place or a totally new experience. Can we afford the change?

The important thing is to make a decision and not get trapped between options 2 and 3.

Entertaining

When we get caught up in serious work and daily life challenges, we tend to forget to have some fun. I myself was guilty in charge of taking work and life challenges too seriously and forgetting to have some good laughs with friends and family, because when everything is gone, they are the ones who will be around. Striking a favorable balance is not easy, yet you need to find that fun spot in your day to make things get less serious and steam off some of that heat. It is important to remember that you can learn something new while being entertained. I observe stand up comedians and watch my favorite speakers, yet at the same time I focus on learning a technique or two that would help me in my work as a speaker and trainer. Edutainment at its best! Find what energizes you, it could be a video clip, a fun act or a time off. You don't need an expensive vacation to feel good, trust me, I've been on one!

Have you noticed that whenever you are happy or having fun you are more receptive to information? Reminds me of my favorite topics at school, I realized later that I liked the topics because of the teachers who made it fun to learn and not the ones who recited the curriculum in a loud voice!

Memorable
Do you really care what people think of you? I see an eyebrow going up! Of course we do, we are social beings and by system or design we were taught to impress someone for something. At school, our parents pushed us to get higher marks with a promise of a reward; the same thing is followed in the university and ultimately the business world. There is this activity called competition that separates the "A" players from the rest of the group and it aims to impress a decision maker in order to help the individual climb the corporate ladder – since the view might be better from the top!

We might argue that it doesn't matter how we want to be remembered, after all, why it should matter? After 10 or 20 years no one would realize or care.

To be successful you have to be present in your society's and network's mind, you actually want them to talk behind your back, but in a positive way. Regardless of whom you are trying to impress, in my humble opinion, people strive to impress two or more of the following:

A. Themselves: People within this group can get harsh on themselves and demand nothing less than perfection. *They feel the need to prove to themselves that, " I will do it better this time, I always did."*

B. Others: They are interested in proving to others how their own work and effort is of value to the well-being of the bigger group and that they are an integral part of their networks. *They sometimes might get caught playing a game of pleasing others and less focused on their own goals and plans.*

C. Beliefs: The ones in this group work and act as per their spiritual beliefs and use them as a guiding compass to the daily activities and have high levels of aligned moral standards.

Who are we trying to impress? Ourselves? Others or our Spiritual Beliefs? I believe we need to have a combination of all three and address the rational and emotional sides of ourselves.

Whenever we feel down or go through harsh times, we may switch to 10/10/80 as prayer can help us keep our chins up. In the same situation another person might decide to follow a 30/60/10 type of an approach.

Each individual can develop this formula and can be either situational or a set approach to life's ups and downs. I am interested in hearing about your formula. This is very necessary as on the road to success we will need to get our acts together whenever we hit a speed bump or a rough terrain. Write yours here ____ / ____ / ____.

"How would you like to be remembered?"

Educational
"How many pages did you read this week?" is a question that we could answer without hesitation ten years ago. In today's fast-paced digital age, the amount of information we absorb might put us under the notion that we "Know" more information or have a better understanding. My 7-year-old Anthony knows what the surgical steps are to retrieve a swallowed battery, thanks to an educational application! But there's a big difference between knowing and doing, don't you agree?

In today's knowledge-rich era, information is all over the place and within a click of a button. However, that shouldn't give us the false notion that now we have better skill sets or thought processes. We pass on many opportunities to learn because of this, as we feel we are safe, since we can look up any information on the spot! Successful people appreciate the value of knowledge repositories, yet they also know where to look for the right information at the right time.

Reflecting on our day-to-day experiences is a great opportunity to learn. I hear people say "Learn from your mistakes!" So should we only wait for our mistakes or the mistakes of others to nod our heads and exhale and get an "aha" moment? Why not develop a habit of reflecting and questioning. Whenever I used to hear a success story, I was worried about what they did and how much money they were going to make;

there is absolutely zero value in this. To scratch more than the surface of any successful experience (yours and others), the following questions can help:

1. Why did they do it in the first place? What triggered it?

2. How did they manage the skeptics, the negative talkers and the frustrations?

3. What were the three most important lessons learned from this experience?

4. If they could go back to "square one," what would they do differently?

5. How did they keep their focus, an eye on the prize so to speak?

6. How did they turn success into a behavior?

7. Who was their role model for success and why?

I sincerely thank you for reading this chapter. You will notice there are great chapters in this book focusing on "the soul of success" and I truly hope that you implement an idea or two to get you closer to your goals and to realize your real potential.

If you put your heart and soul into what you do,
even You can't stop You!

Thank you for allowing me to be part of your life.

About Hagop

Hagop Emrazian partners with his clients to develop practical solutions for workforce learning and management development. He is an energizing facilitator and speaker where he makes sure to push people outside their comfort zones in order for them to realize their potential and get aligned with corporate goals.

With over 20 years experience in the corporate world, he first started his career with Gulf Bank, and later with Agility Logistics as the Regional Head of Learning and Development for the Middle East and Africa regions.

Hagop holds a BSc in Human Resources management and a Diploma in Training and Development as a graduate of the University of Leicester, UK, and a Certified Targeted Selection Interviewer and Facilitator from DDI International.

He is a firm believer in learning from organizations and organizations that learn to adapt new strategies and continually improve their performance. Hagop actively works with students and fresh graduates and lectures and speaks in business conferences, including TEDx.

Currently Hagop is a Sr. Consultant with the RJ Learning Group serving clients in the Middle East and Europe with a primary focus on management development, coaching and team dynamics assignments for multiple business sectors – including banks, automotive, supply chains, hotels, education and construction, among others.

You can connect with Hagop at:
hemrazian @rjlearninggroup.com
www.linkedin.com/in/hagopemrazian

CHAPTER 12

FINDING THE SOUL OF YOUR SUCCESS: HOW MISSION-DRIVEN BRANDING PUTS YOU AHEAD OF THE PACK

BY NICK NANTON & JW DICKS

They had been best friends since they were kids – and, as adults, they had decided to go into business together. They opened one small ice cream shop that turned into a local sensation – ironically, because a sinus condition made it difficult for the one partner to taste anything. They pumped up the flavors in their frozen concoctions to such an extent that it clicked with the college crowd that frequented the area.

The store became instantly successful. On the first anniversary of its opening, the owners held a "Free Cone Day," where they gave away a free ice cream cone to every customer. That and a yearly film festival they sponsored helped make them a vital part of the community. Their local support mushroomed.

But money was still a huge problem – in the winter, there was more of it going out than coming in. They began to study brochures put out by the Small Business Administration that cost 20 cents apiece at the Post

Office. They franchised a couple other stores in the region. They began selling pints of their ice cream flavors to local stores. And finally, they began to see some real money coming in.

That's when they began some soul-searching. These two guys had been almost-hippies who had grown up in the 60's, so they wanted their business to represent that spirit. They wanted to put their social mission at the center of everything they did. They wanted to always have what they called "the double dip" in place – profits and people.

They started with their own people. They put in place a policy that no employee's rate of pay would be greater than five times that of entry-level employees. In 1995, that meant entry-level employees were paid $12 hourly and the CEO could only be paid $150,000 annually.

Then they moved on to the world at large. At the end of each month, the two of them would ask of themselves and the company, how much had they improved the quality of life in the community?

As the company's need for capital increased, they resisted venture capitalist financing, which typically requires relinquishing significant control over the company. Instead, it sold stock to residents in the region, keeping the company in local hands. In 1985, it officially created a foundation, to which the company would contribute 7.5 percent of its pretax profits.

They also made social activism a critical aspect of their operations, putting into action such projects as:

- An original scoop shop made of recycled materials
- Creation of a "Green Team" in 1989, focusing on environmental education throughout the company
- A company bus equipped with solar panels
- The use of hormone-free milk in its products
- A commitment to reducing solid and dairy waste, recycling, and water and energy conservation at the company's facilities

Ben Cohen and Jerry Greenfield's Ben & Jerry's ice cream brand ended up with annual sales of over $250 million by the end of the 90's – and was sold to Unilever for over $325 million in 2000. Today, it's regarded as the top premium ice cream brand in the world – and, even though it's now owned by a giant corporation, it still continues to deliver on its social mission to this day.

Ben & Jerry's discovered the soul of their success by always making sure their business had a soul. No doubt such iconic flavors as Cherry Garcia and Chunky Monkey helped propel them to the top – but, just as importantly, it was also the company's bigger societal mission that encouraged people to both invest in them and buy their ice cream. A 1995 article put it this way:

"As the stockholders made clear, their investment in this ice cream company has less to do with its profitability than how it goes about making its profits. What Ben & Jerry's offers its investors is the chance to buy into a company that reminds them of themselves. A company that is innovative and impassioned about its product, but also values-driven. A company with a freewheeling sense of humor, but also a serious commitment to its community. Business on a human scale, in other words..."[1]

Or, as co-founder Jerry Greenfield himself said, revealing the real secret of their brand:

"...we knew that's what would separate Ben & Jerry's — even more than the great flavors, it was important for us to make our social mission a central part of the company."[2]

To really discover the soul of any business's success, it's necessary to have in place a strong mission that goes beyond the usual profit motive that drives most entrepreneurs. When you're mission-driven, you have the opportunity to create a powerful and lasting brand that can continue to draw customers, grow profits and do good things for the world all at the same time.

Without that mission, however...?

Well, Unilever, the multinational conglomerate that bought the company in 2000, found out the answer to that question. After Ben and Jerry sold the business, the brand went into a slump because, first of all, the brand's true believers thought the founders had also sold out the company's mission – and second of all, that turned out to be largely true.

1. Carlin, Peter. "Pure Profit: For Small Companies That Stress Social Values as Much as the Bottom Line, Growing Up Hasn't Been an Easy Task. Just Ask Ben & Jerry's, Patagonia and Starbucks." *The Los Angeles Times,* February 5, 1995.
2. Harrison, J.D. "When We Were Small: Ben & Jerry's." *The Washington Post,* May 14, 2014.

Unilever effectively shut the founders out of any decision-making and also curtailed the do-gooder missions of the company. To them, all that stuff was just some kind of marketing ploy.

That's why, in 2004, when Walt Freese was named as Unilever's CEO, he quickly invited Ben and Jerry back into the fold to reinvigorate the company's mission – and, of course, the brand itself. Once that mission was again completely back on track, so was the company. How important is that mission to this day?

Well, in 2010, Jostein Solheim, a Unilever executive from Norway, became the new CEO of the company and had this to say about the transition:

"The world needs dramatic change to address the social and environmental challenges we are facing. Values-led businesses can play a critical role in driving that positive change. We need to lead by example, and prove to the world that this is the best way to run a business. Historically, this company has been and must continue to be a pioneer to continually challenge how business can be a force for good and address inequities inherent in global business." [3]

In other words, in the case of Ben & Jerry's, the mission and the business were inseparable. Each made the other all the more powerful. It was the soul of their success.

MISSION-DRIVEN BRANDING: THE NEW PARADIGM

It used to be enough to make customers feel something – even if it didn't necessarily have a lot to do with your actual product or service.

It was "the Age of Emotion" for branding. In the words of Advertising Age:

"Prompted by booms of products and prosperity, conspicuous consumption kicked into high gear, and logic wasn't enough. Your product had to make a prospective buyer feel something. A car was freedom on four wheels, jeans made you rebellious."[4]

Yes, branding used to be all about tugging the heartstrings. For example,

3. "Division President: Jostein Solheim, Ben & Jerry's Homemade," FoodProcessing.com, http://www. foodprocessing.com/ceo/jostein-solheim/
4. Walker, Abbie. "Brands Need to Know Their Purpose and What They Aspire to Be," Advertising Age, February 24, 2014.

back in the 1970's, the classic heartwarming Coke commercial featuring football player "Mean" Joe Greene throwing a kid his jersey would make a nation sigh and open another bottle of Coke. McDonalds' famous song-and-dance "You Deserve a Break Today" campaign would motivate families to give Mom the night off from cooking and go get some Big Macs, while Kodak would sell its cameras and film with sentimental family photos and a goofy Paul Anka jingle, "For the Times of Your Life."

Today? Because you can instantly take photos with your phone, Kodak is virtually out of business. The Coca-Cola Company is under fire for allegedly causing obesity and is desperate to repair the image of its signature product. And McDonalds? In 2013, when it began soliciting positive customer comments on Twitter, it instead got overwhelmed with tweeted horror stories from the public, leading the campaign to be dubbed "McFail."

Technology and the Internet have changed everything. That, in turn, means manufactured emotions delivered by an ad or a commercial will only get an organization so far these days. As the same Advertising Age article goes on to say, "Our brands ask consumers for what a person expects from his or her friends—loyalty, trust, attention, love, time— without putting in the reciprocally requisite work. In other words, brands need to reconsider their motivations and behaviors because no one is buying the be-our-friend act any longer."[5]

In other words, trying to manufacture an emotion without having anything real behind it just won't do the job for a business anymore.

That's why Mission-Driven Branding is a must for this day and age. When an organization genuinely takes on a mission and implements it inside and out, when it is consistent and authentic in pursuing that mission, that organization has a far greater chance of creating loyalty and trust – and of creating an authentic emotional response - than by constantly reinventing its appeal with gimmicky short-term marketing campaigns.

There are two huge factors in play today that are an enormous threat to any company trying to win over customers and clients with superficial marketing tactics:

---

5. Ibid..

1. There's too much information out there.

Abraham Lincoln famously said, "You can fool all the people some of the time, and some of the people all the time, but you cannot fool all the people all the time." That's never been more true than right this minute.

For example, a few years back, the Chik-fil-A restaurant chain was embroiled in a firestorm over its backing of anti-gay policies. At the time, a sweet-looking teenage girl rushed to the company's defense by writing earnest posts on her Facebook page detailing all of Chick-fil-A's wonderful qualities. But, because the Internet is the Internet, somebody quickly figured out that this girl's picture was licensed from a stock photo company - and the media presumed that Chick-Fil-A had most likely set up the fake account to manufacture support for its positions,[6] even with no real evidence to prove it.

In other words, whereas a brand might have been able to get away with these kinds of practices before, there is virtually no chance of it now. Even if Chick-fil-A hadn't put up the fake Facebook account, the Internet "jury" still found the company guilty by association. And this was far from an isolated case – right now, there are now millions of amateur "branding police" actively investigating which companies are trying to pull a fast one and which ones are being authentic.

The Mission-Driven company has a natural advantage in this punitive climate. When it stays true to its mission, an organization can't help but pass the "smell test" on the Internet and elsewhere. It earns respect rather than derision from its actions – and that respect boosts its brand above the competition.

2. There are too many choices out there.

With all the options out there for a consumer, and all things being equal, how is that person going to choose who to buy from? Or perhaps the bigger question is: Why would that person choose to buy from a certain company or individual over another? Being Mission-Driven gives your company the answer to a customer's "Why." By defining how your brand uniquely serves the customer or society at large, you also define the positive role of your brand in that person's life.

---

6. Johnson, Dave. "Did Chick-fil-A's PR use fake Facebook account?" CBSNews.com, July 30, 2012. http://www.cbsnews.com/news/did-chick-fil-as-pr-use-fake-facebook-account/

Let's go back to a few of the brands we already talked about and see how their missions add value not only to the brands themselves, but also to a consumer's buying experience:

- If you want yummy ice cream and you want to make the world a better place, you buy from Ben & Jerry's.

- If you want a good chicken lunch or dinner and want to support a company that shares your values, you buy from Chick-fil-A.

- If you want a smartphone and want to buy from the company with the most innovative and stylish technology, you buy from Apple.

In each of the above cases, the company's mission gives the consumer a strong, concrete reason to buy from them – and to continue buying from them. There will always be plenty of premium ice cream brands, chicken restaurants and smartphone manufacturers to choose from – but Ben & Jerry's, Chick-fil-A and Apple all bring a whole lot more than their actual products to the consumer marketplace. No, their individual missions don't resonate with everyone – but they resonate strongly enough with a large enough base to keep their brands incredibly profitable and continually growing.

Again, being Mission-Driven is not really an option in today's marketplace - it's a necessity. As FastCoExist.com put it, "Today's brand must live and breathe through its core values in order to survive. Purpose is king, and there's no turning back."[7] And, in the words of Charles Schwab's executive vice president and CMO, Becky Saeger, "to be successful today, you must identify your company's purpose and execute like crazy."[8]

MISSION-DRIVEN BRANDING:
HOW IT DELIVERS THE FIVE BIG "D'S"

We'd like to close this chapter by naming what we've identified as the "5 Big D's" - the 5 biggest benefits that a successful mission can bring to any brand:

• DESIRABILITY

The right mission attracts a fervent and loyal customer/client base all

---

7. Blotter, Jennifer. "10 Ways Today's Purpose-Driven Brands Can Bring Their Core Values to Life," Fast-CoExist.com, October 14, 2013. http://www.fastcoexist.com/3019856/10-ways-todays-purpose-driven-brands-can-bring-their-core-values-to-life

8. Adamson, Allen. "Define Your Brand's Purpose, Not Just Its Promise." *Forbes,* November 11, 2009.

on its own. When that mission is organically attached to the brand in question, the brand not only attracts buyers, it also attracts quality employees who want to be a part of the brand's mission. Apple again is the best example of this principle in action, but there's no question the quality of Desirability applies to many, many other Mission-Driven brands as well, such as Disney, Patagonia, or Zappos.

- DISTANCE
Any brand faces the danger of losing its luster over time. Remember when Atari was the only gaming choice in American households? Or when you could find a Blockbuster video store in every strip mall in the neighborhood? In contrast, having a firm mission in place – and, just as importantly, continuing to make that mission relevant (imagine if Blockbuster had been the first to do what Netflix did) – almost guarantees consumer loyalty and an ongoing high profile in the marketplace, allowing a brand to truly go the distance.

- DEPENDABILITY
A mission helps a brand retain a consistent identity in the public's mind over the long haul. That consistency is important to developing trust and likeability with clients/customers and keeping them coming back for more. Walmart's "Always the Lowest Price" mission, for example, drives a constant stream of bargain-driven consumers through its doors, because those consumers know the retailer has a high degree of dependability.

- DIRECTION
A mission empowers a brand to focus on what it does best and provide a strong direction for the company as a whole. For instance, companies like Google and Apple understand they have a mandate to continue to deliver innovative technology that improves people's lives. That mandate, in turns, drives how they do business over the long haul and forces them to concentrate on the direction that defines them in terms of public perception.

- DIFFERENTIATION
Finally, Mission-Driven branding creates a powerful differentiation in the marketplace in contrast to the competition. Ben & Jerry's had that differentiation when they first began as a homegrown socially-aware business – and they quickly lost it when the brand became

just another acquisition by a multinational corporation, Unilever. For those few years, they were just another ice cream brand – and it was easy for their formerly fervent fans to simply pick another ice cream if it was cheaper or more convenient. A mission makes a company more than just another merchant or service provider – it transforms it into something much more meaningful and substantial, a business that truly stands out from the pack.

Of course, we've cherry-picked a lot of successful brands in this chapter to demonstrate the power of Mission-Driven branding. You the reader might rightly ask, "Well, yes, a mission works for big players like Apple and Google, but what real difference does it make to most companies?"

Well, we're glad you asked (even if we were the ones doing the asking for you) – because, it turns out, there is actually a concrete way to demonstrate the overall and overwhelming advantage of Mission-Driven branding.

In 2011, Havas Media Labs, one of the leading global communications and marketing groups, began compiling what they called the "Meaningful Brands Index." For the first time, a detailed analysis of companies that were Mission Driven in one way or another (through CSR (Corporate Social Responsibility) policies, sustainability, community giving, cause marketing, etc.) was done to determine just how this kind of brand activity affected their actual business.

The result? In the 2013 survey, the most recent one as of this writing, the so-called Meaningful Brands outperformed the stock market by an incredible 120%.[9]

Umair Haque, director of Havas Media Labs, had this to say as an explanation of the amazing success of Mission-Driven brands: "People aren't irrational in what they expect. They don't want perfect lives—but they do want better lives. What we consistently find is that institutions don't meet their expectations in real human terms. When they do find companies that are willing to benefit them, they're really happy doing business with them."[10]

And that to us is definitely the Soul of Success!

9. Dill, Kathryn. "Google, Samsung, Microsoft Head A Tech-Dominated List of The Most 'Meaningful' Brands," *Forbes*, June 14, 2013.
10. Ibid.

About Nick

A 3-Time Emmy Award Winning Director, Producer and Filmmaker, Nick Nanton, Esq., is known as the Top Agent to Celebrity Experts® around the world for his role in developing and marketing business and professional experts, through personal branding, media, marketing and PR.

Nick serves as the CEO of The Dicks + Nanton Celebrity Branding Agency, an international branding and media agency with more than 2200 clients in 33 countries. Nick has produced large scale events and television shows with the likes of Steve Forbes, Brian Tracy, President George H.W. Bush, Jack Canfield (Creator of the *Chicken Soup for the Soul* Series), Michael E. Gerber, Tom Hopkins and many more.

Nick is recognized as one of the top thought-leaders in the business world, speaking on major stages internationally and having co-authored 36 best-selling books, including *The Wall Street Journal* Best-Seller, *StorySelling*™.

Nick has been seen in *USA Today, The Wall Street Journal, Newsweek, BusinessWeek, Inc. Magazine, The New York Times, Entrepreneur® Magazine, Forbes,* FastCompany. com and has appeared on ABC, NBC, CBS, and FOX television affiliates around the country, as well as E!, CNN, FOX News, CNBC, MSNBC and hosts his own series on the Bio! channel, *Portraits of Success.*

Nick is a member of the Florida Bar, a voting member of The National Academy of Recording Arts & Sciences (Home to The GRAMMYs), a member of The National Academy of Television Arts & Sciences (Home to the EMMYs), The National Academy of Best-Selling Authors, and serves on the Innovation Board of the XPRIZE Foundation, a non-profit organization dedicated to bringing about "radical breakthroughs for the benefit of humanity" through incentivized competition, best known for it's Ansari XPRIZE which incentivized the first private space flight and was the catalyst for Richard Branson's Virgin Galactic. Nick spends his spare time serving as an Elder at Orangewood Church, working with Young Life, Downtown Credo Orlando, Entrepreneurs International and rooting for the Florida Gators with his wife Kristina and their three children, Brock, Bowen and Addison..

Learn more at: www.NickNanton.com and
www.CelebrityBrandingAgency.com

About JW

JW Dicks Esq., is a *Wall Street Journal* Best-Selling Author®, Emmy Award-Winning Producer, publisher, board member, and advisor to organizations such as the XPRIZE, The National Academy of Best-Selling Authors®, and The National Association of Experts, Writers and Speakers®.

JW is the CEO of DNAgency and is a strategic business development consultant to both domestic and international clients. He has been quoted on business and financial topics in national media such as the *USA Today, The Wall Street Journal, Newsweek, Forbes*, CNBC.com, and *Fortune Magazine Small Business.*

Considered a thought leader and curator of information, JW has more than forty-three published business and legal books to his credit and has co-authored with legends like Brian Tracy, Jack Canfield, Tom Hopkins, Dr. Nido Quebin, Dr. Ivan Misner, Dan Kennedy, and Mari Smith. He is the resident branding expert for Fast Company's internationally syndicated blog and is the editor and publisher of the *Celebrity Expert Insider,* a monthly newsletter sent to experts worldwide.

JW is called the "Expert to the Experts" and has appeared on business television shows airing on ABC, NBC, CBS, and FOX affiliates around the country. His co-produced television series, *Profiles of Success,* appears on the Bio Channel - along with other branded films he has produced. JW also co-produces and syndicates a line of franchised business television shows and received an Emmy Award as Executive Producer of the film, *Mi Casa Hogar.*

JW and his wife of forty-two years, Linda, have two daughters, two granddaughters, and two yorkies. He is a sixth generation Floridian and splits his time between his home in Orlando and his beach house on Florida's west coast.

CHAPTER 13

SOUL SUCCESS IN THE CORPORATE ENVIRONMENT
THE ISOLATION FACTOR: WE HAVE TO TALK

BY DR. MARY E. DONOHUE

Mike Camp is the sort of man I would have liked to have had as a boss. He doesn't see race, ethnicity or gender, he sees potential. But Mike, like many other leaders, has too much to do. We all face that problem at work because we are all being asked to do more with less. We don't think about the people that need to get these tasks and transactions accomplished. We just need it done now.

Turning employees into taskers, however, has a terrible downside. It isolates them, and isolated employees leave.

Mike, and other leaders from around North America, are now utilizing a new system I designed to fight off this isolation and build the sense of belonging and team so rare in the modern workplace. Based on three simple communication principles, I call it Stop, Listen, and Lead.

Stop encourages you to focus on goals, understand what people are saying and how they are saying it. Listen encourages you to understand your inner voice, get the monkey off your back, be your best logical self. Lead teaches you to have difficult conversations, understand how to give and take feedback, and understand how to assess on a weekly basis rather than monthly or yearly.

People learn best with a partner - not in a classroom or on a computer. They learn with a mentor or a mentee from their organization, not some outside expert or consultant. Why is this mentor-mentee relationship important? The internal mentor-leader is the best possible guide to explain how the organization really works, what makes it unique and great, and ultimately reminds the mentee why they were chosen to work for or with the organization in the first place, because of their talent.

Time-stressed managers like Mike rarely have time to develop their teams, even though that is their primary job. These folks are tired, stressed and asked to produce more with less every year. The Donohue Mentoring System (DMS) teaches and gives participants opportunities to deploy the Stop, Listen and Lead method. It provides the catalyst for conversation in the same way that a personal trainer acts as a catalyst for exercise. The trainer tells you what to do, walks you through it, and then encourages you to do it on your own.

Real Life Scenario:
This is the story of Mike and his mentee Kalvin Hardy and the DMS. Mike learned to extend his already amazing people skills efficiently and effectively. He is now a "super mentor," imparting wisdom to many team members at a time. After Mike has mentored someone using the DMS, they inevitably received a promotion and stayed with the company. That's the real payoff: people stay with the company and become more valuable. Mike has also been honored by his company, his supervisors, and outside organizations for his unfailing commitment to developing diverse talent into the next generation of leaders. Mike was one of Diversity MBA's Top 50 Under 50 winners in 2014 because of his commitment to mentoring and inclusion.

Though he didn't know it at the time, Kalvin was suffering from the Isolation Factor. He was young, new and lost after three months in an hourly position in the company. He didn't feel that anyone had his back, and he really didn't think he would stay with the company. The more his supervisor asked him to do, the more he felt lost. Rather than risk losing Kalvin, who had shown great promise to be a future leader early on, he was partnered with Mike in the DMS. Through the DMS he learned how to be a team member, be assertive, and also learned that his company believed in him and wanted him to stay.

The Stop Listen and Lead principles that Mike and Kalvin learned in the DMS were the key to their success.

STOP

If your actions inspire others to dream more, learn more, do more and become more, you are a leader.

~ John Quincy Adams

People in leadership roles have priorities every day. Sure, we try to enter our days with a plan and maximize our time, but then something happens that's outside the plan. What then? Our entire day is thrown off. Things get tricky quickly!

As a senior leader in one of the largest companies in the world, Mike didn't have time for another "time-consuming corporate initiative," but he knew he needed to develop his team in a time-efficient manner. He loved the idea of a system that challenged both mentor and mentee every week.

Mike and Kalvin made a commitment to each other: they would devote 30 uninterrupted minutes per week for 16 weeks. They didn't schedule meetings too late in the week because if something came up there was no time to reschedule.

Leaders must be flexible with their time because it's necessary for managing and developing a team and setting and delivering on predetermined results. Parts of leadership are planned, but it's the ability to adapt to the moment and adapt to the needs of the team that makes the difference. Too often leaders expect their team to adapt to them, which kills innovation and productivity and creates "Yes Men."

When Mike worked with Kalvin, he realized how important it was for Kalvin to know he had his back and would always be there for him. As a result, Mike never missed a meeting. This showed Kalvin how much the company believed in him and Kalvin, in turn, trusted Mike and subsequently the company.

LISTEN

No man will make a great leader who wants to do it all himself,
or to get all the credit for doing it.

~ Andrew Carnegie

After three months of employment, Kalvin told leadership that he felt lost. He'd been really excited about his new job and thought it was a great opportunity—building it up to what he believed it should be. We've all done that before! Then he realized that everyone he thought would be there to help in his transition was simply too busy. But he wanted to go places and contribute, despite the challenges he faced being the new, young guy to his managers.

Kalvin felt how many people feel each and every day: finding out that their goals and ambitions have this disconnect with their soul for success. Kalvin's supervisor didn't want to lose Kalvin so she reached up and out to Mike, a more senior person in the company. Once Kalvin met Mike and started the Donohue Mentoring System, he said he found:

- Guidance about what may be the right direction
- Experienced meetings and interactions with a senior leader of the company that were welcomed, not looked at as "something else to get done"

Through his mentoring relationship, Kalvin learned some really exciting things about his talents and what he had to offer. He also learned about what the company had to offer him. The transformation was incredible. Mike reported that "Kalvin transformed from the hourly associate I'd first met, into a confident leader within four to five weeks."

Taking the time to find out a person's strengths is something management often overlooks and my mentoring system can identify. Through the DMS we challenge future leaders like Kalvin by asking them to improve three areas of development (strengths/weaknesses, commitment, and desired outcomes) and mentors create success by guiding mentees through the company's culture, which typically can take years to operate comfortably in. Mentoring is more than giving time, it's about the well-being of their organization and converting "corporate speak" into personal relationships.

When Kalvin first started at this new job, he admitted that he had no idea what to expect. He was eager to listen and learn. Trying to understand the management's mentality was important to him. Mike, who ran his company's Leadership Academy prior to meeting Kalvin, had learned that as a mentor, he needed to sometimes conduct difficult conversations.

Mike was vested in doing this, realizing that in order to grasp a company's culture and even make shifts to it, you must be able to see the big picture while focusing what the individual needs to improve to become a better employee.

According to Kalvin,

"Mike sort of took me out of my bubble and helped me reach out to others and learn about the company. Really, what we focused on with DMS were the areas of opportunity. I was aware of my areas of opportunity, but I really wasn't doing anything to improve upon them at first. But eventually, I looked at it as a challenge that I wanted to rise up to meet. I knew that other employees were made aware of these same opportunities, but very few of them acted. I wanted to act, and with Mike's help, I could."

LEAD

Outstanding leaders go out of their way to boost the self-esteem of their personnel. If people believe in themselves, it's amazing what they can accomplish.

~ Sam Walton

The process of building stronger, happier people must be individualized. Leaders need a roadmap to make this happen; but training must be adapted to the needs of each worker. After all, when was the last time a "one-size-fits-all" strategy ever worked in business or your personal life? It's an individual effort based on strengths/weaknesses, commitment, and desired outcomes, those three areas of development. For Kalvin, it was about building up his confidence using Mike's strategies and tips within a custom-mentoring plan.

Kalvin, who went from feeling lost and left out to a management position, summed it up thusly. "I'm more confident now in myself and my abilities. Before the mentoring program, I was sort of set in my ways. I would be the person that goes to the desk, does their work, does a good job, but I didn't feel a part of the team, really. Now, since going through the program, I feel like I'm a contributor to my team. I'm more willing to be vocal and speak up about things. One of the things that I learned early on in the program – there was a lesson about knowing your stuff. I took that to heart and I really dived into my job and really tried to learn everything I possibly could to be successful, and to be helpful and serve my customers. That was a great help to me. And then, I took that information that I learned and I was able to go to my managers and say, 'Hey, this area here, there's something going on here. I have examples.' And I was able to point those out and give clear directions."

Previously, Kalvin may have thought those things, but would not have stepped up to vocalize them because he wouldn't have felt welcomed to. This nurturing response in his workplace environment has made him a natural leader. He knows what he is capable of and he's now the person that people go to for some guidance and help, which he is glad to give. One of the most golden of rules about mentoring is:

YOUR PROFIT AND LOSS STATEMENT

It's people first and then the commerce will follow.

A day without action toward maximizing the potential of your workforce is another day in which the people you rely on are only getting by. Businesses are much more than sales plans, organizational charts and products and services. They are an enterprise composed of people. It is up to management to decide whether those people are just getting by and looking outside for a better opportunity or are integral, engaged and excited employees who are aligned with leadership's objectives and poised to become leaders themselves.

It's time to create the relationships that will strengthen and build your business from within. You have a wonderful supply of 'human' resources at your disposal.

... Tap into the resource within

About Dr. Mary

Named as one of the 18 Outstanding Women In Tech, 2015, by *RdigitalLife,* Dr. Donohue is a passionate advocate of revolutionizing today's workforce training through technology and internal talent - not consultants.

She believes passionately in the art of conversation, the value of team and outcome based mentoring.

A cancer survivor who worked with Paul Newman, learned from Robert Kennedy Jr, made her movie debut with former Toronto Mayor David Miller, and was briefly (very briefly) a Supreme with Diana Ross, Dr. Mary Donohue is often described as a force of nature. As Founder of the Donohue Mentoring System™ she designs mentoring systems that provide people with a roadmap to become people developers and achieve a better work/life balance.

Dr. Mary is a world-renowned speaker and TEDX presenter, television personality and columnist. Her work appears in the Huffington Post and Financial Post. When she isn't working, writing or speaking she can be found with her daughter and her husband, who is her business partner, or walking her dogs, along Toronto's shoreline.

Dr. Donohue can be reached at mary@thedms.org, 416 564 2944.

CHAPTER 14

BUILDING A SUCCESSFUL FLESH-AND-BLOOD ORGANIZATION

BY DR. MARIE V. BAÑUELOS

Gymnasts, lazy people, complainers and successful people have all practiced to be what they are good at. So if you keep practicing being lazy, you will be lazy. If you keep practicing complaining, you will constantly complain. If you practice compassion, generosity, patience, working hard and having a bigger vision, you will become better at it with time because you will create the causes to become better. You are practicing to become better.

~ Tsem Tulku Rinpoche

I was always told I had a very unusual management style. I have a tendency to see the humor in everything, expect hard work but act as if it is play, and do not take excuses or complaints but rather encourage creativity that is outside of the box to create solutions. I expect work to be fun and exciting without causing major stress in one's personal life. Maybe I am unusual.

After 35 years in education encompassing 23 years in school administration, I became a superintendent of schools in a small community. I was the first woman superintendent since the district's beginning of more than 100 years before me. Not only was I unusual as a "female" to them, I was just plain different than the District was used to from former superintendents. The district hierarchy was strongly built and enforced with firm rules and old-fashioned industrial-age philosophy. Every department had its own box and each never stepped outside its definitions of the work each was assigned. The district was a machine made of cogs that did not know their relationships to one another, and breakdowns in the "machine" were major crises. I knew this was going to be a fun job as the new superintendent.

My job was to build a close-knit team that understood relationships with each member and had the same vision for success, so it could move forward smoothly with or without me. It was important to me that each person in the organization contributed his/her expertise with all members to make the organizational parts move in sync and precision to address the educational challenges in front of our students and the community. It was time for new "rules" different than the old ones. I began with five ideals that needed to be in place:

1. Participate 100%
2. Play Together
3. Learn Together
4. Work Together
5. Celebrate Success

IDEAL #1: PARTICIPATE 100%

Getting to know staff was extremely important. Not only did I need to know them, they needed to know me. This was the only way trust would be built. I started by being in my office only a few hours a day. The majority of my day was spent by briefly stopping into other offices, visiting schools and being visible to school staffs and students. I made the people more important than paper. The staffs noticed the difference right away. They were used to being left on their own. I, on the other hand, was interested in them as people and made sure that they noticed that I put their welfare first. I also let them see I needed their participation in the organization. After all, it is the people in the organization that will make success happen. Engaged and happy staffs that fully participate make a healthy and happy organization. And I do realize that there are usually those who will resist working together no matter what is presented. My job was to set the expectation and keep reinforcing the ideal. Interestingly, it began to work very quickly to get people involved. Trust comes easy when you tell the truth and are available for conversation.

IDEAL #2: PLAY TOGETHER

It was clear to me that previous rules of the organization had implied expectations. During cabinet (administrative team) meetings with the superintendent, members were not to contribute to conversation but rather wait for "instructions" of what to do. I also noticed all departments in the organization were not represented in this elite group of administrators. This was the group making the decisions for the entire organization without representation of the entire organization. It was clear to me that everyone needed to "play" together if we wanted a strong team. My first step was to invite the heads of the missing departments to our cabinet meetings. Shock was the first response. Current members of the cabinet acted as if I had broken some silent rule of exclusion; the newly-invited departments acted as if they were going to be attacked.

The first meeting with all the organization's heads of departments was almost silent. It was my turn to set expectations. I told them how important their input and collaborative assistance in making decisions was critical to make the organization effective. I told them I needed all of them to keep me up-to-date with their departments' progress, to let me know what they needed to accomplish work. I expected all of them to learn all about the whole organization so if I was suddenly gone, they could carry on without me having all of the information of business. That was the beginning of a big change in how the district did business. Departments got more and more involved when they began to see what they had to say and contribute had value. And even though I did not always agree with what a department perceived as a need, discussion became more thoughtful and tended toward more organizational problem-solving rather than department problem-solving. The team started to come together because we all began to understand we were all responsible for success.

IDEAL #3: LEARN TOGETHER

I actually expected all of my administrators and department heads to read. Not only that, I expected them to read the same book and discuss it during staff meetings! The groans were loud at first but soon subsided when I assigned the first book, *Sacred Cows Make the Best Burgers*. Just the title alone worked to silence groans since the district was in an agriculture/dairy community and the title made them laugh. The theme of the book was to identify outdated practices that served no purpose and to rethink what works better to get what the organization wants to accomplish. The book is humorous and easy to read. We had great conversations about the things we were doing that were outdated practices and wasted time. Relief was tremendous when we began stopping those outdated practices.

One example of a "sacred cow" was in my own office. The practice was to create three-ring notebooks of Board meetings that were kept in bookcases in perpetuity. The office had four bookcases full of these notebooks! I purchased scanners for all of the departments in my office. Our summer work my first year was to scan all documents and store them electronically. We got rid of all the paper, notebooks and bookcases and actually created enough room to have another office and increase the size of the staff's break room. To say the least, the secretarial staff was ecstatic. No more killing tress and no more clutter in the office. Just the change in atmosphere changed attitudes to a much lighter and productive feeling. Of course, reading assignments began to turn into educational and technical books that examined current research. By then, the staff was willing to read and discuss what they learned.

We were learning together, building common understanding, and agreeing on common goals for change. Those are big leaps in an organization. To keep the progress going, we had to continue to learn together and stretch our knowledge not only in technical information, but also in exploring ourselves and our personal and organizational beliefs that may hold us back from success. The group began to build trust to talk about issues that were not before spoken of before we began the process of learning together.

IDEAL #4: WORK TOGETHER

This ideal was the most complicated to infuse. "Playing" together which required deeper conversation and more organizational unity was the first step. Now, actually working together was the big jump in changing how work was done. Playing together helped break down boundaries between departments but the real task was to get them to work together as a whole. The organizational machine is made of flesh and blood, not of metal cogs. There is more work to do to get the flesh-and-blood machine to work effectively together than a metal machine where cogs only have to fit together on the exterior. A flesh-and-blood machine had an interior made of beliefs, concerns, personalities, doubts and trust issues. This was my biggest challenge.

We all had to share a Vision in who we were and what we wanted to accomplish. The rhetoric was always there, and Mission statements, but meaning was never agreed to by all parts of the organization. I think that was because the parts of the organization never saw themselves as part of a whole on the same path.

Now that we had experience of talking together, sharing ideas and solving problems together, and having common knowledge in what we read together, it was time to really work together. That meant we had to envision the same results and identify what each of us was responsible for to make the vision happen. It also meant that we needed to trust each other, especially trust me, to keep everyone informed, involved, and respected, to get the work done efficiently.

We began tearing apart those vision and mission statements that had been in place forever and identifying what they meant to each of us individually, departmentally and as a whole. We had to agree that the vision and mission were important, relevant, and reachable. We defined how each of us could participate in making the vision and mission come alive and what and how each department had to offer to make them come to fruition.

It may seem to readers that this should have happened first. It couldn't. Building working relationships, work ethic, building common capacity by reading and learning together had to happen first. The failure of many organizations is that they move too fast or ignore basic human needs. It is the human cogs that will break and can't be fixed if we ignore basic needs of the human organism of connection and safety. An organization is successful if its contributors are well, feel valuable and are respected.

This Ideal took the longest. The process challenged beliefs and defined who we were and what part we each played in the vision and mission of the district. It helped us all agree we all were important in making success happen. The process of deep conversation, deep self-examination of what individually each needed to contribute, and deep respect for each of our contributions resulted in deep commitment. The real work could now begin.

IDEAL #5: CELEBRATE SUCCESS

Who doesn't love a party? Success sometimes goes unnoticed because we don't build the habit of recognizing success and progress as we go along during a big effort; we have a habit of only celebrating at the end of a big project. Big mistake. We need to party when things go right along the way.

Human beings need to know how they are doing in order to keep going. Positive reinforcement encourages continued forward movement and willingness to keep going when movement seems difficult. Organizations sometimes recognize errors constantly; this practice demoralizes staff and makes staff believe they don't have what it takes to do well. When something went off track in our organization, our groups talked about it honestly. Our ground rule was to "tell the truth faster" so we could work together faster to solve problems. Blame and excuses were not appropriate conversation because they did not solve problems. Any problem identified was a success. Any accomplishment that lead to our goals was a success. We celebrated at least monthly.

Every month I held an all-staff meeting to discuss what we had done that month and to identify all the successes we had toward our goals. I recognized individuals and departments. Departments and staff got funny "presents" of little cost but you would think they got a pricey recognition. We, of course, had cake.

We kept a chart of accomplishments posted on our meeting room wall that accumulated successes all year. Staff used to go into the meeting room to read the successes when they felt stuck or because movement forward was getting difficult. They reported that it helped them see the big picture and that, sometimes, slow movement forward was just part of success. Wise insight.

We accomplished changing our culture in our organization. Culture was changed by action, not belief. We needed to do things differently to make the "machine" be more effective. This organization needed to do things very differently to move forward.

We had very simple Ideals: Participate 100%; Play Together; Learn Together; Work Together; and Celebrate Success. I trust the order in which we did these things because I have experienced that the order works. I have used these ideals in my second superintendency with success. They may have worked because I am unusual, but I don't think so. I think they worked because it recognizes that organizations are not machines, they are people with feelings, concerns, trust issues and fears. Good leaders support human growth not just organizational growth. Human growth will result in organizational growth. The organization CAN have fun.

When I retired, I wasn't sure how the district would move forward under different leadership, but had faith that the organization would continue because their operating procedures were different and had become habit. The rewarding news is, 10 years later, I still hear from that staff and administration. Sometimes they say they want me back because they miss all the positive energy. I remind them that they are the positive energy and they can continue to support each other toward success, and they can do just fine without me.

About Dr. Marie

Marie Bañuelos is a retired superintendent of schools after 35 years in education. For the last three years and currently, Marie supervises student teachers and administrative candidates for the University of Phoenix in California so candidates can meet the rigorous credentialing demands of the state. Marie also founded the Central Valley Kings Foundation, Inc., a California Nonprofit Public Benefit Corporation in 2012 to support community service in several communities and to fund scholarships for high school graduates, who do not normally receive scholarships for college. Marie advises high school student service Key Clubs (Kiwanis sponsored) and helps students develop community service values and strengthen leadership skills. Marie is dedicated to helping all students reach their potential by seeking advanced educational experiences and developing high ethical standards and values.

Dr. Bañuelos is a graduate of the University of La Verne, California, with a doctorate in Organizational Leadership. Marie coaches working administrators and has coached over 100 schools in school improvement, staff relations, and reducing resistance and stress while going through change. She donates her time to the Western Association of Schools and Colleges to accredit high schools, adult schools, private schools and prison schools. Marie has a unique style that is inclusive of all staffs in schools and districts. Her most important advice to schools that are going through difficult times is, "Schools are machines made of flesh and blood. If you break the cogs in these machines, they cannot be fixed as easily as metal." Marie's humanistic style unites staff and leadership to helps schools through difficult times of change.

Marie began her growth journey with Jack Canfield in the 1980s. She participated in workshops that Jack Canfield led for other organizations. When Canfield began his own business, Marie participated in Jack's programs and later managed support personnel for Canfield's workshops for over five years, and contributed to Canfield's "Self Esteem in the Classroom" curriculum.

Marie provides schools and district with workshops on building relationships, problem solving, team building, goal development and action planning. Marie also assists schools and districts to analyze new school legislation and develop ways to meet the new state requirements – while still building strong teamwork in times of regulations and helping schools to identify avenues for self-governance and team decision making for what is best in their communities.

You can connect with Marie at:
cvkfoundation@gmail.com
ree1008@sbcglobal.net

CHAPTER 15

WANT TO FEEL HAPPY AND POWERFUL? – TRY THIS SIMPLE, SUREFIRE PROBLEM-SOLVING METHOD

BY LEM H. TRUONG, PhD

Over my entire life, the key concept that accounts for my various successes is a simple, easy method of problem solving. During the first 40 years, that method helped me: (1) cope with the challenges of a lonely and difficult childhood, and (2) become the first woman in my hometown to hold a Ph.D. degree from an American university and to serve as an Acting Head of Department in the South Vietnamese government before Saigon fell. That same concept saved me from being captured by the North Vietnamese Communists in April 1975. It was my entry ticket to various positions after I arrived in the US for the past 40 years, and it helped me lead a meaningful life as an entrepreneur for the past 24 years.

I. HOW DID THE PROBLEM SOLVING METHOD HELP ME COPE WITH MY PERSONAL CHALLENGES?

Although for a long time I was not aware of the significance of the method I used when I was sad, distressed, or wanted something badly, in hindsight I realize that I was indeed using – more or less systematically

– the following complementary actions to solve my problems:

1. Ask for God's help and believe in His love for me, and

2. Do the best I can on my side, leaving it to God to decide on the outcome.

OVERCOMING MY LONELINESS

Here is basically how I remember I acted when I was about six years old. Every day I came home from school before my mother and my older brother returned. I did not want to be around the cook, who did not like me. So I would go to a small place on the left hand side of my courtyard next to a neighbor's usually empty stable. There I began to jump on the wooden plank sticking out from a thatch wall. I did it for a while, keeping an eye on the street that led to my house, to make sure I could run to meet my mother as soon as she appeared, when she returned from school where she was a teacher. After waiting for a while, sometimes for a long while, I would light a small candle next to a paper vignette given by a classmate that I carried in my school bag. The vignette pictured the Blessed Mary holding the Child Jesus. Then I would say the "Hail Mary" prayer at least five times, together with my own wishes. That was my secret daily ritual, which I would repeat every time I felt lonely, worried or distressed. After that I felt all right, even good. That was one of the things I did when I wanted help. I knew that I always had a place to go.

ESCAPING FROM THE NORTH
VIETNAMESE COMMUNISTS

Another much more dramatic example was the imminent danger I faced on the eve of the Communists' takeover of South Viet Nam on April 30, 1975. It showed how, with ardent prayer and taking prompt action, I was able to save my family and myself from being captured by the Communists. Here is how the story goes:

Following the bombardment of the Presidential Palace by the Communists (four blocks from my residence), on the evening of April 28, 1975, two days before the fall of Saigon, a 24-hour curfew was imposed the next day. Nobody was allowed to go in the streets, and I could not reach anyone to ask for help. The telephone did not work and even the American Advisor from the Embassy had to suddenly interrupt his call, and his line was dead when I tried to call back. I was indeed desperate, even though I pretended to keep my calm so as not to worry my mother. My only resort was to pray and ask God for help. So I went down to my living room and started to pray the rosary, as I always do in such cases. I sat on the couch and prayed and prayed until I heard some commotion in the front yard.

I looked up through the window and saw two senior officers from my Ministry crossing the yard toward the living room. They brought a list of names of my senior staff who desired to be evacuated by the American Embassy. I realized there was no other alternative for me than going to the Embassy myself with the list, curfew or no curfew. It was a desperate act, because I could easily be arrested or shot by the guards policing the streets. But I needed to go to the Embassy to seek help. So I did, by hanging on to the seat of my nephew's scooter. I was unable to meet anyone at the Embassy and could not find help there – neither for my staff nor myself! But the good thing was that at least now I knew that I must leave Saigon with my family if I did not want to risk being captured, and that the staff must be informed of my failed attempt. I also realized how blessed I was to have taken the decision to get out of the house even under clear danger – for that allowed me to see the desperate conditions in Saigon at that time – so I could decide on what to do next in order to escape the Communists.

II. THE PROBLEM SOLVING METHOD AND ITS APPLICATION TO ORGANIZATIONAL CHALLENGES

How do I help my clients address their perennial problematic circumstances?

Fast forward to my nine years working as a Senior Project Officer at the World Bank. I continued to apply that problem-solving method to resolve my own problems and challenges.

It was not until I established my own consulting and training business that the need to pass on this method to my clients to help them deal with their own problems became clear and urgent. Executives and managers who came to the courses confessed to me that they were overwhelmed by many personal and professional problems causing them a lot of stress. And what they were looking for in coming to my training was a time to relax, unless I could find a magic solution to help them effectively handle that perennial challenge. I gave the issue a lot of thought and concluded that I needed to use my introductory class to explore and identify the problems and challenges facing my clients, and make the remaining course a gradual discovery of solutions. The feedback from the clients has been overwhelmingly positive.

Below is a sample of problems that were identified by thousands of participants that went through our various courses:

1. Lack of clear and inspiring visions, missions, and objectives.

2. Inappropriate structures and processes to guide organizational behavior, especially as related to communication and decision-making.

3. Project actions and activities require the cooperation of different units in the host agencies that lack the means and incentives to play their parts.

4. Problems are magnified in inter-sector projects, as these must rely on the cooperation of agencies having different objectives, priorities and resources.

5. Inappropriate, or lack of, management systems.

6. Too many conflicting demands at the same time – too much ambiguity and conflict.

7. Staff lacking competence and motivation.

8. Getting beneficiaries to cooperate in order to implement project activities to achieve project objectives.

9. Delay and shortfall of government counterpart funding.

10. Limited cooperation and support from oversight ministries.

As to how my clients typically talked about their situation when they first arrived:

Mr. B. Y., Manager of a Multi-state Program: "As the manager of a large agricultural program, I have the responsibility for the activities at the various farms covered by the program. That requires me to know first-hand the physical progress in the field and at the same time, to prepare reports to submit to government and donors. How can I be at two different places at the same time? No matter how hard I work, I have not been able to do even an acceptable job! And there are deadlines to respect. I feel so stressed. I get up everyday at 4 in the morning. By 6 am, I am already at the Office. I stay there until 11 pm or sometimes past midnight. And yet I don't seem to move ahead by many inches. My blood pressure has increased alarmingly and my doctor advised me to slow down. I hardly see my children, for when I come home they are already asleep. In the morning, I leave before they even open their eyes!"

Mr. Y. N., a Senior Executive, Coordinator of an Infrastructure Program: "… I am drowning! No matter what I do, it's never enough. The job is challenging and interesting, but I don't seem to get much done despite all my efforts. If you don't mind, I intend to come here to rest." [He looked really sick! In fact many people came because they felt on the verge of breakdown!]

Mr. R.A.C., Coordinator of an Inter-sector Economic Management Project: He talked about coping with political interferences from local politicians, which was a common challenge faced by many if not all indigenous development project managers. Those included orders from on high to use project funds for other personal favors (e.g., misallocation of vehicles, distributing jobs to friends and relatives), and political gains (e.g., buying votes, distribution of favors to party members), instead of for the purpose intended and agreed to, with lenders.

"Given the list of problems and challenges confronting senior executives and managers on a daily basis, how could the LTA training help participants handle their jobs effectively?" That was the question asked by all my clients, either openly or silently in their heart. So I decided to address that question right at the first class of every course, and let them find the specific answers to their needs as the course evolves. The result was astounding. People actively participated in discussion, taking the concepts and process to mentally apply in their specific situation. By the end of the course the levels of enthusiasm and confidence were palpable. That mood was carried over to the job; leading to incredible achievements and more participants kept coming based on the word-of-mouth they received.

As for the method, I retained the basic concept but expanded the method into a 4-component framework. Below is a presentation on how to use that framework to handle organizational problems :

Component A: Determining when and how they should act.

Clients are taught to look at the environment in which they operate in a new way. That environment is pictured as three concentric circles;[1] each one represents the things or people over whom the Executive or Manager has some control or influence or neither. They are:

1. The innermost circle where the Manager has the highest degree of control is "the circle of control – CC"

2. The intermediate circle represents the environment over which the Manager has no control but can have some influence over; it is his "circle of influence – CI"

3. The outermost circle represents the environment over which the Manager has no control or influence. It is his "circle of appreciation – CA"

This new concept is very useful. It helps the manager and executive to act only when they know they have control or at least influence over the things and people within that circle. Therefore they could avoid acting recklessly to fail in situations where they can only appreciate, or fail to act or act appropriately, in situations where they could make a difference.

Component B: Applying a process of problem analysis to determine the specific causes and the corresponding specific actions.

This process involves 3 steps.

Step 1: Determine the specific, actionable causes of each problem.

Step 2: Identify the specific action(s) that need to be taken.

Step 3: Determine which actions fall into which circle.

Component C: Adopting a Strategy of Actions.

This also involves 3 steps.

Step 1: Take those actions that fall in the CC and CI.

Step 2: Monitor the results, by comparing them to what is expected/intended.

Step 3: Free one's own mind from concern for actions that fall into CA.

Component D: <u>Committing to take action and follow through.</u>

This refers to the following actions from the concerned executive or manager:

- Ask for and trust in divine help
- Believe in oneself
- Capitalize on one's strengths
- Continue to learn through feedback.

Over the course of my professional life, it has been personally gratifying to see so many people in executive and project management positions benefit from that Problem Solving Framework. In fact I believe that none of this would have been possible without asking for God's help, believing in His love and, after trying to do one's best, leaving it to Him to decide the outcome.

---

1. The concept of three concentric circles was first introduced in the World Bank in 1981 by William E. Smith, Francis J. Lethem, and Ben A. Thoolen in their paper, *The Design of Organizations for Rural Development Projects – A Progress Report:* <u>Staff Working Paper No.375</u>.

About Dr. Lem Truong

Dr. Lem Hoang Truong is the Principal Partner and Chief Executive Officer at L.T. Associates, Inc., a Washington, DC-based International Management Consulting and Leadership Training firm, serving the professional needs of over 5,000 Senior Executives and Managers from 35 Developing Countries – especially French- and English-speaking countries in Sub-Sahara Africa, over the past 24 years (1989-2013).

Former positions include:

- Senior Public Sector Specialist, The World Bank, Washington D.C. (1981-89)

- Associate Professor, Public Administration, George Washington University (1980 -81)

- Assistant Professor, Public Administration, George Mason University (1979-80)

- Adjunct-Professor, Comparative and Development Administration, Georgetown University (1976-80)

- Director of Programs, American Society for Public Administration, Washington D.C. (1975-79)

- Deputy and Acting Minister, National Commission of Administrative and Civil Service Reforms, South Viet Nam (1973-75)

- Vice-Rector and Professor of Public Policy Studies, the National Institute of Administration, Saigon, South Viet Nam (1970-73)

Education:

Master's and PhD degrees in Public Administration, University of Southern California (1971); Certificate in Advanced Administrative Studies, Manchester University, UK (1964); B.S. in General Management, National Institute of Administration, Saigon (1960); Certificate in Personnel Management, Michigan State University (1956); French Baccalaureate II in Philosophy and Letters (1953).

Dr. Truong has attended dozens of seminars and courses on self–help, leadership and management, given by reputable universities, learning institutions and leading experts in the field – including Dale Carnegie, Conan and Nightingale, Franklin Covey and Jack Canfield.

Dr. Truong has four grown children and three grandsons. She lives in Falls Church, Virginia.

CHAPTER 16

SUCCESS – IT'S ALL IN YOUR MINDSET

BY STEVE RENNER

Have you ever seriously considered the origins of success? Walking through the corridors of history, a prominent and recurring theme has been recorded and passed down by teachers, philosophers and spiritual leaders striving to articulate and define the meaning of life. It is the idea that what we seek is what we find; that happiness, and significance, begins in the mind.

5,000 years ago, Krishna taught that our real, spiritual nature is to seek enjoyment. Krishna believed the universe is driven by duties, rights, laws, conduct, virtues and a "best way of living." He proposed that the ultimate goal in life is to achieve the state of unlimited consciousness and that the manifestations of material energy are simply exhibitions of that being's conscious will and plan.

2,500 years ago Buddha talked about a "cosmic law and order" and suggested that suffering is a result of continually striving after things that do not give lasting happiness. His solution was a list of noble or "right" qualities, which, if developed, would lead to the elimination of distress and set the traveler squarely on the path of contentment and enlightenment.

2,000 years ago Jesus taught, "Seek first the kingdom of God and all things will be added to you." The Kingdom of God is actively sought through service and love towards others, as Christ both personified and taught this concept in all that he did, as recorded in the Bible. Increase,

151

or that which is "added," comes as a result of this conscious effort.

In 1902, author Robert Allen in his book, *As A Man Thinketh*, states, "As a man thinketh in his heart, so is he," which not only captures the whole of a man's being, but is so comprehensive as to reach out to every condition and circumstance of his life.

I became aware at an early age, of success being determined by how the mind can directly influence achievement and secure our place in the universe. Although I didn't know it at the time, I was observing the teachings of these historic philosophers in the world around me, and the lesson was deeply imbedded into my subconscious.

I remember as a boy, my Grandmother telling me, "Thoughts are things" and "Step lively with the rhythm of the universe." It wasn't until many years later in life that I began to understand what she meant.

In his 1937 book, *Think and Grow Rich*, Napoleon Hill states these famous words, "Whatever the mind can conceive and believe; it can achieve." I read this book when I was very young and it has had a lasting impression on me.

I now have my own quote regarding success to add to the collection which I share with all my students, and in most of my public speaking engagements:

"You can accomplish anything you want in this life
as long as you make a decision (to achieve it), firmly
believe it, focus on it with all your heart, all your mind,
all the power you possess, and never give up."

~ Steve Renner

I share that message with you from the experience, having faced and overcome obstacles that most would think impossible. Today I am fortunate to be successful in the Internet services industry. For me, it has been a steep and challenging climb to the top, and as I share my story with you, I hope that you will discover and awaken the unconquerable spirit that lies within you, to pursue your visions and dreams no matter how unattainable they may seem.

You see, I didn't start out with any special education, training, resources or knowledge. I was a just a hard-working construction worker. But, I had a dream and I believed in it so strongly, that it became real. I am living proof that anything is possible if you put your mind to it. And, if I can do it, anyone can.

I started my career, with no formal education. I dropped out of high school in my senior year to pursue a career in music. I traveled the country, playing in night club groups for a number of years, before finally settling down to get married and raise a family of my own. With no real marketable skills, I got a job in the construction trades, and discovered I had a talent for painting. I made my living as a painter, painting new homes, remodels and other similar work. I did this for many years, but something was always in the back of mind that I wanted to do more with my life.

Then in 1995, I became fascinated with this new technology called the Internet. I studied it every opportunity I had, reading stories about Bill Gates, Steve Case, Jeff Bezos, and others who were pioneers in this exciting new industry. The more I studied, the more I became convinced that there could be a real business opportunity here.

In the early days, most companies were trying to figure out how money could actually be made on the Internet, and many people wondered if it might only be a passing fad. In my research, I determined that there was real potential in being an Internet Service Provider. During my spare time, I would go to the library after work and get on the computer, learning all I could about this fascinating new world. As fate would have it, one of the clients I was working for built computers, so I traded painting his house for a computer. Computers were very expensive back then, to the tune of about $3,000.

One day, as I was working thirty-five feet off the ground on a ladder, it began to collapse causing me to fall. The results were devastating. I broke my back, shattered both my ankles, broke one of my wrists and was laid up in the hospital for a month. My ankles were repaired with pins and my back was fused by surgery, but the medical staff was unsure if I would ever walk again.

I was released with a hospital bed delivered to my home along with an electric wheel chair. I had a genuine appreciation for this mobility and the freedom it gave me to function reasonably comfortably at home. Little by little, I was able to get out of bed and sit at my computer where I taught myself web design.

Despite my injuries and uncertain future, I focused all my mental energy on dreaming and planning for the development of my Internet business.

I spent about six months using a walker and then moved to a cane. Eventually I was able to walk again, however halting and ungraceful it appeared. Despite my limitations, I dedicated my strength and passion towards success in this exciting new Internet business venture. Looking back, I see what a blessing that accident was for me. If I hadn't fallen from that defective ladder, I might still be working in construction today.

Instead, I was given the time and opportunity to work on my goals and dreams in ways I never could have otherwise. After much research and experimenting with the online capabilities, I began my Internet business by providing free email. I obtained the software program for creating email accounts and offered them at no cost. At the time, there were few email providers.... like AOL and Juno. This was before Hotmail, Yahoo and the others. Next, I set up a program to offer free websites, and eventually I added free Internet access, through a company called Net Zero. Through some limited promotion, and with the help of a part time assistant, the word got out about what I was doing, and my services "went viral!"

One of the smartest things I did in the beginning was to obtain a software program that could track the people that signed up for my service. There was a notification feature that gave a chime sound when a new customer signed up. So when someone new signed up, I heard a "ding-dong." I'll never forget the thrill I shared with my girlfriend and future wife when I heard the first "ding-dong" of a new subscriber. The second was equally as exciting, but soon it was Ding-Dong, Ding-Dong, Ding-Dong, 24 hours a day, seven days a week, as 15,000 people signed up in the first two weeks.

As time went by, I devised a way to monetize this free service, essentially creating a lead generation service. Subscribers (affiliates) would sign up and pay a monthly fee of $25 and invite other people to receive my free Internet services. Through this program, I assisted my affiliates to build their own valuable database of contacts. The only other affiliate programs that existed at the time were a few adult websites and Amazon.

Out of that success came the need to find a way to pay my affiliates more easily than the tedious process of writing manual checks, which were painfully slow to arrive to my international clients. Out of necessity, once again using my creative mental abilities to solve this, I became one of the first companies to offer reloadable debit cards as a payment method for my affiliates.

This new service was called Cash Cards International. There were many people and companies wanting to use this payment method and it took off even faster than my original Internet services company. Lightning struck again, and I signed up well over 100,000 people in the first stages of the business. Overall we had over 200,000 members using the service. This was my core business for many years until many other players came into this space, and PayPal became the dominant player.

With this new competition, the business was not as lucrative as it once was, and I began looking around for other ways to generate business; and I succeeded in yet another new direction. As it became clear that money could be made online, there were many more people who were looking to learn how to do business online. I saw that there were individuals who made a business out of training people how to be successful online. Some of them had the experience from which to draw their training, and others did not.

My business had done millions of dollars in online sales transactions and I thought, "Heck, I'm as qualified as anyone to teach online marketing." So I put together my own training program and started a weekly webcast to promote my training services. Eventually there were people flying in from all over the country, paying a modest fee to spend the weekend with me, where we worked shoulder to shoulder as I taught them the "ins-and-outs" of operating a successful online business.

As I worked with these people, I realized that they all had needs which I could fulfill. They needed things like domain registration, domain hosting, website building, mailing list services, shopping carts, payment services, and more. All these were services that I was already providing in my Internet service business, and so I began offering these services in addition to my training program. The mission of my business became: *To provide the Tools and the Training businesses need to be successful online.*

The only missing ingredient was traffic. It's the old "Billboard in the Desert" concept. You could have the most beautiful web site, and the greatest online business in the world, but if no one sees it, you won't get much business. So once again, I used my creative abilities, and came up with an Incentivized Traffic solution, and once I introduced this, Lightning struck for the third time, and the business took off again. Since then, we have signed up over 400,000 registered users, in 120 countries around the world.

Over the years, my business has expanded and I now have a lucrative income. It's been a phenomenal trip, but it all started with just a spark of an idea in the back of my mind, which became a reality. I began as a hard-working blue collar guy with basically no formal education who worked in the construction trade. Eventually I was terribly injured. A broken back could have been my excuse to lie around and receive disability, believing that my working days were over, along with any hopes and dreams I had at the time, but instead it was really the opportunity of a lifetime in disguise. That fateful accident gave me the time and ability to focus my mental energy on my dream, allowing this spark of an idea to ignite into an unstoppable firestorm of success.

You have the power to control your destiny, and make your own future. There is truly nothing in this world you cannot do, no matter what adversities or challenges you may face. But it's up to you; and you alone. You can't expect someone to do it for you—and handicaps, whatever they may be, are no excuse. You have the potential within; you possess your own special spark just waiting to explode into all you can become.

Jack Canfield states in his book, *The Success Principals*, "There is only one person responsible for the quality of the life you live. That person is you."

Everyone has visions of a better life for themselves and their families. Maybe it's a dream car, a new house, increased income, or more freedom. I'm living proof that you can make those dreams become a reality. And if I can do it, anyone can.

Success is only a matter of making it happen. Thoughts Are Real: Once you create a thought, and put it out into the Universe, it exists. Like planting a new seed, you need to water it, nurture it, give it plenty of sunlight, and it will blossom into reality.

As theologians and philosophers have taught throughout time, you are directly connected to the Infinite Power of the Universe. There's nothing you cannot do if you apply your mind to it. You can accomplish anything you want in this life, you just have to go out and make it happen. Don't expect to see a dramatic change overnight, but you will see consistent incremental changes over time that can transform your life.

Success is neither magical nor mysterious. Success is the natural consequence of consistently applying the basic fundamentals.

~ Jim Rohn

If You Can <u>Dream It</u> – You Can <u>Make It Happen</u>!

About Steve

Steve Renner is an Internet Marketing Pioneer. He started his first Internet Service Company back in 1998, providing Internet Services for individuals and small business. Again in 2001, Steve pioneered Online Payment services with Cash Cards and V-Cash, and became a leader in this industry.

Then in 2008, Steve created AdView, and incentivized online advertising service that quickly spread around the world. In 2011, Steve started the Acesse search engine, which is now ranked as a top web destination in the world.

Steve makes no secret of the fact that he had a dispute with the US Tax service, the IRS. He went to court and lost his case, had to pay a sizable fine, and spent a year in prison.

Through all of the adversity, Steve has been a survivor. He has gone on to build a successful Internet Services Company, which employs over 100 people, and provides services to small business customers around the world.

Steve is well-liked and respected in the industry, and speaks to thousands around the world at live events. His first book, *Transform*, a collaboration with well-known Sales Trainer and Motivational Speaker Brian Tracy, is an Amazon #1 Best Seller.

Steve is a member of the National Academy Of Best Selling Authors.

Steve also writes music and is an accomplished blues guitarist. Steve enjoys spending time with his family, his children and especially his grandchildren.

You can connect with Steve at:
www.steverenner.com
www.facebook.com/steverenner
www.twitter.com/steverenner

CHAPTER 17

BREAKTHROUGH WITH THE POWER OF EMOTION

BY DR. JIN ROBERTSON

THE AMERICAN DREAM BORN IN KOREA

The funny thing is that my success story is an American Dream story, not a Korean dream. Korea in a way provided me a way to find out what I'm made of, but because of what I endured there, I would have killed myself if I had the courage too.

ICE WASHING

Like many people in my community, my family was poor, and poor in a way that is sometimes hard to explain to people that have not experienced such hardship. My father was a really nice guy, but just wasn't cut out to make money. My family was made up of my sister, who was eight years older than I was, and the rest were my brothers. It was expected that women share in the household chores, and until my sister was married and left, I always shared the daily duties. My mother was not empathetic, and I believe she saw no real value in girls, as they were not held in very high esteem in society – so most of her warm regard was toward my brothers.

When my 20-year-old sister was married, the brunt of the housework fell on my 12-year-old shoulders. Today, I can still remember on a visceral level mornings when I hunched outside, washing laundry with my bare hands in a stream so frigid I had to break through the ice first.

I felt despair, a sense of hopelessness that things would never get better for me; and later the urge to kill myself. I mean if there was a version of hell out there, I already existed in it. How could true death be worse?

At the same time I became so angry. Not the anger where people say, 'That's a bad thing," but the anger that gives you amazing energy and strength. It's like a nuclear power source. I was so angry at the society for treating me badly and making me work so hard, I just screamed inside. I couldn't scream outside, because I was a coward at the same time. But inside I was screaming, 'What have I done wrong?' I never asked them to be born as a girl. I never asked them to be born as poor tavern owner's daughter at the bottom of society. It's not my fault. But why am I being treated as a criminal, treated like dirt?

I stepped outside myself and looked at that poor girl with her battered hands and tattered spirit. I became determined that I am going to help that girl . . . me! I'm going to make her so successful and show the world that I am not dirt. That was the anger which started to hold me up. Whenever I would feel sorry for myself, the anger would shake me into saying, "What the hell are you doing right now? You have to stand up. You have to become somebody. You have to show the world that you are worthy. "

This led me to decide I wanted to become somebody. As I was growing up, my sister would say to me, "You are lazy and dumb and stupid." And I believed her, and acted the role. My new energy and the right person came into my life and changed everything.

THE MENTOR

I was number one in my classroom from the bottom. I was the worst student and stupidest student, at least that was what I believed. My sister almost said I was retarded, and at the time I thought maybe she was right. The truth was I did not do well in school, because I did not see a point. Education was something for boys, and for those in good families with money, not a lowly girl such as I. A teacher, a mentor, a superhero in disguise, provided me with an alternative view.

I began dreaming of becoming this folk hero, Am-haeng-o-sa, who was a justice warrior. I wanted to be that warrior who was respected and who changed the lives of everyone she came into contact with, but this was a folk tale, a dream. How could I accomplish this level of success to become a justice warrior?

I asked my teacher what would make me successful. He told me that getting a PHD would be a huge accomplishment. Aha! a PhD. It was the golden treasure. Of course, I did not ask exactly how I would get one, or how long it would take. All I knew was I wanted one, and I needed to change my life to obtain it. This simple act of kindness from this Mentor changed my entire life.

DESIRE PROPELLED ME

The flames had been ignited and I started to study hard and my grades began to skyrocket. When a teacher told my mother I would be successful, she decided to let me continue my studies through High School. (This was in the 1960's, and this was a remarkable achievement for the girl who was expected to have only up to elementary education)

I discovered when you find your desire to do something, you're so desperate you will do whatever it is to achieve your goals, and over time you'll find real results. And I did find real results.

After I graduated from high school in 1967, however, things became tough again. Of course, my parents couldn't afford college, and my dream was smashed. I became a factory worker, making wigs. It was piecework. I was so unhappy in that dingy environment working as a factory girl, I made many mistakes and nine out of ten of my pieces were rejected.

I wasn't just angry anymore, I was seething at myself for abandoning my dreams, at the world for keeping them from me and because of my incompetence as a factory worker I was hungry because I couldn't afford food.

There was that energy boost again. I saw that girl cracking the ice, and it broke my heart. I was not going to allow the circumstances of my life to break my spirit. I was stubborn and I kept fighting and eventually found a job at a country club as a waitress. It was a step up out of despair, and it had the bonus of taking care of my hunger issue. I ate the food customers left after a meal.

THE BRIDGE I FEARED TO JUMP FROM,
BUT I CROSSED INSTEAD

I had a bird's eye view into the rich and powerful, because in those days only very wealthy people played golf and came to country clubs. I watched them, with their children; witnessed them treating the staff like slaves. I knew I could not endure this for long, and decided only I had the power to change my circumstances. I did it once, and I would do it again. After all, I was a Justice Warrior, and I was undoing what was wrong in my own life.

I began working as a housemaid and fell in love. He loved me too, but due to social status differences between us, he was forced to marry the daughter of a Korean Vice Minister instead of me. I was so heartbroken, and again I was knocked down into a cold and icy despair and depression. I was done. I was finished. I found the courage to jump off a bridge and end the pain. The problem was I could not swim, and so decided at the last moment to not go through with it.

It is important to recognize emotions like anger and problems like depression and feeling suicidal are very real for people. For a desperate person, death might seem like the sweetest objective in life. If there is something resilient in you, something that resists dying, that fights to survive and to ultimately realize your dreams—it can be an extremely powerful force. I lived through it. I continued to fight and overcome my desperation and persuade myself to move on. That struggle gave me strength; and now that it is over, it gives me perspective.

COMING TO AMERICA

I did not jump into the river, but I did cross a metaphorical bridge into a new life with renewed purpose. When we have purpose and focus, then the universe will bend to our wishes. I wished to leave and go to America, and I discovered a newspaper ad for a family in America looking for a housemaid. During the early 1970s, many young Koreans saw America as this golden land full of beneficent Gods and Goddesses. The Koreans perceived all Americans to be like the soldiers during the Korean War and WWII who threw children gum and fancy chocolate. We imagined the streets were paved with gold.

At the same time, applying for the maid's job advertised in the paper would be a huge risk. I was broke. I didn't know anyone in America, nor, as I said before, did I speak much

English. Everyone knew many of those ads were false, that when girls got to America instead of working as maids, they ended up as slaves or prostitutes. It took me two years to raise the money and courage to finally go to America, and of course, the job was no longer waiting for me on the other end.

When I imagined myself as the Justice warrior, I imagined that I would have my PhD. That was going to be my ticket to everything I ever dreamed about, and then one day I would return to my village and I imagined the townspeople who treated me badly or looked down on or ignored me, would follow me, kneel and bow and tell me how much they respected me.

It is this creative visualization (I learned what it was called by Jack Canfield many years later in a seminar he taught) that helped me achieve my goal. My creativity was my salvation. It was the carrot I followed, and the stick was that image of that young teenage girl washing laundry in a frozen river; the one who was kicked and made fun of and hit with sticks. This invoked my anger and I pushed even harder toward that carrot.

LIFE IN AMERICA

I found some jobs in America and married an abusive husband. We had a child, and I felt that anger rise in me again. I could not allow this man to hurt me. I was not that frozen little girl anymore. I decided I was going to kill him, but I looked at my eight-month-old daughter and knew I had to use that anger in a different direction. So I decided to join the US Army. If I was going to kill anyone, at least I would be licensed to carry it out.

I was 28 years old, and my daughter was 8 months old when we set off for basic training. Admittedly, after giving birth to one daughter and subsequently suffering a miscarriage, I wasn't in the best shape. I had trouble doing even one sit up and couldn't even keep up for three minutes to jog with my company.

Yet, I persevered. I never gave up. Nobody helped me as much as I helped myself;

my own fortitude and faith in myself drove me to keep going. I was going to become that warrior no matter what, and the Army became my sanctuary and the gateway to my dream. I started out as a private and retired when I was a Major.

And I went back to school. And went to school and went to school, and at the young age of 57, I obtained that PhD from Harvard University. I did consider finding that teacher from my grade school to ask him why he failed to mention that getting a PhD would take so long and would be the hardest thing I ever accomplished.

THE WHEELS OF MY LIFE TURNED

I gained some fame and notoriety in Korea while pursuing my PhD. I was dealing with some health issues, yet in the process, wrote the story of my life in an attempt to help others. I was quite successful and gained a lot of media attention. I was helping others that were falling down and depressed—through my experiences and story. I had become the Justice Warrior. Well, almost, there was one thing left to do.

I returned to my village where I was born and raised, and much had changed. It was more progressive and there were many more girls going to school and launching themselves into the world. I did meet those people from my childhood. I was nervous and did not know what to expect. They were old people now, but they remembered me, and they all came to me and held my hand.

"You are our hero. We are so proud of you," they said.

They were using the words I had always imagined them using in my dream. I was so happy at the same time I was scared. "Is this my dream?" I thought. "Is this just my dream I am feeling?"

Of course it was my dream – one that I had made into a reality!

TOOLS OF SUCCESS

In my story I demonstrated the keys to my success, and I lay them out here for you. Life can be really difficult sometimes, but if you have a dream, and use these tools – miracles will happen.

Seek out Mentors: Seek people that have the knowledge you need and the ability to guide you. They are around us all the time, so listen to them – as even the simplest of statements can change your life.

Use all You Have: I did not have much growing up, but I used what I did have – my education, my intelligence, and my determination. I found my gifts and used them to their maximum.

Channel your emotions: I used my anger to push me forward. Emotions have energy and if channeled correctly toward a positive goal, they can be the fuel to propel you forward.

Visualize what you want your life to look like: Even as a little girl I saw what I would become, and through many heartaches, trials, failures, depressions, and insurmountable obstacles, I was able to overcome them all with the vision of becoming that Justice Warrior.

About Dr. Jin

Dr. Jin Kyu (Suh) Robertson is an international inspirational speaker and bestselling author, and shares the secrets of her American Dream life.

Born and raised in Korea, Jin worked as a laborer at a wig factory, a waitress, and a housemaid. At 22, she immigrated to America alone with $100 in her pocket to become a housemaid and practically no English. At 28, Jin, the mother of an 8-month-old baby-girl, joined the U.S. Army as a private. Through determination, imagination and sheer will, she retired as a U.S. Army major, received her MA (at 43) and her PhD (at 57) – both from Harvard.

This single mother raised her daughter who was selected as a Presidential Scholar (an honor given to only 141 of 2.5 million high school graduating seniors), who graduated from Harvard (BA) and Princeton (MA), and served in the U.S. Army up to the rank of major.

Korea's major TV network created a documentary series of her American Dream story, which has inspired and motivated millions of Koreans, a number of which were saved who were on the verge of suicide.

Jin is Korea's most popular inspirational/motivational speaker (she has made over 2,200 speeches in Korean, English or Japanese), and is a multiple Best-Selling author of the books chronicling her amazing story that has sold more than a half million copies.

Discover for yourself why every one of Jin's audiences rises to their feet in a rousing standing ovation. You'll understand why Jack Canfield, Harvey Mackay, Pulitzer-Prize winner Ron Powers (Mark Twain) and many others have all recommended Jin's work.

Congratulations! X 400. You took my breath away... I couldn't put the book down. I salute and applaud your incredible determination. May your year be overflowing with more blessings than you can even imagine. P.S. Only in America!"
~ Harvey Mackay - author of the New York Times #1 Best-Seller,
Swim with the Sharks without Being Eaten Alive

Contacts & Booking Information:
jin@drjinrobertson.com
http://www.drjinrobertson.com
http://cafe.daum.net/ilovecon (Korean Cafe)
Mrs. Jasmin Cho Abel; phone 1-917-881-7406 (USA); jas1cho@hotmail.com
Mrs. Suh Inchon; phone +82-10-3685-4632 (In Korea: 010-3685-4632)
suhinchon@hanmail.net

CHAPTER 18

REAL SUCCESS

BY DR. KATE SINER

As Gen Xers, both my peers and I mark the beginning of a new take on how to create that "dream life." It is different than for the Baby Boomers who came before us. Gen Xers are frequently labeled lazy, arrogant, and disloyal, and the Gen Ys to follow have added narcissistic to the mix of criticisms. However, the changes in the economy that include job opportunities and access to wealth have sculpted millions of people who are choosing, or some might say are forced, to redefine success.

Collectively, we are simply not as materialistic. We are not driven by brands, status symbols, or a fascination with power for power's sake. Just like every successive generation, we have our own definition of success, which for many of us includes a bigger focus on quality family time, a greater global environmental awareness, and humanitarian consciousness. The desire for freedom, which motivated may of us to go into business, is more about a desire for free time for our family or to pursue our interests in art, recreation, or study. Our wealth is more likely spent on boutique or green items than on Chanel or Rolex. The times, and the definition of success, are changing.

So, what is this new definition of success? I can summarize it with the following example of vacation options. You and your partner are planning a vacation. You have ample money to spend and are looking forward to making this trip really special. You: (a) get an all-inclusive at a high-end chain resort in some tropical destination where you are certain you will be in the heart of luxury and never have to worry about a thing. Or, you (b) find a creative, eco-friendly, Mom and Pop place on the beach, rent a bungalow, and enjoy top-of-the-line local cuisine. If you answered B), then you know what it is that I am talking about. Wealth is a quality or richness of quality found in all aspects of the experience. Mass-produced, seeming luxury factory-feeling experiences that are marked up in cost and hyped up in benefit are just plain uninteresting. Like low-quality factory food, these experiences don't nourish us and they leave us feeling empty. As a metaphor for the changes I am talking about with regards to success, we might say: "Bye, bye fast food and hello farmers market."

As with any generation, there are limitations and oversights. My generation struggles with apathy like few others. But what do you expect when you are born into a time when everything that used to work is falling apart. A time where you can see the devastation that is the result of people who take what they see as "rightfully" theirs, without considering the effects on their children. However, I believe that when we can harness our collective generational strengths, we have something to teach the world about the meaning of success and the potential purpose of business. And ultimately, we are the movers and shakers of the next few decades. So it might just be time to listen to us.

Real success, real wealth, is the result of personal awareness and a commitment to growth, strong relationships with others, and a sense of purpose or meaning. These three components are essential to an experience of success. Studies have shown that after a person's basic needs are taken care of, there is little difference in their overall happiness as resulting from more money. If people are happier when they have more money it is because they have the inner capacity to enjoy what they have. This is only gained through personal introspection, dedication to relationships, and a sense of meaning.

I. AWARENESS AND PERSONAL GROWTH

One of the biggest secrets in the pursuit of success is that who you are on the inside makes a huge difference to your success. In fact, psychological research shows that our perception is key to whether or not we feel like we have what makes us happy, regardless of what it is that we have. In other words, you can have all the riches in the world, a loving relationship, an amazing talent, or an absence of misfortune, and your mindset will dictate whether or not you are happy about the outside circumstance. So if you are thinking that if you increase your income, lower your work hours, or find the perfect mate then you will feel successful or happier, you may be chasing the proverbial carrot. More effective than a search for a panacea, especially when looking for it in making an extra buck, is to find ways to be happier in your own skin.

Without engaging in self-reflection, gratitude, creative practice and personal development, it is impossible for anyone to create real wealth. Our perceptions can restrict us from seeing the opportunities that would allow us to create positive alternatives, as well as stop us from appreciating what we have. My suggestions for anyone who wants to create real success is that they make sure that their own personal development is part of their plan, and that they use this self-reflection to create businesses and lives that are healthy, wealthy, and happy.

While personal development is an ongoing and life-long process, I can make a few recommendations that will support you in getting more of what will really make you feel successful in your life. You can find over 100 exercises to help you to develop yourself in my book Real Answers.

Know Your Feelings: Many people go through their lives with a limited sense of how they feel. We are not taught emotional development in school or even, for many people, at home. As a result, we lose contact with one of our most powerful means of creating real success. If you are not sure what you are feeling, a simple exercise is to stop for five minutes each day and imagine a situation from your life that evoked an intense feeling. Pay attention to the sensations you feel in your body. These sensations and your feelings are directly linked and work as a road map to help you develop your emotional awareness.

Know Your Motivations: Much of the time people act in ways that have been dictated by their prior experience. Often, this prior experience has little bearing on the current circumstance and stops a person from seeing opportunities to create something different. Take a look at your current circumstance and see if there are similarities between it and other experiences in your life. Knowing why you are reacting or responding the way you are helps put you at choice for new behaviors.

Know What You Want: If you do not know what you want for yourself or what you consider success, then you will not know when you get there. Since we automatically adjust to our new "normal", it is easy to keep chasing something that eludes us. For starters, spend some time writing out your goals for the next year to keep you focused and on track.

II. STRONG RELATIONSHIPS

You know the story: the lonely miser who is surrounded by money but does not have one friend. This is nothing new. Neither is the parent who spends 80 hours a week at work and is traveling more often than not, who wakes up to a grown child that has little affection for him or her and sees them just as a wallet. Or, in another version, a married couple who lose track of their love for each other in the grind of moving up in the world or even just in the process of supporting their family.

In many ways, for many people, success has taken the legs out from under our personal relationships. And unfortunately, the damage does not stop there. Cutthroat business techniques and dehumanizing work environments further destroy our relationships with each other. So if you are one of those people who thinks that you can be successful without tending closely to all of your relationships, I encourage you to think again. Relationships are at the heart of success.

Many of us are no longer willing to sacrifice ourselves or our loved ones for money. We understand that if you do this you may acquire money, but you will never acquire real success. There is no space for an environment that prizes the system of dollar accumulation over the health of the individuals and considers this to be success. This approach is barbaric and would be eliminated were it not for human greed and dysfunction, because it quite certainly does not meet the other important human needs, ones whose sustenance has been so clearly proven to be essential for a good life.

Take a moment to consider these possible ways of strengthening your relationships and amplifying your success.

Everyone Matters: By adopting the attitude that everyone is important, you begin to see the world differently. It is not possible to be successful while hurting others or short-changing them. Look for win-win situations, which will mean that you are surrounded by others who delight in and add to your success.

Make Time For Your People: Want to feel successful? Catch a recital with your kid, have a romantic dinner with your partner, or be there to listen to a friend.

Redefine Success: When we talk about success and wealth, we often think solely of work or career. If we broaden our view to include our relationship with others, how might things change?

III. A SENSE OF MEANING

From as early as we have human record, people have searched for a sense of meaning. And if we want to have a sense of wellbeing, a foundation for success, we need to have a deeper sense of why we are doing what we are doing. A sense of meaning is one of foundational pieces of feeling satisfied with our lives. Institutions from religion to psychology have worked to help people in their search for meaning. More recently, most people have been exposed to the concept of life purpose, the idea that you have something you are meant to do and your job is to discover it. Regardless of what you believe along these lines, having a sense of purposefulness is extremely helpful in creating success.

Below, I have listed three ways for you to create a deeper sense of purpose and increase your feelings of success.

(i). Make a Difference
A person who desires more success in their life would benefit from working more towards making a difference rather than just making money. And I am not talking about giving to charity or doing a couple volunteer hours. I am talking about looking at how they can have the most positive impact in every aspect of their income-generating activities.

(ii). Prioritized Values
Living by our values is key; creating lives that support our values is critical. Every time I work with an entrepreneur I have them define their values, because they are critical to all other parts of development. They help you to feel successful as well as to be successful.

(iii). Care More Than It Makes Sense
If you want to be successful, a surefire way to get there is to "give a damn," as I would say. In the face of uncertainty, care. In the face of

problems, care. When people say that you should not care or that it is hopeless, be brave enough to care. It will change your life forever.

In short, success can no longer be defined by wealth or status in a hierarchy. It cannot be found where profits are more important than impact, or where people do not matter. Real success comes from having all of what makes life worth living and being able to enjoy it. It is largely an inside job, with careful attention given to the details by which we either gain or lose our quality of life, and by which we contribute or detract from others.

About Dr. Kate

Dr. Kate Siner is a personal and entrepreneurial mentor, an author and a speaker.

Her passion is helping you move past whatever is holding you back to embrace all you can be. She helps to identify conscious and subconscious blocks that may be keeping you from your ideal life. Working with Dr. Kate Siner is the opportunity to rid yourself of limiting patterns, thoughts, and habits. You will tap into her diverse knowledge, skills, modalities, and mentoring genius. With a PhD in Psychology and rich personal story, Dr. Kate Siner is the perfect one-two-punch that has facilitated transformational work for thousands of people around the world. She has dedicated her life to her own passion, which is helping people find, develop, and own their personal fulfillment and outward success. She can help you connect to your true self and show you how to take powerful action in your own life.

Dr. Kate Siner has been on NBC, ABC, Fox, and other major network affiliates speaking on fulfillment and success. She's been featured and quoted in numerous journals, magazines, and online resources, and hosts her own weekly radio show *"Real Answers."* She's a winner of the "2015 Women Entrepreneurs to Watch Award" from the Rhode Island Small Business Journal and has spoken on WPRO, MIX Talk of the Town, Consciousness Network, and TalkStream Radio. A certified Core Energetics Therapist, an Expressive Arts Therapist, and Mental Health Counselor, she is also trained in coaching, women's empowerment, hypnosis, leadership, bodywork, and transpersonal and humanistic methods. Dr. Kate is committed to lifelong growth and development and is currently training at the Barbara Brennan School.

While completing her PhD, Dr. Kate worked as a hands-on healer and massage therapist. She worked in hospice, addictions treatment, and private practice. She currently runs a small non-profit, *Larger Visions*, dedicated to helping the women of Guatemala overcome gender-based violence.

Dr. Kate is an avid traveler, bibliophile, and mother of one amazing son. In her free time, she takes tango lessons, paints, and loves to enjoy a thoughtfully-prepared meal.

CHAPTER 19

THE SECRETS OF EXPRESSIVE WRITING

BY NATHAN OHREN

The single most-important innovation in all of human history waits willingly at our fingertips.

Writing down our thoughts – putting abstract ideas into a concrete form so they can be understood, even if only for ourselves – is responsible for nearly all other human accomplishments. Because of this ability, great cities are planned and constructed, as are the highways that connect them. Thanks to this innovation, we raised machines, and evolved them into space-age computers, which now effortlessly and repeatedly perform tasks that were once considered miraculous. The universe is explorable. Justice is achievable. Every advance in medicine, and every Nobel Prize has been awarded thanks to this ability to preserve our thinking.

No other animal can trap its thoughts into such tidy packages and transmit them across space and time, maintaining their integrity, without distortion, dilution or the delusions of our memory and oral traditions. Writing allows collaboration with others, seen and unseen, and even with future versions of ourselves. Because of writing, our ideas, like building blocks, can be joined, organized, and refined to construct new realms of possibility. Thanks to writing, we enjoy the results of centuries of accumulated knowledge and wisdom, exponentially expanding the limits of what's possible in each generation.

EXPRESSIVE WRITING HAS UNIQUE POWER

There is a sacred category of writing, a surprisingly under-utilized conduit for personal growth, which has somehow remained a tightly-held secret. Known as *expressive writing* (also commonly called reflective writing, or journaling), it is the practice of writing down one's private thoughts and feelings for no other audience than one's self.

Many who invest time in expressive writing consider it a spiritual practice, because it fosters safe space in the psyche for honest self-examination. It allows for:

- (Re)discovering one's passions and creativity.
- Repairing relationships.
- Deepening compassion for one's self and others.
- Gaining clarity on troubling issues.
- Focusing on professional accomplishments and career growth.
- Connecting with one's life purpose.

Expressive writing has also proved to contribute positively to one's physical health. Done correctly, expressive writing is not difficult. It does not take a lot of time. And yet it unlocks grand hallways to greater joy and productivity in every area of life.

Ironically, we learn the mechanics of writing in childhood, yet rarely utilize its full power. We put more emphasis on obeying rules of punctuation and grammar, and overlook the magic of examining our own thinking. It is like owning Aladdin's Lamp, never realizing that a Genie yearns to be summoned.

Writing for personal growth is vastly different from merely thinking or talking about it. Anyone who meditates knows that thoughts are like shifting sands of a beach, pushed by the waves of our moods, and the tides of circumstance. Have you ever been in a conversation, and found yourself saying, "No, I didn't say that," or "I might have said that, but I didn't mean it"? And then there's the subtle interference of the thoughts we have of the person with whom we are speaking, which we rarely admit, and barely notice.

Writing promotes clarity, and forces specificity. Pressing our solitary thoughts onto paper allows us to pinpoint and harvest valuable raw material from the heavenly fields of dreams, and ground them, into concrete milestones of our journey. More than just playing within the whims and fancies of our mind, writing empowers us to relate to ideas as solid objects, and transform even the silliest notions into powerful words, goals, and action steps. Interestingly, in Hebrew, the word for "word" (*millah*) is exactly the same as the word for "thing." This underscores an ancient notion that our ideas become manifest by pinning them down with words.

Therefore, writing enables an individual to grasp genuine substance from the flowing river of thought, and not merely bask in the glow of potential enlightenment, which dissipates all too soon. (There's no wonder why New Year Resolutions get forgotten by February.) Writing puts handles on our thoughts, so we can use them to build mental lighthouses that attract more thoughts, directing them into safe harbor, where the precious cargo of self-awareness and self-mastery can be readily unloaded.

The awareness of one's thoughts is the first step to redirecting them. To master our thoughts is the ultimate solution to conquering fears, changing behavior, overcoming addictions, and programming ourselves for success in every way. We overlook that writing is the ideal circuit for harnessing the intellectual currents that flow through our minds.

The incredible power of expressive writing has been mistakenly camouflaged by the innocent accusations of uneducated naysayers. Some of them claim that spending time on such writing is selfish, wasteful, unproductive, lazy, or useless. The stories which follow are a few examples which call out a thundering difference between selfishness and cultivating opportunities that benefit a person's emotional, psychological and professional interests.

Pursuing what is beneficial to one's interests leads to new developments and accomplishments, which in turn benefit everyone. Furthermore, expressive writing helps develop the kind of personal awareness and responsibility that makes it possible for people to make better choices. It promotes the acquisition of much-needed life skills. It empowers the mind, and strengthens the soul.

There are several forms of expressive writing: from list-making to letter-writing, and may include doodling and other artistic expressions. Their common thread is summarized by a quote from Dr. James Pennebaker, President of the Society for Personality and Social Psychology, recipient of the Distinguished Scholar Award for his ground breaking discoveries. "When individuals write about emotional experiences, significant physical and mental health improvements follow."

In 2004, Dr. Pennebaker published the results of scientific and paradigm-changing studies, which produced an unprecedented body of evidence for the power of expressive writing to heal the physical body. Pennebaker showed that expressive writing boosts the immune system, promotes healing of wounds, improves lung and liver functions, and reduces common symptoms of disease and illness. As a result, doctors and therapists now prescribe journal writing as a respectable component of treatment for many types of medical and psychological ailments.

Pennebaker provided empirical support for what journal writers have always known. Some of the world's greatest entrepreneurs, doctors, teachers, scientists, artists, coaches, psychologists, educators, therapists, and leaders in every field of endeavor have credited private journaling as a factor in their health, relationships, financial success, and career accomplishments.

REAL LIFE EXAMPLES

Below are true-story examples from real people whom I have either personally helped, or interviewed on my weekly Internet podcast, *JournalTalk.*

- Mari first began keeping a journal as a form of physical therapy so she could regain control of her right hand, which had deteriorated due to multiple sclerosis. She was able to reverse the symptoms of this condition by writing three pages every morning. In addition to the physical benefits of this practice, her mind and memory also improved because of her newly-cultivated abilities to notice and nurture the many concepts that streamed from her subconscious mind.

- A nine-year-old girl named Addison had been keeping a private journal for several months. One evening she lost her temper, saying some unfavorable things to her brother. Addison was sent to her room, where, without request or instruction, she wrote in her journal to process the experience. When she emerged from her bedroom an hour later, she carried two letters. The first, an apology to her brother, explaining that she only said what she did in order to get his attention. The second letter, written to mommy, apologized for lying about the incident, and expressed her desire to come back into her good graces. Her mother read these letters with amazement and gratitude.

- Christopher was a hard-working account manager, who treated clients expertly, and was intimately familiar with the company's systems and processes. In a short time, he was promoted to management, overseeing a team of other account managers. It seemed by all standards that he was enjoying a prosperous career. But Christopher felt pushed into a role for which he was unprepared, with no training or guidance, and was now expected to resolve really tough issues. He silently suffered, daily questioning his confidence, embarrassed to ask for help, and always under pressure. He feared it was only time before he'd lose his job altogether. I gave Chris a series of daily writing prompts, which helped remind him of his value, track the effectiveness of his decisions, and communicate his ideas succinctly across the organization. Today, Christopher is a manager of managers, and successfully leading multiple teams using similar strategies.

- Shirley, a Jewish woman, age 65, was still plagued by fears of hellfire and damnation because of the harsh Christian beliefs impressed upon her from childhood by her surrogate parents. This anxiety became a major part of her life and caused her much pain and fear. A therapist advised her to write a journal entry in the form of a message to Jesus. The message expressed her deepest fears, confusion, and the need for understanding and acceptance. After a few days, Shirley followed the instinct to write another entry, this time as a response from Jesus. It conveyed only kindness, love, and appreciation. This therapeutic use of journal writing allowed Shirley to heal a deep spiritual bruise that had lasted decades, providing peace and comfort

- Donny and his wife Leslie spent months in angst about whether he should give up a successful career so they could relocate nearer to their family. They had agonized over various options, and replayed pros and cons in excruciating detail. Donny seemed to flip-flop his decision every few days, trying to make his head and heart agree. All the while, Donny stifled to take action, in fear of making the wrong move. He agreed to my unusual writing assignment: to write out his thoughts and feelings from an alternative viewpoint – mentally projecting himself one year into the future, long after the decision was made – and writing as if looking back on today. After just a few pages, a huge weight was lifted. Donny could see clearly what they needed to do. His resignation letter was the next thing he wrote. Donny, Leslie and their families celebrated, and never look back with regret.

After reading these stories, you might be wondering what expressive writing could do for you, and how to get started.

HOW TO GET STARTED

Into which areas of your life are you ready to invite passion, clarity, and purpose?

- First, **don't over-think** the process. Let go of any rules about spelling or grammar, the length of your entries, or the tools you write with. The primary goal is simple: Express your truth. Every journal writer has their favorite formula, but forcing yourself to adopt someone else's method can backfire. Find a way that you enjoy so it can work for you long-term. Write about what is most important and relevant to you in the moment. The only rule about journaling is that *there's no wrong way to write.*

- **Writing prompts or simple questions** are a helpful nudge in a worthwhile direction. My favorite is, "What was the best part of my day?" Or, you might start by writing anything that comes to mind, and if nothing comes to mind, then write about that. If you experience writer's block, then write about your experience of writer's block.

- **Keeping the pen (or fingers) moving** will prevent you from getting "lost in thought". Using a five-minute timer and short sentences often keeps the process easy and simple, so it can become a consistent routine.

- **Be willing to explore yourself and question your assumptions.** It helps to begin each session with a moment of quiet reflection. Observe and document what you notice. As your journaling practice matures, you may learn more about how your thoughts and emotions originate, and become fascinated to note either their simplicity or complexity. *Journaling is mostly about noticing.* Keep this principle in mind, and your adventures will yield fruitful results.

- It's also a good idea to **finish an entry with brief statements of feedback**, answering such questions as: *What do I now notice having written that down?* Or, *How did it feel to write about this today?* Or, *What will I do with this information now?* Journal writing builds upon itself, as the actions you take today become a source for reflection tomorrow.

- **Being completely honest with yourself** generates the greatest discoveries. This doesn't mean being overly judgmental or harsh on yourself. If you have a strong inner critic, writing out its voice gives it a chance to be heard. And do the same for other aspects of yourself, your inner nurturer and inner child. Listen to the family of internal voices and write their tales.

- **Writing consistently** offers exponential benefits, but remember that *journaling is a process, not a product.* It's not how many pages you fill, but whether you are learning. There's no use for worry or guilt over periods you haven't written. There's no sense in "catching up." Rather just stay present.

- Lastly, it's good to **employ some creativity** to keep the process fresh and interesting. Sometimes it is enough to write down a few fun words that inspire you, or swap out your pen for a crayon, or scribe an imaginary conversation with a loved one. Anything is acceptable because no one is keeping score. As long as you are exploring and learning about yourself, you are nourishing the most valuable relationship possible. In the words of my high school counselor:

> *When you become familiar with yourself,*
> *you will know the whole world.*
>
> ~ Phyllis Molloff

CLOSING THOUGHTS

Some people worry that expressive writing might stir up old trauma from the past, or kick-start a downward spiral of anxiety. While this is less common, it is true that writing can make one's hopes and fears feel more tangible. There are a growing number of journal therapists who advocate a more structured approach to expressive writing, to waylay these fears, and still receive the many benefits discussed here. Most people find that with time, journaling helps them to develop strong internal resources to contain – even take advantage of – this effect, and deal with life's issues in an authentic and powerful way.

Journaling enthusiasts have come to appreciate its incredible paradoxes. For example, journaling is simultaneously a simple, straightforward exercise, as well as one that requires great courage and tenacity. Another, it seems equally important to record the most profound ponderings of your soul, as well as trivial aspects of your day. Also, some of the best insights and life-changing realizations from journaling happen when you least expect it.

Above all else, journaling promotes a profound "getting real" with one's self and with life. After all, true happiness is not found in shallow platitudes or optimistic clichés. Success on a soul level begins by seeing things clearly for what they are, and choosing a response with passion and purpose.

If I had to choose between happiness and clarity, I choose clarity.

~ Dennis Prager

About Nathan

Nathan Ohren offers a variety of workshops and focused coaching programs for personal and professional growth, using journal writing as a primary tool. His signature workshop, *Passion, Clarity and Purpose,* helps people get back in touch with the reasons they were born, and to move their lives in the direction of their dreams. He helps people mend important relationships, advance in their careers, and replace long-standing, confusing or frustrating issues with clarity and creation.

In June of 1985, Nathan Ohren had no idea what prompted him to pick up the pen and begin writing in a 200-page, 5-subject, spiral-bound notebook. His first entry began, *"Today was another boring day..."* Perhaps even at the age of fourteen, Nathan expected to invite passion and purpose into his young life.

As a troubled teenager fraught with suicidal thoughts, Nathan wrestled over issues of identity, and finding real truth. He filled his early volumes with pages of heart-felt prayers, meditations and responses to sacred texts. In one poignant entry during his coming of age, he wrote, *"The only thing I can know for sure is that I can't know anything for sure; and I'm not even sure about that!"* Journal-writing itself had become Nathan's spiritual path.

During the next 30 years of recording compelling stories of anguish and ambition, trials and triumphs, Nathan set his course on helping others to find passion, clarity and purpose through journal-writing.

After obtaining a B.S. in Business Administration from California State University at Northridge, Nathan served as a Crisis Hotline Counselor, Area Director for Toastmasters, and holds a successful twelve-year career as Director of Client Services for a leading worldwide software company.

Meanwhile, he has become an eminent authority in the journal-writing community, as founder of Write4Life. He hosts and produces *JournalTalk,* a weekly podcast nominated for Best in Class at the Ninth Annual People's Choice Podcasting Awards. Nathan manages operations and content at EasyJournaling.com, the world's leading resource on digital journaling. He created the *30-Day Digital Journaling Challenge,* bringing together journaling therapists and application developers to help people investigate the opportunities of digital journaling.

In 2013, Nathan earned his Certified Journaling Instructor credentials from the Center for Journal Therapy. He is a requested guest speaker at numerous business and journaling events. His book, *The Journal-Writer's Guide to Staying Started*, helps both new and experienced journal writers maximize the many benefits of journaling.

You may contact Nathan with any personal situation, large or small, to receive his suggestions for writing exercises that offer resolution, strength, or clarity. For a current list of available workshops, or to contact Nathan for a private consultation, please visit: www.write4life.com

CHAPTER 20

THE HORSE-EATING ELEPHANT

BY BRIDGET RILEY

I love horses, I have since I was thirteen. Currently I have a quarter horse I call Brody. One beautiful Spring California Saturday, I went to the barn where I keep him to go for a ride. Usually I go out for trail rides with friends, but this day nobody happened to be around; so off we went.

The trails by the barn are near an area with dense trees and shallow streams; it's very pretty and relaxing. We were about 30 minutes into our ride when out of nowhere blared an ear-splitting sound! Now, a horse's natural defense is to flee danger, so when this noise erupted, Brody's body tensed immediately; he started snorting and wanted to run somewhere - anywhere - he considered safe. I managed to keep him from bolting off with me by staying calm and relaxed in my body, reassuring him we would not be eaten. This was no easy task, but he trusts me and we got back to the barn safely. By the way, that terrifying noise that had echoed through the trees was someone practicing their trumpet (badly) and only three notes at a time. I'm sure Brody thought it was a horse-eating elephant!

I share this with you to illustrate that even though I was anticipating a peaceful ride, you just never know what lies ahead on the trail. But with proper preparation, what could have turned into a nasty accident was an opportunity to reinforce my horse's trust in me. Sometimes, no matter how hard we try, things just don't always go according to plan.

I stepped into the Financial Services Industry as a second career, I was a single mother of two teenagers and my previous career in accounting afforded us a nice house, good schools and plenty of activities. But in 1999, my workplace went through some restructuring. Suddenly the job I had for 12 years and thought I would be in for many more was not to be. I decided that rather than continue in accounting, I would take advantage of the shift. I was ready for a change and made the decision to start a new career in Financial Services. This seemed to make perfect sense: I loved working with numbers; I could make my own schedule and be more available for the kids' after-school activities. It was not as smooth of a shift as I had hoped.

The first few years were exciting, lots of learning, adjusting to a different pace and discovering the joys and fears of being self-employed. Thankfully, it was a great time to be in Financial Services. However, we were at the peak of a bull run that had been going on since the 1950s; stocks were a sexy place to be. So that's where I started, working with small businesses helping the owners with their investments and setting up 401(k)'s for their employees. You could hardly lose in the market at that point, there was an air of invincibility about investments. Load up the pot and it would turn into gold at the end of the rainbow. But all the while, I had a nagging internal conflict between advising clients to be aggressive in the market and feeling it was my duty to keep their money earmarked for retirement safe.

We had a wake-up call to the endless gain mentality in 2002, and it's been a roller coaster ever since. 2002 gave us a 40% "correction" but that didn't sway many. "Ride it out" is what the brokers told their clients. "It will come back." And it did. By 2006 we had regained that lost ground and people were optimistic again, until 2008.

Many of you either personally lost, or know someone who lost a substantial amount either in the stock market or real estate. The point is, no matter how successful we have been, we all have had setbacks; we do our best to live our lives to take care of the people we love. But if we are not prepared for the unexpected, the unexpected can be devastating.

In any setback, positives can be found. Through my change in careers and witnessing of the impact the economic shifts have had on my clients, I have a much greater appreciation for how quickly we can lose what we have worked so hard for. I care a lot about my clients and keeping them safe is always on my mind. My relationship with my clients is for the long haul; this is a process, not a quick fix. My focus is educating my clients and protecting their hard-earned retirement money so they can focus on enjoying their lives.

So, now, my practice is focused on Retirement Income Planning, rather than Accumulation Planning. I work with people nearing or recently retired. I don't deal with risky investments to try to get double digit returns; I prefer to help my clients make more conservative choices. I want to make sure they have a solid plan of how they will receive income in retirement they cannot outlive. I help make sure they are as prepared as possible for the financial instabilities that can and do happen to seniors.

The challenge I constantly run into with my clients is this: How do we start thinking differently about money? How can we shift from the "how much can I make?" mindset to "how can I use what I've made to support myself the rest of my life?" How do we create a lifetime pension for ourselves? How do we leave a legacy and not a liability to our children?

Allow me to share a story I came across recently: Are you are familiar with James "Whitey" Bulger?

Whitey Bulger is a Boston Irish Mobster. He was #1 on the FBI's Most Wanted list, but after 16 years of hiding in plain sight, he was finally caught in 2011 – apprehended in Santa Monica, California, living with his girlfriend of many years in a small apartment. He is now in his 80s and serving 2 life sentences. When the police were going through his apartment with him before he was taken in, one of the officers noticed several 64 oz. plastic bottles with tube socks stretched over them. He asked Mr. Bulger what they were and his response: "I buy the socks at the 99 cent store and they are too tight for my calves, so this is how I stretch 'em out." When the FBI officer asked why he shopped at the dollar store when he had over $700,000 in the apartment, he said "I had to make the money last."

This man, who was convicted of having personally killed or ordering the execution of a total of 19 people and evaded capture for years, was afraid of running out of money! And in this regard Whitey Bulger is not alone; outliving their money is the NUMBER 1 concern of retirees today.

It boils down to this: When you get to the point of wanting to retire, we need to shift from an Accumulation Mindset to a Distribution Mindset. Because, let's face it, isn't having a steady stream of income to provide for your lifestyle needs more important than the amount of money in your account?

I personally believe everything in life is a balance, and this supports my belief. I like to help my clients create a balance with their money and formulate a plan that includes three categories - buckets if you will:

Liquid Money - Safe Money - Risk Money

The Liquid money will be available for emergency or unplanned expenses that come up. The Safe Money will provide you with a steady stream of income to meet your basic lifestyle needs. Then, the Risk Money amount you wish to invest does not have your future resting on it.

So what are the three biggest threats to your retirement income security?

1. Market risk

2. Illness

3. Death of spouse

Let's look at each of these:

THREAT #1 – MARKET RISK

Let's look at Joe and Barbara, Joe was 63 years old in 2007 and hoping to retire at 65. Barbara worked part-time for a local school, which she very much enjoyed and planned to continue. They were savers and had built up a nice savings of approximately $600,000 between the two of them. Unfortunately in 2008-2009 their $600,000 had dwindled to $360,000; by 2011 when I met them, their accounts had recovered to about $420,000. They were still aggressively invested in the market with their broker and Joe still working with no idea when he could retire. They were fearful; it's a different story when you know you will not have a paycheck coming in to replace possible losses.

Solution #1
So what could they have done differently? Maybe rather than leaving all their future income at risk, wouldn't it be a good move to take some

chips off the table, so to speak? Protect the money that will provide you with your base lifestyle needs. The benefits of some of the solutions I utilize are:

- Can't lose principal due to market risk
- Still take advantage of conservative market growth
- Guaranteed income for both lives, even if account is depleted to zero
- Remaining principal and interest paid out at time of death
- Access to up 10% free withdrawals each year

Every other solution still leaves your money at risk and offers no guarantees of lifetime income, which greatly increase your chances of running out of money.

THREAT #2 – ILLNESS

Tom and Joan were retired for just 4 years when Tom had a stroke. Unfortunately it was severe and his care would be more than Joan could handle alone. They had a nice income, but it was not enough to provide for the additional $65,000 cost of care for Tom and still support Joan. They ended up selling their family home and Joan returned to work to make ends meet. Sadly they are not alone. With the increase in longevity, we have a larger percentage of the aging population dealing with declining health issues. Combined with rising health care costs, it can be devastating to a retiree's financial security.

Solution #2
Thankfully the insurance industry has responded to this with some practical solutions. Yes, we have had access to Long Term Care Insurance for years and while it can be very effective, it does have its downsides. Here are a few: it can be difficult to qualify for if you have any health issues already; it's not cheap and if you are fortunate enough to never need to use it, you lose all the premiums you have paid, similar to auto insurance in that respect.

An option I prefer for my clients is a combination Life/Long Term Care policy. These are Life Insurance policies with a rider attached that will give you accelerated access to the death benefit while you are still alive should you have a major health incident or need chronic care. For example, if you were not able to do 2 of the 6 activities of daily living (bathing, dressing, transferring, toileting, continence and walking) you would be able to receive a maximum of 2% per month of the death benefit until it was exhausted. So with a $250,000 Death Benefit policy that would be a $5,000 per month benefit. That way if you need it, it's there, but if you never do, your family will still receive the Death Benefit when you pass away.

THREAT #3 - DEATH OF A SPOUSE

This is probably the most common and least considered of all challenges. Let's look at Jim and Alicia: They had a comfortable retirement with Jim's company pension and Alicia's 403(b) from her teaching job and they both had Social Security income. What they didn't plan for was what would happen to their combined $96,000 income when Jim died. The result was Alicia's income was reduced to $57,600.

While losing a partner is devastating, the financial impact often comes as an additional shock. Not only do you lose a spouse's Social Security income (usually the lower of the two benefits), but you also either lose all, or 50% of the decedent's Pension, depending on the election made at retirement. The average we see in our practice is about a 40% decrease in income.

Solution #3
There are several ways we can address this concern to minimize the impact, one simple solution is to put a Life Insurance policy in place. Then the surviving spouse can place the proceeds in a safe account and draw out the shortage needed each year to make up the difference.

SLEEP BETTER AT NIGHT

Bottom line, I love what I do because I get to help my clients be able to sleep better at night. I meet the nicest people. They have worked hard and look forward to a long and enjoyable retirement. But, between the tumultuous nature of the market and fears of Social Security failing, they are not quite sure how it is all going to come together. A distribution plan is much different than an accumulation plan. How you plan, or fail to, largely determines how the last third of your life plays out.

While no one can anticipate every horse-eating elephant, whatever hurdles you have had in your life, give yourself a break, acknowledge all you've accomplished and discuss your Retirement Income Plan with an Income Planning Specialist. It can save your assets and your sanity. Don't let your legacy be stacks of Dollar Store tube socks!

About Bridget

Bridget Riley, an Investment Advisor Representative and Owner of Bridge Retirement Planning, has been helping people plan for their retirement for over sixteen years. Bridget has always been committed to protecting the assets of her clients. Through her focus on income planning she helps to assure they can have a secure retirement income for life.

With her history in the industry of helping business owners, their families and individuals with their investment and insurance needs, Bridget's goal is to simplify the many complex decisions retirees must make with clear, easy-to-follow steps, while creating customized plans.

Bridget has received comprehensive education and training throughout her career. As a professional concerned with the health, financial, and social issues facing retirees today, she also believes in educating her clients as well to make sure they are prepared for the unexpected and can retire with peace of mind.

You can connect with Bridget at:
bridget@bridgeretirement.com
www.bridgeretirement.com

CHAPTER 21

THE POWER OF HAVING A WORLD-CLASS MINDSET

BY HENRIK ROSVALL

For several years, I was on the road at least 250 days each year speaking and coaching throughout the 50 states and Europe. My programs were focused on how to equip leaders to be peak performers, how to lead high-performance business teams and how to be *In The Zone* as athletes. I took pride in giving my clients and audiences a true experience where they felt motivated, inspired and empowered, while also learning practical and proven tools. I wanted them to feel resourceful so that they could respond, rather than react to the situations they were in.

Then suddenly on Thursday, February 1, 2007, my life as I knew it came to an end...

I woke up paralyzed from my waist down. By the time I arrived at the emergency room ten minutes later, the paralysis had spread up to my chest. I was immediately given medication to stop the paralysis from going any higher, which would have required me to be on a respirator. The doctors had no diagnosis or prognosis. After initial tests, I was told that I would be admitted to the hospital for a few days for additional testing.

Uncertainty, doubt, worry, anger—these emotions could have dominated the next 48 hours of my life. Having been an lifelong athlete, to suddenly be bedridden until further notice was a dramatic change that could have easily felt overwhelming.

Instead, those hours were filled with strong feelings of certainty, confidence, love and optimism.

How was that possible?

That first night, after my family had gone home to get some much-needed rest, I opened my journal and started writing.

"Here I am...everyone has gone home...the phone has stopped ringing... now what? Now it's me and my thoughts that will determine my reality and experience. Because I know that positive thoughts are so important, I have to nurture them, and continue cultivating new ones. How do I cultivate these positive thoughts? Reading uplifting material, including books, articles, quotes. Listening to music also does wonders. Watching the news on the hospital TV or staring at the white hospital walls will not give me what I need or deserve. Why am I so positive? It's simple. It's the ONLY option! Positive beliefs lead to positive results. Period. I choose to play life rather than allowing life to play me. I am not a victim, but rather a messenger to remind us all how precious life really is. Enjoy life, savor each moment! What may seem easy for us is next to impossible for someone else! Be In The Zone! I don't want to recover, because then I haven't learned whatever lessons I am supposed to be learning right now. I want to transform!"

Two days later, I received word that the doctor in charge of my case will soon come to give me a diagnosis. Imagine lying in a hospital bed, paralyzed from the chest down, waiting for the doctor to share what your future holds.

From my extensive experience as a speaker and coach on peak performance, I knew that how I felt when the doctor delivered the test results would directly affect how I interpreted and processed this diagnosis. I just had to feel positive, uplifted and empowered. Therefore, I made a point to repeat positive affirmations over and over again.

I'm a winner!
I expect excellence!
I am courageous!
I love making decisions!
I am proactive!
I play life!
I'm ready! Bring it on!

Finally the doctor comes in with my medical records in his hand. He leans up against the sterile white hospital wall with his left shoulder. Wearing his white doctor's coat, he crosses his right leg over his left shin. Very nonchalantly, he says:

"There is a 99.5% risk that you will never walk again."

That's what he *said*, but that is not what I *heard*. What I heard is that there is a 0.5% chance that I *will* walk again. That's all I needed! Now I was ready to do whatever I needed to do.

The doctor continued: *"In three months, that percentage will go to 100%."*

I interpreted this as "time to get busy." I wanted to have absolutely no regrets after three months. Being lazy, tired or feeling sorry for myself was simply not an option at this point. There was no time for that. I had to take full responsibility for what I *could* control and do.

The doctor walked out of my hospital room. So there we were, my family and I, left alone with this life-changing diagnosis. The doctor didn't care about bedside manner; he could now check me off his list. In his mind, there was nothing else he could do for me because he believed I would be spending the rest of my life in a wheelchair.

Yet in my mind and in the mind of my girlfriend, I would walk again. We never once talked about it; it was just an unspoken understanding. My family and I asked the nurses to bring a wheelchair as soon as the doctor walked out. If I was going to walk, a wheelchair seemed like the first logical step. I had a three-month window. There was no time to waste. The nurses told us that a wheelchair wasn't an option. I had no upper body strength and apparently I would fall forward if I were placed in a wheelchair.

So, plan B…we asked for a wheelchair anyway and strapped my upper body to the seat back. Problem solved! I was mobile again. This was progress.

A few days later the doctor returned with recommendations for various convalescent homes. Since, in his mind, I wasn't going to walk again, there was no point in sending me to rehabilitation. Of course, I had other plans. After much discussion, he agreed to move me to a rehabilitation facility for a couple of weeks with access to physical therapy, a gym and a heated pool.

During the next several months of intense training, I became very selective in who I allowed to be on my "team." The therapists needed to be positive and believe in me. I needed them to show up and be ready to challenge me each day. There was absolutely no time to waste.

For months, I had borrowed a wheelchair from the rehabilitation center. I didn't see any reason to buy my own—it was just a temporary step on my way to walking again. But when a wheelchair sales person showed up with brochures, it was the first time I couldn't think straight. I now had to decide what kind of handles, wheels and size I wanted! I finally ordered a wheelchair to be delivered a few weeks later.

The day the wheelchair was delivered was the very same day I stood up for the very first time. But the training was far from over.

Fast forward to present time. The days, weeks, months and years since that Thursday in February have truly been a journey. For countless hours I've reflected upon how I was able to defy the odds to learn to walk again, and what keeps surfacing is Mindset.

Everywhere we go, we take our Mindset with us. Both in our personal and professional lives, our Mindset either works for or against us. Our Mindset directly affects how we interpret situations, circumstances and events.

Researching the effects that various mindsets have on performance for over 25 years, my paralysis became the Ultimate Case Study. I had to walk my talk and use the same mindset and tools that I had been using to coach leaders and athletes.

Since this journey began, I have become very selective in which programs I present and clients I work with. The World-Class Mindset programs continue to be received so positively because the participants understand the importance of having the right type of Mindset as their foundation, both personally and professionally.

Here are three keys that will help you cultivate a World-Class Mindset that you can operate from consistently:

1. Selective Mind Input

Complete this sentence: "Garbage in, garbage _____." Did you answer "*out*"? That is what most of us have heard growing up. It may be a catchy phrase, yet it is inaccurate and definitely affects our ability to perform at a high level. So, what is the correct answer?

"Garbage in, garbage *stays*."

As you go about your day, is there any "garbage" that you will come across by default by simply being awake? Of course – negative people, news stories, TV shows, videos, online content, social media, and more. Do you *have* to take in everything that comes your way?

What you consistently hear, see and read definitely plays a significant role in how you feel. Can you *totally* control what you hear, see and read? Probably not. Can you influence what you hear, see and read? Most definitely.

If you are serious about having a World-Class Mindset, then make the decision to be active and selective in the input that you allow to affect you on a daily basis!

2. Self-Accountability

Having regrets stinks.

These regrets can be very unhealthy and can feel like they are eating away at your identity. Time is precious and you don't get any more of it, so commit to living your life regret-free!

Having a high level of *self-accountability* is one of the most important skills that you can develop, as the benefits will permeate throughout your life.

Some of the many benefits include:
- Living life with more self-confidence
- Experiencing a richer and fuller life
- Establishing trust with others on a higher level
- Elevated respect from others
- Increased problem-solving ability
- Deepened inner strength
- Increased level of focus which resists distractions
- Achieving and exceeding your goals

What are you doing when nobody is watching? What are you doing when nobody is telling you what to do? Decisions in situations such as these will ultimately influence your destiny.

3. Be a Solutionist

Become a proud member of the small group of people who project solutional thinking in everything that you do. Whether it's personally or professionally, you ultimately choose what you project. By default, it is easy to project the attitudes of those you spend time with. Instead of living your life by default, decide to be a Solutionist!

The benefits are numerous and include:

- Finding solutions because you are focused on finding them
- Feeling like you play life instead of like life is playing you
- Being more respected and having others gravitate towards you
- Setting the tone and modeling what you want to see in others
- Feeling an increased level of daily happiness

Here is a key distinction: Instead of having *problems*, how about if you only have *challenges*? Wouldn't you rather deal with a challenge than a problem? When challenges arise, be a Solutionist!

WORLD-CLASS MINDSET

Mindset matters. Some people may be able-bodied but live a paralyzed life, overwhelmed by fear and stress. Instead, take pride in being proactive, deliberate and consistent in conditioning your World-Class Mindset on a regular basis. With a World-Class Mindset as your foundation, you will approach life with a completely different attitude. Make your World-Class Mindset permeate throughout everything you do and stand for!

Successful leaders, teams and athletes have coaches. They invest in themselves. They understand how important it is to have a Mindset that works *for* them, rather than against them. I challenge us to continue to raise the bar, set new standards and step up. This power to have a World-Class Mindset is in everyone. All of us have the ability to have a mindset that works *for* us. Let's remember that we can make a conscious choice to elevate our mindset!

Let's use our World-Class Mindset to be difference-makers and role models!

About Henrik

Henrik Rosvall, Coach To Champions, is walking his talk – literally.

Paralyzed from the chest down in 2007, doctors informed him that he would most likely never walk again. In what became the Ultimate Case Study, Henrik used the same tools and mindset that he had been teaching for years to defy the odds and eventually learn to walk again.

As President of In The Zone Institute, Henrik has over 25 years of speaking and coaching experience on such topics as mindset, leadership, team building and peak performance. As a highly sought-after international motivational speaker, coach and author, Henrik shares his World-Class Mindset Philosophy with businesses, teams and athletes around the world. World-Class Mindset programs include Keynotes and Breakouts, Executive Coaching, World-Class Leadership Programs, In The Zone Coaching, Home Study Courses and exclusive Retreats.

Henrik mixes humor and enthusiasm with empowering stories to deliver a high content message that equip audiences with practical and proven tools. Participants condition their World-Class Mindsets in a safe, inspirational and highly energizing learning environment.

With his strong passion for serving others, Henrik has impacted hundreds of thousands of lives while customizing each presentation and coaching session.

All C-level executives, organizations, associations and Hall of Fame athletes who work with Henrik share a common bond – they are committed to excellence, raising the bar and maximizing their performance.

A certified Peak Performance Coach and graduate of Jack Canfield's *Train The Trainer* program, Henrik is committed to talking with, instead of at, audiences.

Messages such as *Walking The Talk, Being In The Zone On Demand, Conditioning A World-Class Mindset* and *Overcoming Obstacles* are all in high demand. Because of his high-energy presentation style, Henrik sets a positive tone for conferences when he is hired as a keynote speaker.

Credibility is essential when booking a speaker and hiring a coach. Henrik gets results, earning him extremely loyal clients who hire him time and time again.

You can connect with Henrik at:
Henrik@HenrikRosvall.com
www.HenrikRosvall.com

CHAPTER 22

THE TRUTH

BY DR. FRED ROUSE, CFP

*[**WARNING**: What you are about to read may be hazardous to your current belief system. Please do not continue reading this unless you want to experience the TRUTH.]*

What are the secrets to success in business and in life? That's basically what everyone is looking for.

As you go through your life, and reflect on what's there, you may quickly come to the conclusion that there are no secrets. You are simply reminded of something that you've forgotten. Sometimes, what appears as new is simply something old that's now presented in a way that makes more sense. And, sometimes, you're just in a different place mentally with a different set of experiences that allows you "discover" this new information.

Your personal perception of success in business and in your personal life often is not the same as the public perception of your success.

There are many that believe fame and fortune, exotic cars, travel, mansions and lavish lifestyles are success and that we'd all be happy if we had what "they" have. Others believe that the introspective life of some monk or other religious person in a faraway secluded monastery is true success.

In over 30 years of dealing with select individuals and small businesses with 0 to 6 employees, the vast majority of people would consider success as the ability to live the lifestyle you want, for you and your family, without having to worry about money.

That simple, very basic definition tends to generate a few problems for most people.

FIRST PROBLEM

The first and most basic is that most people can't define what they actually want in life. Stop anyone on the street and ask them what they want and they give you the generic: . . . I want to be happy, . . . I want to be rich, lines.

At some point in time, you may have found yourself with the same answer to that question. You may have that answer now. The problem with that answer is that it gives you absolutely nothing to work with or towards.

In order to move ahead **we need to define what specifically makes us happy**; how much money specifically makes us feel rich. Once we do that and write that information down on paper, we now have something to work with.

As we now look a little deeper into this situation and we ask people and ourselves what you don't want or what don't you like, there is no equivocation, no hesitation whatsoever. We all can rattle off a number of things, situations, and or people that we don't like. We can do that with an amazing unprecedented amount of conviction.

If you may be sensing a larger problem, you're right. We have a hard time defining specifically what we want but have no question in our minds of what we don't want. If you fit in this situation, and most people do – **Please understand that it's not your fault. The system has let you down**.

We've been conditioned to watch hours and hours of TV and cable for our news and information. We actually believe what's on the Internet. We'd sooner text message someone instead of having a conversation with them, and seldom, if ever, pick up a book. People who are not educators and have never taught are passing laws so that teachers are forced to teach to a test. The days that teachers were allowed to develop critical thinking skills in individuals have been replaced with ever-changing legislative initiatives that have put the United States far down on the list of developed countries in both basic and advanced education.

But let's get back to what we can control. Assume that you know specifically what you want as to things, relationships, experiences, lifestyle and money. . . And, that you've written them all down. . . AND, you have a specific date that you want to accomplish or acquire that item, now what?

Basic Assumptions –At this point we'll need to make some very basic assumptions:

- **One, money is not good or bad**. It's just a medium of exchange and is used by some as a way of keeping score in the game of life.
- **Two, each of us only has 24 hours in a day** to accomplish what's on our list.
- **Three, the more money you have the more options you have in your life**.

If we agree on these three points, then we can move to problem number two (remember the first problem was deciding what we want and writing it down).

SECOND PROBLEM

Before we get to the money part, **we need to address the time situation that almost everyone tends to ignore**. You can always make more money. You may not believe that, but we will cover that soon. You can't make more time. Time, and how we use it, is the single biggest and most overlooked factor in our success, a life of mediocrity, and/or ultimate failure.

The *Pareto Principle* comes into play here. It can be phrased in many ways, but it's the 80/20 rule. In a given sales force of 100 people, 80% of the sales are generated by 20% of the sales people. As individuals, 80% of our success comes from 20% of our activities. If we believe that, and you should, then the converse is also true. 80% of our time is spent on activities that don't substantially contribute to our success. Some will barely acknowledge this and take it as a minor point. Nothing could be further from the truth.

Knowing and using the 80/20 rule appropriately, along with your written listing of time sensitive, specific things, activities, relationships and experiences you want will move you closer to actually achieving/acquiring those items than the 90+% of people that have no clue and never decide what they want and never write things down on a consistent basis.

We've covered:

- What you want
- Why you need to write it down
- The reality of time
- The 80/20 rule that controls life

Now, let talk about the money:

Remember, money is NOT the ultimate goal! The ultimate goal, for most people, is to live the lifestyle you want, for you and your family, without having to worry about money. In order to do that, we generally need substantially more money than we currently have.

THIRD PROBLEM

That brings us to the basic question of: How do we get more money?

This is, sadly to say, dependent on our level of education, that of our family and friends, and our personal experiences. The degree of that dependence is ultimately up to the level of desire and the willingness of the individual to form a detailed, time–sensitive listing of what they want, and the single-minded determination to act on the activities needed to acquire the things and situations on their list, and to gain the additional knowledge and experience they need to do so.

Wanting or wishing for more money doesn't make it happen. The odds are not in your favor, nor do you have any control, over winning the lottery. The chances are also good you're not going to be the next Bill Gates or Mark Zuckerberg. Yes someone is, but let's realize the actual odds of that happening and temper that with some reality.

That being said, what can the other 98+% of us do to increase our chances of acquiring the substantial amount of money sufficient for us to be financially secure and not have to ever worry about money?

You could become a Doctor, Lawyer or software engineer if you had the grades, time and money to do that. You could become a professional athlete, actress, actor or singer/musician if you had the physical skill, sufficient good looks and or talent and connections.

However, let's assume that you just don't fall into one of those groups of people. **What can you do?**

The first thing most people do is to look at their existing job and try to get some extra shifts or overtime. This continues to trade your time for their dollars and will never give you the financial security you want and deserve.

Most people don't want to admit that; yet they do have that understanding internalized and try to keep it locked away going through life hoping that things will "work out." They never do, and these folks are working into their 80's, if they live that long, just to survive.

Don't believe me, just look at those Walmart employees, or the 70-year-old waitress at the local restaurant/diner carrying those heavy plates. Do you think these folks were bored sitting at home, or do you think they're working because they need the money to pay the bills and just survive?

Once someone comes to the understanding that their existing job is just not going to get them where they want to go, they generally do one of five different things for more money.

1. One, they look for a second job. This only gives temporary relief. Yes, they are getting more money. However they continue to trade more of their limited time for someone else's very restricted dollars. It does give them the feeling of "doing" something, but remember the 80/20 rule. Is this second job just more activity that sucks your time and moves you further from your long-term goal of financial security? Probably yes.

2. Two, if they have a job that easily translates into a business, they use their existing job skills and start a business of their own "on the side." They have limited to no management or sales/marketing experience but they have a technical skill that they think can make them rich. After six months they crash and burn or they meander along working in their business instead of on their business and effectively just created a second job that moves them further from their long-term goal of financial security.

3. Three, they decide to go back to school to get a different or improved set of job skills. They may end up with a pay raise or a new job at a higher salary and that's nice. It generates a feeling of accomplishment. However, all they've done is to increase their lifestyle without moving much closer to their goal, of long-term goal of financial security. This is more of the 80/20 rule at a higher level.

4. Four, they start looking at all get-rich quick, multi-level marketing, Internet marketing, money-making scams, and work-from-home opportunities. And, if they have more money, the multitude of franchise opportunities. You've probably seen them, the Amway's, Fuller Brush, Avon, Mary Kay and the vending machines. Most everything in this group is sold as an "opportunity." As they get started they know or at least believe that someone is making money. After a few months of time, effort and money, they notice it's just not them.

5. Five, they take a weekend trading or investing course. Here things get more interesting quickly. The course could be anything from "no money down" real estate to buying tax certificates, foreclosed/pre-foreclosure properties, estate sales, stocks, options, or commodity futures. This is a world of charts and projections of what "could" be. By the completion of the weekend course the participants are convinced that they know have sufficient knowledge to take on the pros in the field and win. Within six months to a year most people are out, but it was an interesting exposure to something that could work if they knew more.

Can you save your way to financial security?

If you can cut the 5-30K a year you're spending on mortgage interest and do a better job of tax planning, that could free up some money and you can start to "invest" it.

There are dozens of TV and Cable ads and infomercials. They all show you all the available "tools" they have so you can trade like the pros. There are even several apps for that so you could do it on your phone. But this gets back to number five above, the weekend trading/investing course.

So, working for a living is guaranteed to keep you at the mercy of an employer and you'll never really see the true financial security you want and deserve. You know you need to do something and starting your own business seems to be the thing to do. You've come to that conclusion. Great!

You know that you need more information. This book was a nice start to open your eyes to "other" possibilities. . . but what now? What kind of business? Do I need some specific location or set of skills? Could I, or should I, buy a franchise? Which one? Would it really work? . . . But I don't have the 20K to buy in or the time to train at their headquarters. There are many questions. I hope that I provided some direction and some answers.

You now know that you need to identify and write down very specific things, situations, relationships and experiences that you want. Along with the specific amount of money you need to have for those things and a very specific time frame of when you want to achieve and or acquire them.

You know that your time is limited, and you need to focus 80% of your efforts on the 20% of things that will lead you to your long-term goal. You also know that if you're not vigilant, it's all too easy to spend 80% of your time on things that will give you less than 20% of the result you want.

I want to thank you for spending time with me and allowing me to spend some time with you. I am very concerned for your success. All these things I've shared with you are not some abstract theory. These are personal experiences that I've lived through and that I've helped Clients through. My purpose here is to shortcut your pain, aggravation and wasted time that you may be experiencing so you can reach your long-term goals in the fastest way possible.

I know that there's just so much more to discuss and this is book is very limited because of its format.

I've written a book called: *The END of YOUR EMPLOYMENT – How YOU Can Quit Your Job, Stop Your Money Worries and Start Living Life on Your Terms.* You'll find this book to be an excellent resource so you can start to consider what's available to you as you move towards achieving the true financial security and respect you want and deserve.

About Dr. Fred

Dr. Fred Rouse, CFP (aka: The REAL Money Doctor & Quiet Trader) – his entrepreneurial spirit first showed at age 12 as he started painting hand rails on the row homes of South Philadelphia.

After 5 years in the US Coast Guard and 10 years as a Registered Respiratory Therapist he knew there had to be a better way. He sold Amway, vacuum cleaners door-to-door, Real Estate, Insurance and Mutual Funds.

He studied, eventually became a Certified Financial Planner and started working with select Individuals and small businesses with 0 to 6 employees. He's reviewed thousands of businesses for Clients and been involved with, or evaluated for his own, hundreds of small businesses. He knows what works and what doesn't.

In his early days, Dr. Rouse took a $5,000 trading account to $2 million in two years, and then lost it all in six months trying to make the $2 million into $4 million. The experience, although painful and frustrating, did become a major turning point and teachable moment in his life.

Ever since then he has been on a quest. He concentrated on taxes and started actively studying money. . . First he got an MBA, then a Doctorate in Business Administration, then a PhD in Taxation, and even one year of law school.

He now exposes the conspiracy of *Eight Money Lies* that the government, Wall Street and the Banks have been concealing from the public for decades about money, taxes and trading. And how you can turn those lies around and exploit them into cash and a secure financial future for you and your family, without ever having to worrying about money again.

He is the author of ***The Real Money Doctor's College Student's Money Guide,*** a must-read for High School Seniors, college freshmen and their parents, where he details how to cut through the stress of college, get control of your finances, save yourself and your parents tax dollars and make your college experience something you'll fondly remember. He's a contributing author to the Amazon best-sellers, ***10 Ways for Any Business to Easily Make More Money,*** and ***10 Businesses That People Can Start Online In 1 Day Or Less!***

He is the Senior Trader and Senior Educator for the flagship course he authored: ***The Quiet Trader's EOD Scalping Trading System,*** where he details an easy-to-follow blueprint on how you can retire in 7 years or less in under 30 minutes a day without working a second job or 70+ hours a week.

He is also the author of ***The END of YOUR EMPLOYMENT — 10 Keys to Your Ideal Business, How to Quit Your Job, Stop Your Money Worries and Start Living Life on Your Terms.***

For more information, visit:
http://quiettrader.com/

CHAPTER 23

OVERCOMING OVERWHELM

BY DR. JENNIFER HARRISON

Life can be hectic. I have found that even when things are going well, it's easy to get overwhelmed by stress. So, how do we overcome being overwhelmed? Well, over the years I have discovered seven simple but powerful strategies for dealing with stress. As it turns out, they're also at the heart of creating happiness, health, wealth and success. They've changed my life and I'm excited to share them with you now!

1. <u>BODYMIND</u>

The body and mind are totally interconnected and it is literally impossible to separate the two. I refer to it as the bodymind. To illustrate, you can't have physical pain without it affecting you mentally and emotionally. Similarly, you can't have mental and emotional stress without it affecting you physically. While research continues to show the benefits of things like meditation, I would like to introduce you to a technique from the BodyTalk System that will help to decrease your stress in under 90 seconds. BodyTalk is a WholeHealthcare™ system and I have been a practitioner since 2001. It literally has enhanced my life on every level. One of the basic techniques is called the Cortices (CORT uh sees) Technique. The purpose is to help balance out right and left brain communication, improve brain-body communication, as well as to decrease stress. In addition to teaching the Cortices Technique to my patients and students, I personally use this easy but very effective bodymind self-care tool every day.

2. <u>NUTRITION</u>

We all know that we are what we eat, but did you also know that we are what we drink? When we get stressed, good nutrition often goes out the window. However, one of the best things you can do for yourself is to drink water! Every cell in your body needs water to function properly. Also, when your brain is fully hydrated, it's 80% water. Most people are chronically dehydrated and this can cause health problems like headaches, poor concentration, muscle pain and even kidney stones. I see lots of patients who think that the coffee they drink throughout the day and the wine they have with dinner all add up to the daily fluids they need. Wrong! Both caffeine and alcohol are diuretics which mean they cause you to lose water.

While the research varies on how much water you need to drink each day, here are a couple of recommendations. One is that when you are well hydrated, your urine should be almost clear and not have much or any odor at all. If it's dark yellow and has a strong odor, then you're dehydrated and need to drink more water. Also, be aware of your activity level and climate. For example, if you're doing strenuous exercise or you're spending time outside where it's hot and you're sweating a lot, your body is going to need more water than if you're being sedentary. You also get a bit of water from juicy foods like tomatoes, pineapple and watermelon. If you fall into the category of drinking coffee, pop, and alcohol each day, I would recommend gradually cutting back over a several week period while gradually increasing your water intake. Making the change to drinking more water may seem a bit daunting, but if you work on it every day, you'll be healthier and your bodymind will love you for it.

3. <u>EXERCISE</u>

Our bodies were designed to move. We were never meant to be sitting all day. In fact, a 2015 study found that more than 50% of an average person's day is spent being sedentary, whether at work or at home. It was also discovered that the amount of time we sit during the day is associated with a higher risk of heart disease, diabetes, cancer and even death, regardless of regular exercise! The take home point here is that, while exercise is still very beneficial, we need to be moving throughout the whole day in order to be healthy. In fact, our very lives depend on it!

So the question is, what do you do if you're both sedentary and not exercising? Well the solution is simple. I'm always encouraging my patients to get up from sitting every 30 minutes throughout their day. You can program your computer or your cell phone to remind you to stand and stretch or just move around for a minute or so. The other good news is that 10 minutes of cardio activity done three times a day has the same health benefits as doing a single 30-minute cardio session. For example, if you take the bus to work, get off one stop early and walk the rest of the way. Take the stairs every opportunity you get. After lunch, go for a 10-minute walk.

Whether or not you have any existing health conditions, if you want to start exercising, please be sure to check with your medical doctor before you begin. Also, if you're planning on getting back into a workout routine after being inactive for months or years, be sure to see your athletic therapist or sports physiotherapist and chiropractor. They can make sure you're aligned, ready to start exercising and can help you choose the activity that is right for you.

4. <u>MONEY</u>

OK, you might be wondering, why is a health care practitioner giving out financial advice? Well, I've been studying mind-body medicine since the late 80's and stress, including money stress, continues to be the common underlying cause of most health issues including heart disease, headaches, digestive problems and back pain. Business used to intimidate me. However, as a business owner (I have my chiropractic practice, I teach professional development courses to health care practitioners and lay people, I have a membership web site and I'm an author and speaker), I've had to learn a lot about money management over the years.

While it seems that everyone wants to win the lottery, one thing I've noticed is when it comes to financial issues, most people don't know how to manage the money they already have. Research has shown that the majority of professional athletes who have multi-million dollar contracts, as well as people who win the lottery, will either be back to where they started financially before coming into large sums of money, or they will actually be bankrupt within 5 years!

A simple success strategy to help manage your money more effectively and to decrease stress is to create a monthly BUDGET. There are three steps you need to take:

- First of all, keep track of your monthly income. It may be from a single source like your day job or it might be from multiple sources. (If you're a business owner, you likely already have a system in place to track your revenue and expenditures, but it's also important to track your personal spending and saving habits.)

- Secondly, create a spreadsheet (Microsoft Excel works well) listing all of your monthly expenses. This should include things like what you pay for rent/mortgage, utilities, groceries, car and other loan payments, insurance, clothing, education, charitable donations, entertainment, bank fees as well as money you put into savings and investments. To help with this, keep every receipt from all your in-store and online purchases for one month plus your bank and credit card statements and put them in an envelope. At the end of the month, enter what you spent onto your expenses spread sheet. This will help you to actually see where all your money is going.

- The third thing is to add up all of your monthly expenses and then compare that number with your monthly income. If your revenue is greater than your expenses, awesome! If not, then look to see where you need to cut back on your spending and make the necessary adjustments. If you're deep in debt, you may need to see a qualified credit counselor to help get yourself back on track. Being on top of your finances goes a long way to decreasing your stress as well as increasing your wealth.

5. <u>RELATIONSHIPS</u>

What's the common denominator in all of your relationships, the good ones and the not so good ones? YOU! One of the most important relationships you have is with yourself. If you're not happy with yourself, how can you expect to be in loving and healthy relationships with others? Whether it's with family, friends, co-workers, neighbours or clients, how you feel about yourself will be reflected in all your interactions. Positive self-esteem is not about conceit or narcissism. These are not aspects of true self-love. I'm talking about appreciating who you are, "faults and all." Researcher and vulnerability expert Dr. Brené Brown says that learning to love ourselves and others requires empathy and compassion. Positive self-worth gives "purpose and meaning to life." So, how do you go about loving yourself more?

Well, first, take a look at the people who push your buttons. What's a common theme in your relationships with these people? Sometimes, those we find irritating are actually just mirroring back to us an aspect of ourselves that we really don't like. I have found identifying these aspects to be very helpful in my own self-discovery journey. If the problem is more complicated or you really don't know where to start, you may want to seek out the advice of a counselor or psychologist to help you have a healthier relationship with yourself. BodyTalk can also assist with this.

Secondly, look at the people you love in your life. Who do you love? Are your feelings of love and respect reciprocated? When I say "love", I mean all types of love including romantic love, familial love, friendship love and spiritual love. Love is actually essential for our health. Cardiologist Dr. Dean Ornish says, "the most powerful and meaningful intervention" for coronary artery disease "is love and intimacy and the emotional and spiritual transformation that often results."

So, I invite you to work on nurturing the relationships you have in your life, especially the relationship you have with yourself! This is at the heart of creating health and happiness.

6. **THE BIGGER PICTURE**

What do the Pope, the Dalai Lama and quantum physics have in common? They all point to evidence that there is a force or intelligence that is not only a part of us, but bigger than us. Whether you call this God, Allah, Yahweh, The Great Spirit, The Universe, the Tao or by another name is up to you. Regardless of your religious or spiritual affiliations, it's interesting to note that research shows that people of faith tend to recover better from illness and surgery. Dr. Larry Dossey in his book, *Healing Words: The Power of Prayer and the Practice of Medicine*, outlined research that he found showing the difference prayer made on the wellbeing of everything from bacteria and plants, to animals and humans.

I start off and end each day with prayer and meditation, with numerous prayers for guidance and of gratitude sprinkled in between. University professor Dr. Gary Schwartz in his book, *The G.O.D. Experiments: How Science is Discovering God in Everything, Including Us*, reviews evidence of what he refers to as G.O.D., an acronym that stands for a "guiding, organizing and designing" force. Dr. Amit Goswami, a well-known physicist, wrote a book called, *God is Not Dead: What Quantum Physics Tells Us About Our Origins and How We Should Live.* The book is described as, "a fascinating tour of quantum physics, consciousness, and the existence and experience of God."

In a world that is moving at a faster pace all the time and where stress levels continue to escalate – causing all types of problems – exploring the possibility of a "Bigger Picture" can be comforting and give greater meaning to our lives. It can also provide us with valuable resources to work through life's challenges. In other words, it is a key part of the soul of success on all levels.

7. **PUTTING IT ALL TOGETHER**

Sometimes it can seem overwhelming to make changes in our lives, even positive ones. We feel that we're already maxed out just trying to get through our day-to-day busyness. The key to overcoming being overwhelmed by stress is to make small changes AND be consistent with implementing them daily. American author Mark Twain is quoted as saying, "The secret of getting ahead is getting started. The secret of getting started is breaking your complex, overwhelming tasks into small manageable tasks, and then starting on the first one." Jack Canfield and Janet Switzer in their book, *The Success Principles: How to Get from Where You Are to Where You Want to Be*, expand on this as Success Principle 8 and provide some wonderful strategies for "chunking it down."

I hope you will use the strategies I talked about in this chapter to assist you in overcoming being overwhelmed. Taking these steps will definitely help you

Go From Your Stressed Self to Your Best Self!™

About Dr. Jen

Dr. Jennifer Harrison is a Certified Athletic Therapist, Chiropractor, Certified BodyTalk Practitioner, educator, author, membership website creator and public speaker. She works with an amazing group of people at an interdisciplinary clinic called Active Back to Health Centre in Calgary, Alberta, Canada. She also incorporates a wide variety of techniques into her practice. Dr. Harrison is currently the only person in the world with her training and experience.

Dr. Harrison has instructed at post-secondary institutions in Calgary. She taught Advanced Anatomy and Physiology for seven years at a local massage therapy college. She also did an annual guest lecture on the Role of Chiropractic in Sports Medicine at Mount Royal (College) University for the Athletic Therapy Program for 7 years as well as a doing a guest lecture on mind-body medicine at the University of Calgary. Dr. Harrison has developed professional courses for Athletic Therapists, Massage Therapists and Physiotherapists and teaches across Canada.

In 2007, Dr. Harrison also became a BodyTalk Access Trainer. (BodyTalk Access is a one day course, available to anyone, where you learn five core BodyTalk Techniques, including Cortices, which can be applied for daily self-care or to help family and friends.) In 2009, she was invited to join the International BodyTalk Association Access Review Committee which is responsible for evaluating applications from people around the world who want to study to become BodyTalk Access Trainers.

Dr. Harrison has a passion for writing. She has been featured in Impact Magazine, a Canadian health and fitness magazine, as well as the International BodyTalk Association newsletter, which reaches thousands of people around the world. She posts monthly articles on her membership website www.drjenniferharrison.com which cover topics on bodymind health, nutrition, exercise, money, relationships and something she calls "the bigger picture" where she talks about the merging of science and spirituality. In 2015, she published her first book called, *Stressed Self to Best Self™: A Body Mind Spirit Guide to Creating a Happier and Healthier You.*

After studying the mind and body as separate entities at university (with a psychology major and zoology minor), in the late 1980's she started studying mind-body medicine which demonstrates the interwoven, inseparable link between the mind and body. In 1990, she had a spiritual reawakening and embarked on a new path. Through her personal experiences as well as her studies, particularly with the BodyTalk System and through her church, she has developed a deep understanding of the mind-body-spirit connection and the impact stress can have upon it.

Dr. Harrison embraces the belief that we're all on a never-ending life journey, the purpose of which is to learn from both our mistakes and our successes so we can grow and help others. She also feels that to truly live up to our potential, we need to overcome the pressures of life so that we can go from our stressed self to our best self!

You can connect with Dr. Jen via her web site:
http://drjenniferharrison.com/
Facebook: Dr. Jennifer Harrison
Twitter: @drharrison1

CHAPTER 24

YOU DON'T LOOK LIKE A NEWBORN BABY, YOU LOOK LIKE AN ANGEL...

BY REV. JEANNE FORREST

. . . were my first thoughts, as I beheld the beautiful child God had sent to me. Though only seconds old, his cheeks were smooth and full, his chest also full and healthy in appearance, his skin absolutely beautiful – not red and wrinkled as one might expect in a newborn, and, oh…there were the precious little tight blond ringlets that covered his perfectly shaped head. I was amazed at the extraordinary beauty of the child I had just delivered, as I looked up to see him. He was perfect, and so very beautiful! The nurse was wiping him off, and then he was laid in my arms while the delivering doctor took our picture. He was here! He was mine to love and to cherish, my firstborn child, my firstborn son. His name was Michael.

I can only imagine the awe that Mary must have felt. I'm sure it didn't matter that he was born in a stable – she had given birth to her firstborn son and gently laid him in a manger. There he was, and both Mary and Joseph knew, this child was indeed the Son of God and the Son of Man. This Son would be called Jesus.

I held Michael briefly before he was whisked away to be examined by the head doctor of the hospital in the city of Wuppertal, which on that glorious day of June 7, 1972 was in West Germany. Later the doctor reported to me that all was well, and the child was fine. "Of course he is fine, and so incredibly beautiful," I thought.

The natural childbirth delivery had gone well, although the mid-wife assured me that I made as much noise as the Italian women, and should learn to be quieter, like the Germans. Hey, all I had was laughing gas, and, as I discovered, it doesn't really make you laugh. I was an American, and, if the pains of labor hurt, I could have cared less about the customs of various nationalities. I came from a country founded on freedom and allowed myself the freedom of self-expression. Guess I haven't changed much!

The pain I had been through was immediately forgotten, as I pondered the wonder of new life. Michael was the most precious treasure in my world. I knew my life would never be the same again. I was overcome with awe and joy and felt extremely humble and grateful to God who sent me the gift of this child and allowed me to become his mother. I thought of the years ahead, and knew God had blessed me richly.

My husband came to the hospital shortly after Michael was born, and saw him though the nursery window before leaving for our apartment to call family and friends. I had never been happier, as I held him in my arms. I adored him. He was calm and peaceful... calm and peaceful that is... until another nurse came in grabbed his little head and forced him to my right breast. "No, leave him alone," I cried, but she insisted. Michael became very upset and began to cry. Then, as he would take a breath, I heard a little catch in his throat. The head pediatric nurse had come into the room and grabbed him. "Something is wrong with his breathing," she said. "We are taking him to "Children's Hospital, across town."

As I tried to reach my husband from the hall pay phone, the nurse walked past me with a tiny bassinet headed for the ambulance that would transport them to the other hospital. When I reached David, he said, "I will come right away." "No," I replied, "go to the Children's Hospital and be with the baby." My roommate and I prayed and prayed for Michael to be well. There was no word from the medical staff for two days.

June 9th, I awoke feeling strongly that everything would be all right. But Michael had died at 2:10 am. Now I recognize that when I felt my prayers had been answered, it was really that Michael was free from the bonds of his body and had made his transition back to the heavenly kingdom from which he had come. When the doctor appeared followed by my husband, they didn't really need to speak. Their demeanor told it all. Michael was gone. I would hold him no more, but I would love and cherish him for the rest of my life. He was no longer my newborn baby, but the cherub angel he looked like at birth.

Before releasing me a few days later, the head nurse insisted that I use the hospital office phone to notify my parents. My mother was booked on a flight to come to Germany to help with the baby. I assumed she would still come, and, under the circumstances, I needed not only her but my dad as well. When I called, a friend answered the phone and with the noise in the background, it was clear that my parents were having a party. What a time to tell them that their first grandchild had died!

With David and the nurse standing nearby, I took a deep breath and said, "I am calling from the hospital. Michael died early Thursday morning. He seemed to have difficulty breathing."

Even before my words could have sunk in, I heard my mother say, "Well, you don't need me to come, do you?"

I was stunned! Her comment literally took my breath, and I couldn't speak for a moment or two. I finally said, "I guess not," as if it didn't matter. But it did matter! It mattered so much. I needed both my mother and my father more then than I ever had, and they weren't coming! I wanted to kick and scream!!!

Daddy, ever more compassionate, offered words of condolence and offered to make arrangements with the Funeral Home. As customs would not allow the body to enter into this country, Michael was cremated in nearby Düsseldorf. We sent his ashes back to the U.S. and later distributed them from my Dad's boat in the Chesapeake Bay. I had never done this before, but I wrote the services for both occasions and, though I didn't know it at the time, I look to their writings as the true beginning of my ministry.

The summer was memorable to say the least with the ravages of grief increasing around every corner. The German doctors thought it best for me not to travel back to the states for a month, so we were stuck in

Germany - far away from family and friends with whom we could share our loss.

At that time and in that location, the Germans considered it poor manners to communicate with the mourning. We had many friends in Germany, and all had been most excited about the forthcoming birth, but no one called on the phone or came in person. Our landlord and his wife offered us a place in their family plot - which would have perpetual care - but I would not leave my son in Germany.

A month later we flew home to my parents in Virginia. Having viewed the recent renovations to the house my parents decided we should celebrate our homecoming or something – I'm not sure what - with a glass of champagne. Suddenly, my mother said, "Oh, David, a package arrived for you the other day." (He had mailed two packages before we left Germany, one quite large, the other shoebox size.) I froze… "Where is it," I asked. "On the shelf in my closet," she responded. Well, I don't need to tell you which one it was as I spilled my champagne on the new hardwood floor in the master closet.

Perhaps, Mother didn't realize it was my child in that box, so rather than upset her, I dried my tears, tried to put on the sought-after smile and went back out to "celebrate!" What was it we were celebrating? I still haven't figured that out.

Instead of the joy we had all anticipated, the summer brought with it one hurt after another. The Sunday morning after we arrived, we got up early to distribute Michael's ashes before going to church. As we prepared to go to my dad's boat, I was surprised to find out that my mother would not be joining us. My mother had gone through a terrible shock when her mother had died on an operating table, so death was something she had difficulty dealing with. Thus, she stayed home to "cook breakfast!" That's what mothers do, isn't it? But who cared about breakfast – I was burying my child!!!

Thus it was that Daddy, David and I went alone on that boat ride in the Chesapeake Bay section of Virginia Beach. Again, I had planned the little service: My father's prayers were always very special, and I asked him to offer a prayer; David read the 23rd Psalm; I said a few words and offered a prayer of thanksgiving for the short time that we had Michael and included a prayer of commitment giving him back to God.

David then distributed the ashes into the waters of the Chesapeake Bay.

Breakfast? Oh well ... I was glad we were at least going to church – it seemed appropriate. My family had been the backbone of the church since its inception. I was both surprised and hurt that no mention was made of Michael or even of our presence in the service that morning. The only saving grace was the beautiful solo "Let Not Your Heart Be Troubled" sung by a lifelong friend who had come from NY to Virginia to sing for me. I had sung the piece many times myself, so it was especially significant to me. At least some people know how to respond to grief. We had just sat down to lunch when a car arrived. "Oh, that's the new preacher, I think he's here to talk with you, Jeanne," my mother announced. Not you and David, or the whole family, just "You Jeanne." I didn't care much about lunch anyway, but anything would have been better than talking with this man who had about as much sensitivity and knowledge of "pastoral care" as a dead fly. It was excruciating, and he didn't leave a minute too soon.

Shortly before we were to return to Germany, a family friend, wanting to help, held a large "birthday party" for me. With my plastered smile, we all survived – or did I?

Following graduation from the Duke Divinity School, I invested time and money in intensive training in Chaplaincy and Grief Support. For several years, I have facilitated classes and seminars in Grief Support, Happiness, Discovering Your Life Purpose and Spiritual Development.

In 2011, I began a series of Psychotherapy sessions required for recognition by the AAPC for therapists and Pastoral Care Specialists. After relating the events I have shared with you, I asked a very strange question – one I had never thought of before. I asked, "Why was Michael born?" The therapist didn't say a word, but picked up his Bible and read:

Isaiah 61:
"The Spirit of the Lord GOD is upon me,
because the LORD has anointed me;
he has sent me to bring good news to the oppressed,
to bind up the brokenhearted,
to proclaim liberty to the prisoners; ...
to comfort all who mourn;

to give them a garland instead of ashes,
the oil of gladness instead of mourning,
the mantle of praise instead of a faint spirit."

"But that's what I do," I uttered in amazement.

"The Lord sent Michael to anoint you <u>before</u> the elders of the church would 'lay hands on you' much later," he said.

Amazed, stunned, and humbled – my tears flowed so heavily I had to leave by the back door.

God often uses times of tragedy and difficulties in our lives to help us grow to a new level of understanding and closer communion with God. Through Michael's birth, I learned what it is to love; through his death, I began the preparation for the ministry to which I would be distinctly called many years later.

About Rev. Jeanne

Following successful careers as a Professional Singer, Voice Teacher and Real Estate Agent, Jeanne Forrest received a 'later-in-life' call to ministry. After graduating from the Duke University Divinity School she was ordained and then ventured into intensive studies in Grief Support and Chaplaincy. Jeanne is recognized as a Pastoral Care Specialist by the American Association of Pastoral Counselors and has served in various capacities in Church Ministry. She finds her real passion in the classes and seminars she plans and leads.

A constant learner, Jeanne has studied with such well-known figures as Rev. Jeanne Klauda, Rev. Dr. Richard Harrison, Alan Wolfelt, PhD., Jack Canfield, Jean Houston, Neale Donald Walsch and Deepak Chopra.. For several years she has led classes in Grief Support, Spiritual Development, Happiness and now is particularly enjoying her work in helping others as they go through the process of Defining and Living Their Life Purpose. "It's amazing," she says," in looking back over my own life events, both happy and sad, I now see how carefully God planned my life which has brought me to this point."

Jeanne is known as an author, guest speaker and seminar leader. She is the mother of two wonderful children, Ken and Karen, and their three-year-old daughters, Olivia and Skylar. Jeanne grew up on the banks of the Lynnhaven River in Virginia Beach, Virginia and now resides in Williamsburg, Virginia with her little Maltese, Candi.

Jeanne is available for Speaking Engagements, Seminar Leadership and Private Consultation. Her favorite lecture and Seminar topics include: *Happiness; Living Your Life Purpose* as well as *Grief and Loss*.

She can be contacted at:
Rev. Jeanne Forrest
Cell Phone: 757-503-3550
E-mail: jfjeanneforrest@gmail.com

CHAPTER 25

THE SOUL OF BELIEF: ACHIEVING PEACE AND PROSPERITY

BY KENAN GODFREY

"He who believes is strong; he who doubts is weak. Strong convictions precede great actions."

~ Louisa May Alcott

There is a great deal of joy in believing. At its most pure form, it is hope. Hope makes us all happy. Therefore, we want to believe, it is part of our DNA. We all start out as kids, a blank slate – and then we are molded with the beliefs of our family, our community, our religion, if we have one, and we are even shaped by those whose beliefs we resist. These core beliefs are muddled together to form our identity. We quickly forget the blank slate we all started out as.

As we grow older, we layer more beliefs on top of our core identities; some are helpful and others not so helpful. We tend to call these good and bad habits. If we had a good foundation of core beliefs, the good habits will outweigh the bad habits and we become well-adjusted members of the society. This was the path that I travelled as a young man.

I was a top student in my high school. In my sophomore year I received a full scholarship to college at the age of 15. I continued to perform in college but then, an event that was rare then but all too common now, caused me to come face-to-face with my own mortality. In my freshman year, the campus was ravaged by a school shooting that left two dead and physical and mental injuries to many others. I began to have a spiritual crisis that caused me to begin to question everything. This led me on the path of seeking, which would lead me into a greater understanding of the nature of believing.

I graduated and went into a career in financial services. In my free time, I studied philosophy and religion. Even though I was raised Episcopalian, I really enjoyed the Eastern philosophies. I kept seeking. . . and then I discovered consciousness studies. The study of consciousness is essentially the study of everything – so it was the end of the beginning for me.

If you study anything closely enough, you transition into a study of consciousness. For an example of how this plays out, take the scientific study of matter. We know that matter is composed of tiny particles called atoms, and atoms are composed of even smaller particles, and at the forefront of particle physics is the famed "god particle" or the Higgs-Boson particle which is the smallest particle we've discovered so far. The equivalent in consciousness studies is belief. Belief is what seems to create personal reality and reality seems to arise in consciousness.

My experiential exploration of my own consciousness allowed me to begin to handle the traumatic experiences of my past, limiting beliefs and the beliefs that no longer served me. I was able to achieve a new kind of clarity as a result of this – kind of like the blank slate of a newborn, but with the added appreciation of the journey it took to get there. From this fundamental state of being I felt a sense of peace and prosperity that still resonates.

With a greater appreciation of how beliefs shaped my personal reality, I began to create beliefs at my core identity. The words of Heraclitus came to life – "Character is destiny." My career began to take off after many years of stagnation. It was confirmation for me that what I was doing was working, so I kept on exploring. I should note here that I was not alone in my explorations, and that many of the realizations I had, have been shared by many friends and colleagues from around the world.

The paradox of exploring consciousness is that it is very subjective, but that is exactly what makes it the same for everyone. We all have a sense of the subjective "I". You can't really locate "I". That is one of the things that makes it so powerful. But it is nothing without "You" and

"We". We need "You" and "We" viewpoints to even begin to know the true nature of the "I" viewpoint. This is why consciousness studies must be done within groups of people to provide for verification, validation and agreement.

I began to operate as an "I am" in the world once I had a grasp of this, not as a concept, but as a personal reality. This core identity is pure beingness. I am reminded of when God said to Moses, "I AM WHO I AM" in Exodus 3:14. It takes much practice and training to really experience this, but if you can imagine what it would feel like to exist with no limitations and no definitions, then you are getting close to this feeling. Hours are like minutes from this perspective. It's not like you get a lot done, but there is nothing to be done from this perspective. Everything just seems to flow the way it is supposed to.

When I added beliefs to that core "I am" identity – such as, "I am successful," or, " I am charismatic" – there was little to no resistance to experiencing this as a personal reality. The funny thing about personal reality is that it tends to translate into physical reality very easily. You know how when you feel good about yourself others respond to that, and vice-versa, if you self denigrate and don't feel good, others respond accordingly. The key to making it work is to put the belief in at the core level of "I am." This is easier said than done.

Life is full of distractions. Our attention is demanded from all angles in our society: advertisements, family, friends, work, etc. The mind is conditioned to be constantly occupied. Spending time just being "I am" is not a top priority. I submit to you it should be. There is tremendous power there. Just think about what Moses was able to do. What could you do? Take time to quiet your mind and reflect on this as the first step.

I will be the first to admit that I am not immune to the demands of the world. But knowing that I can renew myself anytime I want to simply by focusing all of my attention on my beingness, I can return to the source of infinite power. I know that within that wellspring there are treasures that only I can bring forth to the world: there is no competition and my only opponent is myself. I have personally experienced many profound things play out in the physical world from beliefs created internally, that I would have chalked up to coincidence if I was unaware of what I was doing.

The biggest takeaway from these experiences in consciousness and in exploring my own beliefs is that the beliefs that I hold as convictions have the tendency to be present in my reality. The level of certainty of my beliefs affects whether or not they become physical reality. The next biggest takeaway is that you can change the level of certainty of beliefs. Notwithstanding limiting beliefs that may be present, what we think we can do is often much less than we are actually capable of achieving.

As I write this, I have been handling some limiting beliefs about working with high net worth clients. I realized that I was feeling inadequate when it comes to interacting with clients of a certain net worth. This is my own perception of my limitations. Just by becoming aware of this belief it seems to almost have magically dissolved. Shortly after having this realization, I ran into a decamillionaire at a fundraiser for his charitable foundation where the seeds of a working relationship were planted. It was as I had always imagined, effortlessly connecting with someone whom I would like to be in relationship with – who has the potential to also become an ideal client for me.

Sometimes, all it takes is a shift in perspective and becoming aware of something to make all the difference. As a financial professional, I help people with their financial well-being, and having an understanding of the beliefs that underlie their personal reality helps me to offer more holistic services to my clients. I can add real value to someone's life by understanding what is really of value to them. It's not money, its what the money means to them in their lives.

Money is just a belief, a measure of life energy expended in service to some other human being. At the core of that belief is the desire for peace and prosperity. Without this belief, civilization itself cannot exist. We can lose track of that in the pursuit of material possessions, which are fine to have, but it's a deadend road to simply pursue material wealth. How do I know this? Look at the most productive members of our society. Their lives are spent providing value to their fellow man and they are rewarded immensely for their service, money is merely the scorecard.

It is important for us to all understand our relationship with money because it is so fundamental to our civilization. Having clarity with our beliefs about money is best understood in the context of having clarity about your core beliefs. Because it is your core beliefs that form your financial character. Your financial character is your financial destiny. If you want to change course, the easiest way is to change your financial character. Your core beliefs inform your financial character.

It's a good idea to take an inventory of your core beliefs about money simply by listing what comes to mind when you think about money. Doing this exercise with a partner is much more effective than doing it alone. You may be surprised by what you find. The deeper you go, the closer you get to the core beliefs. Once you have your core beliefs, reflect on how these beliefs relate to your experience of life.

For example, you may have discovered that one of your core beliefs was, "I don't deserve much money." You may have picked this belief up from a parent or someone close to you as a child growing up whom you admired. You may realize connections on how this belief relates to your experience of reality. By becoming aware of this belief, you have made progress toward moving beyond it.

I hope that I have provided you with valuable information and insights that will help you fulfill your life purpose. I truly believe that being of service is what we are all here for and that we all have unique gifts to give the world through our own perspective. By sharing my experiences with beliefs, it is my hope that I am contributing to a more peaceful and prosperous civilization.

About Kenan

President of Godfrey Financial Group, Kenan Godfrey has been helping his clients reach their financial goals and objectives for over ten years. His holistic approach helps to ensure that client expectations and goals are aligned with their core beliefs. Kenan's multi-generational expertise focuses on creating financial wellbeing for those preparing for retirement, retirees, high net-worth individuals, professionals, small business owners and those in public service.

The number one obstacle to financial wellbeing is the underlying core beliefs a person holds. Gaining clarity of these beliefs and moving beyond them is the answer. Kenan believes it is essential to helping clients reach their personal goals of living prosperous lives into perpetuity.

Building long-term relationships with his clients through regular meetings to review, analyze and recommend adjustments due to changes in needs or goals, is an integral part of Kenan's values-based philosophy.

Kenan began his formal education at fifteen, and he earned his Bachelor's degree at Bard College at Simon's Rock in Massachusetts. He has been recognized as one of America's Premier Experts®. He and his wife reside in Jacksonville and Kenan is a volunteer with many humanitarian and charitable organizations. Away from the office, he enjoys golf, sailing and photography.

Contact information:

Godfrey Financial Group, LLC

Kenan Godfrey
4720 Salisbury Road
Jacksonville, FL 32256
Toll Free: (866) 298-0327
Cell: (904) 755-4557
Fax: (904) 647-2054
Email: kenan@godfreyfinancialgroup.com
Website: www.godfreyfinancialgroup.com

CHAPTER 26

RED FLAGS YOUR PEDIATRICIAN DOESN'T HAVE TIME TO CATCH

SIX PRACTICAL TACTICS PARENTS NEED TO HELP THEIR CHILD SUCCEED

BY KATHRYN THORSON GRUHN

HEATHER'S STORY

The ventilator whooshed in a rhythmic beat, sustaining the frail eighteen-month-old body. The child's mother was checking the gauges and hovering over her like an eagle protecting her nest. The living room had been transformed into a makeshift hospital ward: sterile pads, swabs, alcohol, syringes, and suction tubes – not anything that should be surrounding a baby in her crib. This little girl had an immune deficiency and had acquired polio from the live vaccine. The only things she could move were her eyes and mouth.

As I was adjusting the tracheostomy – the oxygen tube protruding from the child's throat – I asked, "Has anyone ever tried using a

Passy Muir device on her tracheostomy to see if your daughter can make sounds?"

The mother stopped what she was doing and looked at me. "Did you say she may be able to make sounds? I would be so happy if the only thing she could say was 'Ma'."

As I was testing the child's ability to handle a few seconds off the tracheostomy tube, I heard a stifled sniffle. Turning around, I saw a tear slowly make its way down her mother's cheek.

This is what I did for thirty-five years: diagnose children with speech and language problems. I went to college for seven years to gain expertise in my field. But my passion was for each child I worked with to thrive in every area of his/her life to the fullest extent possible.

The child in this story did learn to talk, and she was able to attend public school. While she couldn't walk, she could operate a computer and wheelchair with her mouth. Her parents learned what they could do to improve their child's development, and they made the effort for her to succeed to the fullest extent of her ability.

Parental involvement is crucial for a child's success. From the beginning, I encouraged the parents whose children I worked with to assess and enhance their sons' and daughters' development in all areas. I also taught them as much as I could about optimum child development methods, including following their child's lead and scheduling activities that enhance his/her interests. (Note: I am not advocating "helicopter" parenting. I am suggesting that parents guide and support their children to develop their passions and potential).

After I retired, I thought, what if all parents knew what I knew? What if every parent had access to the same knowledge as the professionals? Wouldn't this empower parents and help their children achieve greater academic success and more fulfilling lives? The answer is YES!

Ninety percent of what a child learns in their lifetime happens in the first seven years.

The heart of success for your child begins with you. Most pediatricians are wonderful and make sure your child is healthy and safe. However, when a child is lagging in talking or some other area, often a parent will hear something like, "Don't worry, your child will talk when he wants to."

Yes, your child may catch up. Some children do. But what if your child is in the tenth percentile, is undiagnosed with Autism, has a developmental delay, or born prematurely? Early intervention with any delays can make all the difference in your child's future.

Let me tell you how you can help your pediatrician, teachers and other health care workers, who have such limited time, to fully evaluate your child – and also how you can aid your child in reaching his or her full potential. It's best to work as partners to give him/her the best start in life. After all, no one knows and loves your son or daughter like you do.

THESE SIX TACTICS WILL HELP YOU AND YOUR PEDIATRICIAN

1.) Monitor your child's hearing.

I once worked with a family whose toddler was acting out and misbehaving. Matthew was very attentive, but he was lagging behind in his ability to talk. With much coaching and rapport I was able to screen his hearing. It turned out that the child had a severe hearing impairment in both ears and needed hearing aids. The parents were so upset that they had been punishing a child for misbehavior when the truth was, he couldn't hear or understand what was expected of him.

At birth, many babies are now screened for hearing using the Auditory Brain Stem Response Test or the Otoacoustic Emissions Test. A small device is used in or near the ear to measure your child's ability to hear. If the infant doesn't pass, the exam is repeated. If the same results are obtained, your pediatrician may refer you to an Audiologist or Otorhinolaryngologist (Ear, Nose & Throat specialist). More screening methods are available as your child gets older.

Here is what you can do:

- Take note if your child is pulling on his ears, crying excessively and can't be comforted, and/or wakes up repeatedly during the night. Your child could be experiencing an ear infection. Medical testing is needed to diagnose this problem, so take your child to the doctor.

- Call your child's name when his back is to you to make sure he can hear. Use a rattle for your baby when he has the strength to move his head to locate sound. If your child does not respond, get medical advice.

- Follow your school-aged child's progress. If she is having difficulty with following oral directions and reading, an auditory processing disorder may be present. Talk with your pediatrician.

2.) Build your child's speech and language skills.

Nathan was brought to me as a frustrated three-year-old who was difficult to understand. He could make only limited sounds, but he was able to understand what was asked of him. He was diagnosed with a phonological disorder and, with therapy, I was able to correct his speech, an early intervention that changed his life.

There are no less than 80 muscles in the facial area and throat, and it takes a year or more for a baby to gain control of them. Muscle strength and movement is important for normal sound production to occur. Eventually, a baby pairs sounds with meaning and he learns words. Over time, words are then combined to make sentences. For a child to learn sounds, he needs to observe the movement of a person's mouth, along with meaningful facial gestures and social interaction. Good speech and language skills will increase your child's academic success, social interaction and emotional intelligence. It is helpful if a parent has an idea of what "typical" development is from birth to seven years. A child's history can be critical in diagnosing or treating a disability in this age group. Any concerns about your child's speech can be addressed by a speech-language pathologist.

Here is what you can do:

- Talk to and with your child. Pay attention to what speech sounds your child produces at each age. Record her sounds and words and share this information with your health care provider.

- Make sure an older sibling isn't doing all the talking for "baby" or that your child isn't spending too much time in front of a screen. This includes a computer, TV or gaming device.

- Read to and with your child. Vocabulary skills are directly related to a child's success in reading.

3). Monitor your child's vision.

Daniel wasn't able to complete his math assignments. His language skills were below his age level and the teacher referred him to me, thinking this was his main problem. It turned out that Daniel was not able to visually line up columns on his paper in order to work his math problems because he had a visual processing disorder.

For normal language acquisition, a child needs to be able to see, so that she can identify objects that can't be touched or heard. If a school-aged child has difficulty reading, but her vision appears to be normal, she may be experiencing visual processing difficulty and an educational specialist may be needed. Photoscreening is a method that utilizes a specially-equipped camera to analyze a child's vision. If further evaluation is necessary, an optometrist or ophthalmologist may be involved.

Here is what you can do:

- Check your child's vision. A simple way to find out if your baby/ toddler can see is to note if she follows movements and looks at pictures you name in a book.

- Provide your child with a visually stimulating environment. Babies need a variety of colors, shapes, sizes and textures.

- Follow your child's progress in reading and math. If he is having difficulty, ask his school's educational specialist to assess for a visual processing disorder.

4). Provide an enriching environment for your child.

I had a parent proudly tell me that her five-year-old daughter, Mary, could count to 100. When I demonstrated that Mary wasn't able to hand me one block when I asked her to give me "one block," the parent realized that while her child had memorized her numbers in sequence, she didn't know what they meant. Mary had a good memory, but she didn't understand number concepts.

Your child's cognitive function determines if her overall intellectual development is on track. The American Academy of Pediatrics recommends that this screening be done by your pediatrician or other health care provider at your child's 9-month, 18-month, and 24- or 30-month wellness checkups. A thorough history will be conducted and you will be asked questions about your child's behaviors and activities and the toys she prefers.

Here is what you can do:

- Read to your child, starting at birth, to give her the necessary sound development, vocabulary and meaningful experiences that will assist her in understanding the world around her. To maintain your child's attention, make sure the books are age appropriate.

- Provide toys and activities that increase your child's creativity: blocks, puzzles, clay and colors will be most beneficial.

- Make note of your child's activities so that you can answer developmental questions accurately at wellness visits. A written developmental history is very helpful to the health care provider.

5). <u>Provide physical and movement experiences for your child.</u>

Randy was an active two-year-old. His parents brought him to me because he had difficulty talking and imitating hand gestures and facial movements. I discovered that he had speech and oral apraxia. With therapy, I was able to get him to communicate with sign language until his speech was easy to understand. I also referred him to an Occupational Therapist to help him develop his fine motor skills.

A pediatrician or other health care provider will monitor your child's physical status at every visit, so regular checkups are important. Growth, weight and reflexes will be tested. If your child's pediatrician believes there is a problem with your child's gross motor muscles (large muscles of the arms, legs and body), he may refer you to a physical therapist for an evaluation. If he suspects trouble with his fine motor muscles (small muscles of the face and hands), he may refer him for an occupational therapy evaluation.

Here is what you can do:

- Note and write down when your child is able to roll over, sit, stand, crawl or walk.
- Take your child for routine checkups with your health care provider at 9 months, 18 months, and 24 to 30 months.
- Build physical activity into your child's routine. Obesity can cripple your child's health. Walks, bicycle rides, outside play and trips to the park are all beneficial.

6). <u>Pay attention to your child's social/emotional behavior.</u>

I saw Jennifer when she was referred to me at the age of twenty months by her preschool teacher because she only imitated words and didn't point, make requests or want to engage in social play. (Because she was "talking" her parents thought she was on track for typical development.) Jennifer was also a picky eater and she didn't play with toys in an appropriate manner. Not only did I work with her, but I also referred her for an evaluation by a child psychologist. She was labeled developmentally delayed and later as Autism Spectrum Disorder. She was placed in a program specializing in children with her diagnosis. Because of her early diagnosis and early intervention, she was able to be mainstreamed in the public school system in kindergarten.

Emotional intelligence (EI) is the ability to recognize and manage emotions and to have healthy relationships with others. A child's EI is a set of acquired skills and competencies that predict positive outcomes at home and in school. People who possess these skills are healthier, less depressed, more productive, higher earners and have better relationships. Positive, age-appropriate behavior is important for a child to be accepted by his peers and teachers. A health care provider or teacher may discuss behaviors and responses that indicate a child's social well-being. A referral to a behavioral or child psychologist or an early education specialist may be in order if you have a concern about your son or daughter.

Here is what you can do:

- Prompt your baby to look at your face and into your eyes. This should be natural by the time your baby is four months old. Smiling, cooing and face time are fun for babies and parents.

- Play imitation games. Stick out the tongue, clap the hands and make facial gestures and see if baby tries to imitate. Lack of imitation of the parent's gestures, sounds or behaviors that are meaningful can also indicate that there may be a problem.

- Have your child's social development screened at his 9-month, 18-month, and 24- to 30-month wellness checkups. Early detection of autism is important and can make an enormous difference in a child's academic and social success.

- Provide opportunities for your child to socialize with peers and adults.

- Instill positive virtues and teach compassion and empathy. Start with manners and teaching your child the Golden Rule.

Why are these six tactics important? Because if there are any physical problems or developmental delays, early intervention can make all the difference in a child's reaching his or her full potential. The person in the best position to detect that a child might benefit from intervention is the one who knows him or her best – the parent or caregiver. Every parent and caregiver needs to know:

- 1 to 6 out of 1000 children are born with a congenital hearing loss

- 1 out of 6 children will be diagnosed with a developmental disability

- 1 to 9 out of 100 children will be diagnosed with a vision impairment

- 3 out of 10 children will be classified as overweight

- 1 out of 66 children is diagnosed with Autism

You are the one who has the most power to ensure that your child thrives and prospers in all areas throughout his or her life. Your attention in the early years of your child's development will empower you to assess and enhance your child's abilities and to work as a team member with your pediatrician to give your child the best start in life.

About Kathryn

Kathryn Thorson Gruhn, MA, CCC-SLP is a Speech-Language Therapist.

When Kathryn was a teenager, her father had a laryngectomy. Attending his voice therapy with him at the Mayo Clinic in Rochester, Minnesota, convinced her that this was the career she wanted. After meeting Mother Theresa in India a few years later, helping others was engraved in her soul.

After finishing her degree at the University of Minnesota – Mankato, Kathryn worked in various school systems for ten years. She earned a Master's Degree at Appalachian State University in North Carolina, with a Certified Clinical Competence, and worked in clinics, hospitals, rehabilitation facilities and developmental day cares for twenty-five more years. Kathryn then opened a private practice, specializing in working with children from birth to seven.

Her most rewarding experience was working in an all-inclusive developmental facility in Charlotte, North Carolina. Physical therapists, occupational therapists, educational specialists and physicians were part of the team that worked together with parents as partners to help each child reach his/her potential.

Inspired by this experience, Kathryn created the *My Baby Compass* series, an easy-to-use child development program that helps parents assess and enhance their child's abilities from birth to seven years of age. Pediatricians love the program because *My Baby Compass* helps parents document a child's developmental history and provides coordinating activities to promote growth in speech, language, cognitive, hearing, physical and social/emotional skills. Using this program, a parent can tell quickly if their child is on target for typical development, and if not, what to do to help their child. Parents using this system are seeing advanced speech and language skills and cognitive growth in their child.

Kathryn is known as *The Positive Parenting Coach* and has appeared on CBS, Fox, and the Discovery Channel. She has published articles in *Baby Talk, CNN Health, How to Learn* and a number of local newspapers. Kathryn speaks locally and nationally, promoting the empowerment of parents and educators as a team.

She is enjoying her second career from her home in the Blue Ridge Mountains. When she isn't speaking or exhibiting, she is singing, playing her dobro, riding her horse, taking care of her grandchild, writing biographies and telling funny stories.

The *My Baby Compass* program is available on Amazon.com as a complete kit, *Birth to Seven Years*, or individually: *Birth to Two Years, Two to Four Years,* or *Four to Seven Years.* You can read Kathryn's helpful parenting blog and follow her on Twitter, Facebook and Linked In.

Here are the links:
Website: www.mybabycompass.com
Blog: www.mybabycompassblog.com
Facebook: www.facebook.com/mybabycompass
Twitter: @mybabycompass or www.twitter.com/mybabycompass
Linked In:
https://www.linkedin.com/profile/view?id=86067807

For My Baby Compass information:
https://www.linkedin.com/company/2495765

Contact by Email:
info@mybabycompass.com or mybabycompass@gmail.com

CHAPTER 27

CELEBRITY TEACHING: HOW TO CREATE CRAVING FANS AND INFLUENCE DECISION MAKERS

BY DAVID WELLS, PhD

My life's dream was to become a professor. I started out in the service industry, but because the pay was low and the opportunities were limited, I eventually moved into commodities trading, sales and ultimately decided to pursue an online PhD. From the start, I felt I was hard-wired to succeed but education was vital to achieving my dreams. I was leaving to attend my graduation ceremony when I received a phone call about interviewing for an adjunct teaching opportunity I had applied for. Over the phone I was giving the details of the interview and what to expect. I remember feeling great attending my graduation and thinking that I may break into the field of teaching earlier than I anticipated. A few weeks later I participated in the interview and conducted a teaching demonstration. I had no idea how to do a teaching demonstration but I reflected on the time when I first enrolled in college and took notes on how my instructor engaged the class. I used the techniques I learned from him and got the job! I remember thinking finally all those notes and preparation finally paid off.

So I worked at one organization in the daytime and taught classes at night. When I completed my new hire paperwork, I remember being asked if I would be interested in becoming a Dean at some point. Up to this point I had asked for positions but never had they just been offered to me. The thought of being a Dean never crossed my mind. I did not want to upset my new boss so I said, "Sure, I would love to, one day." I figured she was just asking me so she could give me more work disguised as preparing me for a Dean ten years down the road. I didn't care though, because I was living my dream of being a professor. To my surprise she was not giving me more work, but giving me more opportunity and mentoring me along the way. She saw in me what most of my other supervisors overlooked or feared…someone who could rise to the occasion and wanted desperately to do so.

I remember being new to teaching and having to go through the faculty training before I could be given a class to teach. However, one day I got a call from my supervisor asking me if I could take over one of her courses because her schedule was heavy due to her recent promotion. Without hesitation I said, "Yes." She said, "Okay, I'll give you one and I'll keep the other one because having two classes may be too much for you since you have not gone through the training yet." I told her to give me both classes. Of course, I had no idea what to do. I knew enough to say yes and figure out how later. I believe when opportunity knocks, you'd better be ready to rock!

I decided that I would make sure students had an incredible classroom experience so that they could request me to teach future classes for them. This was my way of creating my own brand within the university and ensuring I had future classes to teach. So I went through faculty training as I was teaching rather than before I began to teach. My love of learning helped make this process easier. Before I knew it, the students were having so much fun. Before these classes came to an end, I was once again given the opportunity to interview for another position in the university. It was a full-time faculty position with a dual role as an Associate Campus Dean. Again, my mindset is to say "yes" and figure out how later. I got the new position. Thus, I was still working by day with my other employer and for the university at night and on weekends.

I was using all I learned to engage learners. This is what I dreamed of doing with my other employer, but they resisted even the smell of a higher degree of success. I was into my new career as an educator for only five months before I was offered an opportunity to interview for a Dean position. You can probably tell where this is going right? I got the job, left my other employer, and began my new role a month later. How does a person go from having no experience teaching in academia to becoming a Dean in six months? You may say luck was a factor but I believe you create your own luck. After being a #1 Nationally Ranked Dean, I was promoted again about a year later. If you are keeping count, that's three promotions in about 18 months. These promotions and initial hiring were not by accident. There are five steps to help "wannabe" professors get hired and create a craving from colleges and universities.

The first step is that you have to find your signature story before you ever apply for a position. This means you have to think back to a time when you reached your transformational moment. You know the place where you made a conscious choice to transition from where you were to where you wanted to be. Think of this as the bridge. I tell people the bridge is where your story is and this is what makes you unique.

The reason you want to find your story before you ever apply for a higher education teaching opportunity is because you will use your story like a magnet to attract and draw individuals in administration to you instead of those hundreds or even thousands of other applicants. Your story is what will make you unique and thus you want to *find it, craft it,* and *nail it.*

Your story is best used when it bridges your experience with your expertise. This could be your life experience or personal experience coupled with your education or specialized training. Once you find your story, you must identify a metaphor that describes your story, i.e., the flame thrower; the leadership lioness, the management miner, or the tech trapper. My metaphor is the Power Positioner™. This metaphor becomes a phrase you will use to craft your documents, which is the next step.

The second step is to create your resume, teaching philosophy, curriculum vitae, etc., using spin offs of the metaphor of your story. For example, if you are the flame thrower, as you craft your documents you may use words such as spark, ignite, and flicker to describe your experience. An example would be, "Sparked high SOP scores averaging 4.0 over the last 24 months." The word spinoffs sprinkled throughout your documents are vital because not only will this set your documents apart from most other applicants, but it also makes you congruent. What I mean by this is that usually when someone is interviewing you, they are usually asking you questions as they are reviewing your resume. When you engage them by telling them your signature story, they will see words in your hiring documents that further describe your story. This makes your story and documents congruent and gives you a non-verbal head nod from the individual reviewing your information. Your story tied in to your documents also helps the individual be able to share your story with others and makes it easier to recommend you. This is the beginning of creating craving fans…when they can share your engaging story with others and they are excited about you.

The third step is to go and get teaching experience. You can do this by either having a friend who is already in the field help you, by allowing you to guest lecture for his or her class or, you can seek these opportunities on your own. Most colleges and universities have an established process for guest lecturers. I would suggest using the phrase "guest speaker" to help you get in and present in front of a class. The key is to try to get in to guest speak in a course you are qualified to teach. For example, if you are qualified to teach graduate accounting then it is best to guest lecture for a graduate accounting course. You do not have to worry about speaking for hours at a time. You can speak and present for 45 minutes to an hour.

The key is getting the experience. Once you have this experience you can add this on your documents such as your resume or curriculum vitae. To make your teaching experience epic for students use some of the techniques I will mention in step five. Now if all else fails and you can't get teaching experience do not let that deter you from applying for positions. You can use your training experience in place of teaching experience. You might be asking the question, "But what if I do not have training experience?" If you have worked in the workforce for at least a year you have training experience. Almost everyone has trained a fellow employee on something – whether it was Outlook, a process or procedure, the cash register, etc.

The fourth step is to have a *killer* interview. There are unique things you can do to stand out in your interview and have the interviewer on the edge of his or her seat craving more from you. One technique is to use a hook. You can use a hook to garner attention. An example of a hook is to say something like, "You know there are three things I learned from Good Morning America that can command attention in the classroom, make students learn faster, and leave them ready for more." This makes the interviewer want to know what these secrets are that you mentioned. Of course, once you have their attention, you must reveal those secrets. I recommend you keep a roster of three to four hooks you can use throughout the interview process that display your expertise and you can call upon when needed.

The fifth step is to have a mesmerizing teaching presentation. A teaching presentation is when you have to simulate how you would deliver a course if you were teaching their students. It's a mock class performance. The key to having a killer teaching presentation is to know your stuff, understand and include all learning styles, and deliver engaging content and outcomes. I teach people how to use techniques and strategies that other companies have used to engage millions of people every week and have these people pay them to play games. The games I am alluding to are Candy Crush and Words with Friends. While these games are free to play, they try to get players to purchase something as well. These games engage millions of people each week and bring in millions of dollars every week. Have you ever wondered why these games are so addictive? Better yet, what if you could learn to harness the same techniques and strategies that make these games addictive and apply them to your teaching presentation, and have attendees craving to not only participate, but bring you into the organization as the newest faculty member?

This can be done by learning how to use gamification to embed in an already content-rich presentation. The key is to use leaderboards; levels, badges, points, etc., to drive engagement, feedback, and new insights or learnings into the lesson. However, this is easier said than done. The key is to already have a strong presentation and deploy gamification elements in a uniquely positioned manner so it drives motivation for acquiring new knowledge, feedback, and competition even if it's competing with a single player.

This is what having an engaged presentation means. This may take some time to prepare and get right. When done right, the results can charge an entire room full of people and have them clamoring to answer your questions to earn points, move on to the next level (or round), and obtain badges. I have experienced senior executives being extremely engaged and literally falling over each other trying to answer questions to earn points and beat their colleagues. This, my friend, is how you make them crave you!

Here are my five steps for making them crave you:

1. **Develop your signature story**: Be memorable. Have a catchphrase that can be easily shared.

2. **Craft magnetic documents**: Create your documents using spinoffs of your metaphor or catchphrase.

3. **Offer to guest teach**: Guest speak at a local college or university.

4. **Use media techniques for interviewing**: What are your hooks to keep them craving more?

5. **Make your presentation irresistible**: Use gamification elements to make them want more of you.

About Dr. David Wells

Dr. David Wells helps people who are having difficulty breaking into the higher education teaching profession not only get in, but also have institutions and students crave them. As a #1 Nationally Ranked Dean, he is a highly sought-after administrator for advice and training on how to go from steps that are "hit or miss" to strategies "they can't resist." He began his career in 2012 being new to the teaching profession and six months later becoming a Dean. When the dust settled, he was promoted three times in about 18 months.

David believes that in any profession you either "stand out" or "get left out," which is the philosophy he teaches. His goal is to show wannabe professors why the traditional approach to getting teaching gigs no longer works. David developed the SECRET Propeller Effect to help lift off their careers and create craving fans. He shows them how to develop their signature story and teaching metaphor to become the magnet that draws institutions in and craving more.

David earned his Ph.D. from Capella University. He is a Dean of a regionally-accredited university and oversees multiple disciplines. He is a best-selling author in *Wake Up* and *Live the Life You Love: Seizing Your Success,* which he co-authored with Deepak Chopra. David has also been featured in ABC, NBC, FOX, and CBS News for his work with professors.

David, a national speaker, trainer and Dean, has worked with hundreds of professors, including some top award-winning faculty members. He has set records in two different industries, sales and education, while beginning with no experience in either.

You can connect and engage with David at:
Get@DrDavidWells.com
www.twitter.com/DrDavidWells
www.instagram.com/DrDavidWells
www.facebook.com/DrDavidWellsSpeaks

CHAPTER 28

FIND YOUR STRENGTH — SOWING THE SEEDS OF YOUR SUCCESS

BY DAVID RUGGIERI

It's time to think about "where am I heading?"

Say goodbye to those thoughts about where you have been because that time is over, done with. Dreams are amazing, but they can also be distracting. At times, we get so wrapped up in 'what we want' that we fail to take the action to achieve it. Then it passes us by and then leaves us dangling, like the last leaf waiting to fall off a tree in autumn. Something different to think about, become a success story by working with your strengths and begin today to start sowing your strongest and most important seeds of your upcoming success.

Throughout time, stories of success have all begun with a realization of where someone is NOW, and where they hoped they could go. This is a fundamental belief in life as we know it, based on a pattern that has existed for centuries. Once we have a drive to create opportunity through seeking it out and finding it, *we must then set ourselves up to take action on achieving our dreams, fueling them into reality*. This is so powerful and it appeals to the very heart of my nature, a guy who has worked in college education for a large part of his life.

Over the years, I've spent a considerable amount of time helping people invest in tomorrow. I love the actual classroom, as well as the world we all live in, which is an equally incredible classroom for many. It comes down to helping every person I come in contact with make that transition from dormant ideas of success to tangible steps that lead to their success and equally and most important - alignment with what those strengths are. This is that incredible moment where you find the motivation to pursue **your** dreams and make them **your** reality. In case you were wondering...**these things do not happen without your participation**. I'm so excited to share with you some of the insight that I've used to help the distracted become focused, and get people using their strengths to create the change they dream and are entitled to experience

"OUR STRENGTHS ARE OUR ASSETS"

You can only define your strengths through evaluation and exploration.

If you ask most people what their weaknesses are, they can rattle of an entire list of things that they feel they could improve on in some way. However, ask someone what their strengths are and there is seldom an immediate answer to be offered. They start thinking about, approaching it more like they have a fear of giving the wrong answer. *How about you*? Can you answer this seemingly easy question confidently? "How would you describe your greatest strengths to a stranger?"

Oddly enough, many people don't really know what their strengths are. They may perceive what they'd like to be a true strength, but let's face it, just because you want to be elite or great at something doesn't mean that you can or will be. I don't relay that message to be harsh; rather, I want you to understand this so you can begin to focus on what tools you will begin to take out of your toolbox to help you build and find the success you want, and may very well deserve!

It's not an uncommon occurrence for me to see people in college or recently graduated from college with no idea what their strengths are. Maybe they went to college because that was what was expected of them, or they had no other plan. Of course, college is wonderful, but it is classroom experience balanced with a splash of real world living for most students, particularly traditional students (18-25 years of age) that begins to put the building blocks together in such a way that you start to make sense about potential opportunity – and that folks. is the very best place to begin. Know what you want, then see yourself getting it Success is rarely linear – it goes up, down, and sideways, you need to be properly prepared to ride it out.

So, how do we find our strengths . . .

Here are 5 steps that I offer to people who want to find their strengths and achieve the wellness in life that they wish to have. Strength and wellness are sometimes synonymous when it comes to our mindset and our actions. **Don't forget:** *the brain, your brain too, is a muscle*!

1.) <u>Create a reasonable plan and become excited and passionate about what you are undertaking</u>.

Think about these questions:

- What goals do you wish to accomplish?
- What are you wishing to achieve?
- How do you envision the journey that you are going to take?

The journey to success requires effort and energy, which is considerably easier to find and maintain when you are operating from a position of knowing your strengths and defining your passions. Your plan for success is every bit as important as the college education you may need to attain in order to achieve it and the quality of life you are creating for your future self.

2.) <u>Make sure you have a roadmap to help show you the path you will need to take—stay on track or get back on track if you find that you've veered off</u>. It is perfectly acceptable to veer off a bit every now and then, but, get back on track and keep moving ahead.

- This roadmap should include strategies such as:
- The tactics to help you conquer challenges and overcome obstacles

Information that you will need to keep moving forward, such as new things you must learn, what you may want to improve on, and people that you may want to mirror who you can learn from (mentors)

You will also want to take notes and make this roadmap a journal of sorts. Documenting what works and what doesn't is a highly effective way to evaluate and assess your progress, which gives you the intelligence to make tweaks—even if the tweak is to go in a completely different direction and start over with the first step.

3.) <u>Since you are going to fall, make sure you fall forward</u>!

There is no looking back or turning back, only going straight ahead. Will you have setbacks? Of course. You want to make sure that you don't start dwelling on them because I assure you, if you do, you will miss out on something valuable in the present that will help you achieve the success you've set out to find in the immediate future.

4.) <u>Document *every single action* that you wish to take toward achieving your goal</u>.

This will allow you to capture your thoughts and give you the opportunity to remember them the next day. We're all busy and it's easy to forget things that enter our mind (usually at a random moment). The habit of writing them down and transferring them to a to-do list will make that a non-factor. In the words of the great Jedi guru Yoda: "Do not try, do." Write it down! If there is one thing I can tell you for sure, ideas not written down become no idea at all. You will forget them, honestly, you will. Small pad, small pen, small recorder. Your best investment I promise.

5.) <u>Take real action</u>!

In order to achieve the successes we've created from our strengths and passions, we need to become active each and every day in turning them into our reality. Say goodbye to the dream and start living it. All your ideas you've documented in the fourth step should transfer over to your action list, which is where you make sure that you are constantly whittling away and moving forward. No exceptions.

These five steps are simple, and they are only the beginning! But there is another component to having them help you sow your seeds of success that you will need. Here's a hint: *it's not only how we act, it's also what we think.*

THE WAY WE THINK DICTATES THE WAY WE ACT

Thinking is not about reading or following a checklist, it's about having the mental energy to follow through with what you've started.

Consider this scenario: Eric has an idea and he's so excited about it, wanting to absorb every bit of knowledge that he can about it. He wants to be prepared and that's very commendable. He reads book after book, browses endless websites for bits of information, maybe even goes to college or takes some specific study courses, and is relentless in his quest to understand the big picture, as well as the small details. This is commendable, right? I believe it is; I obviously have a passion for learning. Now answer this question:

How far has Eric come toward actually achieving his goal?

Not as far as it seems. Busy work is not productive work. Believing we need to know everything before we start pursuing our success only assures us that we'll keep our wheels spinning. He has two out of the three necessary principles down: **hard work** and **concentration**, but he's failed to incorporate the third principle, which is a **commitment to follow-through**. There are many incredible people out there that know a whole lot about a wide variety of subjects, some even geniuses, but for all practical purposes they are weak and not viewed as successful. Why? If we only think we can do something, there is no way to show that we are correct. There's no gauge or assessment to put what we've learned to the test. You cannot measure potential – only performance!

Here's the real kicker about Eric's scenario. Truth be told, if we really want something and begin to work towards it and, it's meant to be for us, we'll find that *it's not hard work* as much as it's joyful work; *concentration is effortless* because we have our 'eyes on the prize'; and the *follow-through is as natural to us as breathing*. Doesn't that sound incredible? Wouldn't you love to feel that way? You can! But it all starts with belief and a plan. So many people run out of drive after the first disappointment, so many great opportunities lost so early in the game. People choke sometimes much like professional sports team do. Don't dream of success and then lose that dream because you failed to hit something out of the park on your first try. Fall down if you must, stand up and dust yourself off, and keep moving ahead.

START LOOKING FOR THE PATH

There is a path out there that's waiting for you to take it and start walking in the direction of your goals and aspirations.

We've all been guided to a path that others have wanted us to take in our lives; some from a young age on and others due to thinking there were no other options. Influence is everywhere, but I challenge you to start accepting that **you are the greatest influence of your life**. Think about that. It's you in control, you in charge, your life, your dreams; it's all about you because it is you. You decide what influence impacts you, not the other guy.

From today on, know that it doesn't matter who directed you to where you presently are. That is the past and you have an opportunity to do something substantial, a special thing that is done far too little in our fast-paced world filled with endless options. *What you take in today and accept in your life should be better than what it was yesterday, and rich currency towards what you can use tomorrow*. There is no purpose in spending time on repeating where you have been. It is a time waster, and that may well have described you at one time, but it doesn't anymore!

Start a trip to someplace you haven't been yet and take with you those seeds to sow and grow with your strength, purpose, and passion for the right type of success—the blend that is made just for you and by you!

IMAGINE YOUR POSSIBILITIES

Our attitudes are everything.

It really doesn't matter what books you've read about it, each and every one when it comes to attitude states in one way or another: *our attitude is everything*. It drives our behaviors and motivates our reactions. Are you ready to think positively and let the good outcomes drive you? If you don't get motivated by positive outcomes for success, perhaps you will start allowing them to inspire you. Consider this: it certainly beats letting the negative outcomes dictate your physical environment and internal wiring!

Helping people find the ways that they can create amazing lives for themselves that are based on their strengths and dreams is what I'm passionate about, and always look for opportunities to do and impact. Having a career where I can be a part of this process is more fulfilling than I could explain at times. I do know that you can have that indescribable feeling of success through your strengths if you allow yourself to take a journey to find it. In the words of the world-renowned Dr. Seuss, "Oh, the places we'll go!"

About David

David Ruggieri creates power in people – that's what moves them on to reach their goals and personal aspirations. He is all about continuing education and has been quoted as saying, "Education is the great equalizer in our society, without it you need a ton of luck, with it you create opportunity – you do the math!" He serves as Chief Executive Officer of a major college group in Florida, and is a Senior Executive on the subjects of Marketing and Sales. In other words, he is a guy who builds both businesses and people.

Over the years David has been in front of thousands of people "spreading the word" on personal power and personal responsibility. He has personally seen the fruits of those moments and witnessed the success many of his graduates have achieved. He has helped develop people into successful roles by giving them the words, attitude, and inspiration they needed, as he says, to "Fall Forward." He is a believer that all attempts to do something are many times met with rejection or failure, but falling is a part of standing, and falling forward is the best way to keep gaining ground. Even falling forward gains new ground.

David has been selected as one of America's PremierExperts and has been quoted in numerous publications on the subjects of education, marketing, and sales.

Connecting with David is easy. Whether it's a question, comment, or interest in personal growth, you can contact David directly at:
druggieri@ftccollege.edu.
Or on his personal email, druggieri@gmail.com
Or call him at: 407-506-5771.

CHAPTER 29

LIVING PEACEFULLY IN THE EYE OF THE HURRICANE

BY SANDY OLSON

Do you remember the last time you bought or sold a home? Were you excited as you started to look at different properties and all the features they had? Did you dream about what type of neighborhood you wanted to live in? Did you want a pool, a wooded lot, a fenced yard for the dog? Buying a home is the American dream and it can be very exciting finding that dream home. Whether it's your first home or one of many, it can be exciting. The upfront excitement tends to wane however, as the paperwork, inspections, packing and moving reality sets in. As a real estate broker, I get to help people everyday achieve that American Dream. I deal with all kinds of personalities and situations every day, so do the 102 agents that work in my two offices.

If you have ever bought or sold a home, you know that it can be one of the most stressful times in your life. You have to keep your house in tiptop condition. You have strangers coming into your home and it is nerve-racking each time you have a showing: What will people think of my home; will they like it? Will this be the buyer that will bring an offer? What kind of feedback will we receive? Why isn't my home selling? Is my agent doing enough to get it sold? The longer the process, the more the tension builds.

If you have ever had a job change, divorce, death in the family. . . and had to move, you know the feeling of being unsettled and anxious Sometimes the anxiety causes us to do crazy things! We once had a seller spray paint curse words on the side of her house in a divorce situation, and sabotage every showing by flooding either the dishwasher or a sink when the house was to be shown to a buyer. I remember seeing the showing instructions on one property stating, "enter the property at your own risk, divorce situation, wife does not want to sell and she has a rifle." We had another man refuse to go to settlement and put a tent on his property and camped out with a gun just to get back at his wife who was ready to move on. These are just some of many examples that happen in real estate transactions.

Nothing surprises me anymore! Have you ever been in a situation where you felt that your safety was at risk? Realtors have to be concerned about this every day. I had one agent who started receiving letters from a convict in a local jail because he saw her picture in an ad and was attracted to her. An agent was once in an open house on a Sunday afternoon and a man touring the house told her that there was water in the basement, and that she needed come downstairs immediately. You know when you get that pit in your stomach? Something didn't feel right to her, so she said she would wait until the sellers came home in a few minutes (even though they were not due back for an hour). The man left and when she went to check the basement, there was no water. He was trying to lure her down there for who knows what purpose, but undoubtedly not a good one. Another agent was showing a man a lot located in an isolated area, and when she turned around to talk to him, he had his pants down around his ankles... she ran as hard and as fast as she could until she reached the road and safety!

Have you ever had the frustration of trying to help someone and been at the mercy of other people that don't keep their commitments? Sometimes we have to work with people that don't answer their phones, have full voicemail boxes, never return calls or keep commitments Many properties for sale in this current market are bank owned. Banks can be very difficult to negotiate with and many don't have realistic expectations of the local market values and take forever to respond. Some agents get defensive, make decisions without consulting their client and can be just downright unprofessional. Thankfully, this is not the majority, but as anyone who works with other people know, not everyone is on the same level when it comes to customer service and professionalism. Needless to say, the day in the life of a real estate agent can be unpredictable.

Going through a move can be a whirlwind experience and real estate agents need to be the calm in the storm; last minute, unexpected situations happen regularly and it is easy for people to get really angry over something that normally wouldn't bother them at all. We have had educated, mature people fighting over minor items like sliding doors not opening smoothly, a dripping faucet, or moldy caulk around bathtubs. In the big scheme of things, these are minor items, but people get emotionally wrapped up in them when going through stressful times. We have had basements flood the day before settlement.

Hurricane Sandy put all real estate sales at a screeching halt because banks wanted to re-inspect all properties a second time before settlement to make sure there was no damage. That was complete chaos! People had moving trucks packed and sitting full with no place to move to and appraisers were completely overbooked trying to schedule all of these re-inspections; not to mention staying on top of the current ones they already had to do. Needless to say, people were extremely upset. We literally had to stay in the "Eye of the Hurricane" during that storm.

If you have ever lived through a hurricane before, then you know the emotions that can come with it: fear, anxiety, worry and lack of sleep. The wind is howling around you, rain is pouring down and beating powerfully against the side of your house, power goes out and you are in the dark, roads are flooded and you can feel isolated and stranded. The "Eye of the Hurricane," however, is the calm spot in the middle of the storm. The sun is shining, it's warm on your skin, there is no wind, and it is calm and peaceful. Many people live with the emotions associated with the hurricane outside of the eye every single day. These emotions can wipe out your energy and keep you from reaching your full potential

As the leader of my company, which has grown from three agents and one office to over one hundred agents and two offices, during the worst real estate market in history; I attribute my ability to stay in the "eye of the hurricane" to my success. When many offices were shutting their doors and agents were leaving the business in droves, my office continued to grow every single year and is still growing steadily today.

I find that the source of my success is to live in the "eye of the hurricane" as often as I can. I also help to guide the agents in my office to do the same. What do I mean by that?

No matter what stresses come upon us, it is important to stay centered, calm and emotionally stable. When an agent's transaction is going completely haywire, they are stressed and they need my help; me going haywire (or stepping outside the eye of the hurricane) isn't going to help the situation and can ultimately just make things worse. It is important for us to shield our client's from those emotions as much as we can. If we allow other's emotional situations or bad choices to highjack our emotions, we have moved away from the calm of the eye of the hurricane and into the whirlwind of the storm – ultimately pulling our clients right into the storm with us.

Therefore, it is important as the broker and leader of my company to stay in that "eye of the hurricane" – that calm, warm space in the middle of the storm. Real Estate agents are drawn to my company because of the culture, the professionalism and my commitment to their growth and development. They trust that our office will be consistently successful because I am consistently predictable in my commitment to training, technology and helping them solve difficult situations in a calm and centered way. So how do I make that happen? How can we stay calm and centered no matter what craziness is going on around us? It isn't always easy and it takes a lot of consistent practice and continued personal growth and development.

I also can get triggered and step outside of that calm eye of the hurricane; I am only human after all. The trick is to recognize where you are going and move back into the calm as soon as possible.

How do we achieve this success? Several ways:

POSITIVE REINFORCEMENT

Make a commitment to hearing positive motivation every day. There are a lot of very successful people who are committed to daily motivations either by e-mail, videos, text messages or books: including Jack Canfield, Darren Hardy and Tony Robbins – just to name a few. When you hear motivational stories of success, or daily strategies to improve yourself just a little each day, it is easier for you to stay centered and have something to draw strength from when things go haywire. Meditation and spiritual motivations are also good practices to keep you centered.

HAVE A PLAN

Have consistent lead generation systems and daily activities in place. The more leads you have in any sales position, the more choices you have. Then you can choose not to work with someone who doesn't respect you, your advice, or your time. I remember a potential client who would not take my advice on the market value of her home and my suggested sales price. When I asked her how she could justify the difference in the price? She said she felt she could get more for her home than what my recommendation was. She had put a double sink in her kitchen, therefore her house was worth ten thousand more than everything else on the market! She was not willing to budge on that, so I chose not to work with that client.

I didn't feel any pressure to because I had systems in place and had plenty of leads coming my way. Sometimes, even when we don't have the leads yet, we need to make decisions like we do have a large pool of customers to choose from, so that we don't waste time and energy with someone who does not respect our advice.

There are many companies that help with marketing and lead generation systems. I am very lucky to have RE/MAX as a resource for myself and my agents, as they support us with excellent marketing and education, and connect us with some great real estate trainers.

CREATE GREAT PROCESS

Have organizational systems in your business. When things are going crazy around you, checklists, organizational systems and technology to keep things organized are essential to staying in the eye of the hurricane. If you lose paperwork or forget an inspection deadline, you have just added additional stress to your life that is totally unnecessary. Sales people are not always organized, so helping with those systems has also been essential to my success. If you are the leader of your company, find those systems for your people; they are selling and don't have time to always do that research.

LEARN FROM THE MASTERS

You don't have to re-create the wheel. Have coaches and mentors. I have always had business coaches, life coaches, personal trainers, financial advisors, legal counsel etc., in my life. You can't be an expert at everything and it is important to get advice and accountability from those who are experts in what they do. We all drift at times, and when we drift, we tend to leave that calm eye of the hurricane.

JOIN A GREAT TEAM

In addition to coaches, accountability partners in your life keep you from drifting. I have built a culture in my office of being supportive and accountable to each other. While agents are competing with each other for business, we all understand that we are stronger individually when our whole office is stronger. There is an abundance mentality; we know that there is enough business for everyone. They connect with each other to hold each other accountable and support each other. It is important as a leader to encourage and support that.

DELEGATE!

When we try to pile too much onto our plate, we don't have time for the things that keep us centered. There is no way that I could have grown my business to where it is today without surrounding myself with good people. I would be a complete hurricane if I tried to do everything that needs to be done to support my business myself. If you are not at the level to afford employees, delegate other things. Hire a house cleaner, landscaping company or a college student to run errands or do some of your marketing activities. It doesn't take a lot to free you up to focus on tasks that keep you focused and successful. The more you do this, the more money you will earn to hire others to delegate to.

The final advice that I can give about staying in the "Eye of the Hurricane" is to surround yourself with other people who live in the "Eye" as well. The people who make you feel good, support you, and that you can have centered and productive conversations with. You also know the people who take you out of the "Eye." You feel their negative energy when they walk in the room, you can feel that pit in your stomach and you immediately want to resist whatever it is they start to say. I find that the more I stay in the "Eye of the Hurricane," the more I can help those types of people who normally live well outside of the Eye come a little closer to it, or to experience that calm a little more often; and that to me is success!

About Sandy

Sandy Olson is the Broker/Owner of RE/MAX Results in Frederick, Maryland. She helps Realtors build their business by showing them how to become small business owners under the global network of RE/MAX. Sandy believes that professionalism, full time commitment and an emphasis on customer service is what makes a real estate office a success and stand out in the crowd. Sandy is committed to training and facilitates several training sessions throughout the year in her office. She is committed to her agents and grew her office from 3 agents in 2004 to over 100 agents and two offices today. She did this during one of the worst recessions and real estate markets in history.

Sandy graduated with a B.S. Degree in Business Administration from Mount Saint Mary's University in Emmitsburg, MD and graduated from Sandler Sales Institute in Rockville, MD. She holds several real estate-related designations; GRI (Graduate of the Realtor Institute) which is a four week intensive program covering all aspects of real estate; she is a Certified Residential Broker (CRB) which requires additional broker training emphasizing business development and management, she has also earned the Certified Negotiation Expert Designation. She is a certified Buffini Mentor so is able to train her agents with a Peak Producer's program.

Sandy has earned the Merit Award from her local Association of Realtors and has served on the Board of Directors and as President in 2010-2011. She earned the RE/MAX Maryland Outstanding Brokerage of the Year in 2009, RE/MAX Central Atlantic Brokerage of the Year Award for 2014 and numerous awards year after year for office production.

You can reach Sandy at:
sandyolson@remax.net
www.facebook.com/RemaxResultsMD
www.frederickhomesales.com
www.Hagerstown-Home-Sales.com

CHAPTER 30

EIGHT STEPS TO TAKE CONTROL OF YOUR DENTAL HEALTH!

BY DR. CRAIG B. SIMMONS

In the city of Spokane, WA, where I practice, I receive a bill from the city every year for hazardous waste. On that bill it states that Dental Amalgam is a hazardous waste and needs to be handled appropriately in its disposal. *If this material is a hazardous waste then why is it legal for me to place it into people's bodies?* I have to have special filters and traps in the office to dispose of this substance. The removal of amalgam from a tooth also needs to be taken seriously, but so does the placement of these toxic substances into people's mouths. I'm sure there are many people that have had this type of filling or crown placed or removed from their mouths, with no barrier, and the material is getting swallowed or inhaled. A common side effect of amalgam placement or removal is called amalgam tattoos, which is when the splatter of the mercury/silver sulfide filling get ingrained into the soft tissue. When I was just starting my dental career, I knew nothing about the negative side effects of commonly-practiced dentistry. I was just doing what I was taught, until one conversation changed the trajectory of my life and my practice.

After finishing dental school and spending the next three years in the United States Navy as a Lieutenant and Dentist, I was ready to start my own practice. In the Navy, I spent most of my time placing mercury fillings (amalgams) in recruits' mouths. In my private practice, I had no intention of changing the procedures I was accustomed to and was taught in dental school. However, everything changed for me after one disrupting conversation with my uncle.

I called my Uncle Paul one day to understand better how I might be more successful in investing. It was in the early stages of my private practice and I knew that proper investing was going to be a key element to my success. I wanted to know what he was doing with his money to make it grow. I called him out of the blue and the conversation took a turn that forever changed my life and my practice. And it all started with a simple question, He asked me, "Are you OK with the materials that dentists, like yourself, are putting in people's teeth?"

Well, of course I was ok with it. I had been practicing it for years through the Navy. Not only that, it is what I had learned in dental school. There was no reason for me to believe otherwise. I rattled off some information I learned in school and elaborated on the stance of the Dental Associations on certain materials and how they have been approved for use in the human body. Dentists have been using these materials for years, so if someone has a problem, it must be the person not the materials. My uncle didn't agree. He began to tell me how he believed the dentistry and materials used on my aunt contributed to her death. WOW! This was new to me! The fact that materials in teeth could even be harmful did not seem to be an important issue in my training at school.

The conversation ended and the weight of the matter felt like a burden I could not ignore. I didn't have the answers. I didn't know if my uncle was right or not, but ethically, I could not continue my practice in the same manner. If there was the potential that I was putting toxic materials into my patients–I couldn't practice with that.

I decided I was going to not place any more mercury fillings or metal crowns. I just did not feel comfortable putting something in someone's body when there was other material available with less potential toxicity. This began my path to providing holistic dental care. Over time I have seen a pattern that has developed and this is why I have put into eight steps that can be applied to any aspect of your life, overall health, dental health, career, education, and family.

As I transitioned into a Holistic Dental Practice, I found the patients very different from the patients that I had been treating in a general dentistry practice. They had more of a desire to be in control of their

EIGHT STEPS TO TAKE CONTROL OF YOUR DENTAL HEALTH!

health and not rely solely on the professional to dictate to them their next course of action. If they could care for themselves naturally they desired this over a quick fix.

So for the first several years I spent time attending continuing education courses that related to whole body dentistry. I also became a member of different associations for dental professionals. These organizations include the International Academy of Biological Dentistry & Medicine, the International Academy of Oral Medicine & Toxicology, and the Holistic Dental Association. The efforts of these associations helped me to understand the overall health of the patient is first.

As a dental patient it is important for you to be educated about your health and wellness almost as much as it is for me, as the dentist. Here is how you can start the process of being educated on your dental health.

EIGHT STEPS TO TAKE CONTROL
OF YOUR DENTAL HEALTH

Step 1. Desire

As I began to notice more negative effects of dentistry, my curiosity in this worked its way into a desire that I must at least attempt to figure out what, if anything, can I do and how can I apply it to the treatment of my patients. Desire is the first step on the path to take control. Without it nothing can be accomplished.

Step 2. Obtain Knowledge

About 5 years passed, and I was busy building up my metal-free practice in dentistry. One day I was contacted by a dental practice sales broker about a practice down the street that was for sale. I actually had seen this practice for sale a year earlier and when I was notified about it, I saw that it was a Holistic Dental Practice. I did not know what that meant and from what others said upon asking (they didn't really know what it was either) they stated that it was weird and that they did weird things there. So having got that vibe about it I thought it wouldn't be a good idea to buy it so a year later I was contacted by the broker again. This time I decided that I would take a look at the practice as a business and get to meet the doctor so as to find out what this holistic dentistry meant. What I was doing was applying the second step by obtaining knowledge.

I met with the doctor multiple times and asked questions about materials and procedures. I really felt a connection and decided that this was the dentistry that I would like to practice. It just made sense to me. When I took over and the doctor retired, I found the patients very different from the patients that I had been treating in a general dentistry practice. I would say that they had more of a desire to be in control of their health and not rely solely on the professional to dictate to them. If they could care for themselves naturally they desired this.

Step 3. Invest in Self

I had to show that I truly was on their side. So for the first several years I spent time attending continuing education courses that related to whole body dentistry. I also became a member of the different associations for dental professionals. These organizations include the International Academy of Biological Dentistry & Medicine, the International Academy of Oral Medicine & Toxicology, and the Holistic Dental Association. The efforts of these associations to me put the patient overall health first and are very focused on and leading the way and cause in biocompatability progression. By doing this I was both obtaining knowledge and investing in myself. These associations help like-minded people get together and further the cause.

Step 4. Plan

As I gained my education and practiced in the manner which allows the patient more autonomy in their healthcare I came up with a plan. To establish healthy lifelong relationships by working alongside patients in their care I believe that the patients are happier and more fulfilled spiritually, mentally and physically. What a great feeling it is to know that you participated in your health decisions. And when something can be dealt with in a more natural way then there is less intrusion on your well being. Ask yourself, if you have had dental treatment how did your body respond? Do you feel like something isn't right? Do you know what is in your mouth? If you haven't had much or any dental treatment and you are in good health, then it may not seem as important but I urge you to look for a doctor you feel is on your side and puts you first. Some day you may need treatment, and if that happens I believe you will have more trust and confidence in a provider that is concerned about the effects dental treatment has on your whole body.

Step 5. Take Action

I was able to take action in the care and treatment of my patients since I had the desire, obtained knowledge, invested in myself and came up with a plan. I was able to provide what my patients were seeking and looking for in their desire to be in control of their dental health. My staff was also able to work along side me in these efforts because they understood the plan also.

Step 6. Step-by-Step

As a provider this entire process is a step-by-step process. The technology is always changing and may not be available or affordable at present. For me there were steps in being at the forefront of dentistry and its treatments, materials, and ways to be perfomed.

Step 7. Plans change as Paradigms Shift

To me, a major part of autonomy is that I don't know what I don't know. Hence when there is something new that is brought to light on health or materials it could lead to a paradigm shift. When this happens and it will happen then I myself have to be open to the shift and change my plans for care.

Step 8. Never Give Up

Never give up on whatever you do. Be persistent even when there is resistance. If a health care provider is not seeming to listen to you or is making light of your concerns, then maybe you should seek out someone who will. One of my favorite acronyms is F.O.C.U.S., or Follow One Course Until Successful. I admire the many patients I have who have been suffering from one or more illnesses and have not been able to get answers or treatement to help them from their primary care physician nor their dentist. Yet they continue to research and pursue.

IN CONCLUSION

As I gained my education and practiced in the manner which allows the patient more autonomy in their healthcare, I came up with a plan. I want to work alongside patients in their care and build a long-term, healthy relationship that educates the patient and allows them to start taking control of their dental health. You, as a patient, should be more involved in taking control of your health. I have found that you will be happier and more fulfilled spiritually, mentally and physically. What a great feeling it is to know that you participated in your healthy decisions! Ask yourself, if you have had dental treatment how did your body respond? Do you feel like something isn't right? Do you know what is in your mouth?

If you haven't had much or any dental treatment and you are in good health then it may not seem as important, but I urge you to look for a doctor you feel is on your side and puts you first. Some day you may need treatment and if that happens, I believe you will have more trust and confidence in a provider that is concerned about the effects dental treatment has on your body as a whole.

About Dr. Craig

Dr. Craig Simmons is dedicated to helping his patients take action to look after their teeth and overall health. He is dedicated to the education of his clients and continuing education for himself.

Dr. Simmons graduated from Marquette University School of Dentistry in 2000. He served as a Leiutenant in the United States Navy for three years where he completed an Advanced Education in General Dentistry. Dr. Simmons worked in a community dental clinic prior to going into private practice and has been practicing Holistic Dentistry for six years.

Dr Simmons is a Board Certified Biological Dentist with the International Academy of Biological Dentists & Medicine and is a member of the Holistic Dental Association, and International Academy of Medicine & Toxicology.

Dr. Simmons is an Eagle Scout and continues to actively be involved in scouting. He is married to wife Nicole and has four sons.

CHAPTER 31

TREATING DEPRESSION

BY CAROL M. SLINN

INTRODUCTION

This chapter is written to help identify traits and behaviors for those individuals who are unable to recognize what is happening to them now. This information may give some insight and options that would be beneficial for them to have. Please reach out to connect with a professional and/or people who will support you, as well as sharing helpful actions or insights to ensure safety for all those involved. Depression is caused by stress and can be resolved rapidly with recognizable results! And I hope you find my approach helpful.

WHAT IS DEPRESSION?

Depression, in my experience as a trainer/speaker to improve health and behavior, is a combination of specific habitual physical reactions. Reactions that happen automatically. Whereas, a response is a more thought out way of handling a stimulus. These habitual reactions trigger each other similar to a domino effect, in a steady flow from one reaction to another. When a combination of reactions become activated more consistently, the behaviours seem to blend one into another. This will keep the individual " stuck" in an ongoing flow of habitual physical reactions. Even when the physical reaction may seem to be very slight, almost unnoticeable to the individual. This flow may become so familiar to the person experiencing it as a physical reaction, they do not realize how often these reactions are impacting their health and well-being.

This activated flow of physical reactions are memorized in the same way the individual learns to drive a vehicle or dial a phone number. Your physical body remembers the action you've learned by repetition! Your physical body does many things automatically. Generally, people are unaware at a conscious level of what they've been feeling and doing when the habitual behavior is activated. They become so familiar with how the body is reacting, the reaction has become normal to them. Like most habits, once activated, they will be carried out from start to finish perfectly, without thought.

HOW CAN DEPRESSION MAKE SOMEONE FEEL?

Rapid Result Training gives people the skill set, to improve "how" they are physically and mentally responding to everyday situations, or in moments of crisis. When the physical body is impacted by different sensations at the same time, the mental and behavioral reaction change as well. As an example, people may feel as though they have zero energy in their body and/or a foggy mind. They can feel extremely tense or very weak. Each and every habitual reaction brings with it a wide variety of physical sensations.

Feeling afraid, abandoned or experiencing a loss are all habitual reactions. If they are being triggered over and over, it is common for them to form a pattern. When this happens on an ongoing basis twenty-four hours a day, this will leave the person exhausted and less able to improve their situation.

This interaction of habitual reactions is normal. The person experiencing these reactions is not consciously aware, their behaviour and attitude has become habitual. Habits formed by intentional learning, at a conscious or logical level, such as learning to ride a bike, or learning from experience, such as eating food for comfort. Unconsciously learned behaviours may be initiated by physical reactions. If an older sibling hits a younger child often in passing, the younger child may flinch if the older sibling makes a sudden gesture in their direction. During daily situations this individual may experience an ongoing flow of reactions physically as well as ongoing shifts mentally. This is common and normal in my observations.

People living in a safe, secure, and happy environment, without a consistent high stress level, will typically flow from one positive reaction to another easily. Freedom from consistent stressors will enable their physical body to be able to maintain a comfort zone and their mental outlook to be positive.

Crisis moments and traumatic events may initiate unfamiliar reactions. These may initiate a new flow or cycle of reactions that can be triggered frequently. Whatever initiates the cycle of reactions for people varies widely from person to person. Some common situations involve loss. Loss of a job, a relationship, seniority, spouse, pet, or an opportunity. Generally speaking, the more unexpected the loss or trauma, the more common it is for people to experience a severe reaction. Depression is more severe than feeling down or a little sad. It has a far-reaching life-changing impact on the individual. It may last for an undetermined amount of time unless the individual receives help to resolve the ongoing reactions that manifest as flashbacks or severe pain – in some cases without any injury or physical ailment. The time frame required to resolve these often debilitating behaviours depend on the choice of action that person or their family wishes to take at this time.

THE STIGMA OF DEPRESSION

The stigma of depression should, in my opinion, be rethought and eliminated. It has been my experience that people from all walks of life can be vulnerable to depression. Though the initiating experience may vary extensively, it has been my observation that normal functioning people who experience an intense or lengthy exposure to a crisis situation – while suffering from sleep deprivation, exhaustion, or feeling overwhelmed – may experience depression and begin to act out some of the behaviours initiated by depression. They may use alcohol or narcotics to feel temporary comfort. We begin to understand how a person can be worn down physically and mentally, for they are no longer safe from the unrelenting reactions that drain all happiness and strength from the physical body. Mental exhaustion combined with shock can short-circuit the natural ability to cope. Does it make logical sense then, that we as people, have limits to what we can endure before we become vulnerable to depression?

If you or someone you love has ever experienced depression, you would know the frustration, anger, and helplessness of battling an invisible foe as it drains a life away. Depression will cause pain, suffering and the inability to think rationally or realistically.

Clients with depression have shared with me they could do nothing about it. Choice was no longer available to them. Their mind was repeating a scenario they had experienced previously. Or worse, their mind and body felt completely numb.

Thankfully there are several positive actions you can take to help during this situation. Pick up the phone now! Tell someone you trust how you're doing. Connect with family, a friend, a neighbor, your religious counsel, your doctor, hospital, or helpline. These would all be good suggestions of action to take. Make the effort to contact someone, anyone, so there will be someone else who will know where you are and how you're doing! That's right! Do it now! It's so important for you to take this step now.

RECOGNITION

People of all ages tend to 'isolate' themselves when they're depressed. They are generally withdrawn and are not seeking help, they become invisible. Another way to recognize depression is their 'avoidance' of things, people and situations this person used to enjoy. Lack of energy and enthusiasm or physically pushing away from personal contacts are all behaviours that are obvious and easy to notice when people are suffering from depression. They may have more mood swings or cry more readily.

The individual's personal care may no longer be important to them. If you notice your husband, child, wife, co-worker or elderly parent exhibiting signs of depression after being relocated or after a loss there are actions you can take. You may you want to consider seeking professional help for them. Create a positive support system for the individual where they will feel included, secure, and comfortable. Avoid judging them. Name calling, blaming or bullying will have a negative impact and make the person withdraw further. It will also alienate or reduce the trust level between you. Remember, they already feel vulnerable and weak without a negative review.

If you are worried about what other people will think of you, if you're the one feeling depressed. Remember, people never choose to be depressed. Suffering from depression is a realistic possibility with today's stress-filled life. Things can change in a heartbeat. Be prepared and stay aware of how you and your loved ones are handling life's challenges. It's best to be aware of your own health and happiness as a preventive action to assist you in being proactive and recognizing the warning signs of depression.

When a person is depressed, they can be demoralized by their vulnerability and lack of energy. They lack the mindset or skill to shake it off without outside help. The interesting point to remember is, typically, most people are able to respond to kindness, understanding, caring and compassion. How would someone recognize any of the aforementioned actions? They hear the words you say to them, see the actions you take for them, and feel the comfort you bring into their life. Consistency builds trust! They will have a far better action plan for their future recovery with your help.

IMPORTANT STEPS TO TAKE

Words, or rather the right words, play a huge role in everyday life! Positive words lead to positive reactions. Interestingly enough, self talk or your internal dialogue also leads to a reaction! So it is important to pay attention and be aware of your inner dialogue (this gets easier to do on a more consistent basis). With practice, this awareness will become a habit and what a great habit for you to create for your overall well-being . . . now! I encourage everyone to avoid putting this off and just do it! You will notice how different you feel when you say positive supportive things to yourself, rather than blaming or bullying yourself. Make the effort to make yourself your number one priority and best friend and do everything within your power to get help now!

The next step is to start to physically move more. Go for a walk, even if you begin to move just inside your house. Any physical activity is good at this time. Physically taking action, your physical, mental, and emotional state will improve with more oxygen. I realize without energy this is a big step, and it is so worth the effort! Remember, if you need help, reach out to someone.

Take notice of what you are eating? Or, are you eating? How often and in what amount are you eating? Notice if you're drinking enough water to stay hydrated. Avoid drinking alcohol! Many people use this for temporary relief and escape. There are other options available to make you feel better, so seek help now. Even in small amounts, alcohol is a depressant so you may want to avoid all alcohol for now. Also avoid using any recreational drugs because they too may make you feel more depressed after the high disappears.

For those of you that are currently looking after someone with depression, I urge you to seek a social support network for yourself. Speak with a counselor, friend or healthcare professional on a regular basis. Often, I am approached by the caregiver of individuals suffering from depression. They feel as caregivers, they themselves are being impacted by the lack of response or the lack of appreciation they are receiving for their efforts. Avoid the blame game, as this is a game that no one wins. You need to be aware of taking time to get some fresh air, listen to favorite music or have scheduled times with friends or pets, as your attitude may deteriorate without taking proactive actions.

A RECENT TRUE-LIFE EXPERIENCE TO SEND YOU HOPE

Courage and love are powerful sources of energy, and staying creative to nurture yourself or another to stay positive during depression . . . courage to find the help you need! Love yourself enough to open the door so you allow the help to come in! The story below shares with you how one man's courage gave him the strength to find the help he needed to take his life back from depression. With his permission, I was given his story of recovery to share.

Carol is a Canadian who has retained her strong Midwest values while living on the west coast. Few people share her wealth of experiences, personal or professional, but it is her ability to give relief to clients that is key to her success. Carol's unique rapid result training has helped transform the lives of individuals within a day, empowering them to successfully conquer their challenges. When your life seems to be disappearing, planning and controlling change becomes out of the question.

Improving our behaviour is difficult, but Carol can accomplish in a few hours what some people struggle with for years. She permanently improves the physical feelings. By the time the training module is complete, you feel better physically, mentally and emotionally—seeing and understanding clearly and experiencing happiness returning to your life for your future.

Are you overwhelmed by anger, frustration or pain that surrounds you? Are people in your life dragging you down? Is addiction recovery a dream? Then let Carol give you back your strength and happiness. You will rediscover your heath and feel good! Just when my world seemed about to crash, I discovered the relief that she can provide. I know because I have been there. My pending divorce led my lawyer to insist that I work with Carol before the court case began. Without discussion or invasion of my privacy, Carol's pre-litigation training module broke through my inertia – giving me coping skills I still use today.

I met and married a wonderful lady for 18 years when she suddenly passed away. This led me into a pit of despair. Even my faith could not overcome my grief and anger. After a year, my friends kindly advised that I seemed to be "getting angry." Knowing the consequences of that observation, I began looking for Carol, who had initially started training me to understand and improve my responses.

Carol has expanded Rapid Result training to include "Good Health Recovery" training by word-of-mouth referral. I am continuing with Carol's Good Health Recovery training now, and I feel energized and happy! I am sure you would benefit from any training with Carol, too.

Imagine what you will accomplish once you are free from anxiety, anger and depression! And you can make it happen! Take your Good Health Recovery training with Carol who will utilize your skills so you achieve your goals – this is your key to success. She can help you faster as no other can. Training with her is a unique life-improving experience!

Thank you for your willingness to have me share some of my insight and experience with you. I have seen depression wreak devastation on peoples' lives. And I've seen their health and happiness return faster than you can imagine. I hope this information will be of help to you or someone you love. If you or someone you know is suffering with depression, and feel they would like more information on what is available with me, please checkout what training would best suit you or your group at: www.carolmslinn.com. Success is achieved when need meets solution!

About Carol

Carol M. Slinn C.H.T., Trainer - N.L.P.
Trainer, Speaker, Founder of Rapid Result Training

Carol M. Slinn lives in Vancouver's Lower Mainland where she created and utilized her many skills for the past 26 years. She developed Rapid Result Training – an in-depth training for professionals to resolve habitual reactions that are having a negative impact on their lives. Training improved their health, performance and attitude all at the same time without any invasive disclosure being needed. The results are obvious and immediate – improving health, relationships, finances and performance. Carol's passion and compassion is for those individuals who have experienced or are experiencing life's challenging times.

Carol's father and ex-husband were both in the federal police force in Canada – the RCMP. She relates to relocating from western to eastern Canada and back again. Moving every few years to another city or town had a direct impact on everyone. Carol divorced after twenty years of marriage. At this time, her father passed away suddenly, leaving the family grief-stricken.

Carol knew many people who were divorcing. She noticed decision-makers who could interact with ease in every situation, became more aggressive, anxious and depressed. She designed a one day pre-litigation program specifically to help those individuals be comfortable, while making better long-term decisions.

One of her key accomplishments: Gaining recognition within the Life Insurance and Disability Insurance industry for creating a new approach to expedite good health to those individuals suffering and in pain – on long-term disability.

Programs for lawyers, CEO's, airline and marine pilots, police officers, firefighters, lawyers, military personnel, government officials, athletes and people in the film industry make up the list of professionals who have chosen Carol's training over more traditional resources.

Carol understands the time constraint there is when it comes to seeking a solution for yourself. Not everyone can take months or years to find a solution for habitual reactions that are impacting their life now. Her approach is safe, realistic and highly effective—empowering her clients while keeping their pride and dignity intact.

Carol's clients achieve recognizable improvements in their lives after, and often during, their Rapid Result Training. Rapid Result Training modules are designed to achieve her client's' goals in a manner that is effective, interesting and a relief for them! Carol's clients come from every walk of life.

Certification and Professional Development

- Interview Techniques for People After Crimes of Violence – V. P. D.
- Hypnotherapy Certification - United States Board of Hypnotherapy
- Anger in the Workplace – Justice Institute of British Columbia
- Mediation – Justice Institute of British Columbia
- Certified Trainer CE Courses - Insurance Council of BC
- Eating Disorders in Adolescents (Dr. Roger Tonkin) UBC
- Addictions and Relapse Prevention - Canadian Mental Health
- Anxiety Disorders Treatment and Behaviours - Anxiety Disorders Association

CHAPTER 32

ENGAGING THE FEMININE: 5 STEPS FOR SUSTAINABLE SUCCESS

BY DEIRDRE MORRIS

LEARNING ABOUT THE FEMININE – MY STORY

I wanted to scream at Sally to get away from my baby. What I saw so disturbed me that my legs almost ran outside by themselves to retrieve my six-month-old daughter from her arms.

But I couldn't move.

I was indoors nursing her twin sister and, after all, Sally wasn't actually doing any wrong. She was just carrying Caoimhe around the garden, speaking to her so closely that their faces were almost touching.

We were paying for Sally's help, as I wasn't able to manage the twins on my own. New arrivals in that part of Spain, we didn't have a community of family and friends around us. Julian, my partner, had just left for three weeks to go to China on an engineering project and we had hired a woman to stay with me in his absence.

How could I rush out now and tear my child away from her? What sane person would do that? And if I did, what would I say? "Keep your face away from Caoimhe's, Sally. It's not safe for her."

What evidence did I have that this might be true? Apart from extreme turbulence in my body, there was none. Not one single shred.

The peaceful scene of Eadaoin feeding at my breast disguised the torrent of emotions washing over me. With huge effort, I slowly, very slowly, returned to reason. "I'm just being a sensitive new mom. It must be insecurity or jealousy." I told myself.

I never really clicked with Sally. It was great to have her much-needed support and she did love the girls, but ever since our first encounter – something did not feel right for me. We had different values and ideas about life, and in spite of the huge assistance she provided, I found it quite an effort to be around her.

When Julian returned, Sally continued with us from Mondays to Fridays, but I was uneasy. Several times, I shared with Julian what was going on for me. He said I could do what I wanted. But for him all was well. He was able to work, she was helping me and she loved the girls.

On the surface, all was right with the world, but I found these conversations very frustrating. I couldn't permit myself to let her go without his true agreement. I doubted and judged myself, and tried to make the best of it. Wasn't I lucky to have help?

Not long after, Julian returned to China for another three weeks. While he was gone, Sally became ill and went home to rest. Without thinking about it, I took the opportunity to bring our arrangement to an end.

This was huge for me. The girls were a full-time job even with another person's assistance. I didn't have a back-up plan. I didn't consult with Julian. I didn't know if I could manage. I just knew that I had to do it.

I recall that evening sitting on a large Pilate's ball, a baby in each arm bouncing them to sleep. I was physically exhausted, but the relief I felt from taking the decision was totally invigorating. It felt so right.

Over the months that followed, we could see that the girls were not thriving, especially Caoimhe, who had a grey look to her. Her sister too was showing up with unusual symptoms. Concerned doctors informed us that both had Tuberculosis. We later discovered that Sally had been the carrier. If they had lived in another country or time they would have died. Months of intensive treatment followed and eventually we could see their vitality returning. Thankfully everyone (including Sally) finally received a clean bill of health.

EXCLUDING THE FEMININE FROM SUCCESS

This whole experience with Sally was a huge eye opener for me. Why did I have such difficulty honouring my intuitions? Some part of me somehow knew that close contact with Sally was dangerous for the girls.

Like most others on the planet, I have grown up in a world that has emphasised the masculine approach to life – which relies on thinking, reasoning and problem solving to achieve results. Our education systems are a good example of this.

In this model, the feminine world of emotions and feelings has been perceived as irrelevant and inappropriate for the most part (until the birth of Positive Psychology in 2000, which, for the first time, shifted the focus of the social sciences from solving problems to exploring what makes life worth living).

So, we have a bias towards trying to figure things out when it comes to achieving what we want. But the notion that reason and logic are superior to feelings in the story of success is not an absolute truth.

It is simply a product of living in a patriarchal world in which society's rules and values over hundreds of years have been shaped by a masculine understanding of life, one that has perceived our MEN-tal lives as superior to our emotional lives. Women, as my story demonstrates, have been part of this too.

But even if this has been the worldview for many hundreds of years, and is shared by most religions and cultures, it is still nothing more than a collective habit, a stage of our development, a shared story that has served as the backdrop against which our lives have played out.

Until now.

Because, even though this approach to life has contributed so much to our evolution and we have much from it to be grateful for, it is incomplete and we are being invited to take the next step in our collective growth.

EVOLVING WITH THE FEMININE

Each of us is a combination of masculine and feminine, and when we depend solely on the masculine (or feminine) we are not using our full potential. It is equivalent to hobbling around on one foot. It can work for some time, hundreds of years even, but success can only be sustainable when we are showing up in our wholeness.

We are in a time of huge transformation.

Anais Nin observed that, "We are all engaged in the task of peeling off the false selves, the programmed selves, the selves created by our families, our culture, our religions."

We are for sure. Central to this, in my view, is re-engaging the feminine.

Based on my experiences and work with clients, I created FEM – the Feminine Engagement Method™ designed to help you to draw also upon your powerful feminine energy, and birth the success you truly deserve and desire. Below I share the five steps involved:

1.) Form – a clear picture of what you would love.

What is most important to you? In the old approach to life, survival was what mattered and we learned that having desires (associated with the feminine) was unrealistic or selfish.

In addition, this approach focused heavily on 'what already is' in order to determine what is possible, thereby excluding the power of other feminine traits such as dreaming and visioning.

However, the process of visualising what we would love can open the doors to new possibilities and permutations that may have never before existed. This has been understood by some of the most brilliant figures in history. On this, Einstein noted that, *"Logic will get you from A to B. Imagination will take you everywhere."*

2.) Feel – what is really coming up for you.

Contrary to what most of us have learned, feelings and intuitions play a central role in all accomplishment.

Feelings act as guidance to let you know if you are on- or off-track from your desires. Mozart was able to create amazing musical compositions that have stood the test of time because, as he said himself, "I pay no attention whatever to anybody's praise or blame. I simply follow my own feelings."

The process of journaling daily is a wonderful way to connect with, express and come to understand your feelings and intuitions.

It is no coincidence that some of the highest achievers on the planet today, such as Oprah Winfrey, have been journaling daily for years and even decades. When we journal we validate this part of ourselves and integrate the feminine in a very meaningful, empowered way.

3.) Focus – on what is going well.

Our education, medical and legal systems have ingrained in us the habit of focusing on problems and trying to solve them with our knowledge and intellect.

Even so, many thought leaders have observed the importance of feelings in this process. This is reflected in William James' comment that, "Success or failure depends more upon attitude than upon capacity."

Adopting an attitude of gratitude, for example, and focusing on what was good really facilitated me in transforming the situation with Sally.

After tense discussion with Julian (I was super tense!), I remember deciding to harness the power of my feelings and focus on what I was happy about. So in my mind, I began appreciating Sally. Every time I felt unhappy with the situation, I began to appreciate specific things about her for which I was grateful.

I began with the most obvious – like the fact that she loved the girls. But then I decided to focus more and more on what I really wanted and any evidence of that already in my life. In Positive Psychology this is called savouring. I appreciated that she was not there two days a week! I appreciated the feeling of peace I had in her absence. I appreciated feeling so good in the mornings without her.

I redirected my energy from trying to find a solution to a problem (traditional approach) and instead focused on what felt good now. We know from Barbara Fredrickson's research that positive emotions broaden the possible scope of action. In my case, appreciating helped me let Sally go – an option that, prior to that, I just could not access.

4.) Free – yourself from the need for approval from other people or ideals.

The download of patriarchy has been to find approval from parents, partners, teachers, doctors, etc.

In my story, I repeatedly brought up the topic of Sally for discussion with Julian. I was annoyed with him when he could not 'see' what I saw. This was true on the surface. At a much deeper level, I was angry with me for needing him to validate me. I didn't want to hurt Sally's feelings either.

In addition, I was committed to a democratic ideal that Julian and I should agree. This was nice and logical, but it prevented me from doing what my children needed me to do.

5.) Follow – your guidance.

Since we have learned that feelings are superfluous many of us second-guess our intuitions and inspirations.

I have put together what I call the *Pause-Proceed Check-In*, which helps to navigate through these one step at a time.

It boils down to this. Unpleasant feelings, on a particular topic, such as discomfort, unease, anger, etc., are calling you to pause (in relation to that issue).

Pause can mean, for example, that you redirect the conversation, adopt a different standpoint, take a break from a relationship, stop walking down that street, hang up the phone, step back from an investment, renegotiate a deal, delegate that task, put the wedding on hold or take just time out to reflect.

With regard to a topic you are feeling good about, these positive emotions are guiding you to proceed.

Proceed means to continue on the path. It does not necessarily mean that you have to finish the whole journey but it is an indication to remain on track and to take the next step (which might be a baby one).

SUMMARY

Evolution is an on-going process. We have championed the process of summoning the masculine and our mental powers in order to progress. Our next step is to integrate also the feminine and her emotions to propel us forward. Working with our wholeness, engaging the feminine will allow us to realise success that is nourishing, harmonious and sustainable for individuals, families, communities and this beautiful planet.

Bibliography

Fredrickson, B.L. (2004). *Gratitude (like other positive emotions) broadens and builds.*

R.A. Emmons & M.E. McCullough (Eds.). *The Psychology of Gratitude (Series in Affective Science)* (pp. 145-166). Oxford University Press.

Seligman, M. (2000). *Positive Psychology: An Introduction.* American Psychologist. Vol. *55* (1), 5-14.

About Deirdre

Emerging as a thought leader in education, Deirdre Morris is passionate about facilitating a shift in the current paradigm, one that moves beyond the patriarchal model which has dominated for centuries and shaped what, why, how, when and where we learn.

Specifically her work is dedicated to Engaging The Feminine™ in education so that children and adults can show up in our wholeness. She creates and delivers teacher and parent training programs as well as educational materials and kits that support this process (for kindergartens, schools and home-schools).

Along with her partner Julian, Deirdre is co-founder of the School of Positivity Project (Malta), where they are co-creating an educational community, in harmony with nature, based on the principles of Positive Psychology and Success. The curriculum is probably the first in the world, stating as a core intention, to engage both the feminine and the masculine so that children and adults can flourish.

Deirdre's academic journey started out with a B.A. in Psychology from NUI Galway, Ireland after which she completed an M.Sc. in Psychology from the University of London (U.K.), and an M.Ed. in Educational Psychology (Special Needs) from Manchester University (U.K.).

For a decade, Deirdre worked as a community-based psychologist with children and adults with learning disabilities. During this time she observed how the dominant model of education demands that children, teachers and parents ignore very important parts of their humanity to achieve results or fit in to the system. This inspired her to explore alternative models, and she decided that if she ever had children she wanted something different for them.

The combination of overcoming her own fertility challenges, coupled with 10 years of supporting women around fertility, gave her huge insight into the creative process and the roles of the masculine and feminine energies in that. For Deirdre, education begins before conception. Through her work with clients, she created an evolved curriculum for mothers-to-be, helping them to reconnect with their true creative power through her on-line forums, coaching programs and private retreats.

Committed to her own personal and professional development, Deirdre is always learning. She has trained as a Family and Systems Constellations Facilitator, a Neuro Linguistic Programming (NLP) Master Practitioner and as Coach. She is also a Human Design Specialist and student of Shamanic Astrology. She loves to travel, has lived in several different countries, and spent a year in India and Nepal exploring mediation and other healing practices.

Deirdre lives in Malta with Julian and their two daughters and frequently visits Spain and her native Ireland.

You can connect with Deirdre at:
EngagingTheFeminine@gmail.com
www.EngagingTheFeminine.com
https://www.facebook.com/pages/Engaging-The-Feminine/346375585556356?fref=ts

CHAPTER 33

THE CONNECTIVE TISSUE OF RELATIONSHIPS

BY GILA BELFAIR

"I stormed into our bedroom and slammed the door behind me. I was shaken, the doorframe cracked. He comes home late without telling me first; leaves me alone with the kids day after day. He promises one thing and does something completely different. I had no idea how to relieve the pain and frustration that I felt at that moment. I had basically given up… I've been repeating myself over and over again for the last ten years and nothing ever changes. It's like talking to a wall. I've had enough. I don't know what to do with him. I hear myself yelling and don't recognize myself anymore… Sometimes I think that I would be better off alone; I can't carry his weight on my shoulders any longer. I can raise our children without him; I don't want to feel this pain anymore…

I sat down on the bed and took a deep breath. I need to get back to the children as soon as I can. It is bad enough that they hear me yelling so often lately… Then he comes into the room and doesn't say a word, which drives me completely mad. He just looks at me. My first instinct is to tell him to get out of the room. I almost say it, but when I look at him, I can see that he's tired too, perhaps even desperate, and something feels different this time. Instead of yelling and trying to explain my perspective, I just sit there silently. We sit in silence… The anger subsides and I'm surprised to discover that it has been replaced with something new, something softer, like a wave that washes over us. I let it happen, it calmed me down. For a moment I wanted to get angry with him again, to make him understand. But something in my body's reaction changed…"

I listen to her speak. Michal and her husband Raz are sitting together in my clinic and I know that we have reached a turning point. It is clear by the expression on Raz's face. He seems less startled by Michal's booming voice and his silence is accompanied by a smile this time. It is a closed-off smile but definitely a smile. It is our fourth session together. The first one was very tumultuous with Michal being very dominant and taking up a lot of room. In those sessions we worked mainly on the "how": how to listen, how to convey a message, how to escape from the chaos and emotional mess. It enabled Michal to let go, open up and be aware not only of Raz's physical presence, but also of his feelings; that is the moment of connection.

The moment something changes and there is even the smallest sign of emotional availability towards the other person ("I can see that he's tired, too."), connections are made. The more connections that are formed – the stronger the relationship becomes. The process begins when we step outside of our individual stories and allow ourselves to receive something from the person in front of us. A connection is formed, one of the many connections that already exist in the relationship, and more connections to come. I call this series of connections the *connectivity tissue of relationships*. Not only do they enhance a relationship, they also help develop the individual personality of each person within the relationship. Forming and maintaining a good relationship is an enormous challenge. Naturally, many points of contention arise that force us to leave our comfort zone, enabling us to enhance our attributes and qualities and reach a higher level of functioning as we become more flexible, creative, patient, forgiving, enabling, and so forth.

I borrowed the concept of "connective tissue" from the field of medicine, specifically biology. I have adapted this concept to describe the process of building understanding and awareness in inter-personal relationships. There is much to be learned from the role of the connective tissue, which is a perfect demonstration of the saying that "the whole is greater than the sum of its parts". This tissue maintains the "relationship" between the various organs in our bodies. Developing the connective tissue between two people can create something more complete than each one on their own. This is no easy task.

Here I offer a brief description of the role of connective tissue in the human body, and explain what one can deduce from it regarding connections between couples, or any other type of inter-personal relationships, for that matter. Try to imagine the relationship as a virtual body with its own qualities and characteristics. This may simplify the understanding of the important role of the connective tissue.

Connective tissue is **supporting tissue that connects and delineates different parts of our bodies**. Changes to the chemical composition of the basic tissue and the ratio and quantity of cells and fibers create connective tissue with varying characteristics. Connective tissue is designed to **support, serve and protect our organs**.

The skeleton is connective tissue that provides osseous and mechanical support for the body. This firm connective tissue maintains the shape and form of our body and protects vital organs such as the brain, heart and lungs.

The skeleton represents the **foundations** of your relationship. What are the things that are most important to you? Which values guide you in your relationship? What can maintain and stabilize your relationship? In order to identify these things, you will have to consider which aspects of your relationship are most important to both of you. The answers may include openness, loyalty, mutuality, love, sharing, caring, success, personal space, security, prosperity, communication, honesty and more.

Tendons, ligaments and cartilage are parts of tissue that connect the muscles to the skeleton and join the various parts of the skeleton. This connective tissue enables **movement**, and therefore is somewhat flexible.

Once you have identified the foundations of your relationship, the next step is to understand how to apply them. What **actions** do you choose to take that are congruent with the foundations of your relationship? How do you express and implement the things that are most important to you as part of your daily routine? Needless to emphasize, you are two different people and each has their own practical understanding of those foundations. Do your actions correspond with one another? For example, some may express love through emotional discourse while others express it through physical contact (though the two can certainly be combined…work it out between the two of you).

Your fundamental values, like your actions, are consciously determined, but the success of those actions depends upon your beliefs, which are less obvious and accessible as they are based in your subconscious. Be conscious of your internal dialogue because it will determine the ultimate outcome. Your beliefs about yourselves are a form of energetic communication. In his fascinating work *Biology of Belief*, Dr. Lipton reminds us that atoms are comprised of invisible energy and that every structure in the universe (including human beings), emits unique energy. But he goes far beyond this to prove, as an epigenetics researcher, that our emotional system, our beliefs and our consciousness affect the genetic code of the cell! The membranes that form the cell wall receive signals that can alter behavior. He writes that "the true secret of life lies in understanding the elegantly simple biological mechanism of the magical membrane – the mechanisms by which your body translates environmental signals into behavior."[1]

Soft connective tissue: this liquid tissue **serves and protects other organs.** This connective tissue defines the boundaries of the various cells by transmitting signals. In other words, it enables passage of communication substances (such as hormones), in order to share information, and also supports the body by passing nutrients and waste from high concentration to low-concentration areas, and even helps renew tissue and preserve balance within the body.

Soft tissue reflects something deep within you. It is **intimacy** itself. It is the sanctified place that exists between you, which goes beyond your external image and is in fact, a deep, spiritual and emotional journey. It has its own unique pace and holds the key to revealing and understanding your true self. This intimacy is manifested in many different ways. Unlike your foundations and actions which are often manifested externally, so that people who are close to you can say, "we know them and they are this and that," this is a private, intimate world that belongs to you and you alone. If you succeed in building this ever-so-delicate "tissue", you will benefit from a deep and profound relationship. You will each express your true inner selves through the delicate and attentive interaction that you share. This occurs in the most hidden and vulnerable layers of your existence; in the most delicate and sensitive part of your souls. This process becomes possible through attentiveness and a deep commitment to your partner. Trust is built up

1. Dr. Bruce Lipton, *Biology Of Belief* (Hay House, 2005), p.45

over the years as you learn to confidently entrust yourself to another person who observes you and reflects something of yourself. This actual tissue in the body is so delicate that it is almost invisible. It hints at aspects of your relationship that are hidden from the public eye. It is assembled by the small codes, communication, acts of love, giving, caring, commitment and responsibilities that you share. Developing this "tissue" involves discomfort, contention, power struggles and pain, but this cathartic process unravels the deepest qualities that we possess.

Another connective tissue is the **fat tissue** that pads the organs and stores energy (when there is inadequate available food, the body will derive energy from the stores in fat tissue). It also isolates body heat and serves as a shock absorber.

The fat tissue in your relationship is your "savings account." It is the credit that you give to each other, the reserves of your shared commitment that can protect you during times of crisis– whether external (illness, termination of employment, loss of any kind), or something that occurs between you such as burnout and routine. If these reserves exist, there will be more reasons to try to breathe new life into your relationship rather than give up on it.

It is important to realize that these are not "different stages" in the development of the relationship. It does not mean that once you identify the foundations of your relationship, you can sit back and relax. It is important to remain constantly aware of and attentive to all that happens to you as individuals and as a couple. The issues in relationships are as alive as connective tissue. There is constant movement, communication, diffusion, signaling, holding; it is like a dance.

It is imperative to view the success of your intimate relationship as a process that is constantly growing and deepening.

Connective tissue exists between organs. Each organ interacts with other organs while the connective tissue maintains the boundaries between them so that each can perform optimally and contribute its part to the function of the entire body. The heart, for example, has one distinct role and the lungs have another; their roles are not confounded, each knows its place and its responsibility within the complete system that forms the human body. In order to develop a healthy and satisfying relationship, each individual must remain authentic and unique. They must know who they are, acknowledge their value and be aware of their individual existence within their relationship. Maintaining personal space and recognizing your value as an individual is your responsibility to yourself and as part of a couple. This awareness strengthens and vitalizes the connective tissue between you to facilitate an ongoing, genuine and healthy mutual communication.

In conclusion, I believe in the utmost importance of sharing this model and raising awareness of it. In this chapter, I have addressed relationships between couples, but this model applies to all kinds of relationships: parents and children, siblings, extended families, friends, professional teams, different nations, religions, enemies, the environment and more. Understanding and deepening our perception of the role of the connective tissue in the body, and projecting it into our own lives, will enable us to create a more tolerant world. "Enable" is a key word in understanding the connective tissue, because that is its main role: to enable all of the organs to fulfill their roles, their purpose. An enabling world – that is the heart and soul of human success; to enable us to comprehend the bonds between us while respecting each individual's uniqueness.

About Gila

For the last 30 years, Gila has helped her patients to progress and achieve their goals, both personal and interpersonal. She was a social worker for a municipal welfare department, conducted community projects, and was appointed a manager in the department. She taught and trained NLP and guided imagery to therapists and instructors in the field. Gila has her own private clinic for more than ten years now, in which she combines the tools of Gestalt therapy, NLP, guided imagery, communication skills, and more.

During her years of experience she has faced the complexities and challenges that relationships entail. Gila has built a model that enables people to acquire a better attitude as well as the tools to improve their relationships. Her model is based on the roles and functions of the connective tissue in our body. Understanding this connection can assist each and every one of us to implement more meaningful and satisfactory relationships with the people in our lives.

Gila has a B.A. in Social Work from Bar-Ilan University and an M.A. in Communications from Ben-Gurion University. She studied Gestalt Therapy at Tel-Aviv University, as well as NLP Trainer, at the Retter Institute.

Gila is passionate about spreading this message about interrelationship connective tissue. She does so with her patients, as well as by writing, speaking and teaching the model.

CHAPTER 34

MINDFUL MARKETING...
GET TO THE SOUL OF SOCIAL MEDIA SUCCESS

BY JANET FOUTS

I live in the heart of Silicon Valley with innovation buzzing all around me. Businesses start up rich with ideas and the talent to make things happen, and come and go in the blink of an eye. Sometimes the frenzied pace is invigorating, sometimes it's overwhelming. Businesses pivot on a dime and we have to keep up with change and public opinion at the same time—on and offline.

Social media enables us to reflect changes in almost real-time and communicate with our market effectively, even create community around the brand for feedback and develop thought leadership. With today's laser-directed communication, everyone everywhere has the potential to be a social marketer too. It's up to you whether or not you want to reach local, national or international audiences. The world is yours to engage.

That makes our jobs both easier and harder. We are constantly being sprayed with a fire hose of information and must be sure our message rises above the rest and stands out with our values and facts accurately represented. A traditional marketer may quail at the apparent chaos. The mindful marketer sees an opportunity and can rise above the noise to be heard.

THE PROBLEM WITH TRADITIONAL MARKETING ON SOCIAL NETWORKS

When was the last time you saw a post from a brand on a social network and thought to yourself, "Wow, they really get me!" Yeah, that doesn't happen to me much either. More often than not brands post about their product, or maybe – just to be different – share a user comment about how great their product is. Feeling all warm and fuzzy now? I doubt it.

Imagine, for just a moment, how powerful that same message could be if it were like talking to a friend. Someone who knows you, what you like and its impact on your life. If you already had a relationship with the person wouldn't it be easier for you to connect? It's not that hard at all really, it just takes learning to pay attention. I call this mindful social marketing.

Mindful social marketing simply means being mindful of the needs of your market as individuals and the content you create for them. It's about engaging them rather than the traditional "spray and pray" tactics to a mass of unidentifiable nameless drones. I'm not a drone are you? It's a way to tune your messaging for the best possible impact and to streamline your workflow, making you both more effective and more efficient by relating more personally to the human reading your message.

MINDFULNESS IN BUSINESS

The technological revolution brings us glorious things but it's also created an environment in which we are inundated with data and alerts. We need to shut the doors on the hubbub so we can hear ourselves think!

Businesses see their workforce distracted and unfocused and they know they must help everyone to a level of sanity and civility in order to be able to serve the needs of their customers and continue to thrive personally and professionally.

When mindfulness practices are put into place, businesses reap the rewards of focused and happy employees who work better together and think before they act. This informs their day-to-day decisions and their relationships within the company as well as with their customers.

Businesses like General Mills, Proctor and Gamble, Aetna and Google introduce employees to the concepts of mindful business, training their minds to be clearer, more focused and connected as a team, working toward a common goal.

MARKETING IS SLOWER TO ADAPT

Unfortunately in many cases, engagement on social media platforms doesn't seem to carry through. I still see the same old-school marketing tactics, spamming and broadcasting "buy, buy, buy!" without a real focus on the receiver of messages. Marketing feels a little stiff and, well, "markety" doesn't it?

It's time we paid attention to how we interact here with others as thoughtfully as we do when we meet them face to face or sit down with them for a cup of tea.

To respond is positive, to react is negative.

~ Zig Ziglar

Today's Internet user is smart. They see through posts intended to make them take action. They see fakery plain as day. They demand to talk to a real human, considerate of their needs and who responds thoughtfully rather than mindless reactions.

Time and time again, I've seen corporations reap the rewards of a thoughtful 1-on-1 response to a user. Whether it's an answer to a problem the person is having, a simple thank you for a comment or even an apology for something gone wrong, it's the humanity of the response that matters. Not only does the customer feel good about the interaction; but when they tell their friends, an affinity develops between the brand and the community.

MARKETING WITH INTENTION

I invite you to take a moment and look over your last 10 posts to social media networks. If you were someone who's never met you and doesn't know your brand, what would you think of you? Snarky? Insightful? Informative? A walking sales pitch? Now, how do you want people to perceive you?

Certainly we all want to be seen as human and helpful. People relate to other people, not sales pitches and marketing jargon.

MAKING IT WORK

When we create even the smallest social post, it is released into the universe of the Internet. Once it's out there it can't be taken back. How do you want your brand perceived? Think about the user who sees that post out of context and wonders what you were thinking. How can you engage them positively and attract them to your offering? The mindful social marketer is always alert to how what we do affects those we touch, and looks for opportunities to learn, educate, entertain and show respect.

LEARNING FROM OTHERS

I've been working in online marketing for over 20 year and seen fads come and go. I love to dissect how marketers work and learn from how their markets respond to various strategies. This informs how I work with my own clients. Observing what others do and putting it to practice in your own situation helps you be an agile marketer, ready to roll with the punches and changes in the market.

Listen more than you talk. Nobody learned anything by hearing themselves speak.

~ Richard Branson (on the best advice he got from his father)

GETTING STARTED IS SIMPLE – LISTEN

There are a number of social listening tools you can use to search social networks for mentions of your product, service or better yet, the problem that your service solves and what your competition is doing. Use this to learn about the needs of your market and talk to them. Learning to listen enables every marketer to be the best communicator you can be.

WHAT'S YOUR NARRATIVE?

If you want to really get people engaged and supporting you and your brand, you need to have a running narrative that intrigues and engages them over and over. This is at the core of what drives you, and gives context to the stories you share.

Some may say their story isn't big enough or interesting enough to start conversations on social media sites, but hey, wait a minute. Your product exists because there was a need for it, right? Someone, somewhere, had a passion for it.

In the 2005 film Robots, Rodney robot the aspiring inventor remembers the slogan of Bigweld, the company's founder: "See a need, fill a need" – something at the core of every inventor's drive. It inspires our hero to not only solve a problem but also help others, and it revitalizes the company he works for. While the story is endearing, it also tells us what we need to be doing as social marketers.

We need to see the needs, fill them and create a narrative that tells that story in an approachable and relatable way. If our message doesn't resonate with the people we want to reach it falls on deaf ears.

So, let's say you want to reach stay-at-home parents. You have the perfect all-natural product to clean up those messy spills that are part of day-to-day life with kids.

But that's a very small part of their day. What else are their issues? If you're not sharing parenting information, tips and tricks on education, getting kids to eat, home care, kid friendly events and the occasional funny parenting jokes, you're missing out being part of their lives. You're just a blip on the radar when they clean up a spill. But, if you can create a relationship of sharing, learning and laughing together over the little things, parents will treat you as a friend and support you because they like you.

Now think about your story again. Ask your friends and employees what they think about the product. How does it compare to others like it? How do they use it and how does it relate to the rest of their day? Pull all of this information together and you're building your narrative.

FOUR STEPS TO SOCIAL MARKETING SUCCESS: THE FOUR A'S

To be successful using mindful social media marketing, pay attention to these four key elements:

1. Audience
Most sales people create "buyer personas" around the person they want to reach and the characteristics of this person. They know what they like and what they don't like, what their favorite color is, if they prefer

phone calls to email or even a tweet here and there. They know which of the products in their line is the best fit for each one and customize their sales offers to each persona.

As a marketer you may think you know exactly who needs your product, but you may also be very surprised when you do some listening. Do your research and test it against what you already know in your heart. Talk to your sales staff and especially your customers. Adjust accordingly.

Do some searches with those listening tools I mentioned and learn more:

- Who needs your product or service?
- What problem do you solve for them?
- How can you serve them?
- What are their other issues?
- What do they do every day?
- Which networks seem to be the most popular with them?
- How do they talk to other brands, including your competitors?
- What do they share on social media sites?

Know your audience. Put yourself in their shoes and pay attention to what you feel. It's your knowledge of your market that resonates with them and creates that coveted relationship.

2. Affinity

It's a lot easier to talk to people you already know, isn't it? If you've done your homework this is going to be easy. You know your market pretty well by now. How does your story relate to your customers' needs and interests?

- Use your narrative to create opportunities to engage users.
- Answer questions and ask questions.
- Help people solve problems even if it isn't related to your services.

When people connect and feel they know a person at the other end of those Tweets, that affinity develops trust. You want them to understand that you really do care about their needs. You want them to think, "Hey, they really get me." And you DO.

3. Agility

Rules and best practices on social platforms change constantly. Customers' needs change, products change, market needs change too. Your messaging must change accordingly in order to retain trust. You have to be willing and able to respond to changes without hesitation, constantly listening and fine-tuning to serve their needs better.

Being the first person with the answers keeps you at the forefront of people's minds. Become a resource for information about the industry you serve and your market will respond with loyalty. They'll also help you spread the word as a trusted resource.

4. Activate

Once you've established a trust relationship with your market and they see you as a valued resource, they will start sharing the great information you are producing with their friends. They are now your extended marketing team, and will evangelize for you if you give them the power. Activate their desire to serve others by being mindful of what you post. Remember, you're giving them the gift of being a resource for their own networks too. Ask for shares occasionally, but in general make your words worthy of sharing. They will, trust me they will.

SUCCESS!

Success through mindful use of social marketing is achievable and that's a fact. It takes time, oh yes it does, but it is time well spent and will reap rewards well beyond selling one product. As you develop relationships with your audience, they begin to look to you not just as a sales channel, but also as a trusted friend who shares advice and stories that entertain and educate. They share those stories with their friends, and their friends with their friends. That is where the magic happens, all because you took the mindful path to success. Imagine how great that is going to feel!

About Janet

Janet Fouts helps clients realize their marketing goals for social media engagement using mindful business practices to stay focused, build thought leadership and get fantastic, measurable results. She's been an active digital marketer since she created her first website way back in 1993, and she's been in love with the tech world ever since.

Her background as a chef in the fine restaurants of San Francisco led Janet to co-found one of the first venture-backed online communities for the restaurant industry in 1996 which won many awards for design and storytelling, and she was lauded as one of the top business women in San Francisco by San Francisco's *Business Times*. Ever since, she's dedicated her business savvy to nurturing online community through a variety of social networks, websites and blogs. She and her company have received many awards. Most recently she was listed as one of the top 50 Marketing Thought Leaders Over 50 by *Brand Quarterly Magazine* and one of the top 100 Giving Influencers on Twitter by *Give Local America*.

She has been quoted in *USA Today, Forbes Magazine,* and *Thought Leader Life* and her writing is syndicated on several business-to-business magazines online, including *Business2Community* and *Social Media Today*. She has authored 4 books on social media marketing and her 5th is due out in July 2015.

Janet is CEO of Tatu Digital Media, a social media marketing agency in Silicon Valley, serving brands from social good organizations like Human Journey, co-founded by Archbishop Desmond Tutu, to tech startups and Fortune 50 corporations.

Janet is respected as a corporate trainer on all things social media, and conducts seminars around the world on the "nuts and bolts" of how to make social media part of the company's marketing program. She is a frequently requested speaker at international conferences on business, making social media approachable with actionable tips attendees can put right to use. Janet hosts a video podcast show available on YouTube, Spreaker and iTunes.

Connect with Janet at:
Janet@janetfouts.com
JanetFouts.com
TatuDigital.com
Twitter.com/Jfouts
Linkedin.com/in/JanetFouts
MindfulSocialMarketing.com

CHAPTER 35

FROM THE *SOLE* OF SUCCESS TO THE *SOUL* OF SUCCESS

BY JEAN SCHOENECKER, C.H.

I smiled as a gigantic billboard loomed ahead on the highway: "GO BIG. BE SEEN." It was obviously a plug for the billboard company to prospective advertisers, but I knew it was put there for me to see. It was like God pointing out how many spiritual signposts I've missed in my life and that a billboard is now required so there are no mistakes! I was thinking small, and "GO BIG. BE SEEN" was a humorous nudge to move forward on some big decisions that were before me.

A day later, a curious hospital billboard seemed to shout at me: "LIFE IS IN THE LIVING OF IT." Not in the planning of it, not in the worrying about it, not in the managing of it, but in the living of it. Right here in this moment. Now! I contemplated the many ways inspiration and divine personal messages are delivered to me now that I am paying attention and aware.

I didn't always pay attention. I see now that I experienced a good portion of my adult life in a version of default mode. Like a SmartPhone in factory setting I chugged along on my path, oblivious to the fact that I had many more "apps" available to me that I was unaware of and was not tapping into. Operating by default leaves so many capabilities untested and untapped. I know so many others who have also been living that way, fearful of change and mistaking safety for success. Default is not

311

living. Why is it that we have to hit bottom to see from a different place? A job loss after 15 years was the final catalyst for me, but the Universe had provided many clues that I missed.

As the oldest of 6 children of hard-working parents, I embraced my type-A Capricorn left-brain tendencies and I busily went to work performing my duties and living my successful life. I believed I was hard wired for hard work, doing it myself, pushing to be the best, being a leader and never giving up. I was an honors student, competitive, and looking for the ladder of success in all life endeavors. My liberal arts degree did not compel me to any specific path, so I did what I knew after years of working in our family shoe business; I moved to another state and became a buyer for a shoe company.

I immersed myself in my 30-year career in the retail and wholesale shoe industry, which had both benefits and drawbacks for my husband and young daughter. I enjoyed many promotions and job changes over the years. I joked that when other people were at church on Sunday morning, I was in the office working quietly and getting some sort of inspiration. I was so passionate about all of it. In 1998 I joined my dream company, with a brand I loved that was introducing a footwear line. I loved everything about it, and I continued to drive myself to be the best. I was extremely busy being successful!

And, I loved making money, servicing customers, spending days on the road, and running a growing and profitable territory. I happily dispensed advice and created business strategies. Everyone wanted the job I had. Wonderful company. Wonderful people. Luxury brand. Glamour. Travel. I loved it for a long time, until I hit that place that so many others before me have written about. Something bigger began to gnaw at my subconscious. That feeling of "Is this all there is?" really took hold in me.

I was restless. I was discontented. I felt stuck. I went to Jack Canfield's first Maui retreat in 2010, fully expecting to come back knowing what I was to be doing, who I was meant to be, my life mapped out according to the matrix of my yet-to-be-defined life purpose. I bought every self-help book, attended seminars and programs all over the country in search of myself. I was also thoroughly petrified about making a change. Although my heart was yearning for change and expansion, the shoe business was all I knew. I defined myself as an introvert in an extrovert's job, and I was in a familiar, predictable, comfortable, boring groove. What lay beyond was somewhat terrifying to me, and I was confused.

I ignored signs that I had missed a fork in the road. The Universe was giving me a big thumbs down, but I was not paying attention. My "series of unfortunate events" might have gotten someone else's attention, but you already know I need a billboard. Our brand was in decline, and business was challenging. The company was bought by an international behemoth. My Dad was experiencing health challenges. I was diagnosed with chronic lyme disease, and struggled to complete tasks I had performed for years. Years of being gone as much as I was home had taken a toll on our family. I felt like a phantom Mom. I had lost weight and was not taking care of myself. I was not honest with myself, and was not honest with my friends and family. I moved through the motions of my life without actually living it. As Esther Hicks said, "Humans put up with so much mediocrity, it's astounding." I missed the now-obvious signs that my life was amiss.

In 2013, the company eliminated my position, an event that I lovingly refer to as my big "pro-motion" as it jolted me off my familiar center and I had to get into motion in a new way. I was in unfamiliar terrain. At least I got the message that the Universe was hearing me even if I wasn't listening to myself, as I had written a letter of resignation a year prior that I had never submitted to my boss. I found it in my desk drawer when I cleaned it out. I set out on a mission to get my mojo back!

I had defined SUCCESS as absence of failure, as doing the right things, as being the best, and while those definitions may inform success at some level, I now know the "soul of success" to be far more enriching! It escaped me that all that pursuit of "successfulness" was actually keeping me from true success. I no longer buy into the Woody Allen philosophy that "85% of success is just showing up." If the body shows up and the soul stays home, the sweetness of real success can't put down roots. I no longer find joy in "just showing up." I am more interested in how I am showing up and what I am showing up for.

I am, as we all are, always in the process of "becoming," but I refuse to do it by default any longer. I am deliberate about all of my intentions. I honor my own values now, and not others' definition of value. I am embracing all parts of me, and taking responsibility for my choices and my decisions. I am a different person, and my "vocation" does not define me. Success is within, and I am calling it forth.

Bookstore shelves overflow with self-help books. I own many of them. There are a million authors and a million strategies for success, but in the end, all you need is one. It's not on a shelf. It's not in a book or a program. It's not a new process or a new guru. *It's in you. It is you.* This was a revelation for me when I finally got it.

Raymond Charles Barker points out in *The Power of Decision* (1968) that we are born with an emotional need for success and a natural drive towards it. I love his simple success formula:

1. Know what you want

2. Decide it shall happen

3. Act upon the decision

. . . That's the FORMULA. Had I internalized this earlier, I surely would've saved thousands of dollars, hours in seminars, searching for who and what would save me. Jack Canfield amplifies these simple steps into a more detailed program in *The Success Principles*.

If you find yourself in a place of restlessness and yearning for more "soul" in your success, you are in a crowd of thousands. I can only share with you the observations of my journey, where I have taken many steps and missteps. My journey has also been the journey and message of many others. It's not new news but perhaps this is your day to hear and act!

- PAY ATTENTION TO SPIRITUAL SIGNPOSTS, and if you are on the wrong road, turn off now. Do not wait. We don't have to hit bottom before we can start in the other direction. Trust your intuition. Your gut knows. Your soul will respond with elation when you get the message and move in new directions. I heard Dr. Brene Brown say on a call recently "We are so tired of being afraid." It can be scary, but the payoff is so huge.

- PASSION MATTERS. Creating is a sacred process, and what you are drawn to is drawing you. If you are not passionate about what you are doing and creating now, it's time to make some changes. Know that passions change as you do, and follow the passion path. One of my mentors, Janet Attwood, says, "When faced with a decision, a choice, or an opportunity, always choose in favor of your passions." This is a great guiding principle to follow. Life really is supposed to be fun, and there is no fun in tolerating a job or a partner or a circumstance that you are not passionate about! Life is immensely joyful and pleasurable when your passion is high.

- CONNECT TO FIND MEANING FOR YOU. Connect with yourself through meditation for insight and inspiration. Becoming a daily meditator was so critical for me, and that simple process changed the way I view everything. It connected me to something greater in myself, and I began to hear my inner voice and accept its guidance. New ideas and and thoughts were born. There are so many tools to help, and everyone can benefit from meditation. Dina Proctor's 3x3 process is so simple and takes only nine minutes a day. Connect with Spirit often in the way that works for you. I used to think I had to do it all alone, but I now feel a deep connection to my Creator, and have greater trust in myself. Approach connections with others with a service mindset. Only connections can lead you to a whole-hearted living. Soul and heart have to be in the game to succeed.

- BE GRATEFUL FOR ALL PARTS OF THE JOURNEY. Everything has a reason and a gift, even the illnesses, the job losses, and the fractured relationships. I was given the chance to be a better Mom and wife, and spent the summer with my daughter before she left for college. What a blessing! I was given a chance to begin a new career that I love, and now I am able to serve more people in a new and meaningful way. I am so deeply grateful for everything that happened to me. Moving past guilt and blame quickly accelerates the changes.

- MAKE DECISIONS. The day I woke up and realized that I had so many career options was the day my world shifted. I knew I would thrive outside of the shoe industry. Realize that you always have choices and decisions to make, and take responsibility for making them. Procrastination is always the worst decision. If you don't make the decision, someone will make it for you. There are always many more choices than you can imagine from which to choose. Decide to decide, and take even a small step in that direction. Watch the momentum build and your dreams materialize.

- FREEDOM IS AN INSIDE JOB. Bondage is, too. I received a postcard advertising health risk assessments that read, "WHAT'S GOING ON INSIDE MATTERS EVEN MORE." The photo depicted a barefooted woman standing in front of her shoe closet making a footwear choice for her outfit. I laughed, knowing this was another message for me. Life is partnering with us all, and if you feel trapped or stuck, change is required. Pretending that other people and conditions are keeping you stuck is a delusion. Only you can set yourself free.

What if SOUL is the only missing link to SUCCESS in every facet of life? I have come to believe that. Now that I have allowed my soul to speak, I take risks, I am willing to be vulnerable, and I have jumped into a new world, yet I am grounded in a new way. I feel sure-footed on my path. Following my truth has inspired courage and confidence. Pay attention. Go within. Hear your heart.

My friend Patty called me with a message in a Yogi tea bag, which sums it all up:

JOY IS THE ESSENCE OF SUCCESS.

Joy is in you. Success is in you. No one else's opinion of what your success looks like matters. What provides joy and meaning for you is totally attainable, for you were not created to live small or play small. Embrace your essence of success and be the light in the world you were brought here to be. Embody that joy and success moment-to-moment, as that will surely add up to a life of joy and success.

When you touch that place of your own "soul of success," you will know it and know you must follow that path. Your life will never be the same. Go forth in JOY and be who you are here to be!

About Jean

Mother, Wife, Mentor, Friend

Certified Hypnotherapist

Certified Success Coach and Passion Test Facilitator

Certified Truly Heal Wellness Coach

Platinum Leader – Sisel International: purveyor of the world's finest toxic-free products and nutriceuticals

Former road warrior, recovering perfectionist, lyme disease advocate, professional self-help junkie, dog lover, student of life, amateur ice skater, marathon runner, avid reader, heart-centered entrepreneur, fine-wine aficionado, foodie, meditator, uplifter, seeker, snow lover, problem solver, spiritual vagabond.

Jean Schoenecker, C.H. now passionately pursues health in body, mind and spirit for herself and her clients, distributors and customers. She resides in Wisconsin with her husband of 29 years, her dog, and occasionally her college-age daughter.

Reach Jean at: www.thesoulofsuccess.com
email: jean.schoenecker@gmail.com
Or call: (262) 309-2521

CHAPTER 36

THE ENTREPRENEUR INSIDE

BY JEFF POWELL

One of my first memories is of watching TV news footage of American soldiers in Vietnam. I was probably only four but I have a distinct recollection of wanting to somehow help those guys. Now, all these years later, as a disabled veteran, I am dedicated to helping every man and woman who has proudly served our country to find peace and prosperity when they return home, especially when they come home unable to do some of the things they could do before they left.

I also want to share with these heroes the philosophy I live by. No matter what kind of adversity life hands us, when it comes to luck we make our own. I know something about luck and the lack of it. My life has had some very good times, but there were many rough days and some that were downright horrifying.

It was around the age nine when life became particularly difficult for me. My father was murdered and I ended up living with my grandmother in a tough neighborhood. My father's murderer was caught and sent to prison but the death of my father forced me to grow up fast. I didn't handle it well.

By the time I was sixteen, I had transferred from one school to another and gotten into more than my fair share of trouble. But then something happened that changed the course of my life. One day, trying to get into a new school, I found myself sitting in the assistant principal's office. We had just started to talk when she was called out of her office to help a student who had started choking. I followed her and because of CPR training that I had undergone in ROTC, I was able to help save the student's life. It was an eye-opening experience for me; I would never have thought I was capable of doing something so important. For my efforts, I received the ROTC Medal of Heroism and a letter from the state governor. And my journey down a bad road was stopped right then.

A couple of years later, I was tested again. The man who murdered my father had been released from prison and had moved into my neighborhood. One snowy day, I saw him on the street. He had locked his keys in his car. I decided to help and I came out of my house with a coat hanger. I helped him get his car unlocked and after doing so, we noticed that his tire was flat. I offered to change his tire, as well. The man had no idea who I was, or what my connection to him was. While I wanted to tell him, and ask him why he did such a terrible thing to my father, I kept quiet. I'd done what I thought was right for this man – the same that I would have done for anyone. By not confronting him when I had the chance, I knew I had put behind me the worst thing that had ever happened to me. I had forgiven this man. That freed me from the hatred I'd carried with me for most of my life.

Years later, I went on to proudly serve in the United States Navy. However, I became disabled during my last muster at Port Hueneme. Upon my discharge, my commanding officer asked me to continue supporting our fellow veterans. "Sir, yes sir," I responded. "I will do my best."

Initially, I wasn't able to keep my promise. After my discharge, I lost my way. I even ended up homeless. With the help of the Department of Veterans Affairs, I was able to figure things out; I learned how important it is to have supportive and caring mentors.

In 2008, I started "Online Verified Veteran Supporter," a site dedicated to supporting veterans in their need. I wanted to show other veterans how to help themselves by learning simple things like how to search for jobs and what to do if they become homeless. I even took my idea to the Department of Veterans Affairs, where the focus of my goals was to bring people together – including business owners, veterans, and elected officials – to help promote ways that inspire people to help other people.

It's been more than fourteen years since I accepted my CO's request and since then, I've dedicated my free time to supporting our veterans, doing things I would not have thought myself capable when I started. Even during some of the tougher times of my life, my passion was to support the VA and my fellow veterans. In the course of this, I've become an entrepreneur. And what I've discovered is that I had everything I needed for success inside of me the whole time. You have it, too. And if there's one other thing I've learned, it's that there's no time like the present for someone to put his God-given entrepreneurial talents into action. Are you ready to get started?

If so, did you know that just by turning on your computer, you could be taking your first step towards owning a business? Technology has made it possible. With your laptop, a connection to the Internet, and the guts to make it happen, you can change your world. Today could be a turning point. When you run your own business, you make your own decisions. You take your own risks. You make your own rewards. And you'll stretch your potential beyond what you ever imagined.

The fact is, with the possibilities of the Internet, the world of work is shifting. In one direction are lowered expectations and plenty of burger-flipping. In the other is the independence and control that can come from business ownership. Which future is yours? In today's digital age, many of those who once waited for instructions are now giving them instead. Your new dream isn't about following someone else's orders. It's about vision, action, and the commitment to doing whatever it takes to do the things you want to do. To be your own person.

But there's more to it than just wishing for it. Wishful thinking alone will not achieve success. Success is attracted by putting your ideas and concepts into action. So what ideas do you have? If you can't think of a good idea for a business, here are a few questions to help you get started and get the mind thinking:

- What inspires you?
- If you could do *anything*, what would it be?
- What do you do exceptionally well?

- Is there a product or service that you've looked for but couldn't find?

- Can you think of a new or under-served market? *(Maybe the military community?)*

- Is there something that frustrates you, and you know you could do it better?

- Is there something that's missing in your community that you could provide?

- Do you have skills that you can use in a non-traditional way?

There's an idea for a business in there somewhere. The key is to make sure your business idea is different, something unique that's unavailable or hard to find. If you can't find any competition, you may be on to something. But even if there is competition, you can surely find a way to separate yourself from the pack. Find that one thing that sets you apart that others will find valuable.

Have you already figured it out? Write it down. Write it in 100 words or less. This will help crystallize it in your mind. It will make your business idea more tangible and real. Seeing your idea in print will give you motivation.

If you need a little more inspiration, there are plenty of online resources available. Subscribe to the Springwise.com blog for your daily "fix of entrepreneurial ideas." Springwise scans the world for unique and innovative business ventures like the bicycle made from cardboard and the plastic brick that can save millions of gallons of water per year. Check out the crowd-funding sites like Kickstarter.com and Indiegogo.com. You're not after a "me too" product, but you might find some inspiration. You'll also see how some really creative people are presenting their businesses. There is much to be learned from the success of others. *All in all, remember this: your business idea has to be something that will make people stop and take notice.*

But of course it doesn't end with an idea. That's just where it begins. The next step is to get your idea out there. The next step is *marketing* your idea. And contrary to what most people think, marketing isn't complicated or mysterious. We market ourselves all our lives. You did it every time you were transferred and wanted to find new friends. You do it whenever you meet somebody for the first time. Marketing your company means doing the same kind of thing – building relationships with people who want to hear from you, hang out with you, and see the value in knowing you.

The key is to find the group of people who are looking for what you have, the people who want to meet you and your company. Then, you gain their trust and demonstrate the value of doing business with you. This means, first, going where your customers are. And then listening to their reaction to your product or service idea and gaining important knowledge from their opinions.

Think for a moment as to where you might find your customers. Facebook? eBay? Pinterest? Instagram? LinkedIn? You Tube? The Reddit bulletin boards? A coffee shop downtown? A trade show? A networking meeting you found on Meetup? The gym where you work out? The places to meet your customers are almost endless. You don't need an expensive advertising campaign. Just go where the buyers are. Make a list of the top five places your potential customers are waiting for you. Then find a way to go meet them! In this day and age, we are infinitely connected.

Remember to be patient. Building relationships with customers is probably going to take some time. You can't barge into the room and try to take over. It's not about hitting the audience in the face with your product or your idea. It's about getting involved in their conversations and getting them thinking about you. It's about demonstrating how valuable it would be to know you because you have something important to offer. It's often word of mouth. Think about some ways you can get people to notice you.

Your ultimate goal: converting strangers into customers and making them so happy they'll insist that everyone they know do business with you, too. Nothing builds a company better than referrals. If happy customers refer you to their friends and their friends refer you to *their* friends, a business can grow geometrically. At that point, you'll build an unstoppable momentum.

Remember that people like a story. Don't just be a nameless, faceless company with a new product. Be a *person* with a new product and a story behind it. Be you. **Have you** overcome adversity? Did your military service teach you something profound? Do you have a "you won't believe this" tale about how you discovered your product? It wasn't easy to get to where you are. Be proud of your journey and tell others about it. Be memorable.

Your drive and your passion will ultimately lead you to success. I can't teach those things. But my guess is that if you're reading this book, you already have all the motivation you need. You're already the kind of person who is driven to succeed. The rest is mere detail: the right idea, marketed to the right people. This is all within you right now. It's just a question of having it come to the surface. I did it and I had no special magical gifts or talents. I shared with you my story so you could see that I had nothing more to start with than you have now – just a passion for helping veterans and a little dedication to figuring out the best way to do that. . . and to develop my idea and connect with the right people. And before I knew it, my ideas became wonderful hobbies right before my very eyes. I discovered an entrepreneur within and I'm certain there's one inside of you, too.

About Jeff

Jeff Powell was stationed in California, serving the U.S. Navy Seabees, when he became disabled. Upon his discharge, his commanding officer made a final, parting request. He asked Jeff to continue supporting U.S. military men and women, and his nation's future veterans.

Jeff accepted the challenge gladly and committed wholeheartedly to it. Since then, helping others has become his life's mission. The words of Jeff's CO remained clear to him even during the difficulties he had adjusting with his disability, the hardships he encountered readjusting to society, the time he spent homeless, and the years he spent caring for his ailing mother.

Jeff eventually established: VerifiedSupporter.com, a non-profit organization. It's a resource and community forum for all matters veteran. From there, he established other web sites which also serve as helpful resources, including sites dedicated to helping veterans launch successful online businesses.

One of Jeff's sites is Books4Veterans.com. After leaving the military, Jeff attended college to deal with his disability and soon exhausted his book stipend because of the exorbitantly restrictive cost of books. Consequently, he created: **Books4Veterans.com** as a place for veterans and other college students to buy, sell, or donate used books. Books4Veterans.com aims to make the continued studies and self-improvement efforts of our veterans a little easier, and a whole lot more affordable.

The "4Veterans" concept is Jeff's brainchild, or rather heart-child, and his mission is simple: To bring people together – business, government, and veterans – to help and support each other. Jeff likes to say that, together, we can all lend a hand and weather any crisis.

Apart from Books4Veterans, Jeff has dedicated his life to developing many other projects (or "hobbies" as he prefers to call them) for the greater good of all military veterans, their families, and their communities. To date, Jeff has pioneered these veteran initiatives:

Verified Supporter at: www.verifiedsupporter.com

Books4Veterans at: www.books4veterans.com

Homes4Veterans at: www.homes4veterans.com

Running4Veterans at: www.running4veterans.com

Military Veteran Entrepreneurs at: www.entrepreneurveteran.com

Entrepreneur Inside at: www.entrepreneurinside.us

"Serving the community," says Jeff, "is a state of mind, the kind of passion that carries you day-to-day, and that is what drives me every day throughout this journey."

Although life has many challenges, Jeff is one of the most courageous, motivated and dedicated people supporting veterans in the United States today. Jeff truly has the passion for, and a deep insight of, what it takes to help his fellow veterans.

And there is a bittersweet twist in Jeff's life story. Shortly after Jeff's son Jeremiah was born, Jeff lost his mother to a prolonged illness on Independence Day of 2014. Jeff was unwaveringly at her side until the end, and his mother, an avid veteran supporter, left Jeff a final request: "Keep up your good work, my son. Our country is proud of you!"

If you would like to contact or follow Jeff, feel free to doing so at:
Jeff@books4veterans.com
LinkedIn – http://linkd.in/1xYODJ8
Facebook – http://on.fb.me/1FSdCmg
Twitter – http://bit.ly/1C64DLw

CHAPTER 37

WAIT! I THOUGHT I HAD A DREAM...

BY JENNIFER WENZKE

ARE YOU LIVING YOUR BEST LIFE?

Have you been plugging away at life – relatively happy – but occasionally wondering if there could be more to the life you are living? Possibly you are dealing with divorce, loss of a loved one, or a dramatic change in your health or career? After working through a life setback – small or large – many of us, after recovering, revert back to what's comfortable by jumping back into life right where we left off, without making any noticeable mind-shifts?

Unless we take time out of our busyness to identify what's truly important in life, jumping back into what feels comfortable may become our life pattern – causing us to miss out on our best life. When we identify our values and allow ourselves the time to make the necessary mind-shifts to create a new track to run on, we will live the life we have always dreamed of – a life filled with abundant happiness, joy, peace and success.

When I finally took the time to identify my most important values and built my life around them – all I can say is WOW! Possibility after possibility fell onto my path resulting in a life of joy, fun, love and achievement. That is why I am passionate about helping others combat the unproductive mindset of settling for less and instead choosing a life focused on their most important values.

My rocky personal journey has fueled my desire to show others how to create a values-driven life – and why not! The sooner we reach our best life – the better!

WHERE DID MY DREAM GO?

Spring 1982. The holes in the walls can't be covered up with family photos any more. There are just too many holes and not enough photos. He promises he will stop drinking. He doesn't. During the middle of the night, he wanders in to see our son and leaves him lying on a small changing table. The next morning, I find my son smiling up at me, motionless. It is a miracle he isn't laying on the floor. I take my baby and leave.

Fall 1992. The sun is pushing its last bit of light through the window. I move from the couch to the window and shut my eyes, allowing the sun to warm my face. The daily stress of my unhealthy environment is pressing in from all sides – I can hardly breathe. I have done it again – married a man who can't control his drinking or anger. How can a strong, daring, loving, energetic, confident and vibrant woman lose all of her spark and give up completely on herself and abandon her dreams? I take my children and leave the next day.

Fall 2012. I am hiding upstairs in the spare bedroom, sprawled across the bed replaying my life in my mind. I have a wonderful husband, children with successful lives and a career I love. I still feel alone and have doubts about my ability to ever be worthy of success. Tears flood my face. "What's wrong with me?" I am exhausted from hiding behind my perfect façade – fearful that others will find out who I really am and not like what they see. I just can't live like this any more. ENOUGH is ENOUGH!

IT'S STILL ME OVER HERE WITH A DREAM!

At that moment I make a promise to myself. By the time I turn 60 I will set free all of my negative beliefs and leave behind the unhealthy emotional responses that are holding me back from living my best life. I am not sure how I am going to it. But what I do know is that if I don't try NOW I will leave this wonderful world with my story untold – my dream hidden inside my heart. I hire a coach for more money than I have ever paid for anything in my life – outside of a house or car – and I begin my journey of self-discovery.

Summer 2013. I am feeling more powerful than I ever have in my life. My coach is wonderful. We are making great progress. But physically, I feel off. I visit a nutritionist, acupuncturist and physical therapist. Nothing seems to lift the foggy, sluggish feeling in my body. My husband suggests I visit a neurologist – and to our disbelief I am diagnosed with ALS. The life I thought I was going to live is gone. Just like that – POOF! I fall into an even deeper fog. All of the negative beliefs that I have been working on resurface - bigger and bolder than ever before. I hate my disease. I am angry at the world. I feel defeated, hopeless and helpless because I can't do a thing about it - there is no cure.

DUSTING OFF MY DREAM IS SCARY!

After several months of grieving, angry outbursts, isolation and disbelief, I begin to pull my head above the fog. It didn't take long for me to realize that staying home in isolation was giving me as much, if not more pain than the fear I was trying to avoid – the fear of stumbling in public and the sadness on people's faces when they learn about my illness. I need to choose which pain I want to live with – and I choose to leave isolation. So once again I declare: ENOUGH is ENOUGH and I go back to work on me.

I NEVER WANT TO GO BACK!

Each of us has a story to tell – a story meant to be shared. And I believe it is our responsibility to send our special message out to the world and into the lives of those that are waiting desperately to receive it. You may be thinking: what is my special message – how can I access it – how do I know it is the right message – how do I share it? To help you embrace your message and acquire the confidence to blast it out to the world, I utilize many tools and hands-on exercises throughout my coaching process. Each small discovery will add a fresh layer of belief and ultimately the answers to how to live a life filled with joy, fun, self-love, fulfillment, appreciation, confidence, and success.

I love the name of my 5-step coaching process – "MAKE THE LEAP". Why? Try leaping backward - it's almost impossible. All-out leaping with abandon can only be achieved in a forward motion! Some of my favorite exercises in the program include two personality assessments that help you completely fall back in love with yourself, four NLP patterns to release your fears, and my "Claiming Your Fame" exercise. The "CLF" exercise is a personal favorite because it helped me move toward the discovery of my unique gifts, talents and ultimately the message I was meant to share with the world.

CLAIMING Your Fame!

(List everything that comes to mind after each statement.)

C – Challenges & hardships you have over-come:

_____

L – Lose track of time when you do this:

_____

A – Always wanted to do, but never took the time to do:

_____

I – If you could teach what would you enjoy teaching?

_____

M – Message you can't wait to share with the world:

_____

I – Instantly makes you smile:

_____

N – Naturally you are good at:

_____

G – Gifts that are obvious you have:

_____

Y – Your Values – What are your top 5 values?

_____

O – Other people you want to take on your dream with you:

_____

U – Understanding your personal situation – right now:

_____

R – Regret not doing or having:

_____

F – Fears that are holding you back:

_____

A – Answers that you have always wanted:

_____

M – Matters to you most when you look back at your long, wonderful life:

_____

E – Everyone says you are great at this:

_____

It's time to Claim your Fame! Write down the words, phrases and thoughts you notice more than once in your answers. What do you see and feel about those answers? Your natural gifts and passion will be revealed. Decide how you can make them a part of your life.

In order to love what we do and not settle for less, it is important to check-in and truly grasp what our gifts and talents are. And that's not always simple to do. Our true gifts and talents are the ones that come natural to us - and when we are in our gifts we flow easily through life and notice the joy we are experiencing but don't necessarily notice the importance of the joy. We have been brought up to believe that "real work" should feel hard and difficult and when we are working in our gifts we don't always appreciate the significance of the ease. From this day forward, when you are doing something that brings you joy, take notice of what you are doing - who you are with - how you are feeling. Embrace it! Figure out how to use it in your life. It was meant for you all along - to live with - each day of your life. It's God's gift and talent that was chosen especially for you!

HOW TO BUILD A POWERFUL SUCCESS TEAM

In addition to helping women unlock their authentic self, I also coach my clients to reach new heights in their professional life through my success team formula. Why is it so important? Because I learned long ago "If your life is a mess your business is a mess." So it's important to be working on both.

The 9 Ingredients in the Recipe to a Powerful Business Success Team

- Discover your gifts and align your life with your values.
- Attend workshops and events that focus on your personal development.
- Select appropriate networking events that support your business goals.
- Identify and spend time with a mentor.
- Participate in a mastermind group.

- Establish solid referral partners.

- Hire a coach.

- Create a "Signature Speaking System" that features your unique "Side Door" and secures speaking engagements with potential clients in your target market.

- Set up weekly goal accountability with consequences.

LIVING IN MY DREAM IS IGNITING
MY ABUNDANT LIFE!

November 2014. Tonight is "So Now" night, one of my favorite nights of the month. For the past four years I have hosted a group of professional ladies that I lovingly call "So Now". We gather to exchange business ideas, eat a little dinner and have fun. The ladies are magnificent. I begin each meeting with a personal life event story and then share what I learned from that experience – even if the outcome isn't pretty. I never knew, until recently, how many of my stories have inspired the women to take a risk or make a change in their life. I count on their inspirational energy and caring spirit as much as they count on mine.

Our philosophy of helping women to unite and raise each other up into their unique greatness is spreading rapidly with several new chapters springing up across Ohio. Their enthusiasm to help others is unmatched in the networking world. We have declared 2015: The Year of the Butterfly – Embrace your Transformation and Emerge as Brilliantly as a Butterfly!

February 2015 - The snow is falling peacefully from the sky, landing gently on the ground adding new layers over old layers of snow. The neighborhood children are uniting the new layers with the old and artistically transforming them into a beautiful snowman. Other new layers are dramatically plowed on top of old layers off to the side of the road. Then it hits me – I have the luxury of deciding how I want my layers of greatness to be shared. I can choose to combine the energy of my old layers with the new and artistically transform my dreams into fruition OR because of fear, allow my new layers to join the old layers on the side of the road. It is at that moment I decide to gather up all of my layers, old and new, and walk – no, run fearlessly. . . in the direction of my dreams.

About Jenn

Jennifer Wenzke is a mother and wife first, and a speaker, life coach, and enthusiastic networker second. She has an amazing husband, Bob, five incredible adult children, and seven grandchildren between two blended families. She is a slowly-recovering perfectionist, and involved in the never-ending struggle to balance work success with a healthy personal life. Everyday, she is pushing herself to reach new limits to unveil her inner strengths and passions.

As the founder of So Now Coaching, Jenn has used her expertise in Neuro-Linguistic Programming (NLP) to guide hundreds of women through a process of self-discovery while implementing tools that allow women to connect to the personal message they were meant to share. Jenn helps clients identify and overcome fears and other personal challenges that prevent them from living their best life through a 5-step program called "Make the Leap." Through this personalized program, Jenn guides her clients down a path toward joy, fun, self-love, fulfillment, appreciation, confidence, and success.

In addition to helping women unlock their authentic self, Jenn also coaches her clients to reach new heights in their professional life, using her savvy business experience and specialized training to create a detailed action plan to success. Jenn has identified nine ingredients necessary to building a powerful business team, and she ensures that all of her clients implement these in the workplace.

As Jenn was able to reach hundreds of clients through her one-to-one coaching model, she realized that she also had a special message to share with a larger audience and formed the speaking company, Define Your Own Destiny (DYOD). Jenn appreciates the palpable excitement during these speaking events, and the lasting relationships that follow.

So Now Coaching is named after one of her proudest professional accomplishments—founding the "So Now Professional Network for Women." So Now has established a community for women in cities throughout Ohio and helped women rise to their full potential and unique greatness.

Jenn is a Licensed Life & Business Coach, Certified NLP Master Practitioner, and Certified Master Practitioner for the Myers Briggs Personality Assessment. She graduated from Bowling Green State University, and currently resides in Toledo, Ohio.

Two of Jenn's favorite inspirational quotes:

Psalms 18:32, 35: *"It is God who arms me with strength and makes my way perfect. You give me your shield of victory, and your right hand sustains me; you stoop down to make me great."*

Dr. Seuss favorite: *"Today you are You, that is truer than true. There is no one alive that is Youer than You."*

You Can Connect with Jenn at:
Jennwenzke@jennwenzke.com
www.sonowcoaching.com
www.facebook.com/SoNowCoaching

CHAPTER 38

MY SECRETS TO SUCCESS: SMALL-TOWN VALUES AND BIG-TIME DREAMS

BY JOE GLEASON

If one advances confidently in the direction of his dreams, and endeavors to live the life which he has imagined, he will meet with a success unexpected in common hours.

~ Henry David Thoreau

I grew up in a small, all-American, Midwestern town. It was just a couple hours west of Chicago — a little town called Byron, Illinois. When I lived there, it was the type of place where you didn't lock your door when you left for work or school. Everyone knew each other, and when we got our second stoplight in town it made front page news in our little newspaper. It was a great upbringing, and I feel lucky to have grown up in such a safe and nurturing environment. I learned values and principles there that would lead me to live the life of my dreams with purpose, passion, and success.

I discovered at a pretty young age that good news travels fast, but bad news travels faster. If there was something you did that was good OR bad, usually it didn't take too long before most everyone in town knew what was going on! With that, I learned that you want to make sure that you're always doing the right thing. I also learned that when you shake someone's hand, it means something. You look them in the eye and tell them what you promise to do, and then you follow through because your word is your bond. There was a lot of trust with the folks that I lived around and a really strong sense of community among the people, businesses, and daily happenings in our beloved town.

I witnessed how these small-town values parlayed into how my grandfather, Tom Wells, conducted business and how he became a successful, top producer at his company. He worked with local farmers and served as a nutritionist recommending proper diets for the livestock on their farms. My twin brother and I would ride along with him to see his clients when we were little kids. My grandfather spent most of his time strengthening relationships with his clients, and I remember that it was like spending time with family. He'd ask about their latest ongoings, families, and friends. After much laughter and fun during the visit, they'd place the order and off we went.

Because of his ability to create these strong relationships, Grandpa intuitively understood what his clients' needs were and what they were looking to achieve. Some farmers had different objectives with how they were running their farm, and so my Grandpa's job was to discover what they needed and to make sure he understood in order to make the right recommendations. It was never about him making another sale, it was about giving them exactly what they needed.

It makes me smile with pride to remember how Grandpa was always going the extra mile for his customers, too. He would make the effort to put together different feeding bins customized for them. He would go into the warehouse and get supplies for the farmers on his own time, just so they would have what they needed before the deliveries were made. Grandpa also planned and hosted client events, taking some of his best clients to baseball games or other special outings.

I've taken the lessons I've learned from my small-town upbringing and from my grandfather's wisdom and have applied them in my life and in my businesses. Seeing my grandparents live a beautiful, happy life with their extended family and watching them plan so well for retirement inspired me to help others do the same.

In the end, it's not the years in your life that count.
It's the life in your years.

~ Abraham Lincoln

As a financial planner, it's not only about the investments or the tools to me. Just as my grandfather did, I take the time to build relationships with my clients, to understand their needs and desires first. What really revs my engine is empowering people to create their dream lifestyles through a well-constructed financial plan. To me, the dream lifestyle is doing what you want, when you want, with whom you want while fulfilling your purpose. I don't think we came to the Earth to just grow up, go to school, get a job to work for 40-50 years, pay your bills, fight the morning commute, and then pass away. I think that we're here for a bigger purpose, and that's what I like to draw out of people. I give people hope, plans, and strategies to help them live their dream lifestyles.

While spending the time to build relationships with my clients, I uncover their deepest desires and have found that many share common goals:

1. **Traveling:** In my family we like to go on cruises, and a lot of our clients love to go on cruises, too. It's great when clients tell me stories about cruises they've been on from Europe to the Pacific to the Caribbean. I love hearing stories about how they've taken their kids and grandkids on a cruise. Other clients enjoy taking the family to places like Disneyland or Universal Studios. And then we've got clients who have made it a goal to travel to every state in the United States. My grandparents did that in an RV. They drove to every state they could. Then, they flew to Hawaii last.

2. **Spending Time With Family:** This goal is what a lot of folks envision when they think about living their dream lifestyle. For our clients with grandkids, they want to spend as much time as they can with these little ones. And for our younger clients, being able to spend the time with their kids and extended family is priceless. Getting together for reunions, holiday parties, baseball games, and even a weekly dinner gives them precious time where they can grow stronger as a family. I understand where they're coming from because these are activities my own family enjoys.

3. **Enjoying Hobbies:** We have a lot of clients who really want to have the freedom and the ability to enjoy their hobbies and pastimes.

Some people love to go to movies every week while others like to play softball or golf. We've even got clients who are really great at woodworking and making stained glass windows. These are all really cool hobbies. Our clients can enjoy them even more knowing they can afford them.

4. Feeling Fulfilled: Our clients also want to feel fulfilled and a lot of times this means expanding their knowledge. They're learning new languages, taking lessons to play an instrument, and even acting in or directing theater productions. They're continuing or, in some cases, starting their higher education. Being able to nurture their minds in these ways is so important because it gives them a greater sense of purpose in life. I love being in the position to help make that happen.

5. Giving Back: This ties into feeling fulfilled. Many clients work with charities close to their hearts. They carve out time to become more involved besides supporting their charities financially, too. Like many of these goals, I can relate. In fact, my wife, Janette, and I have close ties to a couple of charitable organizations in our community. We organize a gift drive for an organization that assists domestic violence victims and raise money for another which focuses on increasing awareness for autism.

Now, it's one thing to wish or talk about being able to travel, spend time with family, enjoy your hobbies, and give back to the community. All those goals and objectives are wonderful and having that dream lifestyle is absolutely possible, but you have to put the work in.

Plan ahead. It wasn't raining when Noah built the ark.

~ Richard Cushing

The dream lifestyle doesn't just "happen." I believe in preparing for your future through comprehensive wealth management and a full financial plan. Having a plan in place helps you prepare for when critical life events occur such as college tuition, marriage, the purchase of a new home, the birth of a child, retirement, etc. Planning ahead for your short-term goals while you're still working or for your long-term retirement will give you peace of mind and a path for you to follow your dreams. It's important that if you're not going to do the work yourself and have the discipline to really stay on top of that for yourself, that you work with someone who has your best interests at heart.

Whether you create a plan yourself or seek help from a financial advisor, you will want to consider these important components:

Maximizing Your Income: Whether you are working or are in retirement, increasing your cash flow is key to the foundation of your financial success. You can maximize your income by following a budget, creating an emergency fund, and minimizing your debt. As you transition into retirement, it's important to have an income plan in place. You should be aware of your assets, how much you need per month, and the best places to withdraw that money. Having income and savings allows you to enjoy your dream lifestyle.

Planning for Taxes: My Grandpa always used to tell me, "It's not what you make, it's what you keep." It's important that you have your retirement savings constructed in a way, whether it's long-term, short-term, or mid-term, that you're mindful of the taxes. And not just the taxes of today, but the taxes down the road. I work closely with my clients to make sure we're maximizing any tax advantages that we can. The last thing you want is to be surprised with an unexpected tax bill!

Ensuring Proper Protection: It's important to have all of your insurances and protections in place such as life insurance, car insurance, and health insurance to make sure that if something does happen, you have protection. Leverage these tools so that you're not spending all of your out-of-pocket money on any of those life things that happen. Improper protection can derail your plans!

Legacy Planning: You will want to preserve your legacy by creating a plan to transfer your assets to your loved ones. Implementing a legacy plan involves making sure that the dollars you've worked so hard for throughout your whole life will be passed on to your heirs, your loved ones, and your charities easily, efficiently, and without too much hassle.

As you work toward putting all the pieces into place in your financial plan, I encourage you to seek help from a financial professional that you trust to help you navigate through the waters. Having an open mind to new solutions and changing old mindsets or habits will help you live the dream lifestyle you've always wanted. Imagine having the freedom to travel, spend time with family, and give back to others while enjoying life to the fullest!

The most rewarding part of my work is the people — the relationships I get to build just as my grandfather taught me. When I hear about one of my clients retiring, welcoming a new child or grandchild into the family, or paying off a student loan, I share in their joy and success. For me, it's almost like it's happening within my own family! It's my utmost privilege and such a blessing to see their goals being met and to watch them live their dream lifestyles.

[While writing this chapter, my dear grandfather passed away unexpectedly at 89 years old. He left behind a priceless legacy in the form of a large, loving family and innumerable life lessons. He was never "Great Grandpa" to our children, but "Grandpa Great." In fact, Grandpa was "Grandpa" to everyone he met...neighbors, friends, acquaintances, you name it. We loved him for his sense of humor, his unbreakable moral code and his ability to hold such a large and far-flung family together. But more than anything, we loved that he never left anything unsaid. He always told everyone how much he loved them and how proud he was of their accomplishments. My kids will always remember him for the pen in his shirt pocket and his signature "thumbs up." And, all of us will remember him for being a hero.]

About Joe

Joe Gleason learned about ethics from his grandfather, Tom Wells, in Byron, Illinois, a small farming community with just 2,000 residents. During the sales calls, Grandpa Wells would ask his customers about their farms and their families before assessing their needs for his products and services. By watching these interactions first-hand, Joe learned that being in business is about trying to help people.

Today, Joe has brought this small-town approach to Arizona where he continues to apply his grandfather's lessons in his own family businesses: Gleason Financial Group, LLC, which specializes in income and retirement planning; and Gleason Investment Advisory, LLC, which helps clients manage their investments. Operating together, the firms take a comprehensive approach to managing clients' finances.

Using comprehensive fact finding, Joe gets to know clients by identifying their retirement goals. Then through extensive research and planning, he develops a customized financial plan for each client. Maintaining strong relationships with his clients is a priority for Joe, who meets with each client at least once a year and encourages them to call him anytime with their financial questions and concerns. He wants his clients to know he is their financial ally.

His ultimate goal is to empower his clients to create their dream lifestyle – whether it's helping someone achieve the dream of traveling across the country in an RV or making it possible for them to spend more time with their children and grandchildren.

Joe, who holds a Series 65 license, is an Investment Advisor Representative. This means he has a fiduciary responsibility to act in his clients' best interest on their behalf. He is also licensed in life, health, property, casualty, and long-term care insurance. His vast financial knowledge has landed him regular appearances on local television and radio stations, including *Good Morning Arizona* on Channel 3, FOX 10, CBS 5 and ABC 15.

Joe and his wife, Janette, live in Surprise, Arizona, with their three children and their dog, Buddy. They enjoy traveling and attending Diamondbacks and Cubs spring training games.

To learn more about and connect with Joe:
Visit http://www.azfinancialplanning.com
Facebook at https://www.facebook.com/GleasonFinancialGroup
Twitter: @JosephLGleason

CHAPTER 39

LIVE BOLDLY

BY DANNY NGUYEN, CCIM

With more than twenty years of commercial real estate experience, people have often asked how the journey has been for me. I love what I do and I can say that enthusiastically to anyone who asks, without hesitation—always. Making deals, creating the right partnerships and connections, and seeing the results of my efforts is exciting and wonderful. All these things bring me success and satisfaction both financially and in my personal life. Each day is a journey that I enjoy and one for which I am grateful to be a part.

During my time in commercial real estate, I've experienced a transformation that has impacted my entire life. I have this innate joy and happiness when I see my clients benefit from the results of my efforts. Those interested in commercial real estate have been able to develop the portfolios they desire, becoming contributors to their community.

In real estate, creating sustainable relationships is essential, but it is only the start. It's a merger of vision and ideas that lead to amazing things. I have met incredible people, including presidents, senators, governors, government leaders and leaders in the private sector. I've gotten to go on trade missions and submerse myself into different cultures and ways of conducting business. I have taken the opportunity to donate to many charities and non-profits, experienced the overwhelming feelings of gratitude and thanks that come from being a part of mission trips, and so many other things. From each of these experiences, I walk away with a valuable bit of advice that helps me gain a greater connection with the people I meet. And the lessons learned and wisdom gained is priceless…

The journey and *the person that I have become* are incredible and fulfilling. I came to the United States as a political refugee from Vietnam; grateful for the opportunity and knowing that I had much to prove with the incredible opportunity I was given. I've learned a lot and there are six things, in particular, that I want to share with you. It is my hope that you will find the inspiration and guidance to act on them.

(1). <u>Do what your heart and soul desire.</u>

When you seek out a career where your heart and soul meet, you need to factor in these four things:

- Money
- Skills and talents
- Level of joy
- Meaning and purpose

There is no shame in being motivated by money when you are searching for a career. I certainly was because I knew one thing for certain: **I wanted to do better and have more impact.** Money helps! So, when I enrolled in college and later chose a career, I placed a lot of weight on this. Being honest with our motivations is important!

When we are being truthful about what drives us, we can find the balance, inspiration, and drive to succeed in our lives. We create roadblocks and obstacles because we didn't take the time to figure it out. So, to anyone who doesn't know what they are good at, you have to do an inventory of your skills, interests, and everything else and start dabbling in these areas to find the right formula. It will happen, but it won't happen without you putting forth some effort. Here's a bit about what my process looked like:

Driven by a natural desire to become an asset that gave back to my country, had respect for my opportunities, and also for making a name for my family and serving God, I wanted to show this vision to not only my Vietnamese family and ancestors, but to my new country.

When going to college, I had the opportunity to help people set up several small businesses – including nail salons in big shopping malls – and used the money earned to help pay fees and bills during school and not accumulate debt. During that time, I saw the impact of entrepreneurial power and found my passion for commercial real estate.

After graduating from Texas A&M University, I decided to go into real estate. I knew it was the one thing that lit me up from the inside out and made me want to give all I had to being successful at it. Twenty years later, I am still doing that and many of my friends that I graduated with have switched jobs multiple times, still seeking out the job that truly ignites their purpose. I am humbled and grateful for having chosen the right career path for myself. I worked hard to make the right choice

(2). <u>Be willing to pay a price.</u>

The best way to learn success is to study success and then apply it. It takes action! Based on everything I've observed from people, one thing has remained universally true:

What separates successful people from unsuccessful people and happy individuals from unhappy ones is that some are not willing to pay the price for this success or the happiness they want. There is always a price and eventually it must be paid.

I see no reason to not pay the price right away so you have more time to enjoy both success and happiness. Why procrastinate on these amazing rewards that life has to offer? There is no reason. I want to share a personal testament with you about this process and how it played out in my life.

Thirty years ago, my father decided to pay the price for freedom by risking our lives escaping from Communist Vietnam. I was fourteen years old and on a small fishing boat with my father and seventy other people. My mother and five siblings were left behind. It was hard to think that we might never see them again, but this was a risk that had to be taken for a better future for all of us. We ended up spending close to twenty-five days in the Pacific Ocean, enduring a raid by Thai fishermen-pirates – in which we were robbed and the ladies on the ship were raped. We ended up in a Thai prison and a few different refugee camps in both Thailand and the Philippines before we were able to get to the United States.

Was it still worth it? Yes. My father had known that there may be a price to pay and he taught me to accept that. It was a valuable lesson.

All of the heartache and hardship of family separation, almost losing our lives because of a desire to experience a life many take for granted—a life with freedom, whether it be freedom of speech, enterprise, worship, travel, etc. These freedoms are privileges and for millions of people, life is a privilege to be celebrated and be grateful for. It was a catalyst to realize how much I wanted to give back for the opportunity I received and to remind my fellow Americans that freedom is not free, and we must treasure and respect it to enjoy its benefits.

My father and I had to start all over and adjust to our new lives as political refugees. This freedom was the foundation for us to build our future upon, including my career and the person that I have become today. If I could impact you with one thing, it would be this:

Whatever perceived or real difficulties, challenges, or adversities you have, be willing to embark on a new endeavor or journey and consider the price tag that you will pay for that item. This is what will bring you happiness, and your heart and soul will know that what you desire is worth the price. Not doing this is never worth that price—a loss of dreams, opportunity, and joy.

(3). **Believe in God, Yourself, and America.**

In order to believe in yourself, you must have faith in your Creator. There must be something out there that we believe is much bigger than us. If I didn't know this to be true, I would have had a much harder time enduring that Thai prison or those many days lying at the bottom of a boat without a roof and a broken-down engine, looking at the stars and the moon, the rain and the sun, and those waves that came over the edges of that rickety old boat.

People suffered on these journeys. My father certainly did, as well as the others that were around me. Back home, my mother and siblings were, too. How else do you remain strong and committed to the end results in the face of such adversity, if not through awareness of God? It takes you and the universe's Creator.

Faith also goes much further than that. You must also have faith in your country. For me, this country was America. I knew that I'd get there some day and when I did, I'd have to know where I wanted to go from there. It would be the start of another journey. **THIS IS THE PLACE where dreams could come true!**

My belief was so strong that I made sure that I was no longer that political refugee, although those experiences are a fundamental part of me. Today, I am a man who looks out my living room window to see a replica of the Statue of Liberty out there to remind me. I have served as an elected city official in the city where I live in thanks to a voting process that ensures that opportunity due to the United States being a Republic. With work, I have received high accolades that have taken commitment and that I use to make my community better, including the CCIM, which is the highest designation in CRE that a professional can earn. I want to make a positive impact with everything I do. Without faith in America and God, these things would have never developed.

Is it scary? Of course, but it is absolutely worth it! These are all things to think about and to discover the answers you need, it takes faith and action.

(4). Stick with it until you've made it.

Not everything has always come easily for me, which is something that others may not realize. I recall having the intense feelings of failure when I first entered real estate. It was so frustrating!

I was waiting to close my first commercial deal and eager for it to get wrapped up and get that commission check, of course. I was working hard and very aware that my other friends that I'd graduated with and moved on to a 'real job' were getting paychecks and starting to live the dream. They had security and I felt like I had only uncertainty. It was all made worse when someone would ask, "Did you get a check yet?" I'd answer, "No, but I will soon." I claimed it and kept going, not willing to let anything stop me. Deep down I knew I want an opportunity, not security. I wanted the ultimate freedom to determine my own destiny and realize my fullest potential. And I am proud of that because it takes courage.

I had plenty of areas that I could keep gaining experience and growing while I waited. And finally, it did come! It felt great, but once again, it was only a stepping-stone on the journey I was meant to take.

Not only my life, but all lives have obstacles on occasion or perhaps a lot. You may get some unexpected bad news and such. It's what you do with a challenging situation that is important. Do you allow it to stifle you or do you find a way to make it through? You keep going!

It's so easy to get discouraged and quit, but those emotions are the enemy. Self-doubt is about the same as self-destruction. You have to dig deep and figure out what will keep you motivated. Here's what I do:

I think about what gets me going and will get me excited again! Today you are a little better than yesterday, and tomorrow you are better than today. Set goals and measure your own success.

(5). <u>Enjoy success and keep rising.</u>

The easiest way to remember where you've been and where you'd like to go is to keep records, evidence, and notes. These are your assets, equity, and inventory in what you've done and no one can take those away.

I have a habit of counting my blessings in a way similar to how a business owner may go over his profit and loss statement or year-end evaluation. Only my evaluation is not about money, it's about how many lives I have positively impacted in the process, about happiness. Some of this inventory is in my memories, and other parts are more tangible forms, such as business cards, contacts, a phone call, email, letter, postcard, or even a certificate of some sort. These things remind me that I am impacting other lives daily and that I am connected to success through my love of what I do. It feels great and if I do have a 'tough day,' I can access this inventory and get the reminders I need.

Being able to pull up these memories and specific events whenever I need them is how I define success. I could lose everything else but those things would still be positives on my balance sheet. These are the sources of my motivation, inspiration, and empowerment. They are my vitamins, the energy that gets me out of bed each and every morning—at 4 AM. I'm just ready to go because I have so much to go for. **What do you have to get up and go for**? *Take the time to find out today because tomorrow isn't too far away!*

(6). <u>What if I hadn't done it?</u>

Looking back, I sometimes wonder what would have happened if my father hadn't taken that bold move to get us to the United States. Everything would have been different and my life would not be what it is today. What if I had not stepped into this career boldly? Not only would I have missed out, but a lot of the people that I serve, my clients – my community – my city might have missed the benefits as well.

Now that I have over twenty years of real life experience doing something I love and a career that has transformed my life, I am ready to help as many people as I can to step into this career. It will make a difference in their own lives and also create a meaningful impact for their community and city, as well. I've used my calling to be an advocate for freedom and I am on a mission now. You'll find rewards that go beyond explanation and that impact you so profoundly that you may view what's around you from a new perspective—thankful to no longer be missing out on the bigger picture.

Go for it, my friends!

About Danny

With more than 20 years of experience in commercial real estate in Houston, Texas, Danny has *sold, bought, leased, managed,* and *developed* several multi-million dollar transactions for his clients: landlords, tenants, sellers, buyers and investors. Danny specializes on SHOPPING CENTERS, COMMERCIAL BUILDINGS and LAND. Danny is a recognized expert in the disciplines of commercial and investment real estate with his CCIM designation – which is considered by many to be the "Ph.D. of commercial real estate." He graduated from Texas A&M University where he received a Business Administration degree with a concentration in International Business & Marketing.

Danny has received several awards, certifications, an Honorary Degree, and even Proclamations from prominent government leaders, various organizations such as Chambers of Commerce for his economic development, entrepreneurship, leadership, community services, and City and Real Estate Industry contribution.

Danny has been seen, quoted and featured on ABC 13 News, the *Houston Chronicle,* Business Journals, *Forbes, International Toastmaster Magazine,* CCIM "Rising Star" 2007 Magazine, and many others. Danny was also interviewed on a radio talk show hosted by former State Senator Dan Patrick, who is the current Texas Lieutenant Governor, about Freedom and Entrepreneurs, and work ethics.

Danny has actively lead and participated in outbound trade mission trips to different countries, served as a City Councilmember at Large and International Relations & Economic Development Committee Chair – in Missouri City, TX and committee Chair of the Mayor's International Trade Development Council in Houston, Texas.

Danny has been invited to speak with other Experts, International Diplomats, Dignitaries and well-respected leaders on different platforms and on different occasions about Leadership, entrepreneurship, International Relations and opportunity, Diversity and Inspiration. He has recently been invited to speak at the UN (United Nations) and share the stage with Brian Tracy at the Global Economic Initiative.

Danny has also co-created a new six-part training program CD series with Brian Tracy – a step-by-step program to help real estate agents break into Commercial Real Estate and be successful at it.

Boards served and Affiliations:

- Asian Real Estate Association of America – Houston – founding member Board of Directors

- Vietnamese American Chamber of Commerce – Houston – Co-Founding Chair
- American First Tower Owners Association - Board Member
- Houston Association of Realtors® – Former member, Board of Directors
- Texas Association of Realtors® – Former Director, Houston region
- Houston Association of Realtors International – former Honorary Advisory Member
- Entrepreneur of the Year Award 2009 – Houston West Chamber of Commerce
- Aircraft Owners and Pilots Association (AOAPA) – Member
- Rice University's James Baker Institute – Associate Roundtable
- National Speaking Association – NSA Houston – Academy Graduate and Member

As a business and property owner, Danny is a strong advocate of freedom of enterprise and property rights. He is married to Marie Nguyen and they have three awesome boys Jordan, Darrell, and Jacob Nguyen. Danny enjoys horseback riding, singing, playing the guitar, and flying private airplanes.

You can connect with Danny at:
DannyNguyen@DNcommercial.net
or 713-270-5400

CHAPTER 40

WRETCHED NO MORE:
A CHAMPION'S CHOICE

BY DR. NICHOLAS COOPER-LEWTER

ONE MAN'S MESSAGE TO HIS SON AND TO THE WORLD

"Daddy, I want to be a champion," my then 4-year-old son pleaded. I am 59 years older than my youngest son. My son was smiling with excitement as he looked at the cover page of a marketing magazine. His father's face graced the front page and "his Dad" was named the "Soul Whisperer" in the feature story that followed. He knew from watching that I had helped other "boys and girls" overcome the odds and become champions. His twin God-brothers were awesome Division 1 football players, and one was playing in the NFL. He also got to hang out and "run" with Olympic Gold Medalists. Pop Warner coaches felt he had great potential. My son is an excellent, highly-imaginative Montessori student with manners. "We" read books together routinely and my son is a gifted dancer and model.

By seven, he had been a repeated guest at practices and games in men's and women's basketball, softball, and volleyball. Even more special he had been embraced by name and high fives by a championship bound SEC women's softball team. He participated in a keynote "No Limits, No Limits" speech sponsored by a University Athletic Department, which was later placed on YouTube and then sat front row when the women's basketball team rolled over their opponent. "We" even got a signed game ball and took pictures with some of the star players.

"Daddy, I want to be a champion, please help me!" I could have just said, "Just think positive." But one of my most important father-like mentors, Dr. Henry H. Mitchell now in his mid 90's, told me, "Son, experience is the language of the spirit, and even God's love must be mediated to be embraced as real." Words are plentiful and cheap. Remember to put first things first. I had to put first things first.

We represent the spiritual, physical, and mental DNA of all of our ancestors from the beginning. To be true champions, we must embrace all who were capable of "Being." Championship "Doing" follows. We are here because they were successful. We honor their unfinished hopes by recognizing their championship gifts passed on to us for our use. But what were the essential ingredients needed for him to become a true champion? To be more precise, what was the single most important ingredient he needed? We are best at helping people go where we have gone. Beginnings matter. My thoughts drifted to my mothers.

I am my mothers' son. Yes, I said "mothers' son." I did not know for years that I was adopted. I believed that my aunt whose birthday I shared was simply my aunt who used to call me her "ugly duckling." My mother, her sister made up an elaborate story about her C-section. She even showed me a scar across her abdomen. It was these two ladies and their painful search for the one thing they were missing, "the single most important thing they needed to experience" to live a potentiated life and embrace an honorable transition, which has inspired me.

I was a "sacred secret." No one was to ever tell me the truth about "Who I am, really." But even sacred secrets are very hard to keep. Combined with the research and experiences that went into my success as a "Soul Whisperer," I have discovered the most important experience they searched for, needed, and never found before they died.

WRETCHED AND NOT SO PRECIOUS

I want to share some transformational nuggets that each one of my mothers bestowed upon me. "Mama" adopted me to protect the family name. Mama had a husband. "Momma" was my birth mother and was not given a choice in my intra-family adoption.

Mama was Omni-competent. Her chicken and potato salad followed by homemade fresh peach ice cream or strawberry shortcake made waiting for dinner an enjoyable torture. Helping Mama massage the freshly delivered cow manure into the ground around her roses was a smelly chore but it produced a happy spirit when she won the neighborhood rose garden awards. Gathering fresh vegetables for dinner from Mama's vegetable garden lifted her spirits. It made my work to keep the vegetables free of weeds a joy. I learned to sew, cook, garden, play football and basketball, catch, clean, cook, fish, write, dance, paint, and read from Mama.

On my 10th birthday, Mama gave me a book titled *As a Man Thinketh* by James Allen. This was ironic, because on any given day, I did not know what to expect from my mother, because of her growing friendship with alcohol and an intense secret animosity against her sister, my biological mother. Inside her book gift, I found:

Mind is the master power that molds and makes,

And Man is Mind, and evermore he takes

The tool of Thought, and, shaping what he wills,

Brings forth a thousand joys, a thousand ills: —

He thinks in secret, and it comes to pass:

Environment is but his looking glass.

Mama confused me, because of her mixed messages and inconsistencies. On some days, in certain moments, at certain times and without a warning, mama made me believe that there was a hateful devil with imps, or in contrast, a good loving God with angels. If the spirits that she consumed via the bottle were her guides, her actions were devilish and character corrupting. If the spirits that she held secret within her heart, which I came to believe, were good and loving about her were her guides, her actions dealt in uplifting my character. Wretched and not so precious became a routine message as the alcohol became her best friend. This unloving friend kept whispering, "You are wretched." And since we tend to pass on what is within, wretched and not so precious without choice were the lessons I received. I never knew who would be her guide, but my survival, my health, and any potential happiness depended on my accurate and immediate assessment of every situation.

MAMA SAID

Mama often tied me to the bunk bed that my father built with the help of my uncle. She would open the window so that the children in the neighborhood could witness her beating the "devil out of me." My befuddled screams would bring the children running. I did not know how the devil got in me. My godfather was our pastor and he preached that children were from God. Repeatedly, he said, "God was good and hears the cries of children because God loves children." I often wondered, "Was the devil in something I ate?"

Mama was committed to extracting the resident evil from my gullible soul. Mama would tire from her ordained task and often needed to take rest breaks. Too tired to untie my hands, she would retire. The children would laugh and analyze the shortcomings of my naked body. Once mother had rested, she would complete her task of devil removal. The sign that the devil had left seemed to coincide with the evacuation of my bowels. "Clean up the mess," Mama would order. "Clean up yourself and go out and play with your friends." I can remember standing at the kitchen door, looking through the translucent curtains at the seemingly jubilant crowd of childhood friends and feeling a deep hole being etched inside my heart and soul.

What must one say about their mothers? Mama, my mother who adopted me, in a dispirited childlike voice before she died, asked me to remember the book she gave me when I was a child whenever I wondered if she really loved me.

MOMMA SAID

I held my birth Mother's head as she struggled in the final moments leading literally to her last breath. She seemed as if she was running to catch her final breath and smiled with impatient eyes. "It's time to do as your Momma says, and not as I have done. I gave you away hoping my wretchedness, my shame, would not infect you. I have watched painfully how you have spent your lifetime trying to be acceptable and seeking appreciation to prove your right to exist. You have been a champion in training who has never felt like a champion. Momma understands what it means to believe no matter how hard you try that you will never be good enough. Momma sees you. You have mastered how to live a crucified life, striving but never arriving. Momma wants you to try something different, resurrection. Promise me! Get off of my cross, and live your life . . . resurrected." It was the last message my birth Mother gifted me. What is a child to do but say "yes" to the woman who birthed you?

Nugget 1: Who is the Who in Who I am? Biologically, Psychologically, Sociologically, and Spiritually?

At the age of five I read Hans Christian Andersen's *The Ugly Duckling* and instantly identified with the story. The Ugly Duckling found himself in a situation not of his making. No matter how hard he tried to make sense out of the nonsense of his experiences, he could not. He could not love himself because others for unexplainable reasons bullied, hurt, rejected, and excluded him. He did not know who he really was and allowed his crucifying feelings to determine his happiness.

Things happen to us, but things that happen do not have the power to make us into something, unless we let them. I would become a recovering ugly duckling fulfilling deathbed promises to a birth mother and adoptive mother to seek out other ugly ducklings. I was challenged to let them know spring was coming and they would have a chance to embrace the Swan they always were.

The essential most important secret for becoming all we were intended to be begins with the knowledge, wisdom, and understanding of "Who is the Who in Who We Are?" What we value guides our choices. We are Beings who experience emotions and attach values to our experiences. Love, the active substance of God, must be mediated in relationships by people conscious (aware of our spiritual potential) and committed by choice long enough and strong enough for it to be embraced as real. Love is an activity that recognizes our Spirit and the spiritual treasure each of us is, and encourages the full manifestation of God's Intended (or innate) potential in us.

We are Beings that inherit life experiences from others and we ultimately choose what to believe and value about our past, our present, and our potential future. How I interpret the feelings and what value I give them is a key to becoming a true champion. Getting stuck in wretched experiences or in my case a history of many types of confusing, mixed messages, loving and non-loving experiences, and letting experiences tell me who I am allows the "No-s" to rule my life – making winning more import than being a champion. A person may lie and cheat and win. Being a champion is more about character, which bubbles up in times of challenge.

Nugget 2: Champions and Championship Chatter Are By Choice
Understanding what contributed to how we feel is better than dwelling on how we should or ought to have felt. "Shoulds" and "oughts" when we speak of our true feelings, imply the presence of a flaw, a form of wretchedness in our Being. Championship Choices and Chatter start young. We reflect what is modeled consistently and repeatedly heard as truth in our valued relationships. To "feel" is to express a value. Thinking, if it has a value, means "feelings" are present. We value, therefore we are. Love is an activity not a feeling. The touch of love needs to be experienced as unapologetic intentional support. The "why" and the "what" we "say" to our children becomes their inner voice.

Beware of those who require a pat on the head from their enemies to feel good about themselves. Today's challenges are best met by really knowing "Who is the Who in Who I am" and practicing and playing out of that clear understanding. Be and Become who you were created originally to be, more and certainly no less. This will allow the Champion in us to emerge victorious.

Nugget 3: Bio-Psycho-Socio-Spiritual Health and Performance Package
Asking, answering, and evaluating each of the elements in our Bio-Psycho-Socio-Spiritual Champion's Health and Performance Package at each stage of our progress is essential. Sample questions follow which need to asked, answered, and evaluated for each element.

Question 1. What are my requirements today to reach my goal of champion?

Question 2. What do my goals require of me, this day?

Question 3. Have I done what is required today or am I currently doing what is required, this day?

My mothers' did not realize that in their spiritual, physical, and mental DNA were all the successes of our ancestors past. They did not know that deep within them, as part of their multigenerational legacies was a "No Limits" spirit! Champions eliminate the wretchedness planted by others, bad experiences, unhealthy interpretations, mixed messages and traumatizing meanings.

Nugget 4: Daddy, I Want to be a Champion
Son, champions embrace the 'Who' at the center of 'Who they really

are.' This nugget eluded my mothers – we are called to be creative artists and methodical scientists building heavens, even where hells have existed. Taking 100% responsibility for what we have control over and no more or less, is crucial.

Son, the 'Who' in 'Who you are' is the Champion of Champions. Every ancestor who overcame the odds has been a champion. Once we really embrace "Who the Who is in Who We Are," we are in position to create and experience:

Championship Choices – Embrace the best choices in any moment to be and become all we were intended to be.

Championship Chatter – Insist on uplifting and constructive conversations even with ourselves.

Championship Character – Represent well all who have sacrificed, named and unnamed, so we can be here today.

Championship Culture – Build heavens even where hells might exist.

Championship Caring, Concern, and Compassion – Love like you never have been hurt, lead with love even when others choose not to. Love is the creative force that builds heavens.

Son, Who you believe is the 'Who' in 'Who you are' shapes your dreams, influences your outcomes, determines what you are required to do, how much disappointment you can take and how to keep overcoming any odds placed before you in life.

Nugget 5: Son, you are a swan.
My mothers want me to tell you this and to make sure you experience the mediated love of the One who is the 'Who' in you. I refuse to pass on the Wretchedness. Pass on the love, son, starting with yourself. That is what real champions do.

I will love you even when I die. How will you know? It will be in your DNA.

As always,
Your Dad.

About Dr. Nick

Reverend Dr. Nicholas Cooper-Lewter holds a Master of Social Work degree and a Ph.D. in Psychology. He has studied at the Ecumenical Center for Black Church Studies in Claremont, California under H.H. Mitchell, Th.D. and is a supervising Licensed Independent Clinical Social Worker and Marriage and Family Therapist. A grandmaster, he has personally developed an Asian-African American Martial Art style of Kung Fu.

Throughout his four-decade career as a licensed psychotherapist, life coach, mental trainer, optimum performance professional and sports psychology expert, Dr. Cooper-Lewter has served as a senior pastor, tenured full professor, visiting full professor, distinguished lecturer, chaplain resource (mentor), workshop facilitator, and a motivational speaker. He served as a commissioner on the Samuel DeWitt Proctor Conference, Inc., Katrina National Justice Commission, and as a consultant. He has worked with universities, seminaries, churches, agencies, foundations, and institutes around the world. Dr. Cooper-Lewter is called the "Inmate Whisperer" by Capital Trial Attorneys because of his ability to facilitate inmates sharing difficult psycho-social histories. In 2012, he was chosen to be on the cover of the Carolinian magazine, which was the inaugural issue of the University of South Carolina's "No Limits" branding effort. The Carolinian's featured story gave him a new nickname: the "Soul Whisperer."

He "coaches hearts to empower minds" to embrace their God-given potential. His clients and many former students agree that "when the unspoken must be spoken & the unknown must be known," Rev. Dr. Cooper-Lewter is the one to trust. He conducts therapist trainings, he works with athletes at all levels and in all sports to overcome the odds to optimize personal achievement on and off the field, and he assists in the development of Rites of Passage programs for youth. He honors his African, Native American and European ancestry and recommends recapturing the ancient healing folk/spiritual values and practices of "Soul Therapy."

Cooper-Lewter's speaking and teaching abilities have been honored with a number of national teaching and service awards. He is especially recognized for his ability to motivate and inspire others through his personal story of adoption and overcoming childhood abuse. In his practice of Soul Therapy, he helps people eliminate Inceptional Wretchedness from the Who is the Who in Who I Am. Spiritually, Rev. Dr. Cooper-Lewter challenges people to become People of the Resurrection instead of living crucified and stuck at the Cross. Dr. Cooper-Lewter's innovative and successful work with athletes has been showcased in both the national and international media with documentaries on his work. His research and work addressing shame, trauma, grieving, and the power of real love have earned him international respect.

Reverend Dr. Cooper-Lewter's first book, *Soul Theology: The Heart of American Black Culture* that was co-authored with Dr. H.H. Mitchell, has been well received around the world. His book, *Black Grief and Soul Therapy*, has earned him the designations of the Black Jung and the American Fanon. Forthcoming are two works titled *Wretched No More* and *Championship Choices.*

Facebook: Dr. Nick the Soul Whisperer
Twitter: twitter.com/DrNick
Website: Cooperlewter.com

CHAPTER 41

THE HEART OF MY SUCCESS

BY P. RUTH DONESON

As a Life Coach, all of my work is client centered. For me success is all about the results my clients achieve through the work we do together. People seek personal coaching for very different reasons or purposes, but there is always an emotional component, and the outcomes always include some kind of a shift in the way the client views him- (or her) self. The way we see ourselves and how we feel is important to this process because, if you live on this planet, you have been subjected to opinions, judgments, comparisons and all manner of limitative notions and ideas. There are always plenty of people around who will be happy to tell you why you cannot, should not, are not qualified to do, to be, or to have something you want. In such an atmosphere most likely everyone has programming in their minds that causes doubts, misunderstandings, and limiting beliefs about themselves.

I call this faulty programming the "false belief system." Unfortunately, this false belief system can become the premise upon which to base additional conclusions that create more false beliefs. Then, depending on the kind of experience one was having at the time this faulty programming was instituted, some feelings were produced in the body by the emotional system which, if not expressed, will be saved for later. These unexpressed feelings don't go anywhere. They just stay there, in the body, held in place in a state of denial, affecting you on the sly.

Denied feelings are also cumulative. So when new experiences produce same or similar feelings, they trigger the denied feelings into a response largely disproportionate to the current experience. Or if the new feelings are ignored, they too will remain in the body in a denied state.

What we believe and how we feel affects everything in our lives. There is an expression I've heard: "Look around you, everything you see in your life today is the direct result of what you were thinking yesterday." Actually it's more than that. It involves our thoughts, our words, our feelings and our actions. Mostly it's about our beliefs! We don't manifest what we want; we manifest what we believe.

THE UNIVERSE

The Universe is made of energy, and everything that exists in the Universe is also made of energy including us. Energy has always existed, cannot be created or destroyed, moves into form, through form, and out of form, and can be in more than one place at a time. Energy is also the engine of action, the substance of connection, the blueprint for existence of all creation, and it has consciousness. Energy is constantly in motion, always vibrating. It vibrates at higher levels or frequencies when it is vibrating at faster speeds, and lower frequencies when it slows down. The higher frequencies are etheric, and the lower frequencies become dense matter. The Divine Architect of this Universe created It with It's own set of scientific laws that govern It's dynamics. These laws are referred to as The Universal Laws of Creation.

THE UNIVERSAL LAWS AND US

You're probably familiar with some of these universal laws: The Law of Cause and Effect, The Law of Attraction, As Above So Below and many others. The dynamics of the Universe are multi-dimensional, and It's nature is multifaceted. The laws that govern this Universe we live in are always working whether we know it or not. We are using them every day if we are living and breathing. They are unavoidable, and like the laws of physics they cannot be changed or modified in any way. We did not create them, and we cannot affect them. But they do respond to our vibrations we send out with our thoughts, our emotions and our words. We are creative beings; we were designed that way. We are constantly creating in our world. We are creating because it is our nature to create.

Being creates naturally. When we are not creating consciously, we are creating unconsciously.

BELIEFS

Believe is an interesting word. It comes from the words be and live. I remember hearing this when I was in my first year of seminary. When I began my studies there, I made a choice to disregard whatever I thought I knew, so that I could learn the wisdom of these great spiritual teachings. At that time, I felt I wasn't really sure what I believed anyway, and I was in a process of changing my way of thinking and living. So when I heard that believe comes from the words be and live, I said to myself yes! That's it! If I want to really know the truth of it I must live it and be it!

That worked out very well for me, because I consciously chose it, experienced it consciously, and learned the truth of it.

Not so great however, for the unconscious creator, being and living the false belief system, and at the mercy of triggered emotions without any awareness of where they are coming from. That really is what beliefs are. Beliefs are ideas that become the basis of who we think we are and how we live. They start early in our lives. Someone tells us something. We observe something and internalize it. We overhear something. We absorb these ideas like little sponges, without ever questioning their validity. Then, these ideas grow to become the foundation of how we perceive, think and feel for the rest of our lives; unless there is an intervention, i.e., something happens to make us want to change it! These understandings and many others are valuable in my coaching work, because clients always turn up when they are ready to make changes.

THE LAW OF ATTRACTION

The Law of Attraction simply stated is: "Like Attracts Like." It is the law that determines order in the Universe by magnetically drawing similar energies together. The energies of our thoughts, ideas, feelings, and words are being constantly transmitted into the Universe at every moment of our lives. In response the universe sends back to us exactly what we send out. It manifests in multiple forms. Sometimes it draws more of the same kinds of feelings or thoughts. Sometimes it manifests things or ideas, or situations or people are pulled into our lives.

Whatever manifests, whatever we attract, I can assure you it is vibrating at the same frequencies as we are. Some of these manifestations can be messy or chaotic. Remember that expression I mentioned earlier: "Look around you, everything you see in your life today is the direct result of what you were thinking yesterday."

We call that the reflection. What you see on the outside mirrors what is going on, on the inside. Or maybe the people or situations you attracted are similar to the ones that haven't worked out for you in the past. I had a client who told me that she had "married her abusive grandmother three times." We call that a pattern!

But before you start judging yourself or beating yourself up, consider the possibility that the Universe is showing you the reflection, or presenting these similar scenarios to give you the opportunity to get it worked out correctly. This is the big misunderstanding about the meaning of the word karma: I've heard people say, "I must have been a horrible person in my last life to deserve all this punishment I'm getting in this one." It's not punishment! If we haven't completed it, if we didn't get the lesson, if we're still carrying it around in our bodies, we continue to attract more of it.

When I was working as a psychotherapist, I told my clients that from the psychological perspective, they were drawn to the familiar as if it were their comfort zone, their norm. But from the metaphysical perspective, they were attracting what they needed to learn in order to move forward. It's liberating for people to learn there is nothing wrong with them, they're not intrinsically flawed, and they can learn and grow and even heal themselves in the process.

The law of attraction states "like attracts like." It has been said: "the law is no respecter of persons." That means it is impersonal, not selective. It works the same for everyone. It is nonjudgmental. Blame has no place in Creation. We were never meant to judge ourselves, or anyone. It is important however, to be responsible for everything in our lives; it is after all, our creation. As we grow our levels of conscious awareness and understanding, ideas like being completely responsible for everything in our lives take on more meaning. (And that has nothing whatsoever to do with the concept of blame.) Since everyone is always operating at his or her own present level of conscious awareness at any given moment, everyone is always doing the best they can do at the time. Whatever the outcome, it still is true. The question is: what would you rather do next time?

CLEARING THE FALSE BELIEF SYSTEM

Our Divine Creator, in Who's own Image we were made, also designed us each with a will of our own, that we may choose what we create. The equipment we need is already within us and in use. We must engage our Spirit and our Will so we may harmoniously attract what we desire into our lives. The Spirit expresses through the mind, and the Will expresses through the emotional body. They must become harmonious and work together. We need to examine our thoughts and our feelings as well as our beliefs. Sometimes people have quite a bit of success in changing their thinking by using logic and supporting it with affirmations. However that doesn't work well with feelings. This work is best done at the subconscious level with regard to both thoughts and feelings, and particularly with beliefs.

There are several processes that I have been trained in and have been using with clients for the last 25 years. They have all been very successful. The client is in a deeply-relaxed state but fully awake. The processes are interactive and the client is always in choice. The only suggestions that come from me are: for the client to be comfortable, relaxed, feel safe, and that I will be talking with and asking questions of their subconscious mind while the conscious mind observes. Every choice or suggestion for change comes from the clients themselves.

These processes sometimes take a while to complete, but they produce quick results. If the subconscious takes the client into an unhappy or traumatic memory, the client can change the outcome of the experience any way he or she wants to, in his or her own inner world. It's empowering for the client to have control where he or she once had no choice. As the former feelings are now allowed to express, they are no longer affecting the client, instead they have been replaced by the new happy and loving feelings that come from the empowering new experience. They don't forget what happened originally, but they are no longer attached to it.

There are other processes in which the subconscious does not need the client to go into the memories at all. The subconscious confirms the existence of the various causes of the problem or condition being addressed, and the client can then choose to release and clear out every one of them. Then all of these things can be replaced with self-acceptance and self-love. The client can call back all of his or her own energy from everywhere in the Universe. I was with a friend when we discovered that with this process, enormous quantities of false beliefs, old habits and patterns, and unexpressed emotions could be released and cleared without ever having to go into them. I expressed some concern that it might not be as empowering for the clients, if they are not involved in making their own specific choices and changes in the process. She said, "You have the right to undo your creation as quickly as you like!"

Clients come out of these processes looking lighter, younger, clearer, more empowered, and relieved. Within days after the sessions they often call to report a profound experience in which they realize that they don't feel that way anymore.

I have discussed here some of the Universal Laws of Creation and Metaphysical Teachings from my studies going back many years. I have shared many insights, and explained some of the ways they are used in my coaching practice, and how they apply to all of our lives. There is one is essential element that I learned at the beginning of my studies, and it is fundamental to all the rest of it.

LOVE IS THE CHANNEL THROUGH WHICH ALL POWER,
FORCE, AND ENERGY FLOWS IN THE UNIVERSE.

This is the number one primary principle through which all other Universal Laws of Creation work.

What does it mean? I always view these kinds of statements as self-explanatory. It means that EVERYTHING works through love. It is the infrastructure of my coaching practice, and the HEART and SOUL of my SUCCESS. It is also the title of my forthcoming book.

About Ruth

Author P. Ruth Doneson, Founder and creator of Whole Person Life Coaching, is a Spiritual Teacher, Psychotherapist and Life Coach with a private practice in Scottsdale, Arizona. Whole Person Life Coaching was designed to address all four aspects of the person: the spiritual, emotional, mental, and physical aspects. Thus, an internal balance of the whole person can be achieved in the process.

P. Ruth Doneson is also an Ordained Priest, and Metaphysician. A former resident of San Francisco, California, where she attended Balboa High School, City College of San Francisco, and San Francisco State University, Ruth entered a seminary in 1969.

Ms. Doneson attended the Holy Order Of MANS Seminary[1] as a resident member for four years. The Holy Order Of MANS[2] was a Mystical Christian Teaching Order and it was there that Ruth began her metaphysical studies. Many years later, Ruth reconnected with some of her former teachers; and after some additional training, she was ordained to the Priesthood of Melchizedek, through the Gnostic Order Of Christ, by Rt. Rev. Timothy Delbert Wayne Harris on February 2, 1990.

Ruth has continued her metaphysical studies throughout her life and uses this nonjudgmental universal approach to inform her coaching and therapy. Ruth prefers coaching as a profession because it eliminates the hierarchical relationship of client and therapist, and creates a partnership between coach and client. This structure seems to her more comfortable and appropriate for the current millennium, as well as empowering for her clients.

The quality of Ruth's work can only be demonstrated by the self-discovery, self-love, goals reached and successful accomplishments she has helped to facilitate for her clients as she journeys with them on their paths.

---

1. Holy Order of MANS Seminary charter received the California State seal in July of 1968 and was granted the legal right to issue diplomas/degrees by the Bureau of School Approvals in June 1971.

2. In February of 1988, the Holy Order of MANS, having been converted to Russian Orthodoxy, changed its name to Christ the Savior Brotherhood.

CHAPTER 42

BOLD THINKING:
THE WHY, THE WHAT
and THE HOW!

BY RABIAH SUTTON

We are born awake to all of our senses. We naturally explore our environment, we know what we want, we aren't afraid to ask for it and we instinctively take action, we think BOLDLY. As time passes we learn how to speak through use of societal languages and decode body language AND suddenly we adapt the pleasures, fears, prejudices, preferences and expectations of others. Through this adaptation of societal norms, we slowly forget we can think BOLDLY, we begin to forget our true selves, and we fall asleep, lost in.... Are you a sleeper?

~ Rabiah Sutton, BOLD thinker – FWD think™

If you've ever felt asleep in life, as if you are on automatic pilot going through the motions of life, then this chapter is for you.

THE WHY

In 2010, I worked for a Fortune 500 company, I was the youngest person and one of two females on the executive management team. I managed a great team of people and I really liked the business unit we supported. I was married with three kids (Kaci, Joey & Laila), a dog and lived in a single-family home in the suburbs of DC. I had the ideal life and I was about to accomplish another goal, obtaining my MBA from Johns Hopkins University.

During my graduation ceremony, I was looking around and noticed most of my fellow graduates were smiling and happy. But, I was not. I felt gut-wrenching turmoil and I wondered WHY I wasn't happy. During the weekend festivities, I confided in my husband, Jason, that I was not happy. I explained to him that school allowed me to stretch, to think critically, to collaborate with others and to solve problems the way I thought best. At school I was encouraged to be BOLD. I felt alive, I felt awake. I realized my work environment was restricting my thinking by trying to make me conform to their methods and think within their paradigm. Jason looked at me and said, "You need to make the choice that's going to help you create your happiness."

I thought, easy for him to say. Jason was fortunate that his WHY was inextricably compelling and easy to redirect his colleagues back to. Your WHY is what you believe in, what motivates you to take action, in this case your career or business and its connection to making you feel as if you are doing something worthwhile. I can illustrate this no better than comparing my career path with Jason's. I am a Government Contracts expert, meaning I specialize in helping companies find, negotiate and implement work with the Federal government, while Jason has a much more noble career, he is an educator, a Principal in fact. I was always envious that it was very easy for him to set boundaries and think BOLDLY as he was easily able to convey his WHY. I would frequently hear "is it best for the kids" or "how does this action help our students be better people, form better habits, learn better?" He had it down, Jason would never make a commitment that did not support his WHY.

I wanted to be happy and I wanted to exert my innate BOLDNESS, so, without hesitation, right after graduation I resigned from my corporate position and declared that I was starting my own business. I started **FWDthink**™[1] with me, the BOLD thinker, leading the company's growth strategies and well, as a startup, everything else. I was on my way to creating my happiness.

Starting **FWDthink**™ was my opportunity to create a culture that rewarded out-of-the-box thinking. To serve clients in a meaningful way, always focused on WHY the mission was necessary, not just WHAT the mission entailed.

---

1. www.fwdthink.com

THE WHAT

In 2012, I was running a successful company providing growth strategies to small businesses and government contractors, but I was starting to feel stagnant again, so I put my BOLD thinking hat on and reconsidered my WHY. BOLD thinking means taking risks, tackling challenges, stepping outside conventional thinking, shrugging off the judgements of others in pursuit of your own vision. After some thought, I realized my WHY was still the same, but I needed to shift WHAT we were selling. For my company, this meant diversifying my offering. Up until this point, I had only been marketing **FWDthink**™**'s** services to other businesses and I wanted to produce an offering specifically to sell to the federal government. So I went on a 6-month discovery period of figuring out which (WHAT) service the government was buying that I wanted to sell, but more importantly, would align with my WHY of serving clients in a meaningful way, helping them grow their businesses through expansion and enhancement.

We settled on a new offering of professional development courses in two areas: Soft Skills (Leadership, Conflict Resolution, Communication) and Technology (Project Management, Agile Development, Cybersecurity). Training and coaching employees of government agencies, government contractors and commercial companies was fulfilling. It felt like we were doing something substantial, and in the spirit of BOLD thinking, we were doing it differently than our competitors. We vetted our instructors and coaches differently than our competitors, ensuring they understood our WHY and we understood theirs, and that those two WHY's were aligned. We incorporated tools into our trainings that broke up the monotony of "death by PowerPoint" or being talked **at** all day. We deliberately created our trainings to be interactive, multi-modal, and BOLD.

The WHAT is the result of your actions at any given moment in time. These actions may be related to family, work, school, hobbies, or volunteer efforts. Your WHAT is factually-based and necessary, as you must take action in life to make it interesting. But, your WHAT is not what motivates you or draws others to your efforts. Human beings are motivated by their feelings and emotions and this is controlled by the limbic system in our brains[2]. Our limbic system also controls our decision-making abilities and all human behavior. This means that we are biologically predisposed to respond to WHY we are interested in a cause, instead of WHAT that cause is. I believe we are all capable of thinking in a BOLD way and that you must know WHY you are taking action and focus on that instead of WHAT you are doing. Once you identify your WHY, your WHAT will be easy to create. The WHAT should be known, but the WHY is what will keep you on track, allow you to BOLDLY take risks, enable you to reset when you drift off track and compel others to work with you.

THE HOW

SEVEN STEPS TO BOLD THINKING

STEP 1: BALANCE YOUR THOUGHTS

For someone like me who has a thousand new ideas a day, it is still hard to think BOLDLY or otherwise if your mind is cluttered with worry, activity, to-do lists, resentment, etc. You must allow yourself to embrace the power of simplicity. The simplest thing to do is to implement structures and routines in your life, otherwise known as habits. These habits become the framework for balancing your thoughts. To connect our balance and thoughts try sitting in a quiet place, even if the only place you have is your bathroom or the car. Put on some instrumental music you like, you can search for meditation or spa music and set out to actively clear your mind, calm your mind and relax. If you are new to mediating, start with 5 minutes and build up to 20 or 30 minutes per day. I like to do it first thing in the morning, but anytime of day you can get it in, will help.

STEP 2: FIND YOUR WHY

Once your mind is clear, you can begin to reflect on your Why. Simply put, your WHY is what you believe in, what motivates you to take action, in this case your career or business and its connection to how you feel. You may initially think, it's the money or the distinction that motivates you but **IT** is not. Those are the results of your actions, not your motivation for taking action. Try thinking about what you would love to do even if

---

2. "The limbic system supports a variety of functions including adrenaline flow, emotion, behavior, motivation, long-term memory, and olfaction.[3] Emotional life is largely housed in the limbic system, and it has a great deal to do with the formation of memories." (http://en.wikipedia.org/wiki/Limbic_system)

you weren't getting paid for it and then think about WHY you chose that adventure. It could be serving others, it could be making processes more efficient, it could be solving problems, or it could be spreading joy. Don't worry if it doesn't come right away, be BOLD enough to walk away and come back, by the third try you will discover a common theme.

STEP 3: CREATE A SPACE

In my house I have a dedicated space, a sanctuary (a corner) in my bedroom and in my home office, where I go to think. These spaces are setup to allow for the free flow of ideas whether personally or professionally. I have a vision board of things that I want to accomplish or to have or that inspire me. I have tools like music, books, pencils and paper, which stimulate my thinking process. When I am in these spaces I feel calm, relaxed and eager to create. These spaces are clutter-free zones. Do not let a dedicated space deter you. When I first began this journey, I didn't have a dedicated room so I just dedicated the top of my dresser in my bedroom as the space and I placed items that inspired me there and hung my vision board next to it. I would spend short amounts of time (10 minutes) each week standing or sitting in that space and the ideas would flow without hesitation.

STEP 4: EMBRACE YOUR BOLDNESS

Once you get into the habit of calming your mind and being open to whatever ideas come, you will not be able to turn it off. Don't be alarmed this is the exciting tipping point, YOU ARE AWAKE. ☺ You will now harness the ability to think freely, BOLDLY. You will be able to focus on other aspects of your life, but you will also have no problem with your creative expression and thoughts. You will be a BOLD thinking, problem-solving machine!!

STEP 5: WRITE IT DOWN

It is important that you write down your thoughts. Getting into the habit of cataloging what you think will develop your maturity as a BOLD thinker. You will not always have time to act on your ideas right away, so writing them down assures you will remember them later. It also helps you develop your BOLD thinking muscles as you can go back and review your thoughts and ideas, revise them and improve upon them. I have a whiteboard, a couple of journals and a few online tools I use to document all of my ideas and bursts of BOLD thinking. And I, REVIEW THEM REGULARLY (see Step 7).

STEP 6: CONNECT YOUR OPPORTUNITIES

When you clear your mind, begin meditating on a regular basis and take the physical steps necessary to incubate your BOLD thinking muscles, the ideas and BOLD thoughts you document will bring about a shift in the universe. And you will start attracting opportunities to yourself that are directly related to your WHY and your BOLD thoughts. Be mindful of this and actively look out for, and be open to, opportunities presenting themselves. This manifestation could be anything from a job opportunity to a travel opportunity to a volunteer opportunity. The possibilities are endless and will be based on your WHY. In my opinion, the more the opportunity scares you, the more fulfilling it will be. Remember, you are BOLD....

STEP 7: FOCUS, FOCUS, FOCUS

If you are like me, you could spend all day, every day being a BOLD thinker: coming up with creative solutions to problems, ideating, innovating, enhancing and expanding ideas, so this is my word of caution. Do not get distracted by your newfound love of free-flowing, great ideas that align to your WHY and give you hope that you can change the world. All of this is great and I want you to develop your BOLD thinking muscles, but you still have to get things done. So, in order to avoid this taking over your life, I have found it useful to set a time each week that I call IDEAS REVIEW. I block it off on my calendar and I don't schedule any other tasks in that time period. My space is already created, my music, books and vision board are handy for inspiration and it flows easily. This way I can be super-productive throughout the week, knowing I will get my time to sit and think with no interruptions. This is my favorite time. This doesn't mean I don't have ideas and BOLD thoughts throughout the week, I absolutely do. I write them down and wait until my designated time to do any further brainstorming.

CONCLUSION

Most recently, **FWDthink**™'s professional development offering FWDlearn.com has expanded through a new product that guides companies and individuals who want to learn how to sell to the government. This new offering required BOLD thinking but also required using the steps outlined above. I had to remember to take action, to document my ideas, refine them, prioritize them, ensure they aligned to my WHY and look for opportunities to make the ideas a reality. If you follow the practical steps above, they will aide not only in building your BOLD thinking muscles, but your mental and physical organization and all around sense of balance. Here's to you… awakening from the slumber and reclaiming your true self, your BOLDNESS.

About Rabiah

Rabiah Sutton is a growth strategist who partners with her clients to expand and enhance their businesses. She believes every human being is capable of BOLD actions that will make the world more delicious for the next generation.

Described by her colleagues as a "BOLD thinker, who transcends the word "partner" when it comes to delivering quality services, maintaining integrity, and telling her clients what they "need" to hear versus what they "want" to hear. Rabiah founded FWDthink™ five years ago in order to assist a wider spectrum of clients with varying needs. She leads a team of FWDthink™ers that advise clients on Strategy, Growth and Professional Development in the Public (Government) and Private (Commercial) Sectors. Rabiah continually looks for ways to ideate and bring innovative best practices to her clients, and FWD think's products.

A consummate professional, yet down-to-earth realist, Rabiah is well-connected in Federal technology circles through her tireless involvement in key Industry associations: (ACT-IAC, AFCEA, eWomenNetwork, NCMA), and is respected as a person of deep knowledge and understanding. It is because of those qualities that Rabiah has, and continues to build, her solid Rolodex of friends, partners, confidants, mentors, and mentees at the C-Level down to the program staff. She is simply someone you want to know and be around.

Prior to founding FWDthink™, she served as Director of Government Contracts & Compliance at Tyco Integrated Security (TYCO), where she led a multi-functional team of compliance, contracts and GSA administrators dedicated to helping the government-focused business units sell, negotiate and implement their contractual deliverables.

She holds an Executive MBA in International Leadership & Consultancy from Johns Hopkins University; B.A., International Studies from American University; a Graduate Certificate, Procurement & Contracts Management from the University of Virginia; and is a Certified Scrum Master.

Rabiah has been an active member of ACT-IAC since 2011 and won the rookie of the year award in 2012 and the Ginny McCormick New Heights Award in 2014. She continues to volunteer with ACT-IAC and is currently serving as the Chair of the Academy Working Group and Industry Chair of the 2015 Small Business Conference. Rabiah is a member of AFCEA and participates in the AFCEA Bethesda chapter. Rabiah is a lifetime member of NCMA and is very active with the DC Chapter. Rabiah was recently named Managing Director of the DC Chapter of eWomenNetwork.

"If I were looking for a partner to help me navigate the complex and competitive world of doing business with the Federal Government, I'd look no further than Rabiah Sutton." Vice President, Business Development, Fortune 500 Company.

You can connect with Rabiah at:
Rabiah@fwdthink.com
https://www.linkedin.com/pub/rabiah-sutton/5/b46/30
https://twitter.com/RabiahSutton

CHAPTER 43

'HAVENING' — INSTANT STRESS RELIEF – IN YOUR HANDS!

BY PAUL EMERY

THE STORY OF JOE

Once upon a time, there was an important businessman with a lot of responsibilities. He took them extremely seriously and so worked very, very hard every day, even during his days off!

He worked late every night, and even though he took his sleep medication he often had a restless night's sleep. Thoughts would run through his mind again and again and again. He would worry about the economy, providing for his family, health concerns, things that had to be done, things that shouldn't be done, work demands, meetings to attend, the future of his business, the competition, budgeting, downsizing and the effects it would have on his staff. His thoughts were never-ending, so as usual, he woke up feeling exhausted, tired and rather grumpy.

Every day, as he looked blurry-eyed into the bathroom mirror at his aching out-of-shape body, he vowed to find time to get back to the gym again, sometime soon, perhaps tomorrow.

One particular morning, his young children were getting ready for school and as usual, were a little noisy and energetic. Children can be like that, you know! They tried to engage with him as he sat down at the breakfast table, but his patience was a little thin, so he snapped back at them, "Can't you be - MORE QUIET!"

Head down, he checked the emails on his smartphone as his beautiful wife brought him breakfast, but all he had time for was a few mouthfuls and a quick, strong coffee. The first of many these days.

Leaving for the office he noticed his wife looked concerned as he gave her a quick peck on the cheek. He promised to eat later at the office, but he knew that would be unlikely as meals were often erratic, and usually unhealthy at best these days.

No sooner had he got into the office than he discovered an employee had made a mistake. The second time within a month. He exploded with anger. He realized he was over-reacting, but just couldn't stop himself. He was a perfectionist and his staff should be too! But alas, nobody could meet his expectations. Not even he could meet them, so what chance did anyone else have!

The months and years passed by, and nothing really changed at the office – except the work pressure increased, he got sick more often, gained more weight, developed high blood pressure and diabetes, and was on anti-depressants.

But at home things had changed. He now had the peaceful home he previously sought and was living in a new, much smaller home, because his wife divorced him and took the children.

Years later, as he lay alone on his deathbed, he reviewed his life and regretted not handling it better. He regretted not creating, even demanding a better work/life balance. He regretted that he didn't spend more time with family and friends. He regretted not being a better husband, father and son, that he didn't take better notice and care of his mental and physical health before it was too late, and that he didn't prioritize the really important things in life. THE END.

If you were on your deathbed what things would you not want to feel regret about?

What steps can you start to implement today to positively alter the course of your life before it's too late?

STRESS

The so-called plague of the 21st century is on the rise in this fast-paced, technological, high-demanding, ever-changing, conflict-stricken world of ours. Without a doubt, everyone has to deal with stress, and admits to having it to some degree or other at any one time. It is generally agreed that occasional small amounts of stress can be useful. It can help spur you and others into action, drive motivation, help you attain goals and keep you sharp.

Constant, excessive, uncontrollable and unmanaged stress however, has a massive negative impact on people's lives and on those around them. It clouds thinking, creates poor decision-making, decreases work effectiveness and performance, increases negative habits and behaviors, creates poor health and stops people from being at their very best.

Just consider for a moment how it impacts your life.

Stress can be considered unavoidable and blamed on external factors and circumstances, and of course, there are many valid reasons for it. After all, the future is unknown, employees do under-perform and the Internet IS slow! However, it's your internal emotional reaction to these external triggers that is the cause of stress, not the stressor itself. The proof is that many people react differently to different situations. What stresses one person may not stress another.

Some would argue that these emotional reactions are a natural, even appropriate response that can't be avoided, so we're just to put up with them and soldier on. But many also realize that they feel out of control, that they want to be able to handle stress better. They want to be more relaxed, focused and clear-headed, to perform better, and importantly, not to have their mental and physical health impacted quite so much also.

So, we all know too much stress is counter-productive, yet to manage it is easier said than done, right? Well, not necessarily! With the right tools it can be a relatively quick and simple thing to accomplish. So, other than ignore it and hope it goes away (like some try to do) what can you do about it - *today* - to get noticeable, immediate relief?

Apart from some of the usual ways, e.g., medication (potential side-effects and usually doesn't address the underlying cause) and talk therapy (often multiple sessions, advanced time scheduled, expensive and dependent on a therapist), there are other ways you can be helped.

Firstly, there are two practical and basic ways to reduce your stress:

I. EXTERNAL

Find ways to reduce the external factors. For example, through better organization and time management, planning, streamlining and prioritization of tasks, delegate more, clarify expectations and define roles. These strategies you probably already know, but are you implementing them? A little bit of time spent on these would pay back huge dividends. So, wouldn't today be a great time to start?

You could take regular quick breaks at work by removing yourself mentally or physically from the stress source. Walk around a little, have a friendly chat with a colleague or go get some water or fresh air. Perhaps you could listen to a few minutes of soothing or enjoyable music, watch a short, funny YouTube clip, or play a quick game on your smartphone. Perhaps you could get a therapeutic massage after work.

At home you could engage in a hobby or relaxing social activity. You could take time for a nice long, warm bath, go away on weekends or better still, find time for vacations. Perhaps you can turn off your phone during family or personal time, especially at night and more often over weekends. All of this would be helpful in lowering your stress levels, switch off from work and recharge your batteries.

You could exercise or play sports. Even just 20 minutes of walking or swimming has huge benefits, for instance helping to clear and refresh the mind and allowing the subconscious mind to work on a problem. Studies prove regular exercise is one of the best ways to stay physically and mentally healthy. It helps reduce stress hormones, lowers depression, raises endorphins, improves self-esteem and confidence, and increases a sense of being in control.

I know you've heard it before - but eat healthier too! Processed junk food, which is often full of toxins, additives and preservatives, frequently increases stress and negative emotions in many people. Be mindful how you feel after eating a particular food, and especially avoid any identified food during times of increased stress and anxiety.

II. INTERNAL

Find a better, more do-able, quick and effective way to 'self-manage' your stress. A tool you can either use to clear some past bothersome memory, or something you can have to hand in your daily life for when the immediate need arises. You can try one of the usual talk-type therapies – such as psychiatry, counseling, psychology and coaching.

Or perhaps you could also try one of the more alternative or holistic ways to relieve stress, for example:

- Meditation
- Traditional Chinese Medicine
- Massage
- Breathing exercises
- Hypnosis
- Homeopathic medicine
- Yoga
- Nutritional supplements

If any of these options appeal and work for you and you are able to get quick, sustainable and long-term relief, then give them a try.

However, what I would like to propose to you here today is a new way, an innovative way, a ground-breaking way for you to be able to get rapid, relatively easy, long-term sustainable relief from any form of stress whenever you or your family need it.

Let me introduce you to the amazing Havening Techniques which I wrote about in my best-selling book, *The Winning Way,* co-authored with Brian Tracy. Havening will enable you to not only manage your daily stress, but also to eradicate many causes of it – whether from some past bothersome memory, or some present or future concern.

As unusual as the technique may seem, it has been used successfully to clear a wide range of difficult emotional issues – from P.T.S.D, grief and phobias to anger and heartbreak, so it will help you! All you have to do is apply it and experience the outcome. I think you will be truly amazed!

I wholeheartedly agree with Paul McKenna, the renowned therapist and best-selling author when he says: *Havening is going to change the face of therapy across the world. What used to take months to cure can now be done in minutes in most cases. The initial study recently completed by King's College, London shows the remarkable effectiveness of this extraordinary set of processes.* I have myself experienced remarkable results when working with clients either in-person or via Skype!

HAVENING

Havening (www.havening.org) is a 'Psycho-Sensory' therapy that is hailed as a major break-through in modern psychology. Developed by Dr. Ronald Ruden, who, upon studying the brain for more than a decade, discovered that sequences of repeated soothing touch to specific parts of the upper body, alongside lateral eye movements and distracting visualizations, have predictable and calming effects on our thoughts and feelings. In fact, scientifically-proven Havening reduces stress chemicals, increases the feel-good chemical Serotonin and quickly de-links negative and bothersome feelings from thoughts. It is usually performed by a qualified therapist but is also highly beneficial when self-applied.

There are three aspects to 'Self-Havening':

1. Retrieval of an emotion by recall.

2. Havening touch. This entails gently stroking down the arms, face, then hands in a firm but comforting fashion. These areas on the body are shown to produce strong electrical delta waves to the brain's emotional center, the amygdala. These waves in turn release a specific enzyme (Calcineurin), that permanently de-links then releases the specific recalled stress-causing receptors from the amygdala.

3. Distraction techniques. This prevents continuous re-activation of the stress producing receptors.

HOW TO REDUCE A SPECIFIC STRESS TODAY

1. Eyes closed – take about 30 seconds to bring to mind something you are stressed about. Perhaps something that makes you feel angry, worried, afraid, frustrated or sad, for example.

2. Rate your feeling on a scale from zero to ten – zero being no emotion and ten the highest.

3. Then clear your mind completely of the problem, put it out of your mind as you begin self-havening: Cross your arms over and gently but firmly continuously stroke down from the top of your shoulders to your elbows.

4. At the same time, visualize walking up a beautiful staircase of twenty steps. Count aloud (preferably) as you climb the steps in your imagination whilst continuing the arm self-havening.

5. After reaching twenty, continue the self-havening as you hum a tune that makes you feel good, or is neutral in nature, e.g., Row, Row, Row Your Boat. . . Happy Birthday. . . Twinkle, Twinkle Little Star, etc., for two verses.

6. When finished humming, continue self-havening as you open your eyes and look straight ahead, keeping head still. Look hard to the right and hard to the left, hard to the right, hard to the left, hard to the right and hard to the left again. Close eyes again and take a deep relaxing breath in and out.

7. Repeat the entire sequence 1 - 7. But now, instead of self-havening your arms, smooth across your forehead and cheeks alternatively from the center out, as if smoothly and comfortingly washing your face.

8. Repeat the entire sequence again – steps 1 to 7. But this time, self-haven your hands by smoothly performing circular hand-washing-type movements.

9. Finally, with eyes closed, take about a minute to think about your problem again and rate your level of distress as it stands now.

10. Repeat all above – steps 1 to 9 – until you feel the problem has diminished to an acceptable level or has gone.

About Paul

Best-Selling author Paul Emery helps his clients overcome any psychological and emotional barrier to success, and lead better, more fulfilling, less stressful and confident lives by utilizing innovative, groundbreaking techniques.

Paul is great...it helped me! ~ Kate Moss, Supermodel and Icon

UK-born Paul grew up with an interest in personal development and psychology. He studied at the University of the West of England as a specialized counselor/coach. He also studied the works of Anthony Robbins, Jack Canfield and Brian Tracy – later mastering and developing his skills whilst employed in the retail, telecommunications, education and finance sectors.

Paul trained formally as a therapist, and was fortunate to be mentored by such innovators as Dr. Richard Bandler, Paul Mckenna, Gary Craig, Dr. Roger Callahan, Kevin Laye and Dr. Ronald Ruden.

Paul Emery is a certified NLP (Neuro-Linguistic Programming) Master Practitioner, EFT (Emotional Freedom Techniques) Trainer, TFT (Thought Field Therapy) Advanced (Optimal Health) Practitioner, and a Havening Techniques Practitioner.

In 2002, he launched his coaching and therapy practice that thrived by offering a 'Guaranteed Life-Changing Results' service. His goal is to enable clients to become more relaxed, confident and successful, to help them conquer any limitation that may hold them back by bringing out the best they can be in all areas of their lives, in any situation, at any time either at work or at home. Paul also believes in empowering his clients by teaching simple, yet effective tools and techniques to help them manage any stress or challenge that may occur in their lives.

In 2010, Paul's eclectic service, QEPR (*Quantum Emotional and Physical Release*), was awarded the prestigious – *Holistic Treatment of the Year* – by a panel of industry experts for his outstanding contribution to excellence in his field.

He has also developed his own popular, stress-relieving, life-enhancing, light exercise class called *EMER-GIZES*, which incorporates self-shiatsu, Makko-Ho and Do-In exercises, EFT, TFT and Energy Medicine amongst others.

Paul frequently travels internationally, helping thousands of clients around the world from America to Australia. Companies such as Chevron, Credit Suisse, Thailand's

Chiva-Som and Turkey's Richmond (Nua). He's worked with billionaires, politicians, CEO's and doctors, Royalty, pop stars and Hollywood and Bollywood actors.

He has been featured on TV including Fox, Sky, TNT and on the popular Australian CH9 show *Celebrity Overhaul;* on radio such as Qatar Foundation Radio; in international magazines and newspapers - *Vogue, Marie Claire, Harper's Bazaar, Cosmopolitan, Gala, Women's Health, Men's Health, Sydney Morning Herald, OK Magazine,* the *Financial Times* and was featured in the bestselling book, *Ultimate Spa and Spa Treatments.*

In 2014, Paul co-authored a best-selling book with Brian Tracy titled *The Winning Way*, and was inducted into the *National Academy of Best-Selling Authors* in Hollywood where he received a *Quilly* award. Also in 2014, Paul was one of the sponsors of the inspiring TFT Foundation documentary movie, *From Trauma to Peace*. In 2015, he released a video course enabling people to effectively get substantial relief from any kind of ache or pain titled, *Freedom from Pain – Today!*

He provides coaching/therapy in many formats, including one-to-one, in person or via Skype, group workshops, QEPR Practitioner courses, seminars and retreats. Video of the Havening technique can be found exclusively at: www.quantumepr.com/blog/soulofsuccess.

For more information connect with Paul:
paul@quantumepr.com
www.quantumepr.com/blog
www.youtube.com/quantumepr
www.twitter.com/qepr
www.facebook.com/paulemerycoach

CHAPTER 44

IT'S *ALL* ABOUT YOU… UNDERSTANDING YOURSELF FROM THE INSIDE OUT

BY SALLY ANN MARSHALL

It was October 28, 1982 and my 28th birthday. I was blissfully happy. Out of all my friends, I believed that I'd won the lottery when it came to husbands! He was charming, funny, good looking and an excellent cook. What more could you want?

Michael and I had been married ten months and life was going along just as I'd dreamed. We had good jobs, we'd been able to afford a great little first home, and we had an adorable dog.

The plan for my birthday was going to be a splurge, a restaurant that was very exclusive, which takes months to get a reservation. I couldn't wait!

The evening began with a toast of champagne at home while getting ready. Michael and I were – and still are -- lightweights when it came to alcohol. I had never seen him the least bit drunk. For some reason, this day was different. At first I thought it was about celebrating my birthday, however after he finished the bottle and opened another, I wondered how the evening would go. I offered to drive to the restaurant, but he insisted that he was okay to drive.

By the time we reached the restaurant, I could tell Michael wasn't feeling great. He was trying his best to fake it, though, so I went along, knowing that he didn't want to ruin the evening. He'd put tremendous effort into creating something very special for my birthday. As we were being led to our table, he held onto my arm assuring me with every step that he would be fine.

Michael immediately ordered a bottle of wine after we sat down. I whispered that I didn't want any wine, but he insisted! I was confused, but gave him the benefit of the doubt; something I'd become quite good at through the years—in all my relationships, having been taught that growing up. The wine was poured.

Michael became increasingly pale as we looked over the menu. I was fearful at this point that I might be dragging him out of the restaurant soon. Instead, he quickly excused himself and said he'd be right back, thinking I hadn't noticed. It was painful to watch as he held onto the back of each chair while maneuvering his way between the tables to reach the men's room.

When the waiter returned and saw that Michael was still gone, he asked if everything was alright. I made up the excuse that he'd just gotten over the flu and wasn't one hundred percent yet.

I asked for the bill and paid it before seeing Michael out of the corner of my eye, making his way back to the table. I could tell from how he looked that he had, in fact, gotten sick. We exited the restaurant carefully and I was very relieved to be on our way home.

On the ride home, Michael, slurring his words, said how sorry he was for the night. When we got home, I immediately went into the kitchen to clean up, wanting desperately to be alone with my thoughts.

Michael came into the kitchen to get a glass of water and said, "Again, I'm sorry for tonight, but… I need to say something," He paused, and then continued. "I don't know if I will be able to love you the way you love me." I stopped immediately and asked what he was talking about.

"My family wasn't close," he said. "There wasn't any hugging and kissing or ever an 'I love you.' "Sometimes your excitement for life and your eagerness to be close is off-putting and feels fake to me." I really thought it was the alcohol talking, but the next morning the conversation was repeated. Only now that he was somewhat sober, he made light of it.

After that night, there was no question in my mind, what I needed to do. I went into survival mode and began to set about "fixing" the "unloved" man that I'd married. After all, I had helped my friends work through their issues my whole life, and loved doing it; it was like a puzzle to me. I'd been successful many times throughout the years.

What I didn't realize was that I couldn't possibly fix what I viewed as my husband's problems. It took me many therapy sessions and almost ten years to realize this fact. During this time, I tirelessly researched what I considered to be his issues. I couldn't read enough books about the subject or watch enough talk shows focused on it. Every free moment, I was researching. Even though I have heard many times in my life that you cannot "fix" anyone—you can only fix yourself—it didn't resonate.

In the meantime, Michael, with each passing day, week, month and year was becoming more and more distant. It had become a nightmare. The more I uncovered information about what I thought would be helpful, and shared it with him, thinking that I was helping, the more he rejected my input. He began to work later and later and I began to wonder what to do next.

We both had wanted children when we got married. As we grew further apart, however, I think that Michael, deep down, became afraid to have children with me. I didn't let that stop me though, as I'd been programmed to think as a kid, that I was "right."

As we each began parenting the way we had been programmed by our respective families, I quickly became aware of the next red flag in our relationship. I had dreamed of being a mom since I was a little girl, and was confident from my upbringing—I'd been taught that we, as a family, were a "rare breed." Rare, to the point of total exclusion and hiding in a tower, rare. I couldn't imagine that I wouldn't be amazing at parenting. What I didn't know is that Michael had been programmed to think that children were about lots of ice cream. So he naturally assumed that his parenting—which from my standpoint was a "fly by the seat of your pants" method at best, would be the best for our children.

Back to what I knew best, the "fixing process", this time – with a vengeance. Our children needed "my" way of parenting and "my" love. I assumed that my way of parenting was superior to Michael's since I'd come from a more loving family.

We both wanted to nurture, love and guide our two children into adulthood, but we couldn't agree on how to do so. We both had the best of intentions, but our programming got in the way. I set out to prove Michael wrong at every turn. He had to be "right" too, so it became a standoff of sorts.

Time passed—neither of us thinking we needed to change. So there we were, in this dreadful cycle of fighting and accusations. The hurtful words between us were visibly affecting our then school-age sons. I had wanted and intended to be the best mom possible, but instead, at the cost of having to be right, I was creating fear and insecurity in them.

I always loved Dr. Phil's advice and was overwhelmed when one day he said to one of his guests, "When you yell and argue in front of or within hearing distance of your children, you actually change their DNA…you change who they are to become…Yelling, shouting and fighting is not only abusive to your spouse, but is especially abusive to your innocent children."

At that moment, I knew what I had to do. I had to 'stop' making Michael wrong all the time, especially in front of the kids. I would make an effort, but I knew it wasn't going to be easy. It had become so normal for me to correct Michael; I had years and years of programming to unravel.

I began therapy shortly thereafter. My therapist, Donna, asked me after a few sessions, "Have you ever thought about what you could have done or accomplished with the time you've spent focusing on Michael over the years?" I was speechless! In that instant, I realized that my fixating on Michael was distracting me from my own life, my own dreams!

I promised myself that I would only work on me from that day forward. I set out to answer questions such as: Why did I marry him? What is my part in the miscommunication we have come to know as normal? What do I bring to the relationship? What story am I telling, and why?

Asking these questions was how I began to develop a systematic approach to uncovering ME. I hadn't known I had permission to think about just me. How selfish! "Help others, put yourself and your needs last, and you will be rewarded in heaven" is what I was taught. Until that moment, I hadn't realized that with a simple decision, my life could be different. It wouldn't be easy, necessarily, but the effort I put into it had the potential to change everything. What a thought. I wondered – How long would it take me to shift? I was beginning to understand… that would depend on how strongly I was attached to my programming.

At first, I would slip back into focusing on Michael without being aware of it. Donna then introduced me to Debbie Ford's book, *The Dark Side of the Light Chasers*. It sounded odd and scary. Why would I read about the dark side? What does that have to do with me? But I trusted Donna completely and bought the book. It opened me up to my part in not only every relationship, but every conversation and judgment I had thus far. Until then, I hadn't realized the constant judgments I made on a daily basis.

I was happy. I could work on me—what a concept! I began to practice with every thought and every conversation. I was hooked on uncovering patterns in myself, and found out that life was so much easier when I stayed with myself.

As I began to peel back the layers and learn more about my beliefs, I realized on a deep level that I alone had created the misery I felt.

The steps I have created here will help you open to yourself, understand why you are where you are and guide you to take ownership of not only each thought, but every action you take.

1…Get comfortable asking yourself questions.

2…What story am I telling? Is it even true? Do I believe it? Am I willing to tell a new story?

3…What are my triggers? What kinds of conversations create defensiveness or arguments for me? Where did I learn that?

4…Who or what am I using as my excuse for not moving forward in my life?

5…Am I willing to listen and understand what someone else's point of view is? If not, what am I afraid of?

6...Are my beliefs mine or my families? Am I willing to have my own beliefs, thus making my own decisions and living my life while still loving and respecting my family?

7...Ask, in every conversation...Do we have to agree here? Does someone have to be "right" or "wrong"? Or instead, can we both be right? Will anyone die as a result?

It is best to write your thoughts down as they come up. As you move through these questions and become more accustomed to asking them you will begin to come up with your own. Keep a journal or notebook in your car, purse, briefcase, etc. You will be surprised how often answers will pop into your head. With this process, you are truly getting to know who YOU are and why you make the decisions and have the conversations you do. It has been scientifically proven that our thoughts do, in fact, create our reality...so... have fun getting to know and learning to guide and understand who you are from the inside out!

The true gift in it all was the discovering all the programmed aspects of myself and setting about understanding them. I listened to myself in a new way and didn't need to prove anyone else wrong for my life to go my way. My husband got to be himself and I got to be myself. We slowly adjusted to life without fighting. I didn't even have to discuss it all with Michael anymore. With each revelation, more healthy boundaries were drawn. I spoke my truth in a calm way and expected nothing in return. The respect returned to our relationship. I validated myself and started working with the dreams I had put aside, bringing them to life again. Today, life is about listening to each other. We still don't agree in many of the conversations we have, but we are not determined to make each other wrong – which has brought our laughter back again. I am truly grateful that neither one of us bolted as a result of our programming, and even though I was the only one who had therapy, my shifting automatically created a change in Michael's responses. So interesting how that happens.

About Sally

Sally Ann Marshall is a licensed teacher and coach of Louise Hay's work and book, *You Can Heal Your Life.* She is also a practitioner of Chinese Face Reading, which she learned from studying with Lillian Pearl Bridges, a fifth generation Face Reader and the world's leading authority. She incorporates it all with Human Design Readings she is mastering through her studies with Karen Curry Parker. Sally's biggest desire is to help people get to know themselves again, working with a strategy that helps them live their highest expression based on their Human Design.

Sally has a degree in Special Education from the University of Texas, Austin, and has taught deaf-blind, mentally challenged and dyslexic students. She owned a Private Tutoring business for years before becoming a stay-at-home mom. While raising her two sons, she participated in several volunteer organizations in her small town of 18,000, which included The Garden Club, The Moorestown Improvement Association and The Historical Society and was very involved in her church for many years.

Before marrying her husband of 33 years, she worked in a number of different fields, including human resources at Houston Oil and Minerals, and handled scheduling of the auditing jobs, while assisting with college recruiting at Price Waterhouse in Houston, TX. At present, she is a member of the Sundance Institute and a Patron of the Annual Festival in Park City, Utah, and the Women in Film organization in Los Angeles.

When she is not traveling with her coaching and teaching, she lives in Moorestown, New Jersey, with her husband, George. They have two grown sons, Alexander and Christian.

If you would like to uncover patterns that are not working in your life, change your story by getting to know yourself again and allow healing from the inside out, you can connect with Sally at: samarshall1028@gmail.com, or by phone 609.820.0444

CHAPTER 45

FROM FEAR TO FREEDOM
OVERCOMING THE #1 FEAR OF TODAY'S BABY BOOMERS AND RETIREES

BY TERRY A. DENNIS

When I was a kid, my dad sold World Book Encyclopedias. He was one of their top producers. I remember going with him to county fairs in the 60's in his Cadillac filled with giant, heavy boxes of black and brown colored, gold-leafed trimmed books. Of course, my favorite part was sitting on his lap and helping him drive. When we arrived, my job was to help set them up for display on card tables near the entrance. Now, if you know anything about the trunk of a Cadillac, you know that you could fit a small village in there. This was going to be no easy task! I remember him telling me, "There's nothing parents want more for their children than a good education." All I wanted was a snow cone. As I watched my dad talk with and listen to these parents, I began to realize how much he really wanted to help them. He even had me talk with the kids, read with them and show them how pretty the pictures were inside. Once the parents saw how much their child was enjoying it, my dad wrote an order.

In dealing with hundreds of clients over the years, it has become clear to me that 80% of success as a professional has to do with the ability to relate to the emotions of a prospective client. Like parents at a county fair, people tend to buy the benefit they want most. In their case, it was freedom from the fear of having a dumb kid! Virtually all of my clients want the #1 benefit of an excellent retirement plan: Peace of Mind. With this as our goal, no client meeting strategy would be complete without a plan both to address the fears of Baby Boomers and Retirees and to calm those fears with suitable and practical solutions. At the end of the day, our success is found in the success of our clients.

My financial services practice offers many different types of opportunities to investors. We use a variety of asset classes to help the client meet their own individual goals and objectives. From short-term principal leverage, life insurance strategies, to balanced portfolios, to lifetime retirement income – we utilize a broad range of financial tools.

I see many types of clients in different stages in their investment and retirement planning. Some are financially sophisticated, while others have little or no experience and are looking for guidance from step one. Some can articulate their current retirement fears and concerns quite well. Others lack the understanding or vocabulary to share specific fears that may be keeping them up at night. I understand how they feel. Nobody wants to live with fear – especially during their retirement.

I have found that when you help pinpoint these fears and listen (I mean really listen) to them, you provide an emotional connection that puts them at ease and shows that you understand them. Remember, people don't care how much you know until they know how much you care. Understanding a client's fears shows them how much you care.

THE #1 FEAR: OUTLIVING YOUR MONEY

The #1 fear of Baby Boomers and Retirees today is outliving their money. This is commonly known among financial professionals as longevity risk. Today, a 65-year-old couple has a 50% chance that one spouse will live to age 85, and a 25% chance that one will live to age 92. The number of people living to age 90 and older has almost tripled over the last 30 years, according to the US Census Bureau. This actually hits very close to home with me, as all of my grandparents lived into their 90's! With such good odds for living longer, and all the challenges that this may bring, the burning question on most of our minds is, "Will I run out of money in retirement?"

Many retirees today rely upon what I call the "3 Pillars of Retirement":

I. The first Pillar is the IRA, or Individual Retirement Account.

With the disappearance of many private pensions, most of us have contributed to our 'working' retirement plans over our working careers. Depending on the type of employer we had, we typically contributed to a tax-deferred retirement plan found somewhere in the tax code. We're probably familiar with their tax code references, such as "401(k)", "403(b)", "457", etc. There are different plans for those self-employed. Regardless of the type of plan you currently are contributing to, or may have contributed to, the plan and its purpose become the same: An "Individual Retirement Account" that must maximize it's number one goal: to pay you the very best retirement income possible.

It is critical for boomers and retirees today to get as much income benefit as they can. For many, this begins with guarantees. Do we have them? Are they sufficient to meet our increasing retirement income needs? When I meet with my clients in an asset review meeting, one of my favorite questions to ask is: "How much of this (the assets) can you afford to lose?" It's very rare when I get any other answer than, "None of it!" With uncertain markets, low withdrawal rates and the threat of inflation, maximizing this part of their retirement plan is essential. One of the best ways to accomplish this is in an annuity. First and foremost, the money in an annuity is safe and guaranteed. This safety provides the proper and most suitable use of an annuity: guaranteed income. There are many types of annuities out there, so you must be careful when choosing the best and most suitable one for you and your spouse.

Annuities have long been a favorite income vehicle. Military veterans, government retirees, even teachers have enjoyed the income benefits of annuities for many years. There are many good annuities being offered today. My favorite in this economic climate are the newest Fixed Indexed Annuities. These are annuities whose gains are indexed to the markets, thus creating the potential for higher returns and higher lifetime income. The best ones offer very unique options for creating better returns and some will even do it for a small fee *on the gains only – not on the entire account balance*. This difference alone can amount to a higher account balance over time and thus, a higher income when you decide to take it.

When used properly, these powerful income generators can leverage some of the highest retirement income possible. One particular feature is called the "payout rate". This is income to you. Over time, this rate can increase to give you more of a lifetime income. On average, this rate tends to be between 7% and 8% when income is elected. I've seen them as high as 15%! This means that if your annuity grew to a total of $300,000 over time, your payout at the average rate would be up to $24,000 per year for the rest of your life.

This level of income can be much higher than the "4% Rule" income offered in "at risk" investments. Under this rule, your payout would be only $12,000 from the same $300,000 total account value. That's only half as much income! A Fixed Indexed Annuity with the right features can also continue lifetime payments for spouses, help pay for healthcare costs and even index for inflation creating an increasing income for the rest of your life.

II. The second Pillar is Social Security.

As an avid history buff, I find the origins of Social Security quite interesting. They even have some uncanny parallels to what we experience today. Back in the early 1880s, Chancellor Otto Von Bismarck of Germany had a problem. Marxist unrest was spreading across Europe and some of his own countrymen were calling for socialist reforms. To take the wind out of their sails and stave off more radical policies, Bismarck concocted a first-of-its-kind social insurance program wherein the national government would contribute to the pensions of nonworking older Germans.

Along with German Emperor William the First, Bismarck announced the idea in 1881, and the pair made their case to the Reichstag, or German Parliament, that "those who are disabled from work by age and invalidity have a well-grounded claim to care from the state."* Thus, Social Security was born.

---

* *Just a few years later, Bismarck and William also passed an Imperial insurance order — known in German as the Reichsversicherungsverordnung — which mandated certain workers to pay premiums to health insurance funds. This is known today in America as "Obamacare." But I digress ...*

Maximizing our Social Security income is essential. As income guarantees of private pensions disappear, one of the costliest mistakes a retiree can make is underestimating the value of the second pillar in our strong retirement plan. This is yet another type of valuable retirement income stream that protects against market downturns, interest rate declines, inflation and longevity risk — while also providing benefits for a spouse and survivor. Did you know that there are over 22,000 possible calculations to make and 567 ways to take Social Security?

Knowing how and when to take this important government pension can produce hundreds of thousands of dollars in more income to you and your spouse over a lifetime. In fact, according to some reports, the average married couple leaves $120,000 in retirement and spousal benefits on the Social Security table. Let's take a look at just a few popular ways to maximize our Social Security income:

1). <u>Delayed Retirement Credits</u>: Want to increase your social security retirement income by 30% or more? Of course you do! Simply wait to apply for benefits and you will accumulate "delayed retirement credits." These retirement credits can result in a permanent increase in your Social Security benefits of up to 8% per year. Once you reach full retirement age (or FRA), your benefits do not cap out.

As a matter of fact, for each year past full retirement age (typically, age 66) that you delay taking benefits, you will accumulate a permanent increase in your benefits of up to 8% per year up until your age 70. (The amount of the increase actually depends on the year you were born). For example: if you claim Social Security at age 62, you'll get just 75% of the monthly benefit you would have received had you waited until your full retirement age. But if you wait until age 70, you'll get 132% of what would have been your full retirement age benefit. Or put another way, if your full retirement age benefit is $1,000 a month, you'd get just $750 a month if you claim at age 62, but $1,320 if you wait until age 70.

You can find out exactly how much of an increase you would receive by using social security's online calculator found at www.ssa.gov.

2). <u>File and Suspend</u>: This strategy allows your spouse to collect a spousal benefit based on your earnings record while you delay the start of your own benefits. This delay maximizes your own benefit by accumulating delayed retirement credits (discussed previously). However, this only works if you have reached full retirement age. Your spouse cannot collect a spousal benefit based on your earning's record until you have applied for your own social security retirement benefit. The good news is you can file for social security and then immediately suspend your benefits. This allows your spouse to begin collecting a spousal benefit based on your earnings record, letting your own benefit continue to grow.

This strategy will also result in a higher survivor benefit for either one of you. Caution: In order to properly use this strategy your spouse will need to file a "restricted application" which they can do once they reach their full retirement age. If your spouse has not reached full retirement age this strategy does not work. They will receive a reduced benefit and will not later be able to switch from the spousal benefit to their own benefit. If your spouse waits until their full retirement age to claim the spousal benefit they can let their own benefit amount continue to accumulate delayed retirement credits and switch to their own benefit amount at their age 70.

3). <u>Work History:</u> Social security uses your highest thirty-five years of work history to calculate your social security retirement benefit. The highest thirty-five years are calculated after each year of earnings has been indexed, or adjusted, based on inflation. Think of this calculation like an average; if you have a zero as one of the numbers, it will pull the average down. To maximize your social security benefits make sure you have a full 35 years of work history. If you have less than 35 years of work history, or you have many low earning years listed in your 35 years, you can keep working so that some of your higher earning years will bump some of your lower earning years out of the top 35. Of course, you used to be able to "buy back" your benefits and restart them at a higher amount. To some, this sounds much more appealing than having to work longer for higher benefits. However, this was effectively discontinued in December of 2010. Hence, the case to wait to take your maximum benefit.

III. The third Pillar is our personal resources.

Personal Resources such as life insurance, savings and even alternative investments are the third pillar of a strong retirement plan. (For the sake of space, we won't be defining 'alternative investments' here as there are many possibilities in this space and they deserve their own chapter). This is also where our discretionary funds and our liquidity is kept. (And if you're like my dear grandmother, these two are one and the same – the cooking tin over the old gas stove). This can be done in CD's and Money Markets used to pay for vacations, fix up the house or give gifts to the grandkids.

I'm a big advocate of having a balanced approach to capital. Having cash on hand is important for all sorts of life events and emergencies, too. Of course, there can be a price to pay for having quick access to cash. Today's low interest rate environment makes these funds basically non-leveraged. This means that, apart from their liquidity, you won't be counting on this money to help you retire. No worries. We have lots of other things that do it brilliantly.

These 3 Pillars make up the most common combination of retirement income streams amongst retirees today. Given their importance to our retirements, it is crucial to get our retirement income prepared and done right. The best time to begin this planning is in what I call, "The Retirement Red Zone." For most pre-retirees, this is in the 10 years to 5 years prior to retiring time period. This is the best time to not only anticipate our future income needs, but also create the safe leverage necessary to protect our retirement account balances and ultimately, our monthly retirement income itself.

If you are beginning to plan your retirement, or find yourself somewhere in your own "Retirement Red Zone," please see a qualified retirement specialist soon. It may be one of the most important things you do for those golden years.

Dad is retired now and not in the greatest of health. Hasn't been to a fair in ages. But I remember those days fondly. Helping folks learn at the county fair. And I still love helping folks learn – how to protect and grow their wealth and income - over forty years later. Thanks dad.

About Terry

Terry A. Dennis loves helping his clients invest and retire well. He serves clients from all over the country with educated, honest, independent advice. Starting his own company over 25 years ago, Terry has amassed hundreds of personal clients over the years, and created case design that has spanned decades. Terry's expertise in finance and insurance, asset leverage and accumulation, and retirement income planning has been rewarded by several of the world's largest financial groups and associations awarding him with their top honors.

Terry Dennis contributes financial and retirement content to over 400 media outlets worldwide. He has been quoted by major media including ABC, CBS, NBC, CNBC and CNN as well as being featured in *FoxBusiness, The Wall Street Journal, CBS MarketWatch,* and the *Associated Press* on the subjects of best boomer and retirement strategies, social security maximization, lifetime income planning and alternative investing.

Terry has been a featured speaker at the United Nations in New York City where he spoke at the inaugural Global Economic Initiative. He has shared the stage with experts such as Brian Tracy, and is co-authoring a new book entitled: *Soul of Success* with Jack Canfield, as well as being scheduled for a number of television appearances.

Terry is a strong supporter of orphanages and charities including: Wounded Warrior Project, Habitat for Humanity and Toys For Tots. Terry believes in giving back and paying it forward. His newest passion is helping the underserved people groups of the world receive the gift of mobility. He acts as Ambassador and Founders Circle member for www.freewheelchairmission.org, an international charity dedicated to giving freedom to those who need the gift of a wheelchair.

Terry and his family live in the Texas Hill Country. Some of his family's Texas roots go back to the 1790's. Passionate about his golf game, you will find him on the links most weekends playing golf with his buddies Rick (aka "Junior", "Spanky" and "Helen") and "Slammin' Sammy G". Other favorites include Steak Night Saturday with his three grown kids: his good son Madison, darling daughter Amelia and son-in-law Mike; good wine with his buddy Artie; fishing with his buddy Captain Ron; racing exotic cars at the Las Vegas Speedway; lunching with his great clients; photography; painting; and ballgames and exciting brother trips with his brother Tony.

You can connect with Terry at:
Terry@Retirementcaddieusa.com
www.retirementcaddieusa.com
www.retirementcaddiepresents.com
www.easyssi.com
www.Linkedin.com

CHAPTER 46

LESSONS FROM MY TIME IN THE DARKNESS

BY SHANNA LANDOLT

It was 2011 and I had just left my job as a Vice President at a prestigious, retained search firm to start my own company. I was scared. Could I make it work? Or, would I become just another statistic of an entrepreneur who had tried to go out on their own and failed? I was excited about building something that was truly my own. I was tired of building someone else's business without experiencing the rewards of ownership. I also wanted to work from home so I could spend more time with my family. I had dreamed about owning my own business for years, and finally the timing felt right. I did it! I quit my job. I incorporated The Landolt Group, Inc. And then one week later, I learned. . . I was PREGNANT.

Rather than the joy I felt about my first pregnancy – this one was different. I hadn't planned this. This wasn't supposed to happen. The timing was ALL WRONG. I showed the pregnancy test to my husband Paul and the tears welled up in my eyes and I said, "I'm so sorry…"

My pregnancy wasn't easy. I piled on weight quickly and gained 60 lbs. I had trouble breathing. I couldn't exercise. I was exhausted all the time. But I had work to do and a business to grow. And, given I was the bread winner in our family, I couldn't just take time off. So I made the best of it. I loved my job and wanted my company to be successful.

Nine months later, Karrington Paige Landolt was born. The Landolt Group, Inc. had taken off solidly and I was earning double what I had earned as an employee. Just days before her birth, I had won another new piece of business. The person who was supposed to support me after the baby was born had a death in the family and had to go out of town. So there I was in the hospital, hours after her birth, answering emails. I smiled at my husband Paul as he held her and said, "She's definitely Daddy's girl!"

Five days later, I was interviewing candidates while rocking her back and forth in the stroller. I joked that she was getting her training as an entrepreneur early in life. My husband Paul took 6 weeks of paternity leave and eventually we transitioned Karrington over to our nanny during work hours. There was no "maternity leave." Now it felt like my nanny was raising my baby and I was just the "milk machine."

I was the modern career woman, the "Super Woman." I delegated. I grew my business. I managed the house. I breast fed and pumped milk. I led transformational seminars as a volunteer and coached a team. I was the picture of having and doing it all.

The months went on and my business continued to grow. I kept asking myself. "What are the most impactful actions I can take right now?" And I tried not to sweat the small stuff or get distracted. One of the reasons I had started my own business was that I wanted more time with my family. Never in my wildest dreams did I imagine that my life would look like this. Bit by bit, as life swirled around me, I started to get swallowed up by the bleak darkness. My emotions were volatile and unpredictable. I began to lose the ability to feel joy, to feel pride, to feel hope. Eventually I felt black almost all the time.

Six months after Karrington was born, I knew that something was truly wrong. I felt awful. I felt dark and angry. I wasn't myself. Old resentments that I had with people in my life kept resurfacing. Negative events or disappointments that I had "let go of" years ago would come up again and again. I was flooded by raw feelings of anger, upset, disappointment and resentment, as if the events had happened just yesterday.

I would walk up the stairs in my house and would have thoughts about "accidentally" letting Karrington slip through my fingers over the railing. I would walk though a doorway and would have the impulse to bash her head against the doorframe. While my business continued to thrive, I felt alone. And heartbroken.

While I deeply loved my first daughter Brooke, I had almost no sense of connection with Karrington and I felt guilty. I said all the right things – "I love you my beautiful baby." I sang songs to her. I held her. But what I felt inside was anger and resentment. I was worried that I was somehow damaging her. The voice in my head boomed, "You would be better off dead!"

In my heart, I knew that these feelings and thoughts were not right. I knew that I had to stop them. I knew that I could grow to love my daughter. Over the years, I had done a lot of transformational training and personal development. I really believed that anything was possible. By focusing on this belief, I began to experience a powerful distinction – These thoughts and feelings that I was having were NOT ME. That voice in my head was not my voice. It wasn't me. But at the same time, I had no control over it… and it was awful.

One day I woke up and had a revelation. I wondered, "Am I depressed?" I made an appointment with my doctor and she confirmed, "You have a major, severe depression." I was the last person on earth that I would have imagined having depression. But my doctor explained that this was a medical condition. It wasn't in my imagination and it wasn't my fault. The serotonin levels in my brain weren't high enough. Serotonin is the chemical in your brain that affects your mood and social behaviour. That is why I was having those thoughts and feelings. I was relieved. I wasn't a bad mother. I was depressed! It was such an incredible relief to have an answer!

I went home and immediately tried to Google everything I could find about post-partum depression and was shocked at how little there was online. But I knew that first I had to take care of myself. I let go of all of my outside commitments and responsibilities. If it wasn't critical to my business or family, I wasn't doing it. I got extremely selective about where I spent my time.

I reached out to my family and friends and told them what I was dealing with. I didn't want to keep it a secret, because I knew that I might need to reach out for help. There were a couple of times where I was so low and depressed that I phoned my best friend and had her stay with me while another one of my dear friends took the children. Because I had confided in my friends, they both dropped everything that they were doing to help me. I didn't want my children to see me in the fetal position crying my heart out. I am so grateful for the love and compassion my friends extended to me.

I also wasn't sure how to deal with my post-partum depression in my business. Should I mention it to my clients? Was I better not to? In the beginning I kept it to myself and would make sure that when I called clients that I was in a good head space. Later, after the worst of the depression had passed, I started to share what I had gone through. It was surprising how many people shared with me that they had experienced some form of depression at some point in their lives.

One of the medications I tried made me foggy and forgetful. Three times in the same business meeting, I recommended a candidate that I knew my client had no interest in hiring. And each time I brought up that candidate's name, for me, it was like I had never discussed it before. I called my client up the next day and said. "Listen, I want to apologize because I know that I must have seemed out of it yesterday in our meeting." I let her know that I had just started taking medication for a health condition that was temporary and that "I just hadn't landed on the right dosage yet." My client laughed and said that she was sometimes forgetful herself without being on medication!

Then finally after trying three different medications, we found one that worked and one day at the gym I suddenly felt happy. My happiness had been missing for so long that I had forgotten what it felt like. It felt so good to be happy again.

My road to recovery wasn't easy. It took almost a year before I had the experience of loving Karrington. While I knew I loved her, I didn't have the feeling or emotion. (Now I feel my love for her very deeply.) Then one day, before she could talk, she started singing. And she had a beautiful voice. I had been a professional singer early in my career and had performed in the Toronto production of Les Miserables. When she started singing, my heart just opened up. In that moment I finally connected with my precious girl. Now she says to me all the time. "I your angel Mommy! I your ANGEL!" And she is!

My husband and I went to see two separate marriage counsellors so that we could eliminate any patterns that would trigger my depression.

Whenever Paul would get angry (for any reason) it would spiral me into a depressive episode. It took a real toll on our relationship. We even separated for two months while we worked things out.

I also struggled to lose the weight that I gained during my pregnancy. It just wouldn't come off. Finally I said, "OK – that's not what there is to focus on right now." After going through depression and challenges in my marriage, I decided that I could give myself a break. Now slowly, bit by bit, I'm letting that weight go.

One of the things that made the biggest difference for me was creating a way to relate to my depression. Most people say "I AM depressed." As if somehow being depressed is who they are as a person. Instead, I related to it like this: "I HAVE depression and its temporary. It doesn't define who I am as a person. It's a condition that I have to manage like diabetes or a broken leg. Not fun. Not easy. But definitely something I can manage."

Now it's almost four years after I started my company. Paul and I have made peace with one another and we have way more compassion for each other. Karrington and Brooke are beautiful, confident, self-expressed girls. They both know that they are loved. My business continues to expand and I've had the opportunity to be creative in ways I never imagined. I love what I do.

What lessons can I pass on from this experience?

1) The idea of being a "Super Woman" or "Super Mom" is overrated. Trying to do it all isn't fulfilling. Ask yourself "Is this really important?" Choose where you put your focus.

2) When you are really tired go to bed. The work will be there tomorrow. By taking care of yourself you will wake up refreshed and effective.

3) Listen to your body. If your emotions, energy or health are consistently "off," ask yourself, "What is my body trying to tell me?"

4) Its not always our successes that connect us as people. Sometimes it's our struggles and challenges. Be willing to be vulnerable, even in business. When I talked to people about having had depression I thought that it would be a risk to my business. Instead, it made me more connected with my clients.

5) If you are not happy, stop and ask "Why?" . . . "What has changed?" . . . "What can I do differently?"

6) And finally, while success is important - keep in mind WHY you are doing what you are doing. The reason I became an entrepreneur was to spend more quality time with my family and do things on my terms. Stay connected with your "why."

About Shanna

Shanna Landolt, "Your Leading Authority on Leveraging LinkedIn" is Founder of Secrets From a Headhunter and President of The Landolt Group, a Toronto-based executive search firm.

Shanna has been featured as a LinkedIn and Career expert on NBC, FOX, ABC, CBS, CityTV and the Life Network.

She is a contributing author along with Brian Tracy and Tom Hopkins to the book *101 Great Ways to Compete in Today's Job Market*. She is author of the book, *Secrets From a Headhunter: LinkedIn Secrets for Pharmaceutical & Biotechnology Professionals*. She is also the Editor, Recruitment Strategy for *The HR Gazette*.

Shanna invented The Best Referrals Hiring System™. This unique system leverages LinkedIn with technology used by information marketers to produce top referral hires while saving companies up to 50% off their hiring costs.

She also works with Entrepreneurs and Senior Executives to create compelling LinkedIn Profiles that get them found for their expertise.

She has over 15 years of recruiting experience and has interviewed thousands of candidates and placed hundreds of people in 6-figure jobs.

Shanna is committed to people loving their lives and going to work each day doing something they are passionate about. Clients consider her a trusted adviser.

For more information go to: www.secretsfromaheadhunter.com

CHAPTER 47

CHANGE YOUR STORY, CHANGE YOUR LIFE

BY DAWN ROMEO

Success originates with a mindset; a shift in consciousness where you see yourself as already in the beginning stages of what you will manifest. Your thoughts and attitudes work in your subconscious mind so you can identify opportunities where others may not see them. Success comes from allowing your strengths and gifts to unfold without self-imposed limitations.

You cannot escape your perceived limitations by denying your thoughts and fears about failure. Your mind is not easily fooled. If your personal narrative is embedded with thoughts that you are unworthy or undeserving, what you outwardly say, no matter how positive and inspiring, will not create success. If you want more success, more fulfilling relationships or to feel a deeper sense of satisfaction with your life, it is time to look at your personal story and see how it helps or hinders you.

The narrative we tell ourselves about who we are, where and who we come from and what we are capable of, shapes our lives. Our thoughts, feelings and behaviors create the story we tell about who we really are. Who we are, where we come from, the family we were born into and the events that surround our early experiences lay the foundation for the person we will become.

The way we portray ourselves to the outside world may or may not match the way we feel inside. Many people seem to have it all together, but somehow they can never catch a break. They may believe it is the community, family, spouse or employer that is holding them back.

Even when you are working diligently to put the life together you really want; what you are passionate about may be unwittingly standing in your way.

The external circumstances of your life right now are less relevant than your internal subjective view of yourself. The way we feel and the images we hold in the forefront of our mind manifests in the life we live.

If you define yourself as a struggling single mother who barely makes enough money to survive then this will continue to be your reality. How you define yourself will shift your circumstances and opportunities to that end. Let's say you have spent the last five year's New Year's resolutions focused on losing weight, getting out of debt or finding a romantic partner that isn't a jerk.

What we focus on expands, so negatively charged powerful thoughts becomes your reality, your truth. If you believe you are unable then you will be. If you think you can't, then you won't. Henry Ford said, *Whether you think you can or think you can't—you're right.*

Some people are bereft with negative intrusive thoughts:

- You'll never amount to anything.
- You are just like your father.
- You're not smart enough to go to college.
- You're not pretty enough to get married.
- You could never run your own business.

Your world expands or contracts to your beliefs about yourself and the environment around you. If you believe there is a brick wall behind every door why would you bother to try and open it?

Why do we fail? Fear.

When things don't go your way you say, "See, I told you it wouldn't work."

Success is not about everything working for you all of the time. It's about making peace with the obstacles that cross your path, knowing that obstacles will come up. Working through them gives the experience and time necessary to strengthen our character and resolve. Even with the obstacles concerns, and problems you learn to never, ever, ever give up.

When you believe there is a way for you to accomplish your goals, even if you don't know how that will happen, you work differently. Then it becomes a matter of determining what information you need, the contacts you need to make and what changes are necessary to get you to where you want to be.

When you think you aren't capable of getting to where you want to be, you won't put your heart and soul into a plan. A measure of emotional self-preservation comes in and you temper your response by not putting everything you have into it, to save yourself from complete despair if you don't achieve what you want.

Changing your story in a way that lends itself to your achieving what it is you really desire is an ongoing process. After you have established what your new story is, you need to check in on it on a regular basis to make sure it still holds true for you. If an aspect doesn't seem to be particularly helpful it may require more refinement. After working with many people in therapy and workshops, I have identified seven steps that are necessary to changing your story. This shift in awareness is not about becoming perfect. It is about becoming the best *you* that you can be.

SEVEN STEPS TO CHANGING YOUR STORY

1. Determine what you want your story to be.
2. Be mindful of how you speak and think about yourself.
3. Become grateful for people, experiences and the things you already have.
4. Limit your exposure to people who are critical, negative, self-sabotaging and draining.
5. Keep what you are trying to accomplish with you literally or figuratively.
6. Seek out like-minded people.

7. Don't give up!

It simply isn't possible to create lasting change unless you know where in your life you want change to occur. You need to have a goal. It isn't enough to know what you don't want, although that can be a good beginning. Define what you want in as much detail as possible. Imagine what it looks like, feels like and sounds like when you have gotten what you want.

Be kind to yourself. Don't spend precious time beating yourself up for all of the mistakes you make along the way or call yourself names like stupid, unlovable or unworthy. Mistakes happen. It is important to take personal responsibility in every area of your life, but be kind. Using negative self-talk is counterproductive.

By identifying all of the positive things you have in your life you will more clearly be able to identify what you want more of. I recommend that you write down five things each night you are grateful for, as well as meditate for ten minutes each morning on what you want to achieve.

Create a vision board, mind map or any other visual representation of what it is you want to create or bring more of into your life. Take a picture of what you created with your phone – so you can look at it every day to really keep your goals in front of you.

Expand your circle of friends, acquaintances and colleagues so as to include people who are also on a journey towards growth, success or fulfillment. Being around people like this creates enthusiasm and optimism, so watch out!

Remember that things don't always happen on the timetable we set. There are usually more variables then we first imagined. Change is a process not an event. You are your life's work, your magnum opus, so allow yourself to continue to grow.

JENNIFER'S CHANGING STORY

Jennifer is a 32-year-old woman who works as a freelance writer. Jennifer told me she had always struggled with self-esteem and a sense of worthiness. Despite what others would call enormous talent, she felt her writing was inadequate and was often overly critical and emotionally punishing. Jennifer struggled so much with doubt that she began to feel depressed and anxious. When we met she told me she was writing a book, but was struggling to complete it. She found herself procrastinating and feeling depressed.

Jennifer described herself as a fair writer who made enough money to live on, but she did not see herself ever becoming successful. When asked to describe her story of who she was and where she came from, she described a story of fear and lack. Jennifer grew up poor. She lived with her mother and two siblings. They always struggled financially. Her mother worked two jobs just to make ends meet. She explained that her mother never really approved of her decision to become a writer. Many of her friends encouraged her to "get a real job" with a predictable income and pension.

Even though she was able to make a living from her writing, Jennifer spent a great deal of time second-guessing her decision to stick it out. Her limiting beliefs surrounded her in everything she did. She had no idea how these beliefs kept doors around her closed, but she was willing to do whatever it took to overcome her limitations. The willingness to do the work opened up her possibilities by opening her eyes to the choices surrounding her.

Begin on your new path now. Write out your new personal narrative in as much detail as possible. How different is it than the one you have been using up until now? Pick one area at a time to work on to shift into your new story. Start with whichever aspect you want. The key is to be striving every day. Create a list of action steps for the area you are choosing to work on to keep the momentum going.

In Jennifer's case she began by identifying what she needed to do to get her book finished. She recognized several key things that she needed to implement. First was to reread everything she wrote and make notes on what she thought she needed to add and any areas she wanted to change or get rid of. Then she looked at the negative self-talk she had about her writing and capabilities. Jennifer was able to really see how this mindset did not support what she really wanted to do. She was able to pinpoint exactly how her personal story sabotaged her dreams.

Next we worked on challenging each limiting belief she had and construct ones that supported her dreams and goals. She created a gratitude list every night and began meditating on her capabilities for ten minutes every morning. She visualized her finished book and how she would feel when it was published. She practiced mindfulness throughout her day and challenged any negative thought that came up instead of accepting them. Slowly the negativity began to recede and she felt free and inspired.

Jennifer set up a schedule where she worked on her book for a minimum of one hour each day. She minimized her mindless activities like watching television and surfing the internet aimlessly. Her confidence grew and she planned her daily activities and list of what she wanted to accomplish the night before.

She saw the amount of negativity she surrounded herself with and knew this had to change. Jennifer let go of some relationships she recognized were not good for her, and she set limits with others. She explained how negativity had a bad effect on her life, and that she would no longer be able to be around people who were critical, gossiping, or put her down. To her amazement, setting limits was helpful. Some were fascinated by her direct approach to changing what she exposed herself to and shared what their own negativity had caused them. Jennifer was able to act as a mentor and share what she had learned.

In many ways it is easier to declare you can't change because you are too old, lack the resources to create what you really want, are unlucky or never get any good breaks. But this is an excuse. Your excuses keep you stuck because that is what they are designed to do. If you want to make changes you need to shift your thinking. When you accept who you are in the present moment, then you can begin to change. You cannot change what you do not acknowledge.

Come into being the person you want to become in every given moment. Talk about your unfolding life in terms of *when* instead of *if*. In Jennifer's case, it was "*when* I finish the novel" not "*if* I finish it." Use your identifying phrase "I am" wisely. Whatever comes after "I am" needs to be positive. To get to where you want to be, your inward feelings and outward statements need to match.

Ask for help when it is needed. This can be difficult for some in the beginning especially if you have little experience asking for help. You will most likely find the people who love you are more than willing to help when you ask. Talk about what you want to do. Sometimes just talking about it can spark ideas. Others may also have knowledge you are not aware of and point you in the right direction. Therapy, workshops and coaching are also powerful tools in working through a negative mindset so you can focus on creating a life you enjoy.

You are a fully-functioning human being, who like everyone else, is a work in progress. Each day is a new opportunity to develop a deeper understanding of your capacity and capabilities. You can choose to live your life on, and with, purpose. Follow your own path by changing your story and live your life to the fullest in the most meaningful way for you.

About Dawn

A nineteen-year, multi-faceted career qualifies Dawn Romeo, LCSW, LCADC as an impressive and highly effective psychotherapist who understands the core concepts of success and the roadblocks we manufacture to avoid it. Her expertise and education has benefited a diverse client population as she draws upon an impressive background that includes a Master's degree from Columbia University and a post graduate certificate from New York University in Forensic Mental Health. Always looking to help others and give back to the profession, she mentors a variety of clinical staff including LCADC and LCSW candidates.

Concurrently, Dawn offers family and individual therapy from her private practice in Montclair, New Jersey, where she utilizes a holistic approach to treating anxiety and depression and also provides in-depth education supportive of twelve-step self-help groups and relapse prevention.

Truly immersed in all aspects of her profession, Dawn also acts as facilitator and workshop instructor, presenting regularly on topics such as: "What's On Your Bucket List," "Getting Unstuck," "Increasing Intuition Through Balance," "Finding Your Life Purpose" and "Radical Acceptance."

Dawn also coaches select individuals on how to create more success in their lives. Her philosophy of working with an individual's strengths and guiding them on their path towards the life they are looking for in smaller measurable steps, brings lasting success and fulfillment. She works with clients on creating goals from their dreams, and the action steps to get them to the finish line. Dawn is able to assist people in increasing their motivation and consider possibilities they were otherwise unable to see. Her background in psychotherapy gives her a unique take on perceived limitations and ways to break down barriers.

An accomplished writer, Dawn's philosophy holds that success is more than a result of actions and endeavors. She is an inspiring authority on attaining success, and this, coupled with her broad background with so many groups in clinical settings, makes her an authority on the subject. In addition to her many published articles, she will be releasing a new nonfiction book in late 2015.

Dawn holds multiple accreditations and certificates including School Social Worker, Licensed Clinical Alcohol and Drug Counselor, Licensed Clinical Social Worker, SIFI/LCSW Supervision Certificate and is a Certified Clinical Supervisor. She is affiliated with the NASW, Hudson County Chapter.

Dawn currently operates her private practice in Montclair, NJ, and may be contacted by email at: dawnvbr@gmail.com.

To read more or subscribe to her newsletter visit: www.dawnromeo.com

CHAPTER 48

THE FRANKLIN FORMULA — A DISCIPLINED APPROACH TO WALL STREET

BY DARRYL FRANKLIN, PhD

Wall Street . . . Stocks & Bonds . . . Yields & Returns . . . Calls & Puts — They were all intimidating to me.

Out of necessity (I really needed the money), I found myself on Wall Street and began searching for a way to minimize risk and still get a good return. Doing research, I discovered a process that many can use for their own success as well.

I truly believe that a life of purpose is one that makes the world a bit better because we have lived. I hope my living and sharing my story of Wall Street success will be of value to you and give you concrete steps to enhance your own financial success. Let's start with a bit of background . . .

I am a Chicago kid, Southside, born and raised. Mom is a big Cubs fan, Dad a big White Sox fan. I often say I am the product of a mixed marriage.

My dad worked for the federal government. Mom worked for "Ma Bell" as an operator. I still remember coming home from school, picking up the receiver, putting my finger in the "O" on the rotary dial and cranking it all the way around to reach her and let her know I was home. My parents were a great influence on my life as well as my brother's...especially my dad.

My dad grew up without a "dad" in his life. He said his father gave him two things, his last name and $7 for high school graduation. That's the sad part; the happy part is that the lack of a father figure in his life deeply affected him. He made up his mind early in life that when he became a father, it would be much more than just biological, he would be a dad, a true dad, a dad that encouraged and empowered his children. A dad who would shower them with love and support to make them the best they could be—the exact opposite of what he had experienced.

My dad finished high school and went into the Army. It was in the Army where he advanced to the rank of sergeant, something not a lot of men of color experienced in the fifties. It was the Army where he learned discipline, leadership, honor, and the often untapped power that each of us has within us; all of these were virtues he passed on to me and my brother. Pause for a moment and consider the untapped power within you.

One of my earliest memories involving discipline was dad making sure I got on my knees, and said my prayers before bed, and recited the *"Lord's Prayer."* It was the discipline my Dad instilled in me that sets the stage for what I am going to share with you.

Life is full of twists and turns. Heck, how I even wound up working on Wall Street in the first place is, at the very least, a strange twist of fate.

After experiencing what can only be described as a miracle healing on my body (which is another story for another time), I found myself on the path of spiritual yearning. Wanting to know more, I enrolled in Garrett Evangelical Theological Seminary, located on the campus of Northwestern University in Evanston, Illinois. My life changed dramatically as a result of seminary. It took me 5 years, 4 months and 20-some odd days to graduate.

I then spent two years in full-time ministry, praying for the sick, burying the deceased, marrying the betrothed, and providing pastoral care for a 2000 member congregation.

My life took another turn when our son was accepted at an Ivy League college. I was conflicted. Do I continue in ministry at a quarter of what I had previously earned in the marketplace and say "no" to my son's great opportunity, or do I consider other options and return to the corporate world? It's funny how life works.

During this time of internal conflict, I was led to a life-changing piece of ancient wisdom. It reads, *"If any provide not for his own, and especially for those of his own house, he hath denied the faith, and is worse than an infidel."*

After the tears finished rolling down my cheeks, I updated my resume.

In January 2009 (this is right after the financial crisis of 2008), a recruiter from a big-name Wall Street firm saw my resume, called me and asked if I had ever thought of a career in financial services. I said, "I'd thought about it. In fact, I have done well in my personal account but my undergraduate degree is in computer science, and I'm not sure that's a good fit." She responded with something I'll never forget. She said, "Darryl, with your background, a Masters in Divinity, ordained minister, and working on a doctorate – what Wall Street needs right now is some folks with integrity. We can teach you the rest of the stuff." That conversation led to an offer letter and my immersion in a grueling, two-and-a-half-year training program. It was intense.

Along the way I learned a lot about Wall Street, how it operates, and how "the Wall Street System" often impacts individual investors. Fortunately for me, and now for you, I also learned three rules for success. These three rules are the foundation of what I call the *"Franklin Formula."*

I started using the *"Franklin Formula"* investing process in November of 2010 while working for the blue-chip Wall Street brokerage firm, Morgan Stanley.

After enjoying initial success with just two clients, I ramped up the process. The more I shared the process with clients, the more it resonated. The more it resonated, the more I used the process. It quickly became my full-time effort.

Take a look at the following table of results…

2011: 716 trades in client accounts with just 14 losing trades
2012: 719 trades in client accounts with just 12 losing trades
2013: 1310 trades in client accounts with just 7 losing trades
2014: 2428 trades in client accounts with just 12 losing trades

5173 trades in client accounts with just 45 losing trades*

That's a 99.1% success rate!

*Trades refer to the opening and/or closing of an equity/derivative investment.

Like to know how? Be disciplined and follow these rules:

Rule # 1 – *Look at stocks as you would a business partner.*
Before making an investment, I examine my potential new "business partner" and ask a number of questions. For example,

- How long has the company been in business?

- How many employees do they have?

- What was the company's revenue last year? The previous two years?

- Is the revenue rate growing, stagnant, or declining?

- Is the company a leader in its market?

- Is there a moat around the business protecting it from competition?

- What about the management team? Do they have a record of success?

- What do other analysts think of the company's prospects for the future?

Sure, any one of these questions answered in isolation provides insight, but taken as a whole, the answer begins to paint a picture of a company I want to be a "business partner" with.

Finding these types of companies is not hard, but it does take time. It does take a disciplined approach. It takes a system to follow. In following Rule # 1, I have developed a list of forty (40) stocks that I look at every single trading day. I've learned how they ebb and flow, making it easier to follow Rule # 2.

Rule # 2 - *Put the odds in your favor with timing.*
The stock market in general tends to trade within a range. The same is true with the stock of individual companies as well. Once you have identified your "business partner" company, study the range in which it trades. With practice you will get to know when the stock is near the low of its range and when it is near the high of its range. When it's near the low, it represents a good time to buy, near its high, a good time to sell. Space limitations inhibit me from showing detail, but my firm has a website for our *Resource Guide,* where you'll find a list of the websites I

use regularly to help put the odds in my favor with selection and timing. This takes discipline, but it works.

<u>Rule # 3</u> - ***Preserve capital by reducing risk.***
Let's be clear, long-term successful investing is about <u>preservation of capital</u>.

You can't invest without capital in your hand, and if you don't find a way to preserve your capital over the long-term, a bad investment here or there can take months or even years to recover from. I developed the *Franklin Formula* around the idea that I would rather make a smaller return and preserve my capital than swing for the fences and strike out while chasing a big winner.

I reduce risk by lowering our clients' basis as frequently as possible by capturing both dividends and premium using options. This isn't complicated, but discipline is crucial. Let's look at the dividends first. Finish this line, "You catch a cold and begin to sneeze and wheez. To cover your nose or mouth, you reach for a _____?"

Many will answer "Kleenex." The brand name has become synonymous with tissue. Kleenex is made by Kimberly-Clark. If you go to Kimberly-Clark's website, you will likely notice dozens of products you are familiar with. These products generate repeatable revenue for Kimberly-Clark. Kimberly–Clark has been in business since 1872. They have been paying a dividend consistently since 1935. Now there are no guarantees when investing; there is always some risk. But I ask you, "What do you think the odds are of Kimberly-Clark being in business next year? What about paying a dividend?"

Every dividend you collect reduces risk by lowering your basis, and as an investor, I want the odds in my favor.

The second way I preserve capital and reduce risk uses options to lower our basis by collecting call premium. Again, discipline is the key.

Here's a simplified example. Assume I can buy a stock for $10.00 and then sell someone else the "right" to buy it from me for $11.00. I reap the benefit of the $1.00 increase—the difference between my sales price and my purchase price—as well as the option price for selling the "right." This option price varies but in this scenario it could be .10 to .20 cents.

When I am teaching on the subject, I use the metaphor of purchasing a rental building for $10.00, selling it for $11.00 and the dividend and option price are my rents collected while I hold the investment. In other words, we reduce our basis, reduce our risk, and increase the likelihood for investment success.

There are dozens and dozens of books on options as well as a variety of sources for classes. The Options Industry Council (www.optionseducation.org) offers a number of classes around the country and online, most of which are FREE to help educate investors.

When you follow Rules 1, 2, and 3 in a systematic, disciplined way, it becomes easier to have a high rate of success and limit losses. The power of the strategy enables the potential for at least three paydays: 1) the growth of the underlying investment, 2) the income from the dividend and 3) the premium income from the option. While past performance is not an indicator of future success, the *Franklin Formula* serves as a great foundation.

I want you to invest in yourself first.

Study and use the *Franklin Formula*:

1. ***Look at stocks as you would a business partner.***
2. ***Put the odds in your favor with timing.***
3. ***Preserve capital by reducing risk.***

Develop a process and take action, be disciplined in your efforts, and you will have Wall Street success.

Tonight, when I get on my knees to say my prayers, know that I will be praying for you and all those whose lives I have had the honor of touching, hopefully making the world a bit better.

-Darryl

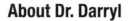

About Dr. Darryl

Darryl Franklin, Ph.D. helps his clients not only dream big, but also bring those dreams to reality as a portfolio manager, planner, and coach.

As a child, Darryl was exposed to a value system that laid a solid foundation of respect for others and building meaningful trust-based relationships. His parents provided a powerful push towards discipline, work ethic, and academic excellence, all instrumental in shaping his financial philosophy.

It is a philosophy shaped by the twists and turns of life. One such twist occurred in 2001, when he experienced a health–related miracle, causing the direction of his life to change. Searching for answers, Darryl enrolled in the Master of Divinity program at Garrett Theological Evangelical Seminary on the famed Northwestern University campus in Evanston, Illinois. This led to his ordination and a two-year stint as a full-time clergyman.

Still not finding all the answers he was seeking, he continued his studies and research at Benedictine University. It was in the writing of his dissertation that some of the answers to life's puzzle began to emerge.

Darryl's life path again twisted when his clergy background caught the attention of a recruiter for a blue-chip Wall Street wirehouse brokerage firm. The well-regarded two-and-a-half-year training program provided a strong financial background, but also exposed some inherent flaws with the traditional Wall Street brokerage model. Believing there was a better way, Darryl founded Oakwood Wealth Advisors in 2012 to serve an underserved niche – working women who just don't have the time to manage and grow their wealth.

Drawing upon his background as a seminary-trained, ordained clergyman, Darryl aligns his faith with the fundamental need to plan for the future, providing a perspective that others often miss. Using his technical and research skills, Darryl discovered an approach to investing which minimizes losses and increases gains. The process is built on a rigorous disciplined approach to investment management, one a client affectionately named the "Franklin Formula."

Committed to the community, Darryl serves in the local church and as a local District School Board member. He also shares his unique life experiences in his lectures, teaching, and writing with an emphasis on helping individuals reach their full potential. In addition, Darryl serves as a business school faculty lecturer at Benedictine

University where he teaches MBA622-*Creativity and Innovation in Business,* MBA653-*Investment Theory & Portfolio Management,* and MBA656-*Investment Analysis.*

Darryl Franklin earned a B.S.C.S. from the Illinois Institute of Technology, a M.Div. from Garrett Theological Evangelical Seminary and a Ph.D. from Benedictine University.

You can connect with Darryl at:
Darryl@oakwoodwealth.com
www.twitter.com/DrDarrylF
www.linkedin.com/in/darrylfranklinphd
www.facebook.com/OakwoodWealth

Other Titles By Darryl Franklin, Ph.D.

- *What Women Should Know About Their Money – 8 Practical Steps For Financial Success*

- *You Can Forget Money Worries If You Follow This Simple Bible-Based Financial Plan*

- *The Higher Power Leadership Model - How The Belief In A Higher Power Influences The Way A Leader Leads*

CHAPTER 49

POOR SOUL, RICH SOUL — DEFINING SUCCESS FROM THE INSIDE OUT

BY VERA GERMANUS, PURPOSE & PERFORMANCE EXPERT

I'm 10 years old and I'm already asking <u>big questions</u>. "Why am I here?" . . . "What should I do with my life?" My sprouting mind had a hard time grasping these tough questions and so do the adults who I ask to answer them. I know they wanted to satisfy my insatiable curiosity, but they fell short on that task. The responses I received were more in line with old world wisdom. "Go to school, just do the best you can. Working is for money, not for happiness." I thought, *okay*, and I tried to make the best of it. However, **I was never content with the answers or the results**.

Mercedes at 20?
Being disappointed in the idea I could find happiness in work, I decided I would at least drive a Mercedes by the age of 20. With a lot of hard work and a skewed idea of how to achieve my purpose, I received high grades that got me to university at 17. There I was, a young bright woman with a great future. I had the perfect scenario lined up: I studied business economics, already got great job offers and had a great boyfriend—a

smart guy from a wealthy family. I was lined up for success, but that was as close as I came to my Mercedes…

No Mercedes!

It was actually during my visits to that boyfriend's family's home that I couldn't help but take notice that something was missing. They seemed to have it all and probably even thought they were happy, but I felt something totally different. <u>I felt no happiness, I felt sadness</u>! Like they were meant for so much more and had given up on that, had even given up on watching their children grow up, just for 'success.' That was unsettling to me. *"If this was success I would not have it!* **I would not sell my soul for a Mercedes!"**

Midlife at 20!

So I was not going to be successful, but then what? I struggled, and although life had its 'feel good moments,' I just <u>didn't feel real happiness.</u> I was never at peace with who and where I was. I longed for alignment—inner peace—but it just wasn't there! I expressed my concerns to a psychologist, wanting to figure it out. She thought that perhaps I was having a midlife crisis. Really? I was already burnt out when I was only beginning. . . when I was only 20 years old.

Life went on . . .

I worked even harder and eventually got my Master's Degree in Business Economics. I went to work and excelled, working with people in the corporate world as an Organization Development Consultant, a Human Resources Manager, and even an Executive Coach, but I still didn't go home feeling rewarded for a great day's accomplishment. *I'd reached the pinnacle, according to traditional definitions, but there was **one huge problem**! <u>My job</u>: teach people to become better in their careers. <u>The reality</u>: my own career didn't make me want to **jump out of bed in the morning.***

No more!

If this is not what I really love, why am I doing it? Each time that question popped into my mind, I was clueless how to change that. Until I found out…I would keep progressing and moving forward, achieving admirable success in the eyes of many that were shallow to me. To put it plainly, it was, "Blah, blah, blah."

There was another problem that persisted in my life, too, which I used to help justify why I was just "putting up." It was my neck. I'd had an auto accident that made my neck become a pretty big concern. However, it gave new meaning to the expression 'pain in the neck.' I couldn't get up, so how could I live my purpose and take full responsibility for my own life and my own happiness?

It really was time to change, but how?

Now what?

Not being someone to remain motionless when I want something, I started to seek out some connection that would help me piece it all together. I learned aura reading and even went on journeys of the subconscious mind where I'd be at a monastery for a few months, meditating and trying to find my answer. *It had to be somewhere inside of me. But where?*

Then it happened, the epiphany. *I had to stand for what I was meant for.* I'll admit that it came with a price. I was around thirty-five and it included the loss of a husband who didn't understand, the loss of my home, and even losing a lot of friends who didn't like my rebellion against their definition of success. It was tough, but guess what? I already felt better!

THREE ENCOUNTERS

I've committed to change; now it's time to find it. I made it a quest to learn from two leading people. That's just what I kept in mind as I headed out on a long trip to Asia. The first was the Dalai Lama, who could help me spiritually. The other was Success Coach Jack Canfield (ranked #1 in the US), who had inspired me from The Secret and made me sense that he could help me find the new definition of success that I was seeking.

1. The Dalai Lama: *Live light*

Making my way to Dharamsala, the home of the Dalai Lama, I hoped to get a glimpse of him. I didn't have an appointment to see him, of course. I just waited. After nearly three weeks, my hope ran out and I thought, *this isn't meant to be.* It was time to leave . . . maybe next time. That night I was set to pack my bags, but I couldn't get it done. I had to postpone it. Guess what? The next morning, the word was out that the Dalai Lama was giving an audience that very day!

I am not a guru seeker, so although I wanted to meet the Dalai Lama, I had little expectation of what he would be like. Meeting him changed that completely! He held my hands for a long time and looked me deeper in the eye than anyone had ever done before. **He looked me in my soul.** When I walked away, I was glowing like a ball of light and it made me cry. I knew that I'd tapped into something special, a concept that would be fundamental in my pursuits. I saw that on top of Buddhism he was showing **that we should all live light.** _Make life easy and joyful instead of heavy and difficult. Live it to the fullest without hurting others!_ This is probably the most difficult thing to do. How do you do that? Suddenly it didn't seem too horrible that I still didn't know my purpose. I had something to work on.

2. Jack Canfield: *Success*

It was time to try to connect with Jack Canfield. This didn't come easily or quickly, though. It took me a few years and luck rather than anything else. I'd kept growing during that time, though, and it further solidified my knowing: everything starts from the inside and works its way out.

Finally, I met him in his home in Maui. Along with another very inspirational man—Mark Victor Hansen. It was great and I was tongue-tied. Honestly, I didn't get out a fraction of what I had to say about connecting people with their soul. "You should have brought that up, Jack would love it," the other people said. I replied, "Should have, could have, but didn't." Even when fate was on my side and I got the chance to interview him 1-on-1, I failed to mention it... I did ask him what he thought of *Purpose as the missing link to the Secret,* though, and we **both agreed that success could only be real success if connected to your soul's purpose.**

3. Me: *Love*

The last important encounter was with someone much closer: **ME!** This encounter started long before the others and is still an ongoing process. How did I get the inner peace I was longing for, as long as I didn't know, love, and accept myself! I needed to get in deep contact with myself and that was the hardest part of all...

So what happened? Learning about myself is what happened! Discovering my true talents and what I was made of. My eyes opened and all I could feel is appreciation for the full me. Which easily turned into love. Love for where I was and who I was: me, my soul, and I.... I could rip myself of all the expectations about me from myself and from the outside world. A heavy weight was taken from my shoulders and from then on I could start living light. Simply by loving myself and using my talents.

That leads me to the final piece that led me to where I am today, which is in a position to help people connect with their soul to become successful.

The truth about success and happiness

— *You do not have to sell your soul to earn money.* You can have success and feel fulfillment while serving the world at the same time. Many people may say that is utopia—it's not. *The truth is that the only way to success and happiness simultaneously is from your soul.* Does utopia exist in our souls? Absolutely!

— *If you do not know your purpose, you do not know where to go.* We know so much now, nothing more important than the understanding that love and joy is bound to happiness. But it still takes one more thing to be successful: **purpose.** Without purpose, you will just live (maybe even light) but go nowhere. Going nowhere means no success. Purpose is connected to the soul and therefore success is connected to your soul.

— *Find that thing that is worth fighting for and pursue it with all you have!* Your higher purpose will pull you up even when you are tired. The more you love what you do, the more success you attract - **new world success**. Toss away the **old world success**, the archaic belief that implies, "*go to school, just do the best you can. Working is for money, not for happiness. More money means more status and success. And that will make you feel happy.*" **Disregard it!**

Focus on these three principles and *success will follow!*

1. Love deeply - Love

2. Live light - Joy

3. Be on purpose - Purpose

Start INSIDE and Work Your Way OUT:

What took me a long time to understand—25 years—doesn't have to take you that long. You have amazing things to do to make this world better by starting with you and what's happening inside of you. That's my focus and that's my soul purpose. Today, I work joyfully and with great commitment to help as many people as possible to start doing what they are born for. *This is what leads to a life of joy, fulfillment and success;* all while adding to the world at the same time. I wish for you to experience that too!

The MOMENT OF TRUTH:

Show your courage and caress your soul with the three questions that can take you from a poor soul to a rich soul.

1) *(Love)* <u>Do I love where I am and what I do</u>?

If you didn't say yes in your brain in a hundredth of a second flat, it's time to evaluate if you are really achieving success through your soul.

2) *(Purpose)* <u>Would I take the blue pill or the red pill</u>?

This question may stump you if you're not a Matrix fan. Let me summarize—blue pill equals the old world success, you do what's expected of you and accept that's your fate. However, the red pill equals the new world success, the one in which you explore your path and find out where your soul guides you.

3) *(Joy)* <u>As I make the choices in my life, do I feel like I am getting lighter or heavier</u>?

Evaluate your steps and how they make you feel. When you do something and it feels good inside of you, maybe even brings a smile to your face, you're walking toward lightness. Likewise, do something that's against intuition or your soul purpose and you might be feeling a bit abandoned . . . maybe even isolated, because you're lost and it's heavy.

Yes, these are three tough but amazing questions, part of a roadmap that is easy to follow, even if you don't know where your starting point is. And from them, the <u>3 Steps of Finding Success</u> emerge:

1. Discover your professional purpose, talents, and what you really desire.

2. Live a life of love, joy and fulfillment.

3. Become successful by doing what you love.

TODAY:

I am living my soul purpose and everything in my life has changed in a meaningful, extraordinary way. And within the people I work with every day, I've seen wonderful transformations because they have taken the bold, liberating step of getting up and standing for what they are meant for. My career is more than a job, it is attached to my very soul—I am thankful for that.

I'm not a mind reader, but I feel quite confident in this statement being true: **you would not be reading this book if you felt that you'd achieved the level of success that really makes your love, joy, and purpose shine**. Understanding that puts you on the right track, but now it's time to act.

I invite you to join me and start living light and connecting with your *soul purpose*. Finding it and incorporating it into your life isn't the end of the journey, but the beginning of a beautiful adventure that leads to amazing results. *Say goodbye to a poor soul and hello to the rich soul*. It is a process of learning that is worth it. Better yet, embrace any opportunity you can to take advantage of what took me 25 years to learn. You may only need 25 hours! Become a graduate of the new class of business professionals.

About Vera

Vera Germanus is a Purpose & Performance Coach and founder of *Purpose & Performance Academy* – a 'new world success' enterprise that specializes in helping clients to discover their talents and find their purpose. The goal is to help individuals gain authentic success in life by doing what they love. Vera is also the co-founder of the Dutch online career academy Happy Worker Academy. Both businesses are attached to her very soul.

Her mission: Creating a movement by *uplifting as many people as possible from the Old to the New Class of business professionals.*

Although Dutch born, Vera has full professional efficiency in the English language. She has earned a Master's Degree in Business Economics from Vrije Universiteit Amsterdam. Vera has a vast business background and has worked at world-renowned companies such as Shell, PWC, and KPMG. Through these experiences, both as a Management Consultant and a Human Resources Manager, she gained a distinct perspective into the corporate environment. With hands-on interaction and observation, Vera was able to pinpoint similar problems consistently surfacing in these environments. It did get her thinking about her own life and career, as well as the way so many others view success. Understanding this became a huge motivator in her looking for a different approach to success than what she was personally experiencing, and knew that so many others were struggling with.

Vera saw an opportunity to positively impact people by helping them seek out what they struggled with most: success and happiness. Research, study, and a very personal soul-seeking journey that included meetings with the Dalai Lama, Jack Canfield and Mark Victor Hanson helped guide her to the place she wanted to be. She became certified as a Talent Coach, grew into her soul purpose, and became a student of Jack Canfield (ranked #1 in the US) to learn more about success. Combining this all made her find a proven system to connect with New World Success or Soul Success.

With her seminars, books, programs and speaking engagements, Vera inspires people around the world *to stand for what they are meant for!* Vera is co-author with New York Times Bestselling Author, Peggy McColl, and multiple New York Times Bestselling Author, Jack Canfield.

Today, Vera travels worldwide, incorporating a personal passion for travel with her career as a Purpose and Perfomance Expert. She lives next to Amsterdam with her husband and two young children. When she's at home, she spends as much time as she can with them. When it comes to important causes to her, she is very passionate about the Save Tibet movement and donates part of her profit to help them free Tibetans and spread the Dalai Lama's message as wide as possible.

For information on how you can achieve success from your soul, contact Vera Germanus at:
www.veragermanus.com
www.purposeandperformanceacademy.com, or
www.happyworkeracademy.com

CHAPTER 50

MAKING THE CONNECTION

BY WENDY BURRUEL

It was almost 40 years ago, but I remember like it was yesterday. I was four years old and I was in our family den watching my favorite TV show, *Bullwinkle,* and I really, REALLY had to pee. While jumping up and down in front of the TV, I was telling myself, "No! Don't come out pee!" and "I'm a big girl. I can hold it!"

When the commercial came on, I ran across the room and right as I reached the hallway, a beer bottle came whizzing down the hall, just inches from my face. I stopped and pulled myself back into the doorway as the bottle hit the floor and smashed open. I peeked down the hall and I could see that my mom was in the kitchen down the hall, hurling beer bottles at my dad who was drunk again. Without missing a beat, I turned back into the den and went back to the TV. Regardless of my physical discomfort, even at this young age I had already learned how to disconnect from situations that made me uncomfortable and to retreat to safety.

Years later, while I was working at Yahoo!, I was asked to help transform a process that was costing the company a lot of money. As part of this process, it was necessary to ask people to do things differently and I had to question why people were doing things the way they were, so as to suggest changes. This made me pretty unpopular sometimes as I could see a better way of doing things, and needed to get people through the transition that no one was really excited about.

One day, I overheard a leader in the organization saying things to people in his group about me that totally undermined my authority with them and he encouraged them not to participate in the process of change with me. I was boiling over with frustration at being undermined in this way, and could not control the tears that were coming, so I retreated to the bathroom and yes…I cried. After I composed myself and regained my confidence, I started to strategize how to better work with this team that was not really excited to work with me. I reflected on how our communication needed to be more of an open dialog and they needed to feel heard. I decided to spend even more time with this group and when I did interact with them, I was conscious to be more open to hearing about their needs as well as their challenges. I kept trying to meet them on their turf, and eventually, I formed a really good relationship with both this particular leader and his team.

It wasn't until years later when I looked back at that event that I could see the parallel from my childhood. When I was threatened (by flying beer bottles or by someone at my office undermining my success), I retreated to safety (in the den or the bathroom). I'm not the only one that has these kinds of triggers or events from childhood that follow us into the office. When events from our childhood come up in our adult lives, we often do things like retreat from others, in order to protect ourselves. This causes disconnection from others and limits our capacity for success, because it upsets the balance of the Connection Pillars of Success (below):

Diagram 1. Configuration of Connection Pillars Of Success

Successful people are connected to THEMSELVES, to OTHERS and to their PURPOSE. These are the people you meet who are joyful, successful and give to others around them. When you meet people who are sad, angry or struggling in their lives, one or more of the Connection Pillars of Success are out of balance.

Here's how those successful people are connected on each of the Connection Pillars of Success:

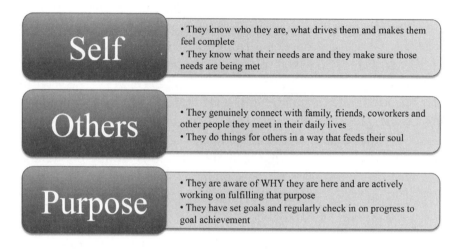

Self
• They know who they are, what drives them and makes them feel complete
• They know what their needs are and they make sure those needs are being met

Others
• They genuinely connect with family, friends, coworkers and other people they meet in their daily lives
• They do things for others in a way that feeds their soul

Purpose
• They are aware of WHY they are here and are actively working on fulfilling that purpose
• They have set goals and regularly check in on progress to goal achievement

Diagram 2. Relationships Within the Connection Pillars of Success

How does this play out in real life? We usually go about our daily life with limited, superficial connections with those around us and we regularly miss opportunities to deeply connect with others when they reach out to us. We give our coffee order to the barista, but don't look her in the eye when we say thank you for the coffee that she's made. In business, we open the door to the office and put on a mask of professionalism that hides our true humanity when interacting with clients and co-workers. This lack of connection at work is profiled in The Connect More Project, which you can view at: www.connectmoreproject.com.

There is a profound cost when we are not connected. The World Health Organization reports that one suicide death occurs every 40 seconds globally, or over 800,000 people per year.* These suicides are the result of a lost connection, where a person feels either real or perceived lack of support and understanding from those around them. Disconnection in the form of solitary confinement is used to punish prisoners in several countries. Those that self-medicate with food, drugs or alcohol will often cite that they are compensating for a lack of connection to others or they feel out of control (not connected to themselves). Disconnection forged from a lack of understanding and agreement over money and religion causes humans to wage war on one another (both literally and figuratively). The latest "trend" in disconnection is cyber-bullying or cyber-shaming, where a person uses the Internet to point to an individual and say, "see…this person is unworthy of connection."

These are all examples of how disconnection can be pretty obvious, but the thing is that disconnection can be subtle and we may not even realize that we are disconnected from others or ourselves. In working with clients, I'm often asked to help untangle situations in their lives, and I find that they are disconnected from THEMSELVES, from OTHERS around them and/or from their PURPOSE. For example, my client Dawn stated that she just couldn't put her finger on why she felt so sad. She owned her own business and was doing well in her career, but no matter what she did, she couldn't shake this feeling of sadness. We walked through what was going on in her life:

- Her marriage of 25 years had ended and she was living by herself for the first time in over 25 years

- Her two daughters had become adults (20 and 24 years old) and didn't need her as they did when they were younger

- When she moved out of her family home, she went from seeing her daughters every day to every few weeks

Dawn felt that her purpose was to be a wife and mother, and both of those roles had changed. Without these primary functions, she became disconnected from herself, and no longer clear on this new path in her life. She was used to doing everything for her husband and kids first, and then caring for herself, so she didn't know how to adjust to putting herself first. As a result, she wasn't doing the things she needed to do for herself. She was disconnected from others as well as she was now living alone for the first time. She was disconnected from her purpose because she had spent so much of her life being a wife and mother that she didn't know what to do in this new reality and felt like she didn't belong anywhere.

I relayed to Dawn that her purpose had been completed; she was a mother to two amazing daughters that were thriving as adults and her marriage was over, so her purpose as a wife was also complete (at least with this marriage). She had other purposes that she could fulfill in her life (friend, business owner, fitness enthusiast, among other things), but she had to fill herself up. She had depleted herself in the process of raising her kids and getting divorced, so her connection to herself was on autopilot. When I asked her to name five things that brought her joy, it took her a long time to find them and when she did, she realized that she was not doing ANY of those things. This disconnection from herself, from others and from her purpose (along with her not doing things that brought her joy) was what was causing her sadness.

We were able to quickly define things that Dawn could do to feed her soul and connect to herself, to others and to find her new purpose. After realizing where she was disconnected and making changes to be more connected, Dawn began to feel happier immediately. Dawn's story is one that isn't easy to see as disconnection because it was only when we looked at all of the Connection Pillars of Success together that it was easy to see that she was disconnected. This is why it is critical to check in with yourself to see if you are operating on autopilot or if you are actually engaged and connecting with yourself and others.

Are you like Dawn and myself? Are you finding yourself retreating from others to protect yourself or are you just not sure what your purpose is supposed to be? If you're not experiencing the level of success that you'd like in your life, chances are that you are disconnected on one or more of the Connection Pillars of Success. Here are some questions to test your connection in each area and suggested action steps to increase the connection to yourself, others and your purpose:

CONNECTION TO YOURSELF

Test Your Connection to Yourself:

1. Who are you? What drives you and makes you feel complete?

2. Do you know what your needs are and do you make sure those needs are being met?

3. Are you on autopilot or are you actively aware of what is going on around you?

Take Action:

1. What are you doing that prevents you from taking actions to connect with yourself? (Stop doing these things)

2. What are you doing today that supports your connection to yourself? (Continue doing these things)

3. What can you start doing today to strengthen your connection with yourself? (Start doing these things)

CONNECTION TO OTHERS

Test Your Connection to Others:

1. Do you genuinely connect with family, friends, coworkers and other people you meet in your daily life?

2. Do you do things for others in a way that feeds your soul?

3. Do you avoid contact with those around you?

Take Action:

1. What are you doing that prevents you from taking action to connect with others? (Stop doing these things)

2. What are you doing today that supports your connection to others? (Continue doing these things)

3. What can you start doing today to strengthen your connection with others? (Start doing these things)

CONNECTION TO YOUR PURPOSE

Test Your Connection to Your Purpose:

1. Are you aware of WHY you are here and are you actively working on fulfilling that purpose?

2. Do you have set goals and if so, do you regularly check in on your progress toward achieving your goals?

3. Has your purpose changed and you're not yet sure what your new purpose will be?

Take Action:

1. What are you doing that prevents you from taking action on your purpose? (Stop doing these things)

2. What are you doing today that supports your connection to your purpose? (Continue doing these things)

3. What can you start doing today to strengthen your connection with your purpose? (Start doing these things)

If you find that you are disconnected in any of these areas, focusing on the area and making conscious connections in each area will help you reconnect to yourself, your purpose and to others. If you find that you are connected in all areas, remember to take some time to focus on your connection with others, because there are some of us that are still isolating ourselves in the den while watching *Bullwinkle*, and we'd love you to help get us across the hall to the bathroom. ☺

* http://www.who.int/mental_health/suicide-prevention/en/ - World Health Organization statistics on global suicide rates.

About Wendy

Wendy Burruel is an author, speaker, and consultant who is inspiring a global conscious movement by encouraging people around the world to connect more openly, honestly and authentically with one another. She maintains that many of us are unaware that we are disengaged from each other, from ourselves and from our purpose in life, and it is this disconnection that drives much of the turmoil in our lives. As a connection expert, Wendy educates her clients on how to see the ways that individual and group interaction impact us on a daily basis and how we MISS THE CONNECTION. We miss connecting to ourselves, to others and to our purpose in life. This disengagement often leaves us depressed and empty, like something is missing – even if we can't quite put a finger on it. Wendy helps people connect to THEMSELVES, to OTHERS and to THEIR OWN UNIQUE PURPOSE IN LIFE. Because of her unique skills, experience, and educational background, Wendy is unsurpassed in effectively helping both individuals and organizations identify missing connections in order to dramatically transform and become more successful.

Wendy has a Bachelor's degree in Psychology from California State University East Bay and a Master's degree from National University. She has studied behavior in clinical settings while training as a therapist and in business while working in Silicon Valley. In her over 20 years spent in the technology sector, Wendy has held various roles, all with a focused effort on making companies better for women, new college graduates and new engineers. Seeing firsthand how people were disconnected from each other in the workplace, Wendy joined forces with Romeo Marquez, Jr. to create *The Connect More Project,* aimed at encouraging people to connect more openly, honestly and authentically with those around them. This effort included a video profiling business people going about their day with each person's internal struggle shown on the screen: http://connectmoreproject.com/.

As CEO of Burruel Group Inc., Wendy drives change for Silicon Valley companies working on increasing their support of women in technology by creating programs that strengthen connections across organizations. She is the author of *College to Career for Tech Women: The Essential Guide for Landing Your Dream Job,* a how-to guide for young technical women to help them find the best job for them and connect with the right people at technology companies in order to land their dream career right out of school.

Connect with Wendy at:
wendy@wendyburruel.com
www.wendyburruel.com
www.twitter.com/wendyburruel
www.facebook.com/ConnectWithWendy

CHAPTER 51

A DREAM VISIT

BY DR. VINCENT MONTICCIOLO

*A smile is the light in your window that tells others that
there is a caring, sharing, person inside.*

~ Denis Waitley

Usually, people who delay going to the dentist don't do it out of lack of care for their mouths. Most of the time, the decision to skip dental care is directly related to the fear and anxiety associated with going to the dentist. Over eleven million Americans experience some form of fear or anxiety about going to the dentist. Many patients refrain from taking proper care of their mouths for many reasons. The anticipated pain involved with repairing decayed teeth, the fear of needles, or a "bad" experience in the past. Avoiding the dentist only leads to long-term consequences and more serious issues, including cardiac, respiratory and kidney diseases.

Sedation dentistry is the use of medication to put a patient in a relaxed state while the dentist performs the dental procedure. The sedative drugs help the patient to become free of stress and anxiety, reduce memory of the treatment, and make the dental appointment a much more pleasant experience, especially in the case of invasive treatments. At the same time, sedation makes the procedure easier for the dentist, allowing him to concentrate on performing the dental treatment in the best possible way.

THE BENEFITS OF SEDATION DENTISTRY

The six main benefits of sedation dentistry for the patient and the dentist include the following:

1. Relaxation:

Dental fear and anxiety are estimated to keep 40% of patients away from the dental office. Many more decide to postpone treatment due to dental fear. Sedation dentistry can transform dental visits into a relaxing experience, with the patient relieved from stress and fear.

2. Comfort:

Patients who are about to have a dental treatment can benefit from the increased level of comfort offered through sedation dentistry. By being sedated, you will feel much less tired after a treatment. Patients with temporomandibular (TMJ) problems, jaw soreness, and difficulty keeping their mouth open will have much less discomfort from the treatment.

3. Amnesic effect:

Amnesia is not only a side effect of dental sedation, but also a benefit. After treatment, there will be little to no memory of the dental procedure. The appointment feels as if it lasted only a few minutes, even if it has been several hours. Certain invasive dental procedures, such as multiple extractions or root canals, can be done without remembering the experience. Many patients, especially those with dental anxiety, will be much more relaxed if they can erase these memories with sedation.

4. Control of the gag reflex:

Reducing the gag reflex is another benefit of sedation dentistry. Gagging, especially if it is anxiety-induced, can be managed successfully with sedation dentistry.

5. Movement control:

Sedation minimizes the mobility of the dental patient. This is extremely beneficial in patients with physical or mental medical conditions who have uncontrollable movements. Special needs and medically-compromised patients are able to have all their dental work safely completed while being sedated.

6. Fewer Visits:

Sedation dentistry can help patients tolerate longer appointments comfortably. Thus, fewer appointments are needed. Complex or multiple procedures, that would require many appointments, can be completed in a few or even a single visit. This is a great benefit for patients with time constraints and very tight schedules.

RETURNING TO THE DENTIST

Sedation dentistry offers the opportunity to tackle a number of problems in one visit. After the procedure, patients have no recollection of the appointment, yet all of their dental issues were treated. Marie hadn't been to a dentist in twenty-five years when she came into my practice. Like many patients who stay away that long, her dental health was affecting her overall well-being. Lacking adequate dental insurance and having a bad experience to local anesthesia prevented Marie from following through with treatment. She sought a second opinion and came to my office for consultation and learned the benefits of sedation dentistry. After such a long lapse in visiting a dentist, Marie came in to have a number of problems worked on while she was sedated. She was able to have many of her issues taken care of quickly. The entire experience was a delight, preventing an agonizing process with multiple and painful visits.

It doesn't even take that long for a situation in someone's mouth to deteriorate to the point where it is negatively affecting their health and self-esteem. Halie had only been away from a dentist for two years, but had a low self-esteem, predominately from her smile being riddled with decay. In one visit, she was able to have a bridge to replace missing front teeth and began the road to better oral health.

Instead of it being a scary day, the biggest memory Halie had of her visit was that it was a breeze. Sedation dentistry allows patients to begin to heal again and have better overall health. We are able to provide patients with a better smile without them having any memory of their dental visit. Much can be done in one visit because the sedation relaxes their body response and relieves their anxiety.

THE EIGHT PATIENT GROUPS THAT SEDATION DENTISTRY CAN HELP

1. Patients with dental and needle phobia

Dental and needle phobic patients are considered as the best candidates for having sedation dentistry. People with these phobias will try to avoid, at any cost, not only dental treatment, but even visiting the dentist. They prefer to tolerate severe pain instead of going to the dentist. Whatever the reason that has caused the dental phobia, sedation dentistry can help these patients to get the oral care they need.

2. Patients with severe gag reflex

Some patients have a very sensitive gag reflex. The fear of choking and gagging can turn dental treatment into an agonizing procedure for the patient. The dentist's work is also much more difficult because he must make very careful movements while working. Some procedures, such as working on back teeth or taking impressions, may be almost impossible for patients with a strong reflex. Sedation methods help patients reduce, and possibly eliminate, the gag reflex issue.

3. Patients with special needs

Patients with special needs, such as Autism or Down syndrome, and those with mental challenges may have a greater difficulty in receiving dental care. Following instructions, remaining calm, using less movements, and the inability to understand that the procedure performed is only to benefit them is hard for anyone. Sedation dentistry techniques can help these patients to receive proper dental care.

Also, certain medical conditions can affect the ability of the patient to control his movements. Parkinson's disease, Cerebral Palsy, and other disorders of the central nervous system can cause uncontrolled body movements. These movements can affect the accuracy of the dentist's actions and increase the risk of injury. Sedation dentistry can relax the body muscles reducing movement, allowing the dentist to complete their treatment.

4. Patients with time constraints

Another problem that many patients face is the lack of time to dedicate to multiple and lengthy dental procedures. Sedation dentistry allows for the opportunity to get treatment in a fraction of the time and in much fewer appointments than traditional dentistry. This can be a great benefit for people with time constraints and inflexible work schedules that would otherwise force them to postpone dental care.

5. Patients who need complex/multiple treatment

Having to undergo a series of complex and invasive dental procedures, such as extensive gum surgery, implants, or multiple extractions, is never a 'pleasant' experience, even for patients without any problem of dental anxiety or physical limitations. Sedation dentistry can help everyone to get the most complex treatments much more comfortably, in a relaxed state, without stress and without feeling exhausted afterwards.

6. Patients with TMJ problems or jaw soreness

Patients with TMJ disorders can find it difficult to open their mouth wide or keep it open through lengthy treatments. They may also suffer from post-operative jaw soreness for many days after treatment. Dental sedation helps to relax not only the jaw muscles but also reduces the overall tension to the body muscles. This makes the procedure much easier and less tiring for both the patient and the dentist.

7. Patients with sensitive teeth or difficulty getting numb

Not all people have the same response to the medications given by the dentist for local anesthesia. Some may get numb with a very small amount of anesthetic, while others may not be adequately anesthetized even with a full dose of local anesthetic. Sedation dentistry can increase the effectiveness of local anesthesia by allowing the dentist to titrate the local anesthesia to the proper amount, allowing the patient to become numb.

8. Patients with past traumatic experiences

Many patients have experienced past traumatic dental visits that have mentally scarred them. Their memory of these appointments has caused an anxiety and fear towards any future dental work. Some of these memories are from their childhood and have increased over the years. Others have had bad recollections of their wisdom teeth or orthodontic extractions. Patients with traumatic pasts, including veterans and domestic violence survivors, would also benefit from the amnesic affect of sedation dentistry.

DREAM VISITS – A GENTLE APPROACH TO DENTISTRY

Sedation dentistry fills a unique niche and can completely transform lives. Patients schedule sedation consultations when they are in pain, losing teeth, or embarrassed about their smile. We're able to change their lives without the complications, fears, or anxieties related to dental work done while you are awake.

Our practice tries to make your appointment the most comfortable dental visit that patients will ever encounter. We try to create an environment of calmness that starts in the waiting room and continues all the way through to recovery. Since many patients come in after having severe dental phobias, sedation allows for them to have multiple problems taken care of in one sitting. This makes the experience a more positive one, preventing them from worry.

WHAT TO EXPECT AT A DREAM VISIT

A visit to the office for a sedation dentistry session begins with a consultation visit to discuss what is needed. Then, a pre-operative visit is scheduled. The pre-operative visit allows the dental team to explain everything to the patient. Instructions are given, and all the risks and benefits are discussed. The patient's vital signs are taken and all their medical history is reviewed, including the patient's medications. Post-operative instructions are also reviewed at this visit. All questions are answered and consents signed. A mild sedative for the patient to take one hour prior to their sedation appointment may be prescribed. This will relieve their initial stress on the day of their sedation appointment. Also, a caregiver must transport them to and from the office on the day of the procedure.

After the patient arrives on the day of their appointment, the caregiver is taken to a sedation lounge where coffee and tea can be found. The patient is moved to the sedation suite and monitors are placed on the patient. The medication for sedation is then added so an ideal amount can be given to reach the desired effect. The standard medication produces an amnesic effect, so they will have little memory of the experience. If a longer and more advanced procedure is needed, a secondary medication may be added.

The sedation used in conscious dental sedation is different from the general anesthesia used in a hospital setting. It has a twilight effect, which is safe enough to do in an office setting. The patient is still breathing on their own. Intubation would not be needed, as is the case if they were under general anesthesia. Thus, less side effects from sedation are seen.

Once a patient is in a fully-relaxed state, we can begin treatment. Upon completion of all the dental procedures outlined during the consultation, the patient awakens without any negative recollections of their visit. Patients often come out of sedation asking when we will be beginning the procedure. They are always amazed and pleased that all the dental care has been completed.

Each evening after sedation, I call my patients to check on them. One night I called a woman and explained that I was calling to see how she was after the visit. She laughed and said, "You know, I woke up at home and I said to my husband, 'We have to get to the dentist! We're late.' And he told me to look in my mouth – we had already been to the office." Sedation patients often have this very same experience.

MAKING DENTAL HEALTH AN INVESTMENT

Besides the occasional physical complication, the biggest challenge to sedation dentistry is availability. Every region varies on the amount of dentists who are certified and can perform sedation dentistry. Of course, fewer sedation dentists lead to further dental neglect. It is important that sedation be an option that is available more globally, because it can be the difference between good health and poor health.

Besides availability, cost is a factor. There is an extra cost for sedation dentistry. When compared to doing many separate procedures with traditional general dentistry, the price is cost effective. Sometimes, dental insurance may cover part or all of the fee. Sedation allows for the dental work to be completed in a safe, comfortable, and efficient manner.

DENTISTRY THAT'S TRULY A DREAM

Lori was a patient that hadn't been to a dentist in five years and was seeing the negative impact on areas of her life. Fear of the dentist, coupled with a sensitive gag reflex, had kept Lori from getting the care that she needed. Eventually, that choice was impacting both her physical health and her self-esteem. Her apprehension had stemmed from one of her first dental appointments when she was a child.

Lori's dream visit changed her life. In one appointment, the problems in her mouth were able to be addressed for the first time in years. A thorough, and deep cleaning improved her oral health, while she was soundly resting. After waking up in recovery, Lori not only had a nicer smile, but also had lost her anxiety of the dentist.

Dental health is imperative to overall health and wellness. Sedation dentistry and dream visits are important because they help ease the fears of visiting the dentist, anxiety over the needles, and pain. Instead of a trip to get a tooth treated being a nightmare, sedation offers an alternative that makes the experience positive. It opens the door to better care in the future, and more self-confidence. For patients that are too busy, too scared, or have been suffering quietly for years, it really is a dream come true.

About Dr. Vincent

Vincent J. Monticciolo, DDS, MBA, JD has a passion for learning that is equal to his passion for helping others. He has created a life where his skills and purpose are combined.

Graduating from the University of Detroit, School of Dentistry, Dr. Monticciolo received many awards and was selected to the Honors Clinical Program. In 2001, he earned his Masters Degree in Business Administration. Also, in 2013, he earned his Law Degree, all while practicing dentistry full time and taking various continuing education courses.

In addition to his family and sedation dentistry practice, Dr. Monticciolo has been driven by opportunities to lead through example, which were first shown in his days as a part-time faculty member at the dental school he'd once attended. Over time, his drive grew into leadership to serve his community, and it was there that everything really fell into place for him.

As inspiration to help struggling individuals who could not afford dental care took shape, Dr. Monticciolo found a way to improve the community he lived in by offering free dental care to a few needy individuals. It was an incredible experience, and Dr. Monticciolo, along with his wife, Dr. Natalie Monticciolo, began to think of how they could take this simple concept and make it grow into something larger. After relocating to the Tampa, Florida area, Dentistry from the Heart was formed in 2001. It has become synonymous with Dr. Monticciolo's energy and efforts to embrace giving back. Since then, Dentistry from the Heart has become a charity that helps coordinate over 250 events in all 50 states, as well as internationally.

Furthermore, in 2012, Dr. Monticciolo started Dental Care Delivered, a mobile dental service that provides care to residents in assisted living facilities and nursing homes around the west coast of Florida. It is another step to ensuring that more people can have the smile they deserve, regardless of their circumstances.

Today, Dr. Monticciolo lives with his wife and two daughters in Palm Harbor, Florida. Aside from his charity work, he enjoys spending quality time with his family and practicing dentistry. He currently practices full time in New Port Richey and Tampa, Florida.

Honors and Awards:

- Honors graduate at dental school
- Academy of General Dentistry Outstanding Student Award
- Comprehensive Dentistry Award

- Frances B. Vedder Society Crown and Bridge Prosthodontics Award
- Omicron Kappa Upsilon (National Dental Honor Society)
- Alpha Sigma Nu (National Jesuit Honor Society)
- Class President in dental school

Memberships and Societies:

- American Dental Society
- Florida Dental Society
- West Pasco Dental Society
- American Society of Dental Anesthesiology
- Society for Special Care Dentistry
- Academy of Dentistry for Persons with Disabilities
- American Society for Geriatric Dentistry
- Florida Health Care Association

www.happydentistry.com
www.dentistryfromtheheart.org
www.monticciolobrand.com
www.dentalcaredelivered.com

CHAPTER 52

YES, TO A NEW NORMAL

BY SUSSI MATTSSON

I'm standing by an open white coffin and I'm looking at my dead mother. She looks so calm and peaceful in a very strange way. It's the first time I have seen a dead person, and still, after 36 years, the picture is very clear in my mind. It's so clear that when I close my eyes I can see myself as the little 8-year-old girl who just lost her mother, standing there in black clothes, with long dark brown hair and big, dark brown eyes, staring at the coffin as an outsider. Her whole appearance expresses emptiness and a loss so huge that she is not even able to cry.

When I think back on the funeral ceremony, my memories are little bit blurry, because I felt like I saw it all through a dense fog. There were several weeping women around the coffin wearing long black dresses, with black kerchiefs on their heads that covered almost their entire faces. Their desperation could be heard in their very loud crying and the bowing back and forth over the coffin. I just stood there not knowing what to do, totally lost in a funeral tradition of the Greek Orthodox Church ceremony. I could smell the strong incense from the bowl the priest swung back and forth, and the whole room seemed so dark. I felt the cold come over me with such force that I completely lost control. I froze and was about to scream out loud – what I saw was that my mother wore jewelry, had white clothes on, and of course - the wig.

Everything was very surreal, and I just wanted to run away to a safe place, close my eyes and wish that somebody could take away all the pain in the picture I saw in front of my eyes.

465

Nobody had prepared me for the funeral. Nobody had actually told me that she was going to die. Yes, I knew she was sick, very sick in fact, but it never crossed my mind that she was going to die. My mother fought cancer bravely for over two years, and at the end she lost a hard battle. It felt that my bridges to security were totally burned.

As we go through life, we always have "normals" in our lives. These normals can be positive, neutral or negative. Our normals can be different for different areas of our lives. These normals can range from having routines in the morning such as going for a walk with our dog, helping us exercise and get fresh air, all the way to other normals that aren't very positive, such as skipping meals, smoking, and constantly living in a state of stress and overwhelm.

Many of our existing normals can be changed if we so choose. Here are several examples where we can change our current normals if we aren't content with them:

- We are eating unhealthy
- We are not getting enough exercise
- We are ineffective as leaders
- We are not spending enough time with our families
- We are going through life on "autopilot"
- We are experiencing large doses of unhealthy stress

The new normal of growing up without a mother became a normal that was totally out of my control. What *was* within my control was how I would interpret this normal and if I would take the role of a victim, or if I would decide to create a new normal where I was proactively deciding how I would interpret this life-changing event of losing my mother as a young innocent girl.

There has been, and *will* be, life-changing events ahead in our lives. How we choose to interpret these events and how we ultimately respond will determine what our normals become. Here is a key distinction that is imperative for us to understand:

We will either respond or react to situations, events and circumstances.

When we *respond*, we feel like we are much more in control, whereas when we *react*, we usually feel out of control. In terms of the normals that we are experiencing in our lives at any given time, the more we can respond and be proactive, the more likely we are to creating deliberate normals. Everyone has normals in their lives, yet very few have made the decision to be proactive about creating normals whenever these normals are within their control. Too often when reflecting upon challenging situations, people assume that "it is what it is" and it cannot be changed.

Sure, sometimes that may be the case, and yes, certain circumstances are outside our control, yet let's commit to living our lives proactively, where we deliberately influence our *controllable normals*. Too many people hold on to their negative normals from the past, thereby limiting their ability to live in the present and eagerly anticipate the future. No matter what trials we may have had or currently have in our lives, we need to remember to be courageous and to take actions that are congruent with who we are. We need to listen to our inner voice and heart and be willing to do what is right, instead of what is easy or convenient. Let's live our lives with authenticity and zero regrets!

Let's also remember that it is the trying times that define who we are and who we are becoming. Our ability to feel pain is a gift and shows that we are human, yet let's not continue to live *in* this pain indefinitely. We all have a purpose, so let's use the challenging circumstances and events in such a way that we take pride in our normals that surround us. Suffering is a choice. So is happiness.

As I reflect upon the countless challenges I have experienced in my life up to this point, there is only one reason that I am happy: I have *decided* to be happy!

I have learned how to build bridges between my past, present and future. I have learned to transform my wounds into wisdom. I have dared to be courageous in my own life, and I have dared to step into my fears. This courage has directly led to increased self confidence, self belief and an ever-expanding comfort zone.

Looking back, I admire the enormous courage and determination that the little 8-year-old girl showed by daring to follow her heart and doing what she so strongly believed was the right thing to do. Having the mindset of "if there isn't a path, I'll create one" has served this girl and now woman, mother, CEO, speaker, author and executive coach, very well.

Let's reflect upon what possible steps can be taken to proactively create New Normals in our lives, where we play life instead of allowing life to play us:

1. Be decisive - let's make the decision that we want to proactively and deliberately create New Normals in our lives.

2. Show courage - let's commit to being courageous and projecting this courage in all that we do.

3. Take responsibility - let's make a 100% commitment to focus on what we *can* control.

4. Use our strengths - let's create endless opportunities in our lives by proactively using our strengths frequently and deliberately.

Wherever you are in life right now and in your personal Journey, it is my sincere hope that you too will find the courage and see opportunities to build bridges between your past, present and future in order to say "YES!" to New Normals.

You can connect with Sussi at:
Sussi@mattssongroup.com
www.mattssongroup.com

About Sussi

Sussi Mattsson, also known as "Sussi from Sweden", is an in-demand International thought leader, speaker and coach. Her interviews have aired on CNN, Fox News and CNBC. Sussi is innovative, walks her talk, and she is not afraid to push the envelope. She takes great pride in being innovative and on the cutting edge. Losing her mother to cancer as a little girl has further fueled her desire to live a life of significance and make a difference.

Sussi is a founding council member of the Global Economic Initiative Forum and has been a featured presenter at the United Nations in New York. She is personally mentored by Jack Canfield and is also a Canfield *Train The Trainer* graduate.

In one of her forthcoming books, Sussi takes the readers on a journey of hope and overcoming obstacles as she describes her compelling life story. In another of Sussi's soon-to-be-published books, the readers are given practical tools and strategies for having a solid mindset, self-awareness and attitude.

In her role as a speaker, coach and advisor, Sussi inspires, motivates and challenges her clients to reach far beyond what they themselves believe is possible. She is licensed by the International Coaching Federation as a Business Coach. Additionally, being a licensed Stress Therapist provides added value to all of Sussi's leadership and coaching programs.

Prior to becoming the CEO of Mattsson Group, Sussi worked as an Interior Architect for 13 years on such projects as ambassador mansions, five star hotels, office complexes, schools in third world countries, and living/working quarters for scientists worldwide. Because of her international success and commitment to get results, Sussi was also recruited by IKEA Headquarters to be the one and only Business Development Manager for IKEA, an integral position she held for five years.

Sussi left this position with a clear vision and a business plan to focus on solutions for the challenge of "How can we best develop successful future leaders who develop high performance teams while at the same time achieving a balanced lifestyle?" All of Sussi's clients, regardless of their field, have one key common denominator: They are committed to developing successful leaders with a Peak Performance Mindset, while at the same time, maintaining a healthy corporate culture. All programs are customized and based upon real life examples. Sussi takes great pride in her commitment to maximizing the performance of each participant.

The interactive learning environment provides practical and relevant exercises from everyday life. Cultivating leadership skills using mental toughness techniques, leaders going though Sussi's programs feel empowered, with a high level of self-confidence and a peak performance mindset.

In addition to World-Class Leadership Programs and coaching, Sussi also offers exclusive Retreats.

You can connect with Sussi at:
Sussi@MattssonGroup.com
www.mattssongroup.com

CHAPTER 53

RUN THROUGH IT: THE SCIENCE OF FLOW AND ULTIMATE HUMAN PERFORMANCE

BY TRISH McCARTY

Our purpose in life is to acknowledge that there is an intelligence within us that's giving us life. That it's both personal and universal, it's within us and all around us, and that our job in life is to remove those masks of ignorance and the emotions that block the flow of the divine within us. And when we begin to move those layers, that intelligence begins to express itself and we become more like it, we become more willful, we become more loving, we become more mindful and its mind becomes our mind.

The only way that you and I will ever do the Super Natural is by doing the Un-Natural. We have to give when everybody else is in lack, we have to show courage when everybody else is in fear, we have to show compassion when everybody else is judging. If you keep doing the Un-Natural over and over again… soon it will start to become Super Natural.

~ Joe Dispenza, D.C.

Is success about showing up? Is there a way to make "Flow" or being in the zone more predictable? The answer is "Yes!" You can work and play in "flow" and help others to do the same. You just need to know how…

I met Peter Diamandis, Founder and CEO of XPRIZE this past September in Los Angeles. Only a few days earlier, I had filed an intent to compete for the XPRIZE and then, presto, suddenly, I am with this very celebrity I wanted to meet. Was this experience by accident, an example of synergy or a direct result of specific predictable choices and behaviors?

Woody Allen said: *80% of Success is just showing up*. I think it's more like 90! Being seen as an interested, committed individual is paramount to building a successful life. Just by showing up, some of the most significant opportunities present themselves and this is the most likely time you will experience "flow." When opportunities seem to be dropping in out of thin air, someone casually mentions something you have been wanting to do and you find it extraordinary, you are experiencing "flow." Then, you must decide to step up, say "Yes" and run through the slightly open door, otherwise someone else might choose to take advantage of the same opportunity.

But is success more than this? Is ultimate human performance about making you "run through it?" or is it more scientifically measured in "flow?"

MINDFULNESS: MIND = BRAIN + EMOTION

What is flow? Flow is trending. In the past people talked about being in the zone…same thing. But it's now being studied as the key to ultimate human performance. It's an optimal state of consciousness in which we perform and feel our best. It greatly amplifies happiness. And flow can happen to anyone! The question here is how can you learn to do it? Maybe it's big wave surf legend, a skier, or your best friend playing the guitar. What enhances creativity, drives innovation, accelerates learning, and helps your neighbor run a 5K run?

Steven Kotler's book titled, *The Rise of Superman: Decoding the Science of Ultimate Human Performance* defined it as: "Flow is like being swept up by the river of ultimate human performance. We are better, faster, stronger. All aspects are amplified." He has researched and interviewed dozens of top athletes and executives, exploring the science behind "flow," an optimal state of consciousness in which we perform and feel our best.

In our super-charged, complex, faster-than-ever changing world… doesn't it make better sense to learn to be in flow? Once, with a group of friends, we floated the Colorado River and decided to create a world record of a human "snake" of floating, interlinked humans. One of the elders on that trip made some remarks I will never forget. He said "Humans are like rocks in the river. They think they can stop the river if they are strong enough, or bold enough, or big enough. But one day they notice the river slides around them and the small pebbles are lifted up to glide with the river's movement. The movement is the beauty, and not predictable. What if a human decided early enough to stay with the flow of life, the river, rather than try to resist and oppose the current? How much more enjoyable would the ride of life be?"

I was in a meeting with powerful business leaders from Phoenix in June of 2002. I had been invited to attend a community forum to discuss Arizona's education problems and how community leaders might possibly help schools to solve some of their problems. I was feeling very passionate about the subject because as a mother, yoga teacher and a banker, I witnessed first-hand how difficult it was for families to live and pay for basic living expenses without a proper education. I didn't think Arizona was doing enough to help families gain financial literacy or any life-skills learning. It was in this meeting of volunteers that I was about to ask a question that would forever disrupt my own life and catapult myself into a completely unknown, unchartered destiny. I accidentally experienced flow.

After hearing one man's explanation of how well he thought Arizona's leaders' kids were doing, because his own three daughters were attending Harvard, my stomach started to rumble. According to him, we should have been concentrating on the kids preparing for leadership from "good" families and stop trying to fix an impossible problem of trying to help "lesser" families ever change their plight of illiteracy and poverty. I couldn't believe this man's naïve thinking but was astounded that no one seemed to be challenging his opinion. Suddenly, without thinking, I realized I was jumping to my feet, talking loudly and asking, "How can you condemn a family to poverty, simply because they have never had an opportunity to learn anything different? What would your family be like, had you never had money, influential friends or learning – to help you become a success? What would happen to your family if for some reason you found yourself without any available assets to pay for anything? What would you rely on?"

I continued as if nearly obsessed, "How can we expect to save ourselves, our families, communities or countries with this narrow-minded way of thinking? We cannot. When people are struggling they are driven to do things from desperation. *Hunger has no conscience!*" By this time my mind began talking to itself, "Trish, what are you doing? These people are your friends and you are making a spectacle of yourself! Sit down before you say anything more you might regret!" I suddenly wanted to stop the river. But the river was about to have me open a school for K-12 kids and I never saw this coming.

What happens when a critical number of people change how they think and behave? The culture changes and a new era begins. It causes an entire shift of consciousness. It is happening, now.

When we talk about people getting into flow, they're usually getting into micro-flow. If you've ever lost an afternoon to a great conversation, or gotten so sucked into a work project when everything else goes away, that's flow. The experience seems quasi-mystical.

My grandson is one of the smartest kids I have ever known, (not because he is mine…or maybe?) His teacher wants him tested for ADHD and perhaps to suggest medication that will keep him focused. I think he needs to be interested. Yesterday, he spent over six hours building a complicated model airplane and, also, painted it. How can a ten-year-old child focus for so long, only to be told there is something wrong with the way he thinks? What and how schools teach needs to change. Being resilient, learning to work with focus and meditation is how humans develop incredible abilities to solve big problems, be creative thinkers and ultimately learn how to be happy.

IS THIS A CLINICALLY MEASURABLE, PHYSICAL PROCESS?

Yes. Flow research started in the 1800s, or earlier. What has happened in the last couple of years is exploding new information about neurobiology.

When George Bush declared the '90s the "Decade of the Brain," money and research flooded into neuroscience. Unfortunately, what or how we teach children has not changed at all.

When it feels like your sense of time slows down or speeds up, and your sense of self vanishes, you are experiencing "flow." What actually goes on in the brain is something called transient hypofrontality. Transient means temporary, hypo is the opposite of hyper—to slow down or deactivate. And frontality is your prefrontal cortex; it's the part of your brain that houses all your higher executive function.

So the old idea about optimal performance is, "We only use 5% of our brain, and flow must be all of our brain functioning at a maximal level." Turns out that's backwards. In flow, huge portions of your prefrontal cortex are turning off. Parts of it start to close out so you can no longer separate past from present from future. And your sense of self vanishes. The voice of doubt and disparagement that's always there, shuts off in flow.

What about the concept of becoming one with everything? You hear surfers, basketball players, musicians and runners talk about, "Oh I was one with the wave." There's a part of your brain called the right parietal lobe that helps you figure out where you are in space. It helps us separate self from other. In deep flow states, energy goes elsewhere and the right parietal lobe shuts down. So, from a neurological perspective, at that point, the brain does believe it's one with everything.

HOW DOES THIS INFORMATION AFFECT THE BUSINESS WORLD?

A study conducted by McKinsey found that the average person spends about 5% of working hours in flow. But if you could increase that to 20%, they estimate that overall workplace productivity would double.

My school, StarShine, has proven that 70% of learning is contextual, so we know a rich environment is another a trigger to flow. A rich environment has lots of novelty, complexity, and unpredictability. Google and Peter Diamandis, Founder of XPRIZE, talk about making a 10x improvement and not be okay with 10% improvement. When you're asking for 10x improvement, you're throwing out all the existing assumptions, and you have to start radically new. You're massively increasing the amount of novelty, complexity, and unpredictability in your employees' work life.

Risk is also a flow trigger, which is obvious for athletes. But it's not just physical risk. What you're trying to do is get the brain to release dopamine, which happens when we take physical risk — as well as an emotional, social, intellectual, or creative risk. Silicon Valley gives people space to fail and take those risks.

MAKING WORK MEANINGFUL

My husband is a musician and talks about being "in the groove," when a song comes effortlessly. Is it possible to lead others, toward this state? What makes some work environments inspire exceptional levels of energy, increase self-confidence, and boost individual productivity? Developing a strong sense of meaning is natural to this extraordinary form of leadership. By "meaning," creating a feeling that what's happening really matters, that what's being done has not been done before and that it will make a difference to others.

MEANING AND PERFORMANCE

Inspirational visions, like Walt Disney's: "Make people happy and it's kind of fun to do the impossible." or Google's: "Organize the world's information." seem to have little relevance to the majority of workers. Research shows that four primary sources give individuals a sense of meaning, including their ability to have an impact on society, community building, and superior customer resources or products.

HOW DO YOU MAKE A DIFFERENCE? (TESTING FOR ALIGNMENT WITH THE COMPANY'S DIRECTION.)

1. What improvement idea are you working on? (emphasizing continuous improvement)
2. When did you last get coaching from your boss? (emphasizing the importance of people development)
3. Who is the enemy?

USE SMALL, UNEXPECTED REWARDS TO MOTIVATE

Sam Walton, founder of Wal-Mart Stores, said of acknowledgement, "Nothing else can quite substitute for a few well-chosen, well-timed, sincere words of praise. They're absolutely free—and worth a fortune."

KNOWLEDGE + MIND, EXPERIENCE + BODY

When people consciously practice gratitude, they are likely getting higher flows of reward-related neurotransmitters, like dopamine. Research shows that when people practice gratitude, they experience a general alerting and brightening of the mind, and that's probably correlated with more of the neurotransmitter norepinephrine.

The mind also can change the brain in lasting ways. What flows through the mind sculpts the brain. "What you think about you bring about." As the mind flows through the brain, as neurons fire together in particularly patterned ways based on the information they are representing, those patterns of neural activity change neural structure. New synapses form as well.

This has also been found among meditators: People who maintain some kind of regular meditative practice have measurably thicker brains in certain key regions. One of those regions is the insula, which is involved in what's called "interoception"—tuning into the state of your body, as well as your deep feelings. A lot of what they're doing is practicing mindfulness of breathing, staying present with what's going on inside themselves.

In one study, researchers compared meditators and non-meditators. However, the people who routinely meditated and "worked" their brain did not experience cortical thinning as they grew older.

So, "showing up" really matters. Not only in our moment-to-moment well-being, but in the lasting fabric of our being. Use the mind to change the brain and the mind for the better. Teach yourself to be in "flow." This is known as "self-directed neuroplasticity." Neuroplasticity refers to the malleable nature of the brain, and it is constant and ongoing. Self-directed neuroplasticity means doing it with clarity, skillfulness and intention.

Attention and focus create who we become, for better or worse. If we rest our attention on the things for which we're grateful, our small and large accomplishments, the wholesome qualities in ourselves and our world, we build up very different neural substrates. And we get more!

William James, the father of psychology in America, said, *The education of attention would be an education par excellence.*

The problem is most people don't have very good control over their attention. And today we are constantly bombarded with stimuli that the brain has not evolved to handle. So gaining more control over attention one way or another is really crucial, whether it's through the practice of mindfulness, for instance, or through gratitude practices, where we count our blessings.

STEPS TOWARD FLOW

- First ten minutes of opening your eyes after sleep, give thanks, it starts to wire your brain.

- Create a sacred morning ceremony. It can be simple but do it for yourself. The habit will ground you, and it will be your greatest predictor of success.

- Teach yourself to be conscious of your choices, words, breath, feelings and responses.

- Look at people's eyes, connect with them and smile. You'll make the world and your brain better!

- Go with the "flow"!

About Trish

Trish McCarty is one of America's leading business strategy and education experts on developing peak performance in schools through school management, technology and processes, shared brand marketing and cutting-edge student resources in brain-based training, self-discipline, self-esteem, motivation and results. She has inspired thousands with her lectures, interviews, published articles and books. She has been an impassioned leader for K-12 education reinvention – alongside her corporate banking and technology backgrounds – serving on many children's charity boards throughout her life. Trish McCarty helps education superstars and professionals have more power and income for reinventing K-12 education. She has democratized the best schools and brought innovation to an audience who traditionally found it difficult to get involved.

Ms. McCarty came into the world with a global view; born in Frankfurt, Germany, as a U.S. Air Force military "brat" and as a child in Tokyo, Japan, where she served on the United Nations Board of Children. She attended Fort Lewis College, in her family's home town of Durango, Colorado with a human biology and neuroscience major and was recruited from there as an executive for AT&T. After five years, she was recruited by the President of Mellon Bank to develop national banking centers. An avid entrepreneur, she subsequently started a bank that grew to $128M in five years and won awards and highlights in national news including INC. Magazine.

Her company opened her first charity charter school, STARSHINE ACADEMY INTERNATIONAL SCHOOLS, in the fall of 2002, for K-12 disadvantaged children, on a crime-ridden street in Arizona. The highly-acclaimed academic "School Eco-Village" is a replicable model for success based on holistic education of a child in health, wealth, happiness, body, mind, and spirit. It integrates the environment and personal health with a community garden and the spirit with music, art and technology. All of the children participate in community service projects integrated into the curriculum to learn economic development and patriotism.

She has created partnerships with the United Nations by hosting "11 Days of Peace and Sustainability" each year from 9-11 to 9-21. The school prototype model integrates the best practices for human growth and spiritual transformation, Human Resources management, sustainability, professional development, data collection and business management. Ms. McCarty is a Lincoln Center Fellow for Arizona State University for Education Leadership and is a partner at ASU Skysong Innovation Center. Yoga is an integral part of the StarShine student curriculum as Ms. McCarty has studied and taught yoga for nearly thirty years.

Trish McCarty is a constant community activist for peace, women in global leadership, and child advocacy. She is married to guitarist and platinum recording artist, Steve McCarty. She has four children and eight grandchildren. Steve and Trish frequently combine their talents in workshops and lectures to spread their message of empowerment, love, harmony, and unity.

To contact Trish McCarty:
Trish@TrishMcCarty.com
TrishMcCarty.com
www.starshineacademy.org
www.eduresources.com

CHAPTER 54

SOUL SUCCESS SECRETS

BY JOCELYNE F. LAFRENIÈRE

Over the years, many extraordinary men and women have inspired our lives with their passion, determination, dedication, perseverance, and loving hearts. Think for a moment of Oprah Winfrey, Bill Gates, Warren Buffett, Mahatma Gandhi, Nelson Mandela, Martin Luther King Jr., and Mother Teresa, to name a few. One common denominator of their greatness is their attainment of soul success. Their lives shine as a testimony to having developed a truly meaningful life, planting seeds of greatness around them to make a positive difference in the world. They are reminders of the beauty in humankind, giving us hope for a better tomorrow.

You too are a being of pure potential, with unique gifts to allow your life to be a success and flourish for your own fulfillment and the betterment of others. Here are ten *soul success secrets* that will lead you on the path of greatness for all to see the unique and true beauty of your soul.

Secret #1: Honor the Desires of Your Heart – Heartfelt aspirations are an expression of the great beauty that resides within you. They are messengers of possibilities for your life. They are true expressions of who you can be. Desires from the heart are blessings coming towards you and those around you.

If you struggle to crystallize your life mission and purpose, start with a reflection of what you want to bring into your life. Ask yourself some fundamental questions: What do I like? What are my skills? What ignites passion in my life? Who do I want to be? What things do I want? What does it mean to me to live my desires?

Look at your natural abilities, and the tasks or hobbies you enjoy. Identify books you take pleasure in reading. Participate in a career orientation program to learn more about career choices. Talk to your friends, family and colleagues for their input on the greatness they see in you. Listen to the small voice of your heart. Consult a good life coach and find mentors who may help in bringing clarity.

Secret #2: Dare to Be All That You Can Be – God has planted seeds of greatness in you. You are gifted with talents, skills, and capacities for the purpose of adding unique beauty in the universe. For this reason, you owe it to yourself and others to be all that you can be. Don't be afraid of big dreams that speak of your greatness. Don't be shy to step out of your comfort zone. If a desire is lingering in your heart, it means it is yours to honor. Know without any doubt that you have the will to turn it into reality.

With greater clarity of your vision, engage in developing your action plan by answering the following questions to move closer to your vision:

- What activities/tasks should I undertake?
- What resources do I need?
- How many times per day, per week, per month should I carry out these activities/tasks?
- By when should the activities/tasks be completed?

Trust your inner guidance to set the stage for a powerful transformation in your life. By creating your desires, you fill your life with enthusiasm, satisfaction, and passion.

Secret #3: Keep Your Mind Captive in Positivity – With an inspiring plan in hand and a commitment to action, your seeds of greatness flourish, and you become the success you are meant to be. With your thoughts captive in positivity, you are not afraid to take a leap of faith. You are confident that today and tomorrow will be happy days. You are grateful for what is yet to come, and your heart is filled with true joy. You maintain a positive outlook and speak words of possibilities.

With daily affirmations and creative visualization, you move forward with confidence, courage, and passion in the direction of your desires. You are comfortable in being uncomfortable. You choose a positive response to all events. You celebrate your successes, small and grand. You cultivate mindfulness where your eyes see the beauty around you. With a positive outlook on life, you let your light shine and fly to new heights of achievement for your personal fulfillment and the betterment of those around you.

Secret #4: Learn from Setbacks – You have the ability to withstand life's challenges and disappointments. Do not be afraid of setbacks. See them for what they are: opportunities to grow and learn what works and what doesn't, and moments to make better choices. They may hold a message that there is a faster or better path ahead, and it's time to identify new paths to travel by. You are fully equipped to bounce back quickly from adversity and move swiftly towards victory. If you stumble, keep moving. This attitude gives you momentum to conquer all your challenges.

Trust in the grander plan of life; setbacks are not meant to impinge on your progress in life but to fully actualize yourself. Facing challenges, choose to activate the power of courage, resilience, determination, and hopefulness. By maintaining a positive attitude, you tackle setbacks with grace, letting your creativity and new ideas emerge with confidence and less stress. You soar high and glide through life with effortless ease. Simply put, you are not overpowered by challenges; on the contrary, you are empowered by them.

Secret #5: Crush Fear and Other Negative Emotions – To create your best life, you need to remain in a high-vibration energy space where confidence, appreciation, and enthusiasm reside. There is nothing wrong in feeling negative emotions for a moment. What is wrong is self-oppression where you are constantly rooted in toxic thoughts and sabotaging your life with disastrous choices.

No one other than yourself can make you feel good. You hold the power to say goodbye to negative emotions and welcome more joy, enthusiasm, and bliss in your life. If toxic emotions consume your heart, take control and restore your well being with good-feeling thoughts. If one good-feeling thought is not enough, then choose another one until you are at peace and well anchored in your well-being zone. Practice makes perfect, so don't be discouraged if you have occasional negative thoughts. Victory is in you.

Secret #6: Embrace Self-Love – You are beautiful, just perfect the way you are. If disempowering beliefs of being unworthy and unloved are within you, crush these beliefs swiftly. Don't be shy about appreciating all that you are. Nourish your mind with new beliefs that you are worthy of blessings and goodness. Recognize that you are of great value. Say to yourself: "I am unique and no one else is like me. I am a beautiful human worthy of love, and especially worthy of my love."

Let God's unconditional love embrace you and fill your heart with self-love. Self-love is the greatest gift you can give yourself. With self-love comes respect for who you are today, with your strengths and weaknesses. You allow yourself to learn, grow, and make mistakes in the process. You accept being vulnerable and are moved to forgive those who have wronged you, living each day with joy in your heart.

With greater appreciation and love for yourself, you value those around you with their unique contributions and gifts. You discover the power of goodness and experience much joy and fulfillment in receiving and giving love to your family, friends, partners, and the world. With an open heart, you create loving, harmonious, and fulfilling relationships.

Secret #7: Open the Gates of Love – There are no riches as deep as love. When you express love, you animate the divine force that is in you. Your soul serves others with joy and compassion. You radiate your light of love and let it shine forever in the hearts of those you have touched over the years. You are love in action with each of your smiles, uplifting words, kindness, patience, forgiveness, and compassion. Love is a call to say I love you. Love is a little surprise to cheer someone. Love is listening. Love is being open to the ideas of others. Love is being patient. Love is respecting others. Love is supporting others in their efforts to become all that they can be. Love is a helping hand. Love is taking time out of your schedule for someone in need. Love is giving back with a smiling heart.

Peace is the song that sings in your loving heart. You stay away from love's poisons such as anger, sarcasm, and oppressive power. You are driven to create a new world where people of all religions and philosophies of life live harmoniously. You see diversity of personalities, ideas, genders, cultures, races, and ethnicities as enrichment, with each person being a source of beauty. You understand that diversity is the basis for expansion.

Secret #8: Be Grateful – Let your heart be rich in praise. Gratitude is a thank you note to life. Take time each day to be grateful and celebrate all your day's victories, small and big. A daily gratitude journal is a great tool to celebrate your successes and your life. Extending gratitude for all situations, good or bad, helps you rise above issues with greater ease. Be grateful for your life, for what you have today, and what is to come tomorrow. Moved by a spirit of gratefulness, you let yourself be excited by another dream and keep a positive outlook on life.

Know that you are rich in talents, friends, love, and all good things. Be grateful for who you are and for all that you have accomplished so far. Appreciate the accomplishments and great beauty you see in others, but most importantly, love yourself and be grateful for your own gifts.

Secret #9: Have Faith that Moves Mountains – Faith in your talents, skills, and capacities leads to wonders in your life and the lives of those around you. You know that no one else can play the same music in the universe. Faith in yourself activates your creative power. It opens your eyes to a world of possibilities. With confidence, you dare to dream bigger dreams to realize your full potential. Most importantly, you launch the full flourishing of your life.

Faith empowers your life with trust and confidence that moves mountains. It fills your soul with inner peace and joy at all times. You see challenges as opportunities for growth and learning. You rise high above your challenges and quickly bounce back. You truly believe, without a shadow of a doubt, that well-aligned thoughts, beliefs, emotions, actions, and faith create the desires of your heart. It is through unwavering faith that you keep your head up and rise to new heights of success.

Secret #10: Share Your Blessings – One who has achieved soul success sees the world as his home and mankind as his brethren. He is inspired to create moments of happiness for others. In sharing, whether it is love, time, passion, gifts, or wealth, he becomes a spark that lights up a prosperity chain.

You do not need to be rich to make a significant impact on other people's lives; a small gesture of kindness brings extraordinary hope. In reaching out to those who hurt, live in poverty, or are in need, not only does it improve your life, but it grants you the ability to help and make positive change in the world. For example, Mother Teresa did not have much money, but she tirelessly spread her love, peace, kindness, and compassion. Nelson Mandela is known for having provided psychological and mental support to other prisoners through his teachings on history, politics, and philosophy.

Giving money carries a double blessing. It gives joy to both the receiver and giver. It holds the power to multiply and transform the lives of your neighbors, thus making your community and country prosper. There is great satisfaction in empowering others to create their best life. By sharing your seeds of greatness, the world never stops expanding with more love, kindness, and generosity. From a serving heart blossoms soul success.

About Jocelyne

Jocelyne F. Lafrenière is an international management consultant, strategist, business and life coach, trainer, and public speaker. She is the author of the truly inspiring book, *Hello, Marvelous You*, in which she genuinely shares her knowledge, experience, and wisdom to inspire people to create their best life.

Jocelyne is the President of JFL International, Inc. which offers a unique and transformational approach that combines leading-edge business advice with coaching and training, enabling enterprises, organizations, and individuals to achieve their goals and drive higher performance more rapidly.

For more than 25 years, Jocelyne has served as an advisor to United Nations agencies, government departments and agencies, businesses, and non-profit organizations around the world. She is a former partner of KPMG Canada, one of the world's largest professional services firms, where she led the International Development Assistance Services of their Ottawa office.

She holds a Bachelor of Commerce degree and is a Chartered Professional Accountant and Certified Internal Control Auditor. She is a Certified Professional Success Coach and Neuro-Linguistic Programming Practitioner.

Jocelyne is known for her business acumen and her drive and passion. As a strategist and management consultant, she helps businesses move to the next level and achieve greater success. As a coach, she enables people from all walks of life to make shifts in their lives and achieve outstanding results. She is an energetic motivational public speaker and charismatic trainer. Her message of creating an enriched and meaningful life is truly inspirational.

Throughout her career, Jocelyne has actively championed the empowerment of women and the protection of children, as well as supporting education. Her love and commitment to disadvantaged individuals has no boundaries. She has been powerfully drawn to a number of opportunities to volunteer and assist with international development issues. Jocelyne is the Founder of the JFL Foundation that advances the lives of underprivileged people around the world through education and entrepreneurship.

She has played an active role in supporting women entrepreneurship. She is a former President of the Quebec Business Women's Network, Outaouais region. Her investment in youth has been wide-ranging, from being a volunteer with Youth Action, to her role as a Board Member of Kids Connection Haiti (Canadian branch) and Save the Children Canada.

She has taught accounting and financial management at the Université du Québec à Gatineau, Algonquin College, and the Building Owners and Managers Association of Ottawa. She has also published several articles on contract compliance matters.

She champions human rights through the JFL Peace Movement. She is a recipient of the Queen Elizabeth II Diamond Jubilee Medal for her significant contribution to the community in Canada and abroad.

For more information, visit:
www.jflinternational.com
https://www.facebook.com/jflgroup
https://www.youtube.com/channel/UC13dL82djmzDC7z5ecRMUcw

CHAPTER 55

YOU CAN HAVE IT ALL:
FOUR KEYS TO SUCCESS IN YOUR PERSONAL AND PROFESSIONAL LIFE

BY JANICE L. QUIGG

You can do anything you set your mind to.

~ Benjamin Franklin

My parents had three children before they were twenty. They dropped out of high school to take care of us. My father got his first full time job with the City and my mom stayed home to take care of us kids. Despite their lack of formal education, they were, and continue to be, two of the smartest people I have known. Although they both came from severely dysfunctional families, they somehow became wonderful parents who taught me so many important life lessons – lessons that have helped me achieve success in both my personal and professional life.

One of the most important lessons my parents taught me early on was that I could do anything I set my mind to. I don't think that they knew who Benjamin Franklin was, but that lesson was one of the gifts I treasure most in my life. I treasure it because it allows me to go through life believing that whatever I want to achieve, I can – as long as I set my mind to it! So far, I have achieved each goal that I have set for myself.

I set my mind to creating a wonderful personal life. To me, that meant finding a wonderful life partner and having a least one child. Guess what? I'm married to the man of my dreams. He has each of the qualities on that checklist that many of us create when looking for a life partner. Sometimes I laugh at myself when I am driving home from work thinking that I am just as anxious to see him now as I was eleven years ago when we were dating!

And guess what else? We have a seven-year-old son, Ryan, who can only be described in my mind as "magical." Ryan is a child whom teachers and friends describe as "having it all." He is intellectually and athletically gifted but most importantly, he has a heart like no other I've known. My husband and I agree, Ryan has alot of "Benjamin" in him – at seven, he sets his mind to something and just executes it!

I also set my mind to achieving a certain level of success as a professional. When I was 12 years old, I came home from school and announced to my parents that I wanted to become a lawyer. No one in my family had finished high school let alone a post-graduate degree. My mom and I had spent many years watching Perry Mason together so she wasn't entirely surprised. My parents were excited and told me that if I set my mind to it, I could do it. When I eventually received my acceptance letter from law school, my parents were so thrilled that they put an ad in the local newspaper! I graduated from law school with honours and have loved being a lawyer ever since. It is indeed true that if you love what you do, you never work a day in your life.

I would like to share with you four keys to achieving success in both your personal and professional life.

FOUR KEYS TO SUCCESS

Key #1: Believe, Plan and Persevere!

When I was sixteen, I was a locker attendant at the local outdoor pool. Being a locker attendant wasn't a bad job, but it didn't take me long to figure out that the lifeguards had a far better summer gig! Although swimming wasn't my best sport, I set the goal of being on deck next summer and I was. But how did I become a lifeguard, when swimming was not my best sport? I broke it down into small steps.

First, I started by believing that I could become a lifeguard. Had I not believed it, I would not have taken the necessary steps to make it happen. Next, I contacted the pool to determine what qualifications I needed. I was told that I needed to complete the Bronze Medallion course. So, I enrolled in the course and failed the test the first time. But I did not give up there. I enrolled in a refresher course and took the test again. I passed the second test and enjoyed many summers as lifeguard, which allowed me to pay for my university tuition (it was a lot cheaper back then), books and a trip to the Caribbean!

You can achieve any goal you set your mind to if you believe, plan and persevere. You must do all three to succeed. Believing is not enough. You must also plan and persevere.

Key #2: Make Smart Decisions!

You can have it all if you make smart decisions which make it easier for you to succeed both personally and professionally. When making decisions about your professional life, you cannot forget about your personal goals, just as you cannot forget about your professional goals when making personal decisions. I always wanted both a challenging career and a happy family life, so I made very deliberate choices that allowed me to achieve both of these goals.

I knew that if I chose to work at a large, international law firm that required me to bill 2000 hours a year, my family life would suffer. So I chose to work at a boutique law firm that allowed me to be home most nights and weekends with my family. I know some lawyers who achieved professional success but paid a high price personally in the form of substance abuse, broken marriages or children who developed behavioural problems.

You must also make smart choices in your personal life. Forget about the old adage, "opposites attract!" Compatibility is extremely important. It is much easier to get along with someone who has similar views, values and goals. If family life is a priority for both of you, then chances are you will have a happy partnership. I have known couples where one spouse is always at the office and, it creates resentment in the other spouse, who is left picking up the slack at home.

Similarly, if you both really want children, then chances are, you will both be really involved in parenting your children. If you have similar parenting styles, then you will be less likely to have fundamental disagreements about how you raise your children.

And remember, people do not generally change! So, to take a very simple example, if you know that your husband is not big on buying flowers and jewellery (but expresses his love in other ways), you better be prepared to live without flowers and jewellery or resentment will build as the years go by and it will permeate the relationship.

Key #3: Be the Best You!

No matter what it is that you are doing, give it two hundred percent! If you do, you will be more likely to succeed in everything you do. This is simple logic – you are half as likely to succeed when you give something half the effort!

If you strive for excellence in everything you do, you will garner trust, respect and admiration from others. You must strive for excellence in both the important tasks and the seemingly mundane tasks because the mundane ones can negatively affect your reputation just as much as the less mundane. For example, if a lawyer sends out an account to his/her client and there is one small clerical error in the account, the client immediately starts to wonder about how many other accounts have had errors in them and how many of them will have errors in them in the future. Similarly, if a lawyer sends a brief to the court prior to a court hearing and there is a page missing or a paragraph incorrectly numbered, the judge is likely to form the opinion that the lawyer is a sloppy one.

So, whether you are performing an important task or a more mundane one, you must perform both to the best of your ability! As a professional, if you consistently meet deadlines, deliver excellent work products and keep yourself abreast of new developments in your area of expertise, you will achieve a high level of professional success.

In terms of your family life, the same principles apply – give two hundred percent to your spouse and children! Each day I strive to be the best wife and mother in the history of womankind, yes I said, womankind! Now, of course, no one is perfect and I am no exception. But I can tell you that making the effort has brought me profound joy as a wife and mother. I have a little boy who tells me everyday that he loves me and, whose eyes literally light up when I walk through the door. I have a husband who will do virtually anything for me and who has made me feel deeply loved for the last eleven years.

One day I asked Ryan why he loved me so much. Of course all kids love their moms but I wanted to know why he loved me so much. He turned and looked up at me with a shy smile and said "because you are so nice to me mommy."

I have often said to my husband that I want to write a book about marriage and parenting and entitle it, "Just Be Nice!" Go out of your way, I mean really out of your way, to be nice to your spouse and children. Treat them like you treat your friends who don't have to stay with you! Go out of your way to say kind things, to tell them that you love them every day, to hug them, to be accommodating, to be flexible, to be forgiving, to be interested in what they are talking about, to be fully present, to play, to listen and to say thank you every chance you get! I promise you, you will get it back tenfold.

Key #4: Give First!

What I have noticed over the years is that the more good I do for others (without any hidden agenda) the more it is returned to me, sometimes with lightning speed! It's like a boomerang! The key is to give first. If you want your employer to be good to you, then be a great employee first! If you want to have a wonderful husband, then be a wonderful wife first! If you want to have magical children, then be a magical parent first!

As a lawyer, I have spent many years volunteering as a mentor, teacher and pro bono lawyer as a way of giving back to my profession. What I have found is the more I give (for the sheer joy of giving), the more I receive in so many different ways.

Similarly, the more I give as a wife and mother, the more I receive back from my family. I once asked my husband why he was so good to me and he replied, "You make it easy because you give so much to me."

CONCLUSION

I have spent the last few weeks thinking about what "the soul of success" means to me in preparing to write this chapter. Not once did I think about "money," "power" or "prestige." While some have suggested that I have achieved such goals, I have never been in pursuit of them. The essence of success is making a difference in the lives of others and having as much fun as possible along the way.

About Janice

Janice Quigg is a member of the firm, Glaholt LLP, practicing exclusively in commercial litigation with specific concentration in the construction law field. She has represented suppliers of construction-related materials, contractors, developers and surety companies in the construction industry.

Janice frequently speaks to the legal community and industry groups on construction law issues. She has been a member of the Ontario Bar Association Construction Law Executive since 2001 and is currently Past Chair. Janice is a Trustee of the OBA Foundation and Council Member of the Ontario Bar Association and the Canadian Bar Association. Janice has been part-time Professor at George Brown College.

Janice obtained her B.A. (Hons.) from the University of Toronto and her L.L.B. from Osgoode Hall Law School.

You can connect with Janice at:
janicequigg@me.com
Twitter: @quiggphotos

CHAPTER 56

OWNING YOUR POWER

BY KANTA MOTWANI

Understanding who I am and being fully aware of myself has brought tremendous joy, clarity and success into my life. The vibrant health and inner peace that I am enjoying today is the result of practising a set of rules I have followed with faith and perseverance which now allow me to live my life to 100%. So I want to share that set of rules with you so that you too can enjoy that peace and calm.

We may experience disease, loss, conflictive relationships, and so much more, but we are not meant to suffer. We are not our conditions and experiences. Suffering is, at the root cause, just a choice that results from attachment.

It wasn´t always that way for me and, there is no fatigue worse in the world than when you don´t know who you are. Allowing past negative experiences, and other people to drain your positive energy, will completely exhaust you and cause you to become overwhelmed ultimately by what you don't want in your life. This is what happened to me.

My life was flooded with painful experiences, for which I paid a very high cost emotionally, health-wise and physically, as I was in a position where I was either regretting my past or fearing the future.

I was born in Spain in 1969 to a traditional Indian family. My father comes from a family of bakers. At a very young age, he worked and attended to his family demands, while facing challenges during the partition of British India in 1947. My mother is a teacher and completed her education after her marriage. In those times, it was very common to have an arranged marriage in India, but this not being the case for my parents, meant many tensions and controversies within and between both families – until life-changing circumstances blessed them with a move to Spain. My dad arrived there in 1967 and was followed a year later by my mother along with my two siblings.

My dad started working as a salesman while my mother worked as a private tutor. They worked very hard, and struggled to raise us. Both of them did their best for us as they saw it then, however, I only appreciated and truly honoured my parents with my heart for bringing me into this world when I started living my life 100%. It was almost after thirteen years of residency that my dad took a risk and started his own business, which turned him into a renowned, successful businessman.

My dad became a workaholic whilst running the business in Spain and yet still very governed by the demands of his relatives who were well established in India. This led to a very negative environment at home, and I grew up seeing my mother having panic attacks as she tried to protect herself from my dad´s and his family's psychological aggression and abuse. They saw women as having a traditional Indian (role). I spent my teens working hard at school and for my dad´s business. I was constantly undervalued by my dad in front of his employees, put down and belittled, compared to others and reminded of my value and limits as a woman. This negative and hostile situation created a sense of fear in me and every time I heard my parents or anyone raising their voices, I started experiencing shivers and these symptoms lasted for years. I started resenting men, money and even the concept of family.

During my childhood, I used to experience a space of complete tranquillity in which I was immersed, the sensation was as if I was no longer a physical body. I was a very intuitive child, and had an extraordinary ability to sense and predict future events – knowing without knowing why. I never shared this with anyone, as I was afraid that I might be perceived as being different.

I completed my higher education in England, which gave me a welcome opportunity to learn, grow and break away from the stressful environment at home. But being far away from home made little difference to me as I was still living my life from a fear-based perception. By the time I wanted to take certain decisions about my life, a little voice in my head would remind me of being underserving and not good enough. I became a victim of my family circumstances, cultural beliefs and traditions, which held women back from achieving their full potential. I was becoming overwhelmed by negativity and despair.

As I returned back home after my graduation, I was no longer in the space I created for myself; I was clashing between two different personalities. One part of me wanted to prove that I was worthy but the other was a victim of fear and circumstances.

In my desire to prove myself worthy, I worked hard and long hours to successfully establish a Computer Lab. I worked for the public and private corporate sectors, and achieved recognition and success, but because I never asked for help, and wanted so much to prove myself, I became overloaded with work. These long hours spent at work were filling the gap of discontent I felt about life. In the meantime, I was also experiencing high levels of stress. I became a prisoner of the negative perceptions of others towards me, and of my own limiting thoughts and beliefs about myself and my potential – which had been ingrained in me through my upbringing without even my conscious awareness.

I became the greatest pleaser on earth, I was way over-giving, constantly beating myself up in the work environment and within the family for not being good enough. In-spite of all the challenging circumstances, I was always trying to keep everyone happy and content, I just couldn't handle anymore distress or tension and agreed to everything for the sake of peace. My personal relationships too were just abusive and a total failure.

I felt fully depleted after my energy was drained over the years. Three months after my parents eventually separated, I became bedridden and fully dependent on others for all my personal needs, as I was unable to stand up physically on my feet. I lost the complete power of my legs.

I was blaming my circumstances, life, my parents, my ancestors, the world and several times even God. The more I resented, the worse my condition became. I accepted that it was my bad Karma, and of my entire family generation, as I was told, hence my suffering didn't stop.

I tried to understand the root cause of my experiences through the path of religion and believed that "I will never attain success in my life," and gave my power over to religious experts and astrologists.

I tried every medical advice and was admitted to different hospitals. Sadly, nothing helped and in fact made things worse, as I was subjected to aggressive medications, steroids, and radiation.

I was labelled with different disease names, and tried to understand their causes. I started translating clinical trials reports altruistically for an organization in Barcelona. I invested time reinforcing ideas of tumours, arthritis, sarcoidosis, and other names I was labelled with. Hence, I created subconscious beliefs and experienced symptoms which I never even had before, and so I started vibrating in resonance with the morphic field of these diseases.

I lost the business, money, and got into debt. I became very quiet and introverted as nothing mattered anymore and I accepted things the way they were.

My mother always says, accept whatever takes place in your life, learn from it and move on. However in my case, I repeated the same mistakes time and time again under different circumstances. I am going to explain the reasons why this happens since a great percentage of the human population experiences the same.

Science through Quantum Physics shows that every thought is a wavelength of energy that vibrates through neurons and communicates information to our brain and body through signals. When I was experiencing a negative situation during my childhood, my body reacted with shivers due to feelings of insecurity, and so later, every time I met with a similar event my body cells reacted automatically and I subconsciously responded in the same way. This explains that every neuron is either programming its memory cells or it's activating a previous program.

While we consciously want to react in a different way, the subconscious program is automatically activated, and in my case I was conditioned to react in that way, so how we condition our energy-thoughts can produce a long-term effect. I describe some studies using scientifically-proven methods that can contribute to transformational changes in the life of any individual in my new book, *My Life Journey to Self-awareness.*

I never lost my greatest assets: my energy, faith and perseverance. And although it took me almost eighteen months, I learned to walk again by myself unaided, and to detoxify my body from all the chemicals and bacteria.

Suddenly, during times of quietness I started experiencing those spaces again, those that I experienced during my childhood, and as I allowed myself to travel deeper and deeper into this personal tranquil space, my oasis of calm, there was an amazing sense of liberation, joy, and unexplainable expansion. I wasn't aware of how this was happening and how could I go back into that space again. All that I know is I was travelling there on a personal journey and this space meant I enjoyed immense peace and calmness within. As a result, I started to improve and get better and better.

I travelled to India a few years later and met a great visionary who works for the development of humanity. Shri Bhaiyyu Dada, unlike other spiritual leaders, didn't allow me to dwell on those limited beliefs and blind faiths that I was carrying in every cell of my body.

I learnt to meditate from him and experienced different dimensions in consciousness. As soon as I cleared my subconscious resistance to create change, I understood who I was, and my life took a complete 180-degree turn. I took full charge of my own destiny and became the Master of my life.

I don't want you to wait for as long as I did to start living your full human potential, so from what I have learned about myself on my journey, I would suggest ten positive steps for you to achieve freedom from suffering and negative experiences:

1. Let go of the past to focus your energy in the now, and give yourself and others the gift of forgiveness. This is the greatest act of courage, and the sweetest present to yourself for your freedom and success.

2. Drop assumptions – to avoid anger, resentment, disharmony and unnecessary stress.

3. Surround yourself with positive people, not those who drain your energy and leave you feeling negative and in despair.

4. Enjoy positive thinking and behaviours that build an optimum subconscious programme in your brain. Practice thoughts that make you feel good about yourself and others.

5. Change your internal world to manifest the changes in your outer world. Take full responsibility for your life and enjoy good mental, emotional, spiritual and physical health, and don´t blame others for your negative experiences.

6. Start to love and value yourself and think of yourself as an asset. Focus on your strengths, and develop the aspects of patience, faith, and perseverance. These will take you to where you want to go.

7. Trust the intuition and divine guidance that lies within you. What others think or say about you or your capabilities is only their consciousness perception and not your ultimate truth.

8. Believe in yourself. Every experience you have in your life is a great opportunity for you to become more self-aware. You have the potential to do and become anything you want in your life, and no matter what it takes, believe that you can do it.

9. Practise meditation and experience different dimensions in consciousness until you reach the sense of nothingness. This will bring clarity, and increase your power of intuition. As you raise your awareness, you will release limiting beliefs and subconscious resistance to change, so take full charge of your own destiny and become a Master of your life to start living your life to 100%.

10. Finally spend time in the company of great mentors and empowering Gurus, and learn from them, taking charge of your own life, awakening the inner power in yourself to be and live the change.

In love, to your freedom and success.

About Kanta

Kanta Motwani is a Certified Professional Holistic Therapist whose talent and approach has inspired many individuals to lead a healthy self-aware life. She helps her clients take responsibility for their emotional, physical and spiritual health and guides them through transformational healing tools and coaching to support them in raising their own level of awareness.

Kanta´s life circumstances created an ardent desire to give hope to people by telling them about her own story and how they too can take responsibility for their lives and begin to enjoy freedom and good health. She left behind a career as a Computer Based Trainer and IT Instructor as well as her business during difficult and negative circumstances. She overcame these barriers and started to study energy medicine and energy psychology. She is passionate about the many opportunities which she has been offered through the art of healing and is committed about sharing and supporting others.

Kanta has combined her wealth of knowledge in science-proven methods that she studied along with spirituality. Kanta uses her passion to enjoy a vibrant and healthy life motivating her clients to accomplish their goals and access their inner guidance through experiential coaching and the practice of meditations.

She has successfully coached and empowered women and men from all walks of life, ages, races and religious beliefs by bringing clarity into their lives and guiding them to live as they always knew they could. She has personally been coached by the Canfield Coaching Group, which, in addition, has helped her to successfully support people to experience transformational changes as she continues participating in the Canfield training programs.

Kanta is a graduate from Thames Valley University in London. She is the President at a non-Lucrative Association that contributes to international humanitarian projects and is the founder of Surya Awareness Academy®.

She is the author of the forthcoming book My Life Journey to Self-awareness, a public speaker, facilitator and practitioner of various healing modalities. She owns a private consultancy in Spain, delivers Teleseminars and workshops on Personal Development, and provides coaching services and remote healing sessions worldwide. She has developed a 90-day Sadhana Program to transcend the ego – inspired by the meditations she has learned during her stay in India in the company of Spiritual Masters and Saints.

Kanta is a trained, certified Aura and Chakra Counsellor and Biofeedback® Trainer from the Auramed Institute in Germany, Dorn-Breuss Massage Therapist by the DMTA-UK, Facilitator of Quantum Entrainment®, ACP Angel therapy Practitioner, Certified Holistic Professional Therapist – Homeopathy L4 and Practitioner of Be Set Free Fast® Energy Psychology method by Dr Larry Nims.

She contributes with her writing on digital press channels and Alternative Health Magazines in Spain. Her goal is to challenge blind faiths, stereotypes, fixed values and limiting belief systems from our society, and to help people use their full potential and own their power by raising their levels of awareness.

http://www.kantamotwani.com
km@kantamotwani.com
www.twitter.com/Surya_Awareness
www.facebook.com/kantamotwani1

CHAPTER 57

THE SEVEN SOUL SHOES OF SUCCESS

BY KATHY ANDERSEN

The secrets to your success are the shoes you step into each day. Just as you choose the shoes you wear to best match the activities of your day, so too, you must choose the "soul shoes" that will match the power you need in your day. Master the powers in the Seven Soul Shoes, and you will be unlimited in your success.

As I reflected on *The Soul of Success*, I thought deeply on the meaningful "aha" that I could bring you in this chapter. I wanted to integrate all of my experiences and learning on success from people and places around the world—from helping people realize their dreams for over 20 years; from my studies and work at Harvard University, in India, Haiti, and elsewhere in the world; from the teachers I have been blessed to meet, including the dear Jack Canfield; from my childhood of sexual abuse, and having nothing when I left home at the age of seventeen, to now having prosperity in all aspects of my life.

Through those reflections came **The Seven Soul Shoes of Success**. These are the representations of all the powers you need on your journey to your most extraordinary successes. The most successful people have mastered the powers of success, and so can you.

So, what are the Soul Shoes of Success, and why are there seven?

1. The Creator Soul Shoe—the power of dreams.
2. The Warrior Soul Shoe—the power of strength.

3. The Sage Soul Shoe—the power of wisdom.

4. The Magician Soul Shoe—the power of manifestation.

5. The Adventurer Soul Shoe—the power of discovery.

6. The Hermit Soul Shoe—the power of time.

7. The Caretaker Soul Shoe—the power of love.

There are seven soul shoes because seven is one of the most powerful and significant numbers. Throughout the ages, "seven" has represented creation and completion. It is found in contexts representing divine perfection, and the fulfillment of a divine mandate. Your journey is one of constant creation and completion, ultimately resulting in the fulfillment of your divine mandate.

With each step on your journey to success, you are confronted by challenges, opportunities, doubts, fears, hopes, risks, rewards, obstacles and distractions. You are confronted by people who may help or hinder your success. You are confronted by questions of purpose, meaning, ethics, character, responsibility, the difference you will make, and the legacy you will leave. You are confronted by the barriers you create for yourself, which are often greater than any barriers others create for you.

Your soul shoes enable you to step into the powers you need to move through challenges and opportunities. They reveal the next step YOU need to take. That step is uniquely yours. You cannot compare it to anyone else, be directed by those around you, or copy the steps of others. This is YOUR journey. It is unique and divine. You are able to be your most extraordinary by the powers you choose with each step.

After you read each soul shoe, you need to do three things to step into the power of each:

1. Ask yourself which challenge or opportunity requires the power of that soul shoe.

2. Ask yourself which specific aspect of that power you most need to apply to move forward.

3. Ask yourself the one thing you can do today to apply that power.

Remember, your answers are within you, and this chapter seeks to guide you to your answers.

1. THE CREATOR SOUL SHOE

The Creator Soul Shoe represents your divine power to create the vision for your life. The Creator evokes the powers to dream, inspire, and express. It connects you to your deepest passions, potential, opportunities, desires, aspirations, universal energies, and eternal life. It activates and awakens your divine being within. Your Creator shoes allow you to step forward guided by your highest power.

The greatest power you summon standing in the Creator Soul Shoe is to dream.

The Creator Soul Shoe is aligned to the seventh chakra, the Crown chakra, and is a receiver and giver of energy and consciousness. You see your place and power in the world. Standing in your Creator Soul Shoes, you can connect to your deepest passions, creativity, inspirations, and ideas, and allow those to guide you through the challenges and opportunities before you.

The challenges through which your Creator Soul Shoes enable you to step are those that prevent you from stepping forward due to not knowing to where that step will take you. You feel blocked. You feel doubt about the purpose and meaning of your activities, and whether you are achieving your greatest potential.

The opportunities into which your Creator Soul Shoes enable you to step are often at the commencement of an exciting venture, a new business, or a new phase in your life. You need to tap into your greatest vision, potential, creativity, passions, and dreams in order to achieve your most meaningful success.

Now, identify a challenge or opportunity in your life that requires the power of the Creator, and the one thing you need to do today to apply your Creator power.

2. THE WARRIOR SOUL SHOE

The Warrior Soul Shoe represents your courage, bravery, resilience, resourcefulness, strength, determination, perseverance, survival, discipline, strategy, command, decisiveness, and hard work. The Warrior Soul Shoes will enable you to fearlessly battle the forces that work against you as you journey toward your dreams. In these shoes, defeat is not an option.

The greatest power you summon standing in the shoes of the Warrior is strength.

The warrior is aligned to the first chakra, the root chakra, and activates the powers to rise above challenges and be triumphant. It is your survival center. In these shoes you are a master strategist who draws on all elements of battle—from brute force to diplomacy. You learn from each step, refine your strategy, re-assess the landscape, develop new moves, and act decisively. The Warrior is well-trained, and has recruited the best people to succeed through every opportunity and challenge.

The challenges through which your Warrior Soul Shoes enable you to step are the forces that oppose you, appear insurmountable, involve great risk, question your abilities, raise doubts, and generate fear. They call upon every drop of persistence, bravery, boldness, determination and strength within you.

The opportunities into which your Warrior Soul Shoes enable you to step are those that provide the greatest reward, are most purposeful to you, take you closest to your dreams, thrill you, and excite you. They enable you to break through to new levels of meaningful success.

> Now, identify a challenge or opportunity in your life that requires the power of the Warrior, and the one thing you need to do today to apply your Warrior power.

3. THE SAGE SOUL SHOE

The Sage Soul Shoe represents your highest wisdom, mindfulness, knowledge, faith, intellect, and judgment. In your Sage Soul Shoes, you feel centered, calm, and tranquil as you stand in your ultimate and divine truth.

The greatest power you summon standing in the shoes of the Sage is wisdom.

The Sage is aligned to the fifth chakra, the throat chakra, and allows you to connect to your higher wisdom and express that in your physical world—in your actions, words, decisions, and endeavors. You are your most intelligent in your Sage Soul Shoes. All you do is guided by your infinite intelligence, your highest wisdom, your divine being, your truth, and your authentic self.

The challenges through which your Sage Soul Shoes enable you to step are those filled with deception, hidden agendas, opposing interests, conflict, complexity, and multiple "truths." These are situations in which you must remain centered in your higher wisdom, and patiently allow the next step to be revealed.

The opportunities into which your Sage Soul Shoes will enable you to step are those that present new and complex endeavors, require you to call upon your greatest intellect, leap to another level of impact, and succeed through wise and thoughtful decisions and actions.

Now, identify a challenge or opportunity in your life that requires the power of the Sage, and the one thing you need to do today to apply your Sage power.

4. THE MAGICIAN SOUL SHOE

The Magician Soul Shoe represents your transformational powers to manifest all of your desires. In your Magician Soul Shoes you stand in your highest power to bring all that you have imagined, dreamed, and visualized into your reality. You are the change-maker. You bring all that is beyond you into reach and transform the seemingly impossible into the possible—as if by magic.

The greatest power you summon standing in the shoes of the Magician is manifestation.

The Magician is aligned to the second chakra, the sacral chakra, and activates your most creative and transformational powers. The Magician Soul Shoes stimulate your powers of visualization, your action orientation, your power to remove obstacles, your ability to generate creative solutions. In your Magician Soul Shoes, you act, "wave your wand," and manifest all you desire.

The challenges through which your Magician Soul Shoes enable you to step are those that are filled with seemingly overwhelming obstacles, difficult people, entrenched attitudes and beliefs, financial barriers, complex relationships, multiple interests, time pressures, resource constraints, and those that generate doubt of your own capabilities.

The opportunities into which your Magician Soul Shoes will enable you to step are those that provide the greatest ability to create meaningful transformation and change. These can dramatically transform your current state into your desired state, if only you can "magically" manifest them, which, powered by your Magician Soul Shoes, you can through visualization, focus, and action.

Now, identify a challenge or opportunity in your life that requires the power of the Magician, and the one thing you need to do today to apply your Magician power.

5. THE ADVENTURER SOUL SHOE

The Adventurer Soul Shoe represents your powers to boldly venture beyond your comfort zone, to step into unexplored territory, "walk on the edge" of discovery, and be unfazed by the height of the mountain or the vastness of the ocean. You step fearlessly into the greatest vision and divine mandate for your life.

The greatest power you summon standing in the shoes of the Adventurer is discovery.

The Adventurer is aligned to the third chakra, the solar plexus, and evokes your power of confidence and fearlessness. You turn inertia into action and move forward. You leap into discovery, venture into unknown territory, step beyond familiarity, and take risks. You are daring, bold, and comfortable with the uncomfortable. You feel the ultimate power of your freedom to "step out."

The challenges through which your Adventurer Soul Shoes enable you to move are those that require you to step into unknown enterprises and unfamiliar territory—where you may feel doubt, fear, and uncertainty. You may need to give up feelings of comfort, safety, and certainty to move forward.

The opportunities into which your Adventurer Soul Shoes will enable you to step take you in exciting new directions, and powerfully catapult you from where you are to where you want to be. These opportunities will stretch you, and take you as far as you dare to travel.

> Now, identify a challenge or opportunity in your life that requires the power of the Adventurer, and the one thing you need to do today to apply your Adventurer power.

6. THE HERMIT SOUL SHOE

The Hermit Soul Shoe represents your powers to expand time through solitude, retreat, meditation, and quiet time. In these shoes, you gain the breakthrough "aha" moments that escape you in the busyness of your day.

The greatest power you summon standing in the shoes of the Hermit is time.

The Hermit is aligned to the sixth chakra, the third eye chakra, and enables you to see the answers that lie within you. In these shoes, you see beyond all that is limiting, to all that is limitless. You experience peace, relaxation, patience, and awareness. You see things from a higher perspective that allows you to uncover breakthrough solutions.

The challenges through which your Hermit Soul Shoes enable you to move are those where the next step is not apparent. You need to apply new knowledge and approaches, and adapt to new forces. You must see and think differently. The only step forward is to "step out," and experience the breakthrough, "aha" solutions.

The opportunities into which your Hermit Soul Shoes enable you to step are those that enable you to "leap-frog" toward your dreams through new thinking, approaches, and solutions. They require new capabilities, and will keep you awake at night as you search for solutions. In your Hermit Soul Shoes, those solutions will be revealed.

Now, identify a challenge or opportunity in your life that requires the power of the Hermit, and the one thing you need to do today to apply your Hermit power.

7. THE CARETAKER SOUL SHOE

The Caretaker Soul Shoe represents your powers of self-love and love for others. In these shoes, you connect to your self-actualized self and your higher being to create meaningful and lasting endeavors that transform your life and the world.

The greatest power you summon standing in the shoes of the Caretaker is love.

The Caretaker is aligned to the fourth chakra, the Heart chakra, and activates love, kindness, compassion, justice, wellness, harmony, and nurturing—for yourself and others. You are aware that your individual success can only be maximized when your ventures generate a greater good. In these shoes, you make your greatest difference in the world. Your success is reflected not only in the things external to you, but also in the inner sense that you are fulfilling your divine mandate.

The challenges through which your Caretaker Soul Shoes enable you to move are those where there are great insecurities, threats, vulnerabilities, pain, distrust, and opposition. In order to move forward, people must feel genuine care and trust for their wellbeing, beyond only material outcomes, a bottom line, or return on investment.

The opportunities into which your Caretaker Soul Shoes enable you to step are those that can create positive change for you and others. These provide a path to follow your most purposeful pursuits, and your greatest causes. They reinforce your belief that you can create the change you want to see in the world.

> Now, identify a challenge or opportunity in your life that requires the power of the Caretaker, and the one thing you need to do today to apply your Caretaker power.

MASTERING THE SEVEN SOUL SHOES OF SUCCESS

Mastering the Seven Soul Shoes and harnessing the power you need to achieve your most extraordinary success requires only your simple daily practice. So too, daily practice is the secret to mastering any aspect of your life.

Luckily, each day we are presented with practice through the challenges and opportunities that arise, and each day you have the Seven Soul Shoes resources to help you.

Here's to your success!

www.7SoulShoes.com

About Kathy

Kathy Andersen is an award-winning author, motivational speaker, television talk show host, leadership and change consultant, success coach, media guest, business person, and social entrepreneur.

For almost 20 years, Kathy has helped people transform their visions for change into realities. Kathy holds a master's degree from Harvard Kennedy School with a focus on international development, leadership, organizational development, and management. Kathy is a Master Class trained consultant in Adaptive Leadership from Harvard Kennedy School, and has also undertaken several executive programs at Harvard Kennedy School and Harvard Business School on management and leadership.

A spirited speaker and workshop host, Kathy has spoken at numerous conferences, and held various workshops and retreats throughout the United States and internationally. Kathy frequently appears on national media in the United States speaking on topics including change, leadership, and success. Kathy is a regular writer for the *Huffington Post*, and the host of the new Lifetime TV show, *Live Life Forward*, commencing in 2016.

Kathy's clients have included international public and private corporations, non-profit organizations, educational institutions, country governments, Major League Baseball players, equestrian athletes, private philanthropists, and other individuals. Kathy is currently collaborating with Sheryl Sandberg, Facebook COO, and Sheryl's Lean In Foundation to undertake success and empowerment programs for underserved women and girls. Kathy is also managing a Clinton Global Initiative America Commitment to Action to lead underserved youth to success.

Kathy's five-time award-winning book, *Change Your Shoes, Live Your Greatest Life*, took readers on a journey of personal transformation. Kathy's second book, *Change Your Shoes, 365 Life Resolutions*, gave readers an inspirational daily journal to achieve their dreams. Now, in *The Seven Soul Shoes of Success*, Kathy brings you the "soul shoes" you need to step into your powers and achieve your most extraordinary and meaningful successes.

Originally from Australia, Kathy "changed her shoes" from corporate high heels to hiking boots after a childhood of sexual abuse by her father left her looking for meaning and purpose. Her travels took her to the richest and poorest countries in the world. Now, Kathy finds meaning and purpose pursuing her dreams and helping others achieve their dreams. Kathy lives in Miami and now calls the United States home.

You can follow Kathy on Facebook, Twitter and other social media, where you will find resources to help you "change your shoes" and step into all you desire in your life and in the world.

www.KathyAndersen.com
email: Kathy@KathyAndersen.com

CHAPTER 58

THE ART OF BUSINESS

BY ROBIN OSBORN

It was a warm June afternoon in 1984. My twin brother and I walked alongside each other donning the words "double" and "trouble" on the top of our graduation caps. Shortly after our commencement, my Dad walked up and handed me an envelope. I unfolded the neatly-typed letter, which had been typed using an IBM Selectric II typewriter on his company letterhead. The letter read: Robin E. Bokelman – you are hereby granted a prepaid one-way Greyhound bus ticket to any U.S. destination of your choice. I heard my Dad cackle with laughter as I read it. I did not find the joke to be funny at the time, today I treasure it!

Sadly, four years after graduating high school my father tragically passed away. My older sister Diane, twin brother Ray and myself became business owners in one day. We had 40 employees, I was 21 years old.

What I learned first hand over the course of the next few years, more importantly than earning the respect of the customers, was earning the respect of the employees would be monumental in our long term success.

What I have found to be true in managing employees is it parallels effective parenting. When my boys were young, about once a year as I tucked them in at night I would ask them, "What do you like that mommy does?" and "What could I do better?" The thing that always struck me was their answers to what could I do better. I remember my oldest son Tanner telling me his timeouts were too short! He said you practically let me out of my room before I barely get back to it!

As I learned something new each time I listened to their responses, what I realized was that they wanted to be held accountable, and valued being heard. They were asking for boundaries and let me in on it at a very young age. Their pure of heart responses helped me to become a better parent.

What I have learned to be true through connecting with employees is that they essentially want the same thing. By asking and really listening to what my boys had to say gave me an opportunity to raise my own bar as a parent. What I found with employees is 'asking not telling' allows an opportunity to raise your own bar as a leader. I have found sitting face-to-face with an employee and simply asking them what do they like about their job? As well as what could we do better? Leads to greater insight and clarity in navigating the business as a whole.

Asking and making your employees needs a priority builds trust, and with trust comes loyalty. Being an effective leader comes down to getting real simple and clear on what the needs are, taking action in the best way possible to serve your employees, as well as your organization. Our average employee has been employed for over 20 years!

A few years ago, I was really struggling with growing our small family business. We were stuck doing the same thing and getting the same results. I remember going to bed night after night and waking up with these 2:00 am thoughts: "Where will our cash flow be next month? . . . How can we focus on increasing sales when we can't afford to hire anyone? . . . What should we do with the personnel conflict? . . . How can we change it?"

Frustrated and exhausted, I reached out to a business coach named Tommi Wolfe who suggested I read the book *Traction®* by Gino Wickman. As I read *Traction®*, a huge sigh of relief came over me. The more I read the more things came together with what we needed to take action on within our organization. Finally, a system we could implement to get crystal clear on where we're going and how we're going to get there! I knew deep down the Entrepreneurial Operation System (EOS®) would bring the clarity we so desperately needed in addition to help us get control over our business. What I did over the course of the next six months was work diligently implementing the EOS® process into our small family business, Chromal Plating Company.

The journey began with the executive leadership team, and over time we introduced it departmentally to all levels within our organization. We successfully changed the way we operated our business from a leadership perspective, as well as made a plan to grow our company.

The philosophy of *Traction*® advocates a healthy leadership team approach, building a team of people that defines your company's vision with you. These leaders all have clear accountabilities and must be able to take initiative over their respective departments. Everyone must remain open and honest about all issues, and be willing to fight for what is best for the company as a whole.

So what is EOS® all about? Think about your business having six key components. Every business, big or small, or any industry has six key components, and to the degree you can strengthen those six key components, everything has a way of just falling into place.

1. VISION COMPONENT™:

First, the VISION COMPONENT™ consists of getting your leadership team laser-focused on creating a clear picture of where your company is going and how it will get there. The first tool we used in EOS® is the Vision/Traction Organizer™ (V/TO™) shown below which is a simple two page document. (A short tutorial on the V/TO™ is located under EOS® Tools on my website.)

THE EOS MODEL™

THE VISION/TRACTION ORGANIZER™

ORGANIZATION NAME:

VISION

CORE VALUES	1. 2. 3. 4. 5.	3-YEAR PICTURE™
		Future Date: Revenue: $ Profit: $ Measurables: What does it look like?
CORE FOCUS™	Purpose/Cause/Passion: Our Niche:	• • • • •
10-YEAR TARGET™		• • • •
MARKETING STRATEGY	Target Market/"The List": Three Uniques: 1. 2. 3. Proven Process: Guarantee:	• • • • •

THE EOS MODEL™

THE VISION/TRACTION ORGANIZER™

ORGANIZATION NAME:

TRACTION

1-YEAR PLAN	ROCKS	ISSUES LIST
Future Date: Revenue: $ Profit: $ Measurables: Goals for the Year: 1. 2. 3. 4. 5. 6. 7. With your cursor in the last row, press Tab to add another row.	Future Date: Revenue: $ Profit: $ Measurables: Rocks for the Quarter: Who 1. 2. 3. 4. 5. 6. 7. With your cursor in the last row, press Tab to add another row.	1. 2. 3. 4. 5. 6. 7. 8. 9. 10. With your cursor in the last row, press Tab to add another row.

By answering the following eight questions and filling out the V/TO™, we will clarify exactly what your vision is.

The 8 questions in the VISION COMPONENT™ are:

1. What are your core values?

2. What is your Core Focus™?

3. What is your 10 year target?

4. What is your marketing strategy?

5. What is your three-year picture?

6. What is your 1 Year Plan?

7. What are your quarterly rocks?

8. What are your Issue's?

2. PEOPLE COMPONENT™:

Remember the Greyhound bus I was granted a one-way ticket for? Well there is a new bus within our company that relates to the People Component™ of our business and it is based on getting the "RIGHT PEOPLE in the RIGHT SEATS." The magic happens when you get the right people in the right seats. You no longer need to push your team because the vision is automatically pulling them. Your leadership team now lives in a 90-day world of setting quarterly Rocks. Rocks are the biggest priorities of/for the company as well as the individual.

So how do you get the right people? Getting the right people is aligning your company core values that are developed in the Vision Component™ with who you are hiring, reviewing, or firing. We use a tool in EOS® called The People Analyzer™ that establishes a minimum standard bar created by the leadership team. The bar is used to identify who fits and who doesn't within your organization. The power of setting a bar is your managers now have absolute clarity on what is acceptable and what is not. Once managers know your expectations, they will hold their team accountable.

The next powerful tool used in the People Component™ is the **Accountability Chart** – which has the most impact of any EOS® tool. Starting with the fundamental belief that there are only three major functions in any business and those three functions make every

ACCOUNTABILITY CHART

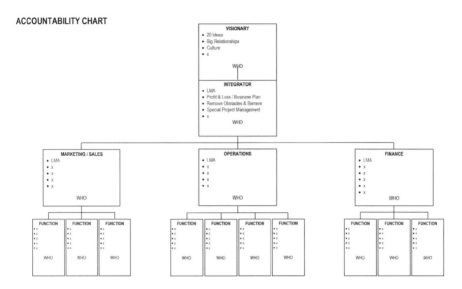

organization run, regardless of whether it's a start-up business or one of the largest in the world.

Right Seats

V - VISIONARY. The visionary is typically the owner, co-owner or founder. Visionaries typically have 10 new ideas a week. Nine of them may not be great, but the one that is keeps the organization growing. Visionaries are creative in thinking and great solvers of big ugly problems (not the little practical ones), and fantastic with important clients, vendors, suppliers, and banking relationships. The culture of the organization is very important to them, because they usually operate more on emotion and therefore have a better barometer of how people are feeling.

I - INTEGRATOR. The integrator is the person who harmoniously oversees all the major functions of the business. They are in the business day-to-day generally very good at leading, managing and holding people accountable. The Integrator is the glue that holds the company together, great at special projects and operates more on logic.

The standard organization has 3 basic seats. SALES/MARKETING, OPERATIONS, and FINANCE. The seats are customized to fit your company's structure. Occasionally Sales/Marketing is split into two seats.

One is a Sales seat and one is a Marketing seat. The same can be true for operations, but it is unique to your particular company. Depending on the size of your organization, you will end up with anywhere between three and ten major functions on that front line. As long as you stay focused on what the right structure is for your organization, the right number will come.

3. DATA COMPONENT™:

The Data Component™ consists of a SCORECARD and MEASURABLES.

What get's measured get's done. Everyone must have a number! Numbers create accountability and cut through subjective communication between the manager and direct reports. A Scorecard is a custom tool you create using 5-15 high-level weekly numbers that are vital in managing your business. Your scorecard becomes a 13 week navigational dashboard to being able to predict, prioritize and systematize your business.

With the Vision Component™ strong, People Component™ strong, and Data Component™ strong you start to create a lucid, transparent, open and honest organization where there is no where to hide and as a result your going to start to smoke out the issues. Which leads us to the fourth key component, which is the Issues Component™.

4. ISSUES COMPONENT™:

By strengthening this component you get great at solving problems – setting them up and knocking them down, making them go away forever. EOS® uses a tool called IDS, which stands for Identify, Discuss, and Solve. Most organizations are really good at discussing the heck out of an issue but not great at solving it. This tool allows you to dig, dig, dig, down deep to the root of the problem and solve it once and for all.

5. PROCESS COMPONENT™:

The fifth key component is what we call the Process Component™. This is really the secret ingredient to systematizing your business through identifying the core processes that make up your business – getting everyone on the same page with what they are and everyone following them, so you're getting consistency and scalability.

6. TRACTION COMPONENT™:

The final key component is what we call Traction®, which brings discipline and accountability into the organization taking the vision down to the ground and making it real. This is accomplished by living in a 90-day World in your organization with your *company* Rocks as well as *individual* Rocks. Secondly, the weekly Level 10 Meeting™ is the most powerful action you can take for your business. The Level 10 Meeting™ is an effective time-management tool.

The five points of an effective weekly meeting pulse must:

1. Be on the same day each week.

2. Be at the same time each week.

3. Have the same printed agenda.

4. Start on time, and

5. End on time.

The Weekly Level 10 Meeting™ Agenda

Segue	5 minutes
Scorecard	5 minutes
Rock review	5 minutes
Customer/Employee headlines	5 minutes
To-Do List	5 minutes
IDS	60 minutes
Conclude	5 minutes

VISION, PEOPLE, DATA, ISSUES, PROCESS and TRACTION are the six key components, and to the degree you focus on six and only six things in your business and strengthen those six key components, everything has a way of falling into place.

It's simple, are you running your business or is it running you? By making small simple steps each day to achieve your vision will catapult you and your leadership team to break through to the next level. What's important is getting crystal clear on what that picture looks like. When you start with the end in mind your business will no longer be a blank canvas, but an amazing picture with a systematic plan. If you are not sure where to begin, take out a blank legal pad and a pen. I promise you, through this simple exercise, all of the right thoughts will come to mind. I call this exercise: *The Art Of Business*. Enjoy creating your business masterpiece!

About Robin

Robin Osborn has spent the last 28 years of her life at the helm of her small family business in Southern California. It is an entrepreneurial journey that she began at the age of 21. Robin has an intuitive understanding of her customers' and employees' needs. She successfully leads a staff of 31 employees and the organization boasts an employee retention record of more than 20 years.

A few years ago, Robin's business, and her frustrations, hit the ceiling. She was up at two in the morning, her mind spinning and her dissatisfaction with her business was reaching its peak. Robin was tired of doing the same thing in business and getting the same results. Her business was stuck – she was facing personnel conflict, profit woes and inadequate growth.

Searching for answers for her business, Robin came across Gino Wickman's *Traction®*. It was there she would find inspiration, not only to change her business, but to change her life.

By applying the EOS® Worldwide Entrepreneurial Operating System (EOS®) to her business, Robin found the relief and freedom that she'd only dreamed about. Robin is one of 105 hand-picked World Class Implementer's for EOS® Worldwide. As an implementer, she is a champion for her EOS® clients, providing entrepreneurs the business principles and real-world tools they need to get the results they want.

www.thetractionexpert.com

EOS Model™

CHAPTER 59

IT'S ALL ABOUT FASHION –THERE IS NO SECOND CHANCE FOR YOUR FIRST IMPRESSION!

BY ULRICH KELLERER

FASHION as an expression of personality.

FASHION is a way to express your own style.

FASHION to impress others.

FASHION to represent your value in society.

FASHION is see and be seen.

But stop!!!

THERE IS NO SECOND CHANCE FOR YOUR FIRST IMPRESSION!

In fractions of a second, our brain decides whether something is good or bad. All the stored data and impressions give us just the visual impulses for immediate assessment and categorization.

There are not only impressions perceived by the eye, but also odors and gestures have a direct signal effect on us.

The ability to store and analyze these impressions can help us to make the right decisions and to attract the right people and situations.

Only limited psychological knowledge is required here.

From earliest childhood there is only one maxim:

Do everything to attract Attention!

What children have learned right from the cradle is applied successfully throughout life.

FIRST IMPRESSIONS IN COMMUNICATION

There are certain countries that have perfected these communication skills to true mastery. All Mediterranean countries as well as the U.S. have made the "talk to everybody" a general philosophy of life.

Only those who ask questions are entitled to answers.

In today's world, where all information is permanently available, people use all kinds of Social Media – i.e., Facebook, Twitter or LinkedIn. Emails, SMS, MMS and Skype are ways to interact with all people at any time and share all kinds of information.

Everyone becomes a designer and creates his own desired image, and thus influences his public image.

But there really is too much of a good thing, exaggerated soul-striptease certainly has never done any good for anybody.

What do I do to my environment and how do I filter the information that is shared? Here as well, the so-called "instinctive feeling" helps a great deal and should be an important component in dealing with others.

Appearance and Reality
Nowhere the difference between appearance and reality is as small as in the fashion world.

Here it is possible to cover up inner problems with the desired public image. Whoever appears stylish blinds his environment and lets personal deficits take a backseat.

You only have to stand apart from the herd, and everyone will believe the performance is authentic. You simply hide behind your self-created façade and play your desired role.

Myth "Fashion"

Since the onset of human civilization, fashion has always been a possibility to keep up with the times and to express your personality.

There have always been trends and general rules that fit every era.

But who sets the trends?

The general understanding of fashion was subject to the respective beliefs and customs. At all times, religion, culture, status, politics and life situations played a major role in determining what was in fashion.

Certain trends repeat themselves time and time again, and the designers of this world cannot reinvent the wheel.

Fashion is much more complex than just reducing it to clothing.

Fashion and Intuition

Even if you want to express your feelings, fashion helps to emphasize your own mood.

You can project your mood through clothing to show how you feel inside.

Since we spend our whole day at work with people, and even in private seek the company of friends and acquaintances, we develop a sense of how we act on others.

This is where fashion helps to represent our current mood. Unfortunately, many women tend to compete against each other when it comes to fashion. Here the usual "competition" is fought out via clothing.

In addition, of course, there are the comments by others about your clothing. Again and again, you're confronted with other people's visual appearance and are misled to judge others wrongly.

The more confident and relaxed we deal with the issue, the more attractive we are to the environment.

Yesterday and Today

Whereas in former times, we looked specifically for availability of fabrics and materials as well as good fit and production capability – and included convenience and everyday use. Today, in a globalized world, anything and everything is available at any time (i.e., Internet, Online Shopping 24 hours).

This hasn't made things any easier because expressing your own style is a challenge, and the best way to display the way you feel inside.

However, in a world where you make hundreds of decisions every day, consciously as well as unconsciously, fashion is a little ambiguous.

Let's take a closer look at the categories of fashion freaks:

1. The Conservative Type
He does not want to catch the eye of others with clothes, furniture, or cars that are outside his own safe, predictable and reasonable style.

Being adapted to his environment at work, his neighborhood and society, he puts emphasis on stability, predictability and familiar territory.

He is also perceived that way from the outside, and all is well for him.

2. The Flamboyant Type
He has no problem with eye-catching colours. Instead, he shows the world that colours and extravagance are part of his life.

He wants the outside world to see how brave and extroverted one can face this world.

He presents himself on a daily basis and lets his flamboyance become his own trademark.

3. The Eco-Type
A long time ago, he made the decision to behave in an environmentally-friendly manner on this planet.

The dwindling resources are used by him wisely. Not only the use of organic food and ecological furniture is a must, but also clothing that is manufactured without pesticides and other pollutants.

Usually you will notice this, but that's also an expression of his philosophy of life.

4. The "Not-Interested-In-Fashion" Type

He is distinguished by the fact that talk about fashion annoys him. He cannot (and doesn't want to) understand the emphasis put on fashion in society.

He deliberately shows that his focus is on other things. He avoids the mainstream and trends. He does not allow himself to be influenced by the media and lives his own life.

5. The "Price" Type

Everything that he considers to be fashionable depends on his attitude to obtain a bargain. Under no circumstances will he pay what he thinks is an overcharged price, but feels only comfortable at the "red price" (Discounts of 30%, 50% or even 70%).

At this point, he buys and considers himself a "Smart-Shopper", even when style suffers.

6. The Fashion Freak

He steps forward to show the world how intensively he copes with fashion.

He is up-to-date, fully informed about current fashions and trends and uses every possible opportunity to display his taste in fashion.

He enjoys full attention and puts time, money and vigor in to impress his environment.

7. The Casual Type

In a world that provides more and more leisure time for everyone, the casual type wants to live in a comfortable and pleasant way.

Accentuating his relaxed attitude of life, he feels good in casual wear.

"Feel 'at home' in the world" is his motto, and he neither overrates the whole thing nor underestimates it.

8. The Elegant Type

He affords the privilege of treating himself in a world that more and more finds itself left without etiquette and good manners.

He has a strong feeling of self-worth and surrounds himself with precious and beautiful things.

So is his outwardly recognizable style.

9. The "Stay-Young-Forever" Type
Fights himself and his elapsing timeline. He joins each and every trend to stay young.

Be it cosmetics, clothing, or accommodation, he (or she) wants to be praised with expressions that confirm his (or her) youthfulness.

More often than not, his behavior isn't suitable for his age, but the desire to be young justifies the means.

10. The "Who-Cares" Type
Since he avoids all hype about fashion and trends (and refuses to understand them), he apparently lives a relatively easy life.

One should ensure that supposed easiness does not turn into negligence. A certain superficiality is a distinctive fact, and rarely does he step out of his comfort zone.

BUT WHICH TYPE ARE YOU?

Different types of questions and answers allow you the possibility of figuring out what fashion-type you are.

If you consider the decisive statement, things can only get better. You have to understand that:

There is no 2nd chance for your first impression.

We, as humans, have different ways to perceive our environment and our fellow humans.

There are eight different types of people in the world:

1. The Extroverted
He puts his whole energy into the outside world.

He is open-minded and lives for outside things. He is perfectly able to adapt to his environment. For this he gains recognition and confirmation.

That promotes his self-consciousness. He must try to be where everything happens. He has a talent for improvisation. Principles are alien.

2. The Introverted
He turned his back on the outside world.

He is difficult to understand. He lives in his own internal world that is fulfilled, and he is very principled. Oftentimes, he just listens to conversations instead of joining them.

He likes to withdraw to his own world of ideals and ideas.

There is often tension between reality and inside world.

3. The Theorist
He strives to understand the outside world intellectually.

He loves order and looks out for generalities and generalizations.

4. The Aesthetic
He is highly influenced by the outside world and processes his impressions for self-expression.

[In this category you will primarily find a lot of artists.]

5. The Socially-Minded
Helping others is his destination.

He feels at home in health care and the social professions.

6. The Power Monger
He wants to rule and take a leadership role.

He is convinced of his ability to lead and strives to influence his fellow humans accordingly.

7. The Sentimentalist
He lives off of moods and is of a romantic nature.

The right words, actions, and ambience are important to him.

He just wants to feel good.

8. The "Visual" Type

He perceives his world with his eyes.

Everything he sees is scanned and evaluated immediately. Within a fraction of a second, what has just happened is found good or bad.

He relies on his trained instincts and notices positive as well as negative changes in his own picture of this world.

FASHION AND LEISURE

In a world where everything is always available, leisure activities are becoming more and more important.

When you're on vacation and travelling, you just like to feel comfortable and therefore choose comfortable clothing, like T-shirts and Bermuda shorts. Polo shirts and swimwear are an expression of your desired holiday feeling.

Clothing is worn here which can rarely be seen in everyday life. It's all about vacation, which means just pure relaxing.

FASHION AND IMAGE

Fashion offers everyone the opportunity to create his own image and to emphasize it accordingly.

Anyone can represent their own "brand", and cultivate this individual form of expression.

Self-confidence increases by skilfully combining clothes that suit your type. Creativity is stimulated here as well.

FASHION IS LIFESTYLE!

As with all expectations, when it comes to fashion one thinks of the fulfilment of longings.

Too many magazines and TV shows create a suggestion of a make-believe world.

However, everyone is only human after all.

So, live in the here and now!

You can achieve anything with a pinch of humor.

Those who do not live as themselves will run after every trend forever.

With this in mind, have fun in the world of fashion.

And remember . . .

"Fashion is Fun!"

About Ulrich

After finishing high school, Ulrich Kellerer went to work for six months in France and travelling became his passion. Being at Fashion Fairs in Italy-Florence, France-Paris, Berlin, Dusseldorf and Munich in Germany, he got well-known in his fashion field.

Ulrich started his career in the fashion business in the early 80's, when he took a sales position at Marc O'Polo and Mason's. His strong selling skills and tenacious personality quickly made him Sales and Product Manager, and finally CEO and shareholder of the company Mason's.

He then started his own trading company called Faro Fashion together with his wife as a partner. Faro Fashion specialized in the import of high-end Italian fashion wear. In 1998, Ulrich and his wife Inge and their Team took over the distribution of the brand **Closed** in Bavaria, Germany, which they have done for more than 17 years now.

Ulrich Kellerer advises his clients on latest fashion styles and trends. Most recently **Closed**, a leading European fashion company for women's and men's sportswear, appointed him their official fashion broker and location scout.

American celebrities and trendsetters, such as Brad Pitt, Tom Cruise, Patrick Dempsey, Sarah Jessica Parker, Katie Holmes, Drew Barrymore, etc. have been supportive in establishing **Closed** as a recognized brand in the US.

In 2012, Ulrich came to Philadelphia to attend a seminar with Steve Harrison and met Jack Canfield for the first time. Jack recommended that he write a series of books like he did with *Chicken Soup For The Soul*. So Ulrich's first book, *It's All About Fashion*, started here.

A media summit in New York showed Ulrich how the U.S. market worked. A further meeting with Steve Harrison and Jack Canfield in Philadelphia made his second life possible, including writing books and living for a new purpose.

Since 2013, Ulrich reads for charity every week in a nursing home, where he lost his mother seven months ago.

You can contact Ulrich at:
Ulrich.kellerer@t-online.de
www.facebook.com/ulrich.kellerer
www.twitter.com/KellererUlrich

You can find his website/blog at:
ulrich-kellerer.com or ulrich-kellerer.de

CHAPTER 60

SAFE SOULS:
TRANSFORMING RELATION-SHIPS AND BUSINESSES THROUGH THE POWER OF KIND, CLEAN AND CLEAR COMMUNICATION

BY LORI LOSCH

THE ORIGINS

I recently had the privilege of spending time with Sir Richard Branson on Necker Island, his gorgeous private oasis in the BVIs. Various events took place throughout the week—kite surfing, tennis tournaments, business mastermind sessions, theme parties and more. About 25 people attended, representing 15 different companies. During one of the masterminds, each company's leader was asked to present a 10-minute TED-style talk. The topic?

. . . An idea that has added at least $250,000 to the company's bottom line.

My husband Ken Losch, Founder and CEO of Advanced Green Innovations and Trillium Residential, asked me if he could share Safe Souls—a distinction I created and he subsequently implemented in his own life. I loved that a gathering of international business leaders would soon be hearing about Safe Souls. It has significantly impacted my life, has wildly benefitted Ken's businesses and has been transformational in our personal relationships, so we'd love for Safe Souls to go global. The world needs more kindness and this formula has the power to usher it in.

SEEDS OF SAFE SOULS

My mom taught me my first lesson on how to be a Safe Soul. She was the embodiment of the saying, "If you don't have anything nice to say, don't say anything at all." She didn't tolerate gossip, triangulation or criticism (GTC). I might come home from school and complain, "My teacher did this or that. It was so unfair!" My mom would invariably say, "Let's take a step back. What were you doing to provoke that?" Or, "What might be going on in his world to cause that sort of mood?" While these cross-examinations drove me crazy, I did learn to approach challenges and conflict from a different perspective. I started seeing people with compassion rather than criticism. This compassion, coupled with my super-sensitive and highly intuitive nature, had me long for kindness to permeate every relationship. The Safe Souls formula must have been percolating in me even back then, as I recall my dad saying, "You don't have a mean bone in your body." And I longed for everyone to follow suit.

My sensitive disposition and my mother's DNA likely created a natural or inherent kindness, but after I had experienced many personal betrayals, I committed to never deliberately causing someone to feel betrayed. I didn't want anyone to feel the discomfort I had felt in so many instances. This was different from inherent kindness—it was a commitment to kindness and to protecting people's souls. Have I done this perfectly? No. Can I think of a few major betrayals where I came out swinging defensively and have done damage? Yes. Am I proud of that? No. A fight-or-flight instinct can powerfully kick-in when we feel threatened. Growing is a process. None of us will do it perfectly.

SAFETY IS OUR OWN RESPONSIBILITY

As infants, kids, teens and young adults, we have various caretakers— parents, babysitters, teachers and perhaps older siblings. They are supposed to guide, teach and protect us. They are meant to keep our little soul beings safe. Sometimes they do a fantastic job and we wind up with perfectly healthy souls and sometimes they don't and we wind up with souls full of holes. This is life—we remember, feel, grieve, forgive and hopefully move on gracefully.

As adults, however, we are not only responsible for the souls around us, we are also the keepers of our own souls. Harming another is obviously wrong, but continually putting ourselves in harm's way is soul suicide.

When I met Ken, I noticed that he, some of his friends, certain family members and many colleagues, often gossiped, triangulated like Bermuda and were quite critical and judgmental. When I mentioned this, he refused to admit they were being toxic and harmful. He said, "You're just being an overly-sensitive woman," and, "This is how guys talk and kibitz with each other."

I pressed.

"Ken, I feel unsafe, particularly in your home. The fighting and backstabbing has me in a constant state of stress. No wonder there's so much strife—unkindness is rampant. One person is all nice to another's face, but will turn around and say, 'he's such an idiot' behind his back." The abundance of negativity literally made me feel sick and nervous. So, I did my best to effect change, but failed.

Some of Ken's colleagues also felt unsafe to me. After sitting through a few meetings, I couldn't help noticing how much they gossiped and how critical they were. Cutting people down was just a part of their normal conversation.

The boardroom had a wide street view so you could easily see the many beautiful, colorful and eclectic people passing by outside. During meetings, the team members would say things like, "Wow, look at the size of her ass." Or, "What a ridiculous outfit." Or, "That guy's clearly trying to be too cool for school."

Why were these well educated, successful and outwardly kind (at least to me) people being so critical? When I mentioned it to Ken, he didn't understand or agree with my perceptions. "You're just being super-sensitive again. This is how guys act."

But I just couldn't accept it.

After unsuccessfully trying to effect change, I took a stand for my soul. "I can't be in this environment anymore. I love you, but I'm not going to spend time at your home or office." At first, Ken didn't get it, but my strong position had him take notice. If he wanted me fully back in his world, he had to consider my observations.

Then the proverbial penny dropped.

Ken said, "When I would leave the boardroom for a bio break, I would go really quickly so I could be back ASAP. I didn't realize it or have the words for it, but now I know that my soul wasn't feeling safe. If they're constantly criticizing others behind their backs, they're most probably doing it behind mine."

Once Ken understood Safe Souls, he quickly implemented it throughout both companies, in his friendships and with his family. When people get it and adopt it, it's transformational. Many testimonials have come to us declaring they have never felt as happy and productive at work as they do at AGI and Trillium because they know their souls are safe. Many friends have said they feel so free in our presence because they know they will not be criticized or judged for being themselves. Others have said they are so grateful for the distinction because they didn't even realize they were being toxic. Conversely, a few have been unable to adopt Safe Souls, and with these people we unfortunately spend very little time.

THE FORMULA

So why isn't the Safe Souls message simply: Be kind to one another.

In their book, *Switch: How to Change Things When Change is Hard*, Chip and Dan Heath explain why just saying something vague like, 'be kind,' isn't effective. According to their research, sometimes resistance to change is simply lack of clarity. Humans need specifics. We might agree that being kind is a great idea, but we need direction on *how* to be more kind.

Sometimes to define light, we first need to define darkness. So, I looked back on my life and analyzed the times when my soul had been shattered. What were the common denominators in each situation? It became clear that three things were consistently present—gossip, triangulation and criticism. Refraining from these became the foundation for Safe Souls.

I also pondered the situations where I felt the highest levels of kindness—both in my actions and in the actions of those around me. Four things were consistently present. These became the Tools for Transformation.

Then I looked at a few, overarching, and powerful mindsets for which to strive. These became the Fourth and Fifth Dimensions.

All aspects of the Safe Souls distinction are specific ways to increase your kindness quotient. The clearer the direction, the more significant the change, the safer the soul.

NO GTC

No Gossip – there is never a place to maliciously discuss someone behind his back.

No Triangulation – if you have a grievance with someone, don't air it with a third party. Rather, go directly to the source of the grievance. This is kind, clean and clear communication, not a triangle of muck.

No Criticism – live and let live. Don't criticize or personally judge another's actions, choices, life philosophies, style, religious beliefs, etcetera.

A caveat to No GTC is when you are managing people. Being responsible for someone's work performance obviously calls for managerial discussions, constructive criticism and performance reviews. Do these responsibly—with the intention of improving the organization and increasing the individual's capacity for contribution.

TOOLS FOR TRANSFORMATION

After committing to the basic formula of No GTC, how can you amp up your kindness quotient even further? You can use the four Tools for Transformation.

1. *Clearing Conversations* – A Clearing Conversation is often the toughest, but most rewarding practice, to implement. Have you ever just known that the energy between you and someone else was not clean and clear? That there were unspoken words and emotions swirling around? That something was bothering you

about someone or you sensed that they were bothered by you? I think we all have. What did you do with that tension? Ignore it? Avoid the person? Brush it off? What if you want to live above such muck and mire? You can have a simple Clearing Conversation.

This is such a basic concept—it feels a bit like suggesting you brush your teeth before bed—but, unfortunately, Clearing Conversations are not very commonly practiced. They're uncommon because they can be uncomfortable. And a person's reaction to your desire to clear the air is always an unknown. Nonetheless, I can tell you that 98% of the hundreds of Clearing Conversations I've had have gone extremely well. The exceptions have been with those that just can't get vulnerable, be real with their emotions and commit to a higher way. It's sad when these conversations go wrong, but when they go right, they are magical.

2. *Committed Conversations for Action* – These strategic conversations with a safe third party are meant to eliminate the possibility of a Clearing Conversation going awry. If you are in an overly-charged emotional state and a Clearing Conversation could do more harm than good, it can be wise to consult a third party first. The caveat is that you must commit to the Safe Soul sounding board that you will immediately schedule a Clearing Conversation with whomever you have the conflict. Ideally the Committed Conversation for Action will be with someone who is not in the same sphere of influence as the person the grievance is towards. This could possibly muddy an otherwise clean and clear relationship.

3. *Covering People's Backs* – If we all have each other's backs in conversation, it ensures that No GTC will be respected. It's not only a commitment to refraining from GTC personally, but when you encounter it happening with others, you address it and shift the conversation to positive comments and praise about the subject. When people know their backs are covered, they avoid the flight, fight or freeze mode—they are liberated to love, to create and to self-actualize.

Why do we sometimes feel unsafe? It's Caveman 101. It's instinct. It's in our DNA. Cortisol and adrenalin course through our bodies when we don't feel our backs are covered. We shoot into sympathetic mode. We run, we fight or we retreat. Our bodies don't know the difference between the threat of a Bengal tiger attack and a group of friends betraying us. Both cause considerable stress and our bodies respond.

4. *Public/Private Praise* – Praising publicly and privately perform different functions and both are infinitely valuable. When we praise in the company of others, it generates palpable energy, excitement and love. It can even cause people, who may not have seen praiseworthy traits in someone, to suddenly see the light. Private praise is more intimate. It can help solidify and enhance relationships between two people.

THE FOURTH AND FIFTH DIMENSIONS

If **No GTC** is an elementary level distinction and **Tools for Transformation** high school, then the **Fourth and Fifth Dimensions** are courses at the college level of Safe Souls.

It dawned on me a number of months ago that during the span of a few days—and, yes, it did coordinate perfectly with the lunar cycle!—Ken could do nothing right. He was irritating me at every turn. His words were jarring, his motions were annoying and I didn't even want to be in his presence. I became emotionally aloof and physically distant. He was highly confused.

Then it dawned on me that I was being toxic. *I was not practicing Safe Souls in my thinking.* My mind was full of criticism and judgment. The Fourth Dimension is about being mindful of practicing Safe Souls even in our thoughts—especially in our thoughts—as our thoughts become our attitudes and our attitudes often become our words. Why not keep them empowered so we can become empowering?

When I noticed I was being an unsafe soul towards Ken, I pulled out a few tools. First, I washed my mouth out with **SOAP**:

- **Stop**
- **Own** It (admit my error)
- **A**pologize
- **P**raise (transform my negative thoughts into positive ones).

Then I had a Clearing Conversation. He graciously forgave me and we had a good laugh about what a Holstein I had been.

I never beat myself up when I temporarily fail at being a Safe Soul. In fact, if we claim that people never irritate us or that we never harbor unsafe thoughts, we would be lying. The transformation is in how fast, once we notice the deviation from our commitment, we course correct. Do we humble ourselves and quickly confess our error, restoring the other's sense of safety and our own integrity?

The Fifth Dimension includes gossiping about, triangulating with or criticizing ourselves. And if you don't think one person can triangulate, you have not heard the committee in my head! Acknowledging and clearing our own thoughts and emotions is vital.

The saying, *Beware of the naked man offering you the shirt off his back…* is poignant. We can't be safe for others if we aren't safe for ourselves. We can't offer love if we don't harbor self-love. We often criticize ourselves more than we would criticize our worst enemy.

Have you considered your self-talk lately? I encourage you to jot down the opposite of any GTC thoughts you have about yourself. Replace, "I'm so freaking lazy," with, "I am a productive and active machine!" Trade, "Why do I get frustrated?" with, "I live life gracefully." Exchange, "I'm such a bad auntie," with, "My nieces and nephews love me!" Get it?

If we all practiced No GTC, used the Tools for Transformation and adhered to the Fourth and Fifth Dimensions, we'd live in a world of immense positivity and productivity. Kindness would be rampant. Peace would rule. People would be empowered. We'd soar way above our basic needs for safety, shelter and sustenance. Love, kindness and prosperity would abound, and . . .

THE UNIVERSAL GOLDEN RULE WOULD PERMEATE HUMANITY.

This is my vision. Will you join me?

About Lori

Once a multiple-award-winning realtor in Vancouver, Canada, Lori Losch recently relocated to Phoenix, Arizona and launched several new careers as: a mobile app developer, children's book author, adult nonfiction author and a workshop creator/facilitator.

Part adventure nut, part creative businesswoman and part philanthropist, she has summited Mount Kilimanjaro and Mount Kenya and has trekked to Mount Everest Base Camp in the Himalayas, as well as the Salkantay and Inca Trails in the Andes. She supports organizations that advance prosperity and healing, as well as animal welfare, in the countries she explores.

As the cofounder of *We're Making it Our Beeswax,* a women's empowerment program, Lori has trained rural Zambian women in the art and business of beeswax candle making, sales and marketing. These skills enable them to create an income for themselves and their families, where previously there was little hope of doing so.

Lori also cofounded the *Answer for Cancer Tour,* a 2-month/20,000-mile motorcycle tour amplifying the message of cancer prevention. She rode forty-five states and seven Canadian provinces on her Honda CBR600 sport bike, helping to raise $500,000 for the cause. In doing so, she brought cancer-prevention strategies to untold thousands via live events, radio talk shows, TV interviews and print media.

While serving on the Canadian board of *Prevent Cancer Now*, she designed and developed a mobile app called *Prevent Cancer: 365 Daily Tips* to help fund the organization. In keeping with her love of inspiring healthy living, she also created *Stretch Guru*, a popular mobile app series designed to mitigate an athlete's risk of injury. HealthTap doctors rate Stretch Guru: Run in the top 10 paid-for running apps.

Lori's children's books, *Bumbles ... finds her way home!* and *Bumbles ... saves Naipoki!,* serve to entertain and educate children, and to bring awareness and financial support to the causes they champion. They are available through Amazon.

But perhaps the closest endeavor to her heart is the Safe Souls movement. Lori's book, *Safe Souls: Transforming Relationships and Businesses Through the Power of Kind, Clean and Clear Communication,* is due out in early 2016 and she is currently presenting its content in a workshop format. She has a vision of a world exploding with kindness, where all people are empowered to self-actualize because they feel free to be themselves—knowing their 'tribes' have their backs.

Lori lives with her amazing husband, Ken, and their sweet and hilarious dogs, Parker and Milo.